John,

Thanks for all the help
interest in the post.

Ian

THE PROFESSIONAL-MANAGERIAL CLASS

The first Stirling Professions and Management Conference was held in August 1993. Over 100 participants were drawn from the UK, Europe, Australasia and the USA and 75 papers were presented.

The main theme of the conference was the character of late twentieth century UK management, with a strong emphasis on the changing situations of professionals who have long been the bulk of the UK's managers. Over 30 of the conference papers are being published in three co-edited books as part of Avebury's Stirling School of Management Series. *The Professional-Managerial Class* (edited by Ian Glover and Michael Hughes) deals with the more general aspects of the main theme. *Professions at Bay* (same editors) focuses on the situations of over ten professions as they face the processes of managerialism, commercialism and consumerism. *Beyond Reason: the National Health Service and the Limits of Management* (edited by John Leopold, Ian Glover and Michael Hughes) is effectively a sector case study of the main themes. It asks whether 'science plus will' in the form of managerialism, allied to commercialism and consumerism are likely to make the National Health Service more effective, or debilitate it.

The Professional-Managerial Class

Contemporary British Management in the Pursuer Mode

Edited by

IAN GLOVER
MICHAEL HUGHES
Department of Management and Organization
School of Management
University of Stirling

Avebury

Aldershot · Brookfield USA · Hong Kong · Singapore · Sydney

Published by
Avebury
Ashgate Publishing Ltd
Gower House
Croft Road
Aldershot
Hants GU11 3HR
England

Ashgate Publishing Company
Old Post Road
Brookfield
Vermont 05036
USA

British Library Cataloguing in Publication Data

The Professional-Managerial Class: Contemporary
      British Management in the Pursuer Mode
      1. Management - Great Britain 2. Professional employees -
      Great Britain 3. Executives - Great Britain
      I. Glover, Ian A. II. Hughes, Michael, 1947–
      658'.00941

Library of Congress Catalog Card Number: 95-83596

ISBN 1 85972 027 7

Printed in Great Britain by the Ipswich Book Company, Suffolk

Contents

v

Figures and tables

List of contributors

Stephen Ackroyd is Senior Lecturer in the Department of Behaviour in Organizations, The Management School, University of Lancaster and an organizational consultant. He has researched widely in private and public sector organizations, and his books include *Data Collection in Context*, with John Hughes (second edition, 1992) and *Public Use of New Technology* with John Hughes, (1992).

Andy Adcroft gained his first and masters' degrees at the University of Wales, Aberystwyth, where he was taught by John and Karel Williams. He has since lectured in Business Policy at the University of East London and also teaches at Queen Mary College of the University of London. He is particularly interested in questions of industrial policy.

Peter Armstrong is a Professor in Sheffield University Management School. Most of his publications have been in the fields of industrial sociology and industrial relations. Over the past ten years, however, the bulk of his research has been on the social and organizational aspects of accounting.

Mike Bresnen is a Lecturer in Organizational Behaviour at Warwick Business School, University of Warwick. He has published widely on the construction industry and his current research interests and publications also include work on leadership, managers and professionals in manufacturing, and subcontracting/buyer-supplier relations.

Annette Davies is a Lecturer in Organizational Behaviour at Cardiff Business School, at the University of Wales. Her research interests are in professional change in the public sector, commercialization in accounting, corporate culture and technological change.

James Dingley is a Lecturer in Organization Theory and researcher with the Centre for the Study of Conflict at the University of Ulster. His research is in the sociology of Durkheim and moral regulation, professions, and national identity and ethnic conflict.

Michael Fores is a writer and lives in London. He was a Senior Economic Adviser with the Department of Trade and Industry and a researcher at the London School of Economics, the University of Cambridge, the City University and the International Institute of Management in Berlin. In the 1970s he led research which eventuated in the Finniston Committee of Inquiry into the Engineering Profession, the Education for Capability movement, and many changes in education. He has published widely on engineering, management, science and other topics.

Ian Glover is a Lecturer in the Department of Management & Organization at the University of Stirling. His main research interests are managerial work and occupations in the UK and abroad.

Jerry Hallier is a Lecturer in the Department of Management & Organization at the University of Stirling. His main research interests are the psychological contract, job insecurity and human resource management on greenfield sites.

Colin Haslam is trained as an accountant and worked for British Nuclear Fuels Limited before taking an undergraduate degree in his mid-20s. His research interests include the world cars business, the European Union, deindustrialization, privatization and managing the postindustrial economy. He is Reader in Business Policy at the Royal Holloway College of the University of London in Egham, Surrey.

Michael Hughes is Professor, Deputy Head of the School of Management, and Head of the Department of Management & Organization at the University of Stirling. He is coeditor of *Rethinking Organization* (Sage, 1992).

Paul Jeffcutt is Senior Lecturer in Organizational Analysis in the School of Management of the University of Hull. His research work concerns Management and Organization Studies in a postmodern world; focusing on the cross-disciplinary development of organization theory, the process of organizational transition and the organization of management education. He is author of *The Management of Transition* (Sage, 1995) and coeditor of *Understanding Management* (Sage, 1995).

Sukhdev Johal worked for ten years in a family run business in the garment industry before taking his first degree at the University of East London where he now teaches in the Business Policy Section. He has collaborated with Colin Haslam on many research publications and is currently writing a PhD thesis on tertiary education.

Ian Kirkpatrick is a Lecturer in Human Resource Management at Cardiff Business School, University of Wales. His research interests include bureaucracy and control and new public sector management.

Peter Lawrence is Professor of Comparative Management in the Business School in the University of Loughborough, England. His main interest is in management in other countries, and he has written books about management in East and West Germany, France, Sweden, the Netherlands and the USA.

David Lawrenson teaches industrial sociology, at the London School of Economics. His main publications have been concerned with accountants, engineers and other professionals. His current research is concerned with the aerospace, railway engineering and motor vehicles industries in Europe.

Robert Locke is Professor of Economic History at the University of Hawaii at Manoa. He has done extensive research with publications in comparative management education, and has lectured widely on the subject in Europe, America, and the Pacific area. His most recent book is *Management and Higher Education since 1940* and his next is *The Collapse of the American Management Mystique* (OUP, in press).

Richard Whipp is Professor of Human Resource Management at and Deputy Director of Cardiff Business School of the University of Wales. His main research interests are strategic change and the institutional analysis of sectors.

John Williams is a distinguished Welsh social historian whose classic publications include a history of South Wales coal mining and an abstract of Welsh historical statistics. Since the early-mid 1980s, he has combined this interest with teamwork on manufacturing, competitiveness and the European community. He recently retired from a chair in the Department of Economics at the University of Wales, Aberystwyth.

Karel Williams trained as a nineteenth century social historian and published a collection of essays on the nineteenth century Poor Law, *From Pauperism to Poverty*, (1981). He has been working on problems of national decline since *Why Are the British Bad at Manufacturing?* (1983). More recently he has concentrated mainly on the cars business from Henry Ford to Toyota. He is currently Reader in the Department of Accountancy and Finance at the University of Manchester.

Acknowledgements

This book arose out of the first Stirling conference on Professions and Management in 1993. We are grateful to all the participants in that conference who helped shape the debate and the content of all three books in this series. In particular we would like to thank four of the contributors, in the order of their appearance in the book, Peter Lawrence, Robert Locke, Michael Fores and Peter Armstrong, for contributing ideas over many years, ones which helped to shape this book.

Sarah Anthony at Avebury was a very understanding, flexible, and dynamically upbeat editor who always managed to solve our technical problems.

Again we are greatly indebted to the tremendous skill and dedication of Terry Middleton who remained calm and good-humoured throughout the particularly difficult task of coordinating the editors' contributions along with numerous other tasks around and during the start of a busy semester.

Abbreviations

AACP	Anglo-American Council on Productivity
AFofL	American Federation of Labor
ARCUK	Architects' Registration Council of the United Kingdom
BL	British Leyland
BLMC	British Leyland Motor Company
BMC	British Motor Company
CEO	Chief Executive Officer
CIOB	Chartered Institute of Building
DGB	German Union Federation
DES	Department of Education and Science
DMS	Diploma in Management Studies
FDP	Free Democratic Party
EU	European Union
FME	Foundation for Management Education
GM	General Motors
HND	Higher National Diploma
HR	Human Resource(s)
HRM	Human Resource Management
IIA	Institute of Industrial Administration
IPD	Institute of Personnel and Development
ITT	International Telephone and Telegraph (Company)
IQS	Institute of Quantity Surveyors
JCT	Joint Contracts Tribunal
JIT	Just-in-Time
MBA	Master of Business Administration

NATO	National Atlantic Treaty Organization
NPM	New Public Management
OB	Organizational Behaviour
OR	Operational Research
PEP	Political and Economic Planning
RIBA	Royal Institute of British Architects
RICA	Royal Institute of Chartered Surveyors
SCALA	Society of Chief Architects of Local Authorities
SOPs	Standard Operating Procedures
SPD	German Social Democratic Party
TWI	Training Within Industry
UAW	Union of Automobile Workers
UMTRI	University of Michigan Transportation Research Institute

For Alexander Wentworth of West Kilbride, MM (1914-)

What kind of heroes
Here for us now
Where leaders, stone preachers
Minnows on flow
But how long the lights
Over Viewfield
And this night will day see no more[1]

There's a vision
Coming soon
Through the faith
That cleans your wounds
Hearts of olden glory
Will be renewed

Down the lens
Where the headlands stand
I feel a healing
Through this land
A cross for a people
Like wind through your hands

There must be a place
Under the sun
Where hearts of olden glory
Grow young[2]

---

1   From The Old Boys, by Calum Macdonald, of Runrig, from Recovery, Ridge Records, 1981.

2   From Hearts of Olden Glory, Calum and Rory Macdonald, of Runrig, from The Cutter and the Clan, Ridge Records, 1987.

Part I

INTRODUCTION

1 British management in the pursuer mode

Ian Glover and Michael Hughes

Introduction

In this, the first of the three books using papers from the August 1993 Stirling University conference on Professions and Management in Britain, we are concerned with a number of related general aspects of the state of management in the UK in the early to mid-1990s. The three general concerns of this volume are to explore the character of late twentieth century UK management against a background of comparative and historical evidence, to consider the interaction of the forces of professionalism and managerialism in the UK, and to speculate about the kinds of manager, management and organization which are likely to emerge from contemporary developments.

The chapters in this book have been grouped under two headings, namely Context and Evidence. The first five, in the Context section, offer a number of general ideas about and insights into the character of UK management and management in general. There are six chapters in the Evidence section, and they address a number of more specific issues and concerns. However the main background idea, which influences all of our thoughts about these papers and the contemporary state of UK management, concerns the fact of the UK's economic decline relative to competitor nations of the last century or so, and the response of the country and of those who manage its economy to that decline. Is it sensible, we ask, to think of the UK and its managements as being in a 'pursuer' mode, as engaged in a genuine attempt to recover lost economic ground? Our suspicion is that it does make some sense to think in such a way. Thus, we suggest that while there is not a great deal of evidence of a large amount of lost ground being regained so far, we are suggesting that the right issues are increasingly being confronted, with the general direction of change starting to look vaguely positive. The pessimism of a generation ago -

'things are getting worse' is nowadays increasingly qualified - 'things will get worse before they get better'.

The professional-managerial class, management, and the pursuer mode

We employ the term professional-managerial class in a very similar way to Ehrenreich and Ehrenreich (1977). It contains managers and professionals and supervisory employees of virtually every kind, and most owner-managers and business partners. It lies below owners and higher executives of large organizations and above ordinary employees. Thus it comprises the vast bulk of those who form a given society's 'managerial stratum', almost all those who plan, organize and supervise the work of others (Glover, 1977, Chapter 1; Whitley, 1989; Tsoukas, 1994). The term expert and managerial labour would be another adequate substitute. Conflict between its professional and managerial, or its innovating and controlling elements, can be real and sometimes severe but it is rarely destructive of the class or stratum as a whole.

For Armstrong (1989) 'the core feature of management within capitalist social relations of production is an agency relationship ... [containing] contradictions between the inevitable dependence of employers and senior managers on trust and the fact that this is expensive, which gives them incentives to dispense with it ... in favour of deskilling and monitoring of management work'. To understand this was to understand the 'micropolitical and historical dynamism within capitalist management organisation'. As Armstrong has in much of his other work, we would supplement these points with Abbott's (1988) depiction of professions and professionals forming a loosely knit open system of competing management-level occupation groups, who compete both outside and within employing organizations for power, public esteem and administrative support.

If we use the English language and a number of assumptions and definitions employed widely in most of the English speaking countries in a rather loose way, we might, although as is explained below it would be misleading, apply the notion of a professional-managerial class across management and organizational hierarchies in virtually every country. To do this we could think of managers as those who plan, organize and supervise work, and professionals as those who also do these things but whose expertise is more specialist and who spend a lot of their time developing techniques, products, services and knowledge, and in producing information, help and advice for colleagues and decision makers. All of these tasks and forms of expertise demand the use of initiative and expertise to direct and control events. However the actual nature of management-level and expert 'professional' occupations, tasks, qualifications, expertise and divisions of labour varies considerably between sectors of employment, and yet even more so, and often very dramatically, across national frontiers and between groups of nations with similar or related as well as different historical traditions (Granick, 1962; Maurice, 1972; Fores, Glover and Rey, 1976; Sorge, 1979; Locke, 1984, 1989;

4

Glover, 1985, 1992; Sorge and Warner, 1986; Lane, 1989; Albert, 1993; and Hampden-Turner and Trompenaars, 1994). All of these writers have discussed different aspects of, and most have broadly compared, what Albert (1993) called the Rhine and the neo-American versions of capitalism, and what Fores and Glover (1976) called *Technik* and (later, Business) Management. The former tends to emphasize the value of production, process, the long term, management *in* specialist activities, and the more positive side of the state's role in economic life. The latter, the neo-American or the (Business) Management Model, stresses consumption, outcome, the short term, management *of* specialist activities, and the more negative side of the state's role.

It is now widely known that UK managers and professionals have long been less highly and less relevantly qualified than their counterparts in most major competitor countries. Traditionally they were liberal arts or pure science graduates, professional specialists of various kinds, or less highly qualified, or not qualified at all. The UK educated, until the 1980s, a far lower proportion of each age cohort to degree level than was the case in the other relevant countries. Before the 1960s most UK graduates had studied liberal arts and pure science subjects. The universities were more concerned with the production of a governing class, traditional professionals such as lawyers, doctors and clerics, and academics and teachers, than with managers and professionals such as engineers and accountants for employment in wealth creating jobs in commerce and industry. The graduates in liberal arts and pure science subjects, employed in government, in very senior posts in the civil service and elsewhere, formed an elite of *custodians* (Glover, 1977). Others, like Granick (1962) and Wilkinson (1964) have used terms like (gentlemanly) 'amateur', 'generalist' and 'philosopher-king' to describe them. As Wilkinson explained, they were designed in large part to be guardians of the UK's imperial and other governing traditions. They have been praised for integrity, intelligence, cultivation and objectivity, and criticized for ignorance of matters technical and of other relevant specifics, for intellectual narrowness, disdain for industry and 'trade', and even for personal eccentricity.

The systems of competitive examinations whereby graduates of Cambridge, Oxford and other traditional and prestigious universities were recruited into the administrative classes of the Indian Civil Service and the home Civil Service were set up in the 1850s and the 1870s respectively (Reader, 1966). In government and in many large and prestigious private and public sector organizations the highest posts came to be occupied, between then and a century or so later, by custodians. However there was something of an historic vacuum in the education and training of expert specialists and middle managers for most kinds of employing organization. This was filled to a large and significant extent, although often very imperfectly, by *professionals*.

A professional occupation is a partly self-governing and self-qualifying one. It sets its own standards just as the guilds were given power to do so by the medieval state. It has its own body of knowledge, both academic and practical. It controls entry to itself and exercises discipline over its members. Professionals are,

5

literally, employed to 'profess': they supply expert advice, information, help, services, ideas. Professions are ideally suited to the provision of disinterested, expensive and often confidential advice and expertise to individual clients who depend heavily on the quality of their work. A sense of responsibility to clients, the community, to society and ultimately to whatever or whoever is regarded as the highest Authority of all is a key distinguishing feature of professionalism. Therefore professions are traditionally commercially-oriented expert senior occupations only in part. They are not mere trades, not only because their education is much more theoretical than that of tradespeople, but also because they do well by doing good as well as by selling their services in the marketplace. Obviously the emphasis on the interests of clients and the community and on the development of expertise, or one's 'practice', for its own sake, is not always compatible with the goals of many commercially-oriented employers of professionally qualified people. On the other hand such employers can be important sources of material and other support for professional work and self-development. Similarly, the large bureaucratic organization with lots of rules and regulations can sometimes strangle professional creativity and responsibility, and sometimes give them considerable support and space to grow in.

Increasingly in the twentieth century, universities and other institutions of tertiary education have become involved or more involved with the education and training of professionally qualified, and with other forms of expert and managerial labour, such as business studies graduates. Against the background just described there have been two major ways of organizing management and employment in the UK (Glover and Kelly, 1987, pp. 171-173). One is custodian-dominated and may usefully be called the *metropolitan* approach because of its association with London, government, other very large and prestigious employers, and Oxford and Cambridge universities. It has been at its most typical in the civil service and many larger companies. Top jobs are staffed by graduates in traditional academic subjects, because of their lack of vested interest in technical detail, and for their potential for manifesting the 'helicopter quality', the ability to see the whole picture and to make important decisions accordingly. Such people were expected to work in most employment sectors, supported by technical and/or professional specialists such as engineers, accountants and surveyors. This approach was and still often is used widely in all sorts of UK organizations in many parts of the world.

The second approach is professional-dominated and can be called the *provincial* one. In many respects the opposite of the first, its raw material tended to come from lower down the social scale, less often from major public schools and Oxford, Cambridge and other prestigious universities and more often from grammar and comprehensive schools and 'redbrick' and former technical universities and former polytechnics like the universities of Sheffield, Strathclyde and Brighton respectively, and from professional practices and offices. In this instance professional and other specialists dominated top management positions. In local government, especially before mid-1970s and later reforms, and below the unpaid politicians on councils and their committees who made policies, there were and still

6

are, even in the post-1970s era of superimposed corporate managers, professional 'empires' of borough, burgh, county and so on architects, engineers, treasurers, surveyors and so on. In the fragmented, ultimately provincial yet in many other respects cosmopolitan construction industry top jobs have long been shared amongst civil and other engineers, architects, surveyors, accountants and others, depending largely on the type of work being done and the kind of firm or public sector department. In the public corporations and nationalized industries before privatisation in and since the 1980s, and often in their successors since, engineers of various kinds, accountants and (although these are in some key respects not professionals at all) marketing and sales specialists have long been powerful and often dominant. Professionals have also normally dominated consultancies of many types, many of which have grown out of traditional professional firms like accountancy, architectural, engineering, legal, marketing research and surveying partnerships or practices.

Over the last thirty or so years, as higher education has expanded and become much more vocational than in the past, with considerable growth in the output and kinds of professionally qualified and other vocational graduate, the two models have tended to converge, just as individuals are increasingly likely to be both graduates and to be professionally or otherwise vocationally qualified. However this development of an increasingly broad, varied and mixed range of relevant qualifications, many of them innovative, although a clear, definite and strong move in the right direction, has not led to a situation in which the UK managerial stratum matches the kind of broadly and relevantly educated *technocrats* to be found in France, Germany, the Low Countries, Scandinavia and elsewhere in continental Europe. Such technocrats may be said to have begun to be produced in France in the 1560s. Their production in France grew considerably in Napoleonic times and it was copied by the German states and by other Continental countries in the nineteenth century and after. Such people, such as French and German Diploma Engineers, are both specialists and generalists, high powered experts and very broadly educated to about what English speakers would think of as masters degree level. Their secondary education is much broader than that available to the vast majority of school students in the UK, where apparently naive politicians make statements about a 'gold standard' (what happened to the original Gold Standard?) of A level GCE passes. Such people, once qualified, and when they are engineers, are commercially, financially, socially and politically as well as technically competent. They include, if they are not engineers, products of higher administrative and commercial courses, who go on to occupy senior posts in business and government. Nor are such people more than occasionally monolingual.

As noted, the general trend of UK higher education has been to become increasingly vocational, and professional education and training have been made significantly broader than in the past, so that accountants know about marketing, and engineers about money and markets, and so on. Rapid and considerable growth in the numbers of business, social scientific and cognate graduates has been accompanied by equally urgent - by historic standards - growth in management education, so that many existing job holders and new graduates have been 'topped up' with management courses and qualifications.

In the 1970s the beginnings of government's concern with UK management quality, historically predictable but certainly highlighted by the first 'energy crisis' of 1973-75, relied partly on Anglo-Continental comparisons and eventuated in, among other things, the government's 1980 Finniston Report on engineers, the engineering profession and manufacturing, which stressed the lack of an 'engineering dimension' at the higher levels of many UK organizations. (Finniston, 1980; Jordan, 1992; Sorge, 1994). In the 1980s, however, attention was diverted from this central weakness - in many foreign eyes at least - of UK management.

Glover and Kelly (1993) listed reasons why this happened. First, the growth of business and management education described above, while a positive development as such, occurred in a society in which management had often had an arms' length quality for decades, and in which there had long been a preference in many quarters for apparently parasitical 'business' over productive 'industry' (Veblen, 1921). This meant that business and management education were often seen as alternatives to, rather than as partners with, engineering and other higher technical and professional education.

There was also the late 1970s, early-mid 1980s, distraction of concern with the 'impact' on employment of new microelectronic technology. Such concern tended to take the form of a fixation with the perceived threat, which unfortunately ignored the older and increasingly important problem of national ambivalence towards and lack of competence in exploiting new opportunities positively by developing all forms of technology, old and new. Similar distractions included the early-mid 1980s urgent interest in youth unemployment and youth training, vital and valuable in theory, of course, but often feeble in practice; and the habit of that time of blaming UK difficulties on the 'world economy', with commentators regarding themselves and their compatriots as economic victims as opposed to actors. Finally there was the problem of a tendency to look to Japanese management and/or society for possible solutions, often through the eyes of writers from the USA, a country which had been a traditional source of inspiration for the UK, partly because of commonalities, many unfortunate for both countries, in language, social and economic aspirations, political culture, education and training, occupation formation, knowledge use and divisions of labour.

In particular, and like the citizens of the UK, those of the USA had an education system which produced far more (US style) custodians and professionals than technocrats, which lacked a very strong Germanic feel for *Technik* - literally engineering but once more helpfully described as "our word 'technique' with a capital 't' and a knighthood" - and which believed in 'management' as an enabling generalism with holders of business and management qualifications as potential top job holders in virtually any sector of employment, regardless of their experience. Populist UK and US management writings like those of Peters and Waterman which often used Japan as an example encouraged the advocacy of inevitably short

8

termist organization level solutions to problems which are at bottom societal ones, often trivialising cross cultural understanding and reducing the chances of genuinely useful learning from abroad in the process. The history of Anglo-German conflict, closer to home and longer than that of Anglo-Japanese conflict, also probably reduced the readiness of UK people to learn from Germany and other western European examples such as those of France and the Benelux and Scandinavian countries. Yet whenever the Germans, or the Japanese, or indeed North Americans or anyone else have been successful, it has usually been because they have got very closely down to the task in hand, giving up any bad habits of arms' length management.

Other factors diverting attention from the real problems and weaknesses of UK management over the last fifteen to twenty years have included 'globalization', a real phenomenon which is nonetheless often exaggerated, partly in order to divert attention from local needs, national weaknesses, and the growth of regional economic blocs like the European Union. Globalization is a glamorous notion which excites more people than persistent weaknesses in medical, business and management and higher engineering education, for example. Also sociology, the subject which might arguably be and which indeed sometimes is most useful for helping people to understand such issues, was discredited by the immaturity of the outputs of some of its recruits of two to three decades ago, and by the vested interests in higher education, various professions, business and politics whose members often rightly derided its callowness, and far less creditably, feared its capacity for exposing injustice and for debunking the incompetent.

In the 1980s, and in a country wearied by industrial and industrial relations problems, and sceptical about the motives of many of its public servants, services tended to receive more favourable attention *vis-à-vis* manufacturing, and the private sector (and its professions) more than the public one (and its). The commercial, financial and human resource aspects of management tended to find more favour than technical ones. Thus the 1980s was the decade of the Management Charter Initiative and burgeoning MBA courses, with the strongly free market societies of the USA and Japan, the latter often *via* business and management gurus writing in the USA, and not social democratic and engineer- and *Technik*-dominated Germany, key sources of inspiration and ideas. Professional modes of working, especially those to be found in the public sector, were increasingly regarded as archaic, too preoccupied with notions of technical virtuosity and service, too little with commercial and financial performance. Society, it was felt, needed freeing up and speeding up, through privatisation and other forms of deregulation and through more assertive, better qualified and proactive management. Professions had to join this movement or go under, to 'move up or get out'.

Managerial controls, and managers as such, were increasingly imposed on professionals in most sectors, private as well as public, along with deregulation, cost-cutting and the development of internal markets. Deindustrialization, and more obviously positive economic developments, helped to add differentiation and rationalization to the process of commodification of professional work and

9

employment. Within professional occupations, there was a tendency for their junior members' work and employment situations to deteriorate and for those of their senior members to improve (Ackroyd, 1995). Professionals have resisted such changes by asserting needs for their specialist and often unique forms of knowledge and skill and by criticising the technically and ethically shallow and limited character of much managerialism and the forms of knowledge and skill that it deployed (Glover, 1995). They have also colonized enemy territory by increasingly taking postgraduate and postexperience management courses, usually at masters level.

The picture of UK management that emerges as the start of the third millennium approaches is far from coherent or simple, but a few features and trends do have a certain firmness about them. Qualifications have grown in number and diversity, and while strong elements of the metropolitan-custodian plus provincial-professional patterns remain in many sectors, for example, banking, the civil service and armed forces, insurance, some large manufacturing and retailing companies and former nationalized industries and public utilities, the general trend has been towards much greater specialisation and complexity, fragmentation even, of managers' backgrounds, qualifications and employment (Leggatt, 1978; Handy et al., 1988).

The fragmentation and uncertainty which is a characteristic of UK management, and of the various markets within which it operates, are reflected in its investment of time, effort and money in such management fads and/or philosophies as business processes re-engineering, and human resource and total quality management. Emphasis on the customer is combined with that on efficiency and unity. At the same time, and while such investment can be criticized for superficiality, for trying to impose, at the organizational level, behaviour, attitudes and skills which perhaps ought mainly to have been inculcated by parents, teachers and lecturers, thinking about management and organization have been becoming significantly more sophisticated than they were in the 1970s and earlier. There is indeed something of a dialectical quality about much recent management thinking and approaches to management education and training (Glover and Chia, 1995).

Research and thinking about how managers act, behave and think, about so called 'managerial work', has gradually replaced, since the 1940s, the calm, rational, logical, planner, decision maker and organizer of the early twentieth century management thinkers like Fayol and Taylor with the active, intuitive wheeler dealer of those of the mid-late twentieth century like Carlson, Mintzberg and Kotter, and more recent thinking is likely to replace the latter with a synthesis between the two, so that competent job holders come to be seen as those capable of both modes of behaviour, of using each as the situation demands (Glover and Martin, 1986; Wentworth and Glover, 1996). Similarly, thinking about the optimum scale of employment and government has changed from 'big is best' to 'small is beautiful', through to a realization that size, as such, is unimportant as long as its effects are positive or neutral.

10

At a higher level of analysis, that of the economic and political organization of developed societies, the 'thesis' of organized capitalism, the state of affairs for thirty or so years until the 1970s, is replaced by the 'antithesis' of 'disorganized capitalism', as the scale and pace of change fragments national economic, political and social structures. But countervailing tendencies offer hope of a 'synthesis', as regional economic alliances grow and as various types of international agreement develop. Dominant intellectual influences change in a similar fashion. Modernist faith in progress in industrial societies is complemented by the apparent fragmentation, diversity, cynicism and anomie of postmodernism. Then a more balanced approach develops, one more concerned with achieving what is possible and ignoring what is not, with perhaps, advanced industrial societies in a proto-stable condition collaborating with less developed societies with the aim of ultimately engendering a relatively stable and hopefully self-sustaining world economy and society.

And regarding the use of knowledge of how management is performed in other countries and on how best to educate people for management-level work, the same kind of pattern is also apparent. In the first case specific foreign management techniques were borrowed naively with no reference to the usually very different nature of the cultures whence they sprang. Then, in the synthesis, judicious adaptation and use of some foreign practices and rejection of others, is followed. In the second, it is first felt that either native wit or a trained mind in a non-relevant subject, or a general(ist) degree such as a bachelors or masters in business is all that is needed. Then there is much more emphasis on sector- or organization-specific learning, knowledge and skills. Finally the desirability of people being both generalists and specialists is accepted. (Anglo-Saxon Business Management or Western or modern 'either-or' is replaced by *Technik* style or Eastern or postmodern 'both-and', to stretch several points somewhat!).

The chapters

There are a number of specific and general points about relationships between managements and professions, professionals and managers, and about the current condition of the UK, economically, socially and politically, which we could have made above. However we will now introduce the chapters so as to variously deepen and broaden the discussion, before we address them.

As noted, our Context chapters are concerned with general ideas about and insights into UK management. It is therefore fitting that Chapter Two is a typically stylish, amusing, deceptively simple and provocative one by Peter Lawrence, on its distinctive characteristics. The chapter contains numerous international comparisons, based on the author's very extensive experience of studying and characterizing and comparing management in different countries, including the USA, Canada, Germany, France, the Netherlands, Sweden, Saudi Arabia and Israel. Lawrence asks what would someone from one of these

11

countries think? He then points to such general UK managerial tendencies as the belief in and practice of generalism, a related belief in and practice of mobility between specialisms and employers, faith in independent and inspirational rather than trained and programmed leaders, an emphasis on informal interaction and patterns and systems of working, 'Management versus *Technik*', a belief (unusual in other countries) that conflict is a sign of failure rather than normal or healthy, faith in the use of discretion as opposed to straightforward or blind following of procedures, strong faith in commonsense rather than doctrine, mild forms of conformity and compliance ('do it our way, win our approval'), and a very strong emphasis on the use of humour for handling stress, smoothing paths and soothing feelings. Lawrence only explains these phenomena briefly, individually or together, but he does link them to UK management's high levels of tolerance of ambiguity. He associates the imprecise, implicit and indirect character of the English language with a national talent or genius for 'fudging', and for accepting the unpredictable and ingenious, rather than law-like, nature of a great deal of life. This he clearly regards as a strength, and as a virtue deliberately chosen, and perhaps greatly needed in an era and a society very much in transition which have been experiencing a lot more in the way of failure and disappointment than they were once used to.

In his chapter, Robert Locke, an experienced historian and student of education for management level work in major industrial countries (Locke, 1984, 1989), compares and comments on post-1945 US, German and Japanese ways of managing. The major emphasis is on the US approach but there is plenty on Germany and Japan, and references to other countries, including the UK, as well. For us the main point of Locke's chapter is the concern with the three economies which are most often held up as examples for the UK. Locke describes the US ways of managing as a mixture of Taylorist deskilling and mass production at the operational level, and management at the corporate level concerned with money and markets rather than products, production, and producers. The USA had invented 'management', as a 'fourth production factor' (Hartmann, 1963) over and above land, labour and capital. Big labour and big government entered the equation as a consequence of the interwar Depression and the Second World War. Governments learnt to use Keynesian demand management to eliminate wide swings in business cycles and, with managements, to use collective bargaining to accommodate the demands and wishes of organized labour, up to a point.

Supremely successful, economically as well as militarily, in 1945, Americans felt that their system was far more effective than those of socialism and the narrowly national capitalisms of Western Europe. Teams of managers, specialists and workers from the UK, Germany, France and other European countries made many trips to the USA under the Marshall Plan between 1945 and the mid-1950s to borrow ideas. NATO and private agencies like the Ford Foundation were also highly involved in the export of US expertise. However there was serious resistance to change in West Germany and Japan.

Germany differed by practising codetermination, by the way in which the German state helped companies to rig markets, by rejecting US ideas of personnel and human relations management, advertising and public relations as bogus, and by preferring close and 'real' contact with workers, based on shared technical expertise between superiors, subordinates and others. There was no US style manipulation and deskilling of workers. The practice of *Technik* persisted, described by Locke as 'the unique blend of knowledge and skill which constitutes their chief contribution to modern engineering'. And the German state sought to develop and protect the rights of individuals.

Japan was distinctive, first, by modernizing economically, from 1868 onwards, while still more or less feudal socially and politically. Before 1945 Japanese society operated as one consisting of clearly superior or inferior people. It was made up of groups which moulded individual identities and actions. Market forces were and often still are derided. Government and business direct events. In theory power is concentrated and used fairly as far as individual and their expectations are concerned. Japanese engineers originally went to the West for knowledge and skills, and they taught skilled craftsmen in their factories on returning home. This cemented the Japanese working union between engineers and skilled labour. Harmony followed the conflict between companies and unions experienced in the intense period of industrialization from 1890-1940. When unions developed they were company ones and workers identified more with their firms than with their class. Status rather than class conflict moulded and reflected conflict in particular and relationships in general.

After 1945 the Japanese also successfully resisted US attempts to impose American managerialism. American attempts to change Japanese education and labour relations were circumvented and subverted. Japan did not, nor does not, really have either 'management' or 'labour relations' of the American kind. Everything is more informal, cooperative and consultative, group-centred and participative. Harmony is a goal which large company managements are expected to pursue and everyone in a company is expected to be both a thinker and a doer. Experts, in a sense, do not exist, because, as in Germany, nearly everyone is one.

Locke compares and discusses efficiency and its correlates in the three countries. Emphasis on the long term and on employee participation and skills are depicted as giving the Germans and the Japanese serious advantages over the Americans. The Germans' legalistic system of codetermination is seen as having held German industry back slightly by substituting relatively formal employee representation for the more urgent and informal Japanese approach to participation. For Locke, if the Americans were to catch up, to be as successful as they had been in the past, they would need to be more sanguine about the role of governments in directing events, and less sanguine about the efficiency of free markets, and they would also (although many US employers already have) need to work hard for harmony and cooperation in the workplace and against the traditional adversarial approach of US industry.

The focus of the chapter by Paul Jeffcutt is the development of the human science of management, both as a realm of knowledge and as a practice, and with its links with complex organizations and the idea and the reality of progress. For Jeffcutt, management's main concern is manageability, for overcoming 'the tension between order and disorder in the achievement of progress in modern society'. The search for manageability is characterized by a restless search for ultimate answers, experienced as an accelerating succession of management fads. The main vehicles for practising management and achieving progress are large scale complex organizations.

F. W. Taylor and scientific management were the starting points for linking theory and practice. While scientific management had not been an unequivocal success in practice it had been a channel for previous and contemporary inputs from the human sciences into management thinking. Previous inputs came from a century or so's management disciplinary and control practices, human scientific thinking and influential ideas about sociocultural evolution. Around 1900 management thought was focused on the rational pursuit of material progress, and on large complex organizations. 'Scientific' approaches to worker discipline and the influencing and regulation of consumption and of the social order in general were developed with the help of professional expertise. However progress brought new restrictions as well as new procedures, and generally the restrictions were associated with rationality and freedom from an irrational past. Increased confidence and assertiveness on the part of management meant that its visible and controlling hand increasingly replaced the invisible one of the market.

During the twentieth century the very explicitly rational 'high modern' kind of management evolved into something more complex. It involved a wider range of human sciences and practitioners and its concerns began to embrace all of society, not just organizations. An 'apparently insatiable will to progress', involving the restless pursuit, consumption and discarding of 'fads', had seen, since the mid-1980s, a redefinition of the concerns of the 'Management avant-garde', "from 'systems' and 'structures' to 'culture' and 'symbolism', from the 'technical' to the 'artistic' and 'authorial' and again to the management of uncertainty and disorder which 'earlier prophets and prophecies had been incapable of solving". The modernising momentum of Management was now in a 'late modern' phase. Its implicit ambition was to 'achieve the impossible' task by 'resolving the ambiguities of undecidability.'

Although Jeffcutt does not discuss such critiques of the elite power structures of most organizations as those of Child (1972) and Clegg (1989), and although he writes as if open systems and contingency perspectives had been followed only by the 'eminence of organizational interpretation', thus perhaps giving an impression that 1970s' and 1980s' accounts of strategic choices and contingencies of intra organizational and interorganizational power and conflict had been less influential than they were, he does identify much of the thrust of recent changes in thinking about management and organization. He does this partly by identifying the link between the growing concern with their 'softer' aspects and the articulation of

14

difference in postmodern thought. His analysis helps us consider, perhaps with the help of cross cultural comparisons, the study of societal effects and other broader and longer interpretative considerations than organization level ones, and whether the growing sophistication of organization studies in the UK and elsewhere might be part of a process of managerial mystification involving neglect of often crucial material and institutional or social components of culture, as well as a vehicle for educating people in the complex realities of employment, work and organization.

Michael Fores in Chapter Five explores the nature of professional knowledge and how it is used by professionals. He notes the tendency, in educated English-speaking circles, for each profession to be dignified with 'its' science and how professions are often seen as having certain preprogrammed, 'scientific', 'rational' and machine-like characteristics. Fores calls science 'a constructed body of provisional knowledge of the ... world about us, in whose construction the identity of individual human beings should have been excized, as much as possible, from influence'. He argues that professionals do not work in preprogrammed 'scientific' or 'rational' ways but in ones characterized by art and technical skill, which is in a constant state of development through doing. To think of human 'systems' (complex and partly preprogrammed groupings of interconnected individual actions, such as Marx's 'capitalist system') as being machine-like, was to dehumanise them by eliminating dynamic human intervention.

Fores differentiates engineers and scientists very carefully. Engineers constructed machines, to make them relatively predictable servants of human beings. Scientists conducted research so as to 'log' (as in 'bio-logy, socio-logy') observations of events and objects. Scientists tended to overvalue the importance of their knowledge and often dramatized their methods into a single discernable 'scientific method'. Unfortunately this led people to believe that 'applying science' to unpredictable and different tasks would make them less so. But the effective person, for Fores, is a 'specialist, dynamic risk-taker', whose 'operations are typically impossible to log on to paper by outsiders'. If human skills could be understood, as by scientists, they would be converted into machine ones, and people would do other things.

He defines three modes of rationality. One is that of someone who is broadly predictable in the eyes of others. Second, there is the 'rational' behaviour of uncritically obedient people. Third, there is someone who is rational in Weberian terms, who calculates and compares alternative outcomes before acting. For Weber (1923, pp. 338, 339) such behaviour exemplified a 'Rational State' which 'has existed only in the Western world'. This alone allowed 'modern capitalism (to) flourish (and) its basis is expert officialdom and rational law'. Marx (1887, pp. 492-639) had stressed what for him were capitalism's machine-like features, but Weber had gone even further by his exclusion of everything 'ritualistic-religious and magical' from what he depicted as something like a machine-governed utopia.

Fores then turns to ways in which prominent writers on science tend to confuse science as a social process of inquiry and as its product, a body of knowledge. Most definitions of scientific processes and products over emphasized rationality, and all this confusion helped to draw respect and attention away from the active and unpredictable skills needed in all human endeavour. Western bourgeois people had generally been taught to think of scientists as being specially rational and those classed as 'artists' as being specially creative and imaginative. Yet science was just as creative and imaginative as any other complex and unpredictable human activity. It was not machine-like and would not produce anything if it genuinely tried to be. By 'flirting with a' rational, 'calculative ideal of humanity, such as Max Weber's - a dynamic ideal.... more appropriate for the operation of electronic computers, levers and steam turbines than for human beings', professionals were seeking status and perfecting an image of themselves as much less skilled than they were in reality. All of these syndromes under discussion conspired systematically to downgrade enormously valuable technical skills, first in the eyes of formally educated people, and then in the eyes of other people, unless they had the confidence as well as the experience and commonsense to think otherwise. These, in our eyes, are important arguments with strong implications for understanding the nature and context of rationalist and self-aggrandizing professionalism, scientism and managerialism.

From the character (Lawrence), history (Locke) and pretensions (Jeffcutt, Fores) of management, we now consider the discussion of its limitations in Chapter Six by Karel Williams, Colin Haslam, Sukhdev Johal, John Williams and Andy Adcroft, henceforth known as Williams et al. These authors begin by noting how much economic and political hope has been vested in management, and how politicians in most countries have entrusted managers with the task of delivering the economic goods, sometimes in order to be able to avoid blame if success does not follow. The chapter has two main sections and a shorter concluding one. It focuses on productivity in the manufacture of cars in France, Germany, and especially, Japan and the USA. It disputes the meaning of many international comparisons of productivity, "challenges the 'lean production' assumption that management.... can always deliver cost reductions, and argues that American owned car companies have structural handicaps which are beyond management". The first section, on the problems and issues of measurement, argues that 'most American and Japanese car assemblers are average performers which share common problems about cost recovery'. The second argues that orthodox techniques for measuring productivity do not identify the causes of differences in performance, and that these are often beyond management control, and thus specifically, that American car companies labour under the handicap of having to pay for extra costs to do with 'the distribution of employment, social charges, and exposure to cyclicality'. In the third section it is suggested that 'if the problems of the average (American) car company are beyond management, political intervention and regulation cannot be ruled out'.

Williams et al. criticize business school gurus and management consultants for deploying harmful myths about Japanese management and productivity and 'lean production'. Managers were being asked to deliver impossible performance improvements when the real problems were very often to do with structurally distorted competition and interindustry and international differences in wages and social benefits. The proselytisers of heroic and 'excellent' managers in consultancies and business schools could help by admitting this.

Finally on this chapter, it has the very specific strength of briefly but pointedly describing France as something of an economic success story. This is useful in our opinion because if more UK and other people understood France's economic and political history since the eighteenth century along with her achievements and influence on other countries, there would be unexpectedly large gains in the general understanding of economic performance.

The six chapters in the Evidence section only *tend* to be more specific than those in the previous one on Context! The first and last of the Evidence chapters, by Dingley and Armstrong, are certainly, and respectively, notable for their partly theoretical ancestry and broad practical implications. All of the other four chapters also have some very general implications.

Dingley's chapter explains the moral aspects of management and the historic value and the great contemporary *potential* of professions and apprenticeships. He starts with a ringing declaration against the limitations of contemporary business school interest in business ethics and corporate responsibility. Too often, this was a 'legalistic or public relations' matter, 'a means to an end... something to be manipulated and calculated (and) not... a natural extension of a pre-existing moral order or community that should command our uncritical deference'.

The idea of the employing organization as a moral community would conflict, for Dingley, with the prevailing emphasis on economic ends and rational efficiency, which precludes such non-economic considerations as moral ones. Thus there is little interest in why (it is assumed) we behave economically, rather than in how, in which there is great interest. Economic laws are deemed to be fixed and impersonal. To support this, organizational behaviourists similarly assumed that interpersonal, occupational and organizational actions follow scientific laws of human behaviour.

Such views had 'relatively modern' origins. Utilitarianism and political economy had combined, from the second half of the eighteenth century, to try to replace the old order of aristocracy, guilds, mercantilist corporations and professions with something more flexible, impersonal and just, something more democratic and less oligarchic. The new order was to be based on the market. But for Durkheim (1933, 1957, 1970), the anomie inherent in an atomistic society of hedonistically self-seeking individuals 'morally' impelled to pursue their own happiness and pleasure, was not a price worth paying for breaking down old vested interests. The old order had made economic, moral and religious matters interdependent, so that all work and all divisions of labour were subject to religious sanctions, for example.

Dingley goes on to focus on the medieval professions and guilds. The former, lawyers, doctors and priests, had professed to God, the highest moral authority, and were blessed in the church, part of its organization and subject to the supervision of collegiate religious orders. Their 'calling' made them agents of God's will.

17

Ideally they professed only to God and did not represent or seek payment from clients and were thus free from monetary and other temptations. They could be trusted because they served God, not Mammon. Through their collegial, organic self-regulation they performed moral functions which helped to cement different parts of society together.

Similarly, the medieval guilds, while definitely part of trade, and serving Mammon more than God, perhaps, also fitted closely into the moral-economic-religious order. Guilds put the community's interests above their own when they regulated and protected trade. Their members were expected to be of good character, to produce work of a good or better standard, and to refrain from exploiting consumers or each other. They had civic responsibilities like policing and elements of tax inspection. Their lengthy apprenticeships were designed to produce people who were good citizens and Christians as well as good workers. The ideal and practice of fraternity was interwoven with all that they did, and the church was the final arbiter in their affairs.

When medieval society went into decline so did the professions and the guilds. However the professions found, in various ways and especially in the English-speaking countries, a new lease of life with rural development, industrialization and urbanization and the growth of new occupations. Part of the reason for the decline of the guilds and professions had been a loss of moral purpose when they began to abuse their privileges, partly for mercenary reasons. However when the professions re-established their role in the British Isles during industrialization it was partly by rediscovering their moral purpose. Their resurgence, that of the reformed public schools, and the partly new Victorian ideal of a gentleman all went together.

Dingley goes on to contrast the concern of Durkheim's sociology, for order, solidarity and harmony, with the utilitarians', and Herbert Spencer's, faith in the unfettered pursuit of 'individual economic self-interest through the market'. Durkheim had felt that the latter was as often likely to produce amoral or immoral, as moral, behaviour. The utilitarians' spontaneous economic cooperation, for them the basis of society, was not in fact spontaneous, but a socially-derived product of pre-existing social relationships. The utilitarians' pleasure principle, their driving force for progress, was badly flawed because much of the change demanded by progress was painful, and only a few people usually had a vested interest in it. Durkheim believed that at work, to be moral was to be social and vice-versa: unrestrained pursuit of self-interest would lead to disorder and inefficiency. But utilitarianism could combine with the ongoing division of labour in an industrial society to produce economic and social breakdown, as fragmented lives and the unbridled pursuit of pleasure combined to overcome society's collective conscience or consciousness.

For Dingley those writers on economic life who had been influenced by Durkheim, but who had played down the centrality of religion and morality in his work, feeling that they were practical people concerned only with the 'real world', were only displaying 'their own limitations'. Management without morality was simply manipulation and doomed to fail. For Durkheim, God was a creation of social intercourse: the social consisted of both God and morality, and religion was a product of everyday life, which restrained our potentially destructive passions. Therefore it followed that managements should develop, in fragmented industrial societies, moral communities within their enterprises. Increased awareness, on all sides, of the social and moral character of economic life, with people showing restraint and responsibility towards each other, and developing shared identities in constant dialogue with each other, together constituted a *sine qua non* of civilized life. Dingley felt that the often shallow and manipulative nature of contemporary interest in organizational culture reflected a relatively uncivilized state of affairs. He also felt that prosperity and happiness could only be secured 'over the long term through a sense of obligation to a greater good than our selfish ends and (that) this is only possible in a social context'.

Such arguments parallel those of Anthony's (1986) in advocating a kind of proactive, benevolently paternal, and reflective management, with authority based on expertise, experience and moral capacity, as a solution to the destructively single-minded pursuit of economic self-interest. Both Anthony and Dingley might have usefully put greater emphasis on the *shared task*, or the processes and products of work, as a fundamental and highly fruitful focus of moral and social concern. Lawrence (1980), Albert (1993), Lane (1989) and Locke in his chapter and elsewhere, have argued that it is the emphasis on *Technik*, on the content and processes of work, on its practical, real, outputs and purposes, which lie at the heart of German and other economic success, and relative social harmony. Such writers both realise and explain how there is more to such success in the form of wider educational, social and political arrangements, embodying much that characterized the medieval corporations of professions and guilds, which surround, support and help constitute the ethos, focus on and processes of *Technik*. Also, and in the recent language of North American management gurus, UK and other managers are often asked to 'thrive on chaos'. The arguments of Dingley and of the other authors just referred to suggest that they are being asked to make a virtue out of necessity.

Complementing Dingley's evidence from the past and his concern for the future, is the chapter by Ackroyd and Lawrenson, which is concerned with how past events led to the present condition of UK management. Their main subject is the UK vehicles industry (namely cars, railway engines and other rolling stock, and aircraft) in the past 60 years of this century, and especially in the 1950s. They note how its relatively small scale (by world standards) operations had long fitted the model of flexible specialization of Piore and Sabel (1984), being very unlike the 'Fordist' US approach of vertical and horizontal integration and large scale use of unskilled labour. For Ackroyd and Lawrenson this *could* have helped it to evolve into something highly suited to the markets and conditions of the late twentieth century. Yet it had largely failed.

Ackroyd and Lawrenson describe the 'craft flow' system of vehicle production in use in the UK for most of the nineteenth century. Skilled labour had been used to make cars, unlike the USA, where it had not been when 'Fordism' developed, because it was relatively plentiful here but not there. Again unlike the USA, the UK market was a relatively small luxury one until the 1950s. The craft flow system of production was in use for most of this century for railway engines, rolling stock, aircraft, and for much of it for cars, and senior engineers moved between these sectors quite extensively.

Craft flow production was a complex, relatively unified and more efficient elaboration of the 'static build' kind, under which one gang of skilled workers produced and assembled a product in one place. It was not mass production, never a UK version of the American or any other kind of it, but it made varied use of its methods, including flow line technology. In the largest UK car firms it was a form of flexibly coordinated volume production. Skilled workers and senior engineers were often involved together in decision making with little direct management control of labour. Firms tended to be under capitalized but nimble in the sense of being quite readily adaptable to technical changes and changes in demand. Skilled labour was always at the centre of things and detailed knowledge of production was needed at all levels. A high proportion of workers served lengthy apprenticeships. Senior engineers received much of their training, often as 'premium apprentices or engineers', on the shop floor. Unlike trade apprentices, who only learned one craft, premium apprentices worked with craftsmen in all the main trades, not to learn all their skills, but to understand them and their users properly. For most of the first two thirds of this century, the premium apprenticeship was fundamental to the training of management across most of the UK vehicles and other sectors. Engineers and managers often lacked university qualifications but they did understand the content and pacing of work. They worked *with* skilled workers, not just over them, in relations of mutual technical dependence.

In the interwar period and in World War Two and after, this system seems to have worked with reasonable effectiveness. It might have been developed and adapted after then to cater for increasingly sophisticated consumers. Engineers needed to learn, at university level, about markets and money, along with engineering and scientific subjects, and the education of apprentices should have been developed in similar directions. What actually happened, however, was broadly negative and sometimes disastrous.

In a relatively few years after 1945 the production of cars and railway engines and rolling stock was 'modernized and rationalized' through dramatic and at times superficially successful attempts to replace it with Fordist mass production. Managements imposed Taylorist controls on production and new forms of management accounting. Amalgamations made companies larger but they were still under capitalized. The changes were due to a burgeoning love affair with US ideas and methods and to partly associated changes in internal divisions of labour in management. As with large US corporations, but somewhat later, engineers began losing out, in a systemic fashion, to accountants and marketing managers, with head offices starting to lord it over factories across large swathes of UK industry. Resultant industrial relation problems were, and in retrospect still often are, blamed almost entirely on trade unions. There was a significant withdrawal of investment from large scale vehicle manufacture in the 1950s and 1960s. Undercapitalized but relatively skilled and nimble companies had turned into larger but much less skilled clumsy ones which were equally or even more short of capital. The greatest mistake, overall, was to replace ostensibly unsophisticated but in reality very relevant skills and approaches to management, with ones developed three decades earlier in the USA, for which the writing was already on the wall. The process was exacerbated by technically ignorant and unsympathetic banks who sought the replacement of engineer-directors by accountants.

Ackroyd and Lawrenson go on to discuss the vicious circle set in motion in the 1950s, of large scale rational and overly tough US style management, which brought into being a self-fulfilling prophecy of the factory as a cost and as the cockpit of conflict, whereas before it had been the core and the hope of the typical company. Engineering-based management was derided and elbowed out with engineers being replaced by accountants, marketing and sales, and personnel directors in boardrooms, and with the development of engineers being increasingly neglected or imposed on them from outside and above (see Armstrong's Chapter 12 in this book; Sorge, 1994; Glover and Kelly, 1987, Chapter 6, and 1993). Ackroyd and Lawrenson discuss various arguments of Armstrong (1984, 1986, 1987) and suggest that he had been a little too concerned with the fine details of why engineers lost out to other groups of managers, and not enough with the changes in dominating philosophies of management. Thus they argue that UK vehicle industry's problems were systemic, products of long term and fundamental historic trends, and almost certainly beyond the capabilities of existing, or indeed present and future managements. At this point it may be fruitful to remember the definitions of technocrats, professionals and custodians at the start of this chapter.

In Chapter Nine, Kirkpatrick, Whipp and Davies take us to the public sector and to the effects on the professions of NHS consultant and academic librarian of the so-called New Public Management (NPM) of the 1980s and 1990s. This had been imposed by successive Conservative governments since 1979 across the public sector and on the professionals who made up large parts of its management *cadres*. Public sector professionals were seen, in New Right eyes, and along with bureaucracy, as agents of collectivist welfare policy, and as being self-interested and ineffective. Kirkpatrick et al. ask whether the balance of power between public sector professions and management had shifted, and if so, how, where, and to what extent?

The authors first emphasize the diffuse character of New Public Management and the variety of its effects. They also explain how professional monopolies and autonomy on one hand and public sector bureaucratic structures on the other have often worked very well together, and that it was wrong to assume, as many had, that they were diametrically opposed. NPM had emerged after the election of the Conservatives in 1979 as part of a government effort to transform the state's role in providing welfare and other services by cutting their cost and re-commodifying their provision and otherwise radically altering their organization. NPM took two main forms. One was 'executive', the other 'market' NPM. The former involved the top-down imposition of managerial, financial and other controls over professionals. It lasted mainly from 1979 to the late 1980s. The second began in the late 1980s and it involved restructuring, along market lines, of the parts of the public sector which could not be privatized. The planning and delivery of services were separated. Vertically integrated hierarchies were broken up and replaced with a nexus of contracts negotiated through 'quasi-markets' of public, private and voluntary providers. In social care this meant an increasingly mixed economy, increasingly using voluntary and private agents. In the NHS it meant the purchaser-provider split, and in local government it meant compulsory competitive tendering. Executive NPM had a strong, 'rational' and proactive style; market NPM was more involved with the rhetorics of customer care, culture change, internal markets, human resource management, decentralization, quality, consumer rights, empowerment and so on, and was less obviously inimical to professional control and autonomy. However the degree to which the ideology, the aims and practices of NPM were actually antiprofession, as opposed to 'pro-managerial', was very uncertain.

Kirkpatrick et al. discuss the general issues surrounding NPM and professions at some length. The strength of managerial *cadres* and of professional groupings within different public sectors would influence, for example, the degree to which 'side' increased its power or the ways in which mutual accommodations and alliances developed. Also, if executive NPM was imposed through and by a managerial *cadre*, as in the NHS, rather than through professionals themselves, as in higher education, higher levels of conflict would normally result. Professionals would tend to lose out when the emphasis on NPM was on value for money and close performance monitoring. They might find ways to extend their collegial and relatively autonomous modes of working whenever 'culture change' and the advocacy of 'excellence' involved such phenomena as flat structures, team working, empowerment and so on. Under such conditions professionals, or at least their priorities, could be incorporated into or be involved in a renewal of their power within management.

Regarding NHS consultants, Kirkpatrick et al. first noted how research has generally emphasized their ability to resist NPM-type threats to their strength. Their own study was of four hospital units in England and Wales, and took place from 1991 to 1993. All four had been developing internal markets and all had been given Trust status. The positions of consultants were very dependent on 'the parallel shifts in the roles of other groups in the NHS'. Consultants had been closely involved in developing the first strategic plans of hospital trusts. They had also benefitted from changes affecting line management. Senior clinicians working as clinical directors had become directly responsible for revenues and costs, as part of their comprehensive responsibilities for their specialities. They were often keen to use business management techniques to gain access to new services of revenue, and were developing marketing skills. On the other hand nurse managers and financial staff were also being empowered by the development of quasi-markets. Decentralization was tending to favour doctors' professional autonomy in the short term, but in the longer one general managers were being constrained to re-assert control over the system so as to ensure greater consistency of behaviour. Also the imposition of market criteria on professional work was having various other consequences for the latter. For example reductions in numbers of hospital beds under policies of expanding outpatient care could mean reduced opportunities for continuous patient observation and thus for research work, and the free exchange of information between professionals was likely to be inhibited as well.

Academic librarians were traditionally less well organized than NHS consultants although they had been quite successful in achieving market closure over many years. However NPM had had quite strong effects both on how university libraries were funded and organized and on librarians' professional roles. Many libraries, following the 1985 Jarratt report on university management, had been turned into independent cost centres and senior librarians were becoming part of a professional-managerial class, whereas their junior colleagues seemed to be being pushed down into the roles of glorified clerks with a mixture of general and specialist information technology skills. For consultants and other senior professionals, too, however, the way forward seemed to be a technocratic via a professional-managerial one, whereby 'experts trade in some of their traditional autonomy and develop integrated expert/managerial roles'.

Glover and Hallier examine one of the last twenty years' most prominent management fads: human resource management (HRM). In the early 1980s, when university budgets were being cut and many erstwhile radical academic sociologists were starting to study the managerial, employment, economic and social 'impact' of the growing use of information technology, many teachers of personnel management and industrial relations also coincidentally became teachers of HRM. Many equivalent retitlings of jobs and departments in the 'real' world also occurred. HRM was not a new notion: it had occasionally been advocated, and more occasionally applied, since the 1950s. It is currently often assumed that it has replaced or will replace personnel management in most places of work. It is usually differentiated from the latter by the use of such words as strategic, proactive, integrated and individualistic. Thus the HR manager is involved in strategic decision making with his or her work being integrated into that of line management. It is not a staff, service providing, function like personnel management. It defines the employment relationship as one best regulated at the individual level, as best freed from the complexities of collective arrangements. It is designed to anticipate and avoid employment related problems through the creative and mutually beneficial employment and empowerment of staff, not to be merely reactive 'like personnel management'. Employee commitment to the pursuit of organizational or managerial visions and missions is also a central concern.

The paper casts doubts on HRM's integrity and on the degree to which it is more than just managerialist rhetoric by reviewing evidence on its origins and nature.

It also, suggests, however, that HRM is a good idea, one with great potential, even if it was developed partly for the wrong reasons. First, however, a number of moral, political and practical doubts about HRM's value are expressed..

The varied meanings of and the ambiguity surrounding the notion of HRM are discussed. Such ambiguity is linked to the great variety of tasks and functions associated with it at different times and in different places, and to its often cosmetic or status concerned use and prescriptive and threateningly managerialist implications. Its beginnings in the USA and later inroads into the UK are noted. So too is the way in which personnel specialists long used the rhetoric and institution of professionalism to stake managerialist claims, using 'soft', 'hard' and other varieties of personnel management rhetoric as the economic and political climate changed. The 'hard' and 'soft' difference is seen as particularly relevant for HR managers. They are seen to switch from being advocates of such euphemistically and morally monstrously termed phenomena as 'downsizing (rightsizing)', and performance related pay on the one hand, and large scale employee development on the other. HRM specialists sought to enhance their credibility and power by associating themselves with strategic management. However the latter's nature, the language used to describe management education and so called management competence were all notoriously hard to pin down, adding 'to the air of politically useful vagueness surrounding HRM'. More helpful uncertainty came from the rapid, rather confused development of vocational education and training in the UK since the 1950s, and from divisions within the UK's middle classes, between its 'tough' and 'caring' elements.

Data from several studies of the recent use or lack of use of HRM in the UK are discussed. Evidence was generally ambiguous, with plenty of rhetoric and enthusiasm, with far less, if any, indication of anything like a sea change in managerial and employer behaviour. Recent UK academic debates about HRM tended to have 'a critical and slightly disillusioned quality'. This was not only because there had been far more preaching about than practice of HRM. Its main goals, for several critical writers, were greater manipulation and control of labour, and the diversion of managerial responsibility for employees to the hidden hand of the market.

The context of HRM is then explored more fully. The authors consider the argument of Reed and Anthony (1992) about an apparent tendency of much contemporary business and management education to produce a 'barbarian elite'. Future managers were not learning how to secure the moral commitment of subordinates. Glover and Hallier suggest that even Reed and Anthony use some managerialist assumptions and accept some managerialist aims, while not disagreeing with their general case. However Glover and Hallier then argue that a more historical and comparative approach to understanding the genesis and character of HRM is needed than any of those so far available.

They attribute HRM to the character of the Anglo-Saxon Business Management approach to work and employment. HRM was thus felt necessary in situations in which arms' length attitudes towards the technical details of tasks prevailed, when as in the UK and North America, parenting and education had often failed to equip members of workforces with appropriate knowledge, skills and other qualities. HRM was 'predominantly a US creation' which had spread to the UK, mainly in the 1980s. In Germany and other more economically successful countries, HRM style thinking was much less apparent. Employers there did not need to develop, manipulate or control their employees as much as in the UK. Strong vocational education and training traditions made this unnecessary. Fashion and opportunism were less powerful influences, with management fads far less influential, and bolt-on management courses, designed to 'top up' narrowly educated people, far less common.

The authors then ask whether HRM can, nonetheless, have a viable future, and answer in the affirmative. However good full time education and training might become, employers still needed to give almost everyone some training and to employ them as effectively as possible. Further, and ideally, they should develop staff for the long term. They would do all this more effectively by providing staff with skills and technical and academic knowledge in occupation specific, sector specific and organization specific ways. In doing this they would move beyond the self-interested professionalism of the personnel management tradition with its emphasis on the general applicability of its techniques, to a situation in which skills in adapting and improving techniques in specific situations were expected. It would also help if managers developed their own and their associates' moral and social awareness in ways suggested by Reed and Anthony (1992) and by Dingley in his chapter in this book. However Glover and Hallier conclude by explaining and regretting the probability, in their eyes, that while HRM can have a viable future, it is unlikely to do so across most sectors of employment for a long time.

Mike Bresnen's chapter deals with construction, a sector which has always been fully commercial, except when employing units like local authority and other direct labour organizations are publicly owned, but within which professional practices and firms have generally played very important parts. Professionals such as architects, surveyors and engineers are important in construction because the industry's products are generally very large, bulky, expensive and of major significance to purchasers, whose needs are complex.

Bresnen reminds readers of the major public criticisms experienced by architects since the 1970s and tells them how they have also lost their previous "pre-eminent position as 'leader' of the construction project team". Traditionally construction projects were organized in complex although fairly predictable and similar ways between designers, builders, controllers of costs and the building trades. However economic development, deregulation and growing inter and intra professional competition and the 'strategic manoeuvring' of building contractors had led to many changes.

The ways in which the construction industry and its professions developed since the middle ages are outlined briefly. By the early nineteenth century the roles of architect, engineer, quantity surveyor and main contractor had been established.

Technical developments had led to the growth of new specialisms, notably in engineering and surveying. Clients ranged from individuals to very large companies and the government. Public authorities and some large companies employed their own design and building staff. Contracting work out meant less control over design and building but was less expensive otherwise. Many clients developed relatively long term relationships with construction professionals and companies, so as to try to get the best of both worlds.

In the 1980s, recession led to major reductions in employment in the industry, with very significant job losses amongst its professionals, especially architects. Public sector work was also much reduced, with much more of it being contracted out. Cost cutting in the private sector had similar results there. Deregulation of the architecture and surveying professions, from 1981 to 1986, allowed both architects and surveyors to work for construction and limited liability companies, and introduced price competition. Since 1986 government pressure on the professions to become more commercial had continued.

The traditional construction project had the architect as designer, specifier and supervisor of the main contractor, a general builder who undertook much of the work, and who subcontracted the rest out to specialist trades. The quantity surveyor measured, itemized and costed the contract, which was between the client and the main contractor. The architects' situation is ambiguous because his or her role is to protect the client's interest and to decide on whether additional work specified by the main contractor should be done, and to adjudicate on its cost. The architect is thus the project manager but this was not fully reflected in the contractual relationship with the main contractor. Also, while the architect is the generalist designer who introduces or helps design variations to take account of specific site conditions, many of the relevant variations concern structural components of buildings and 'building services' like heating, lighting and ventilation, about which architects have little specialist knowledge.

Architects frequently come into conflict with both clients, main contractors and subcontractors because of this. Moreover the splits between design (architects), and cost estimating and control (quantity surveyors), and builders, have notoriously slowed down the pace of both work and innovation in construction. Further, the basic model was known by the many and often complicated variations from it, which had generated many problems of understanding and communication. Finally, the rigid vested interests of the parties meant that builders had no input into design, that managerial coordination was very complicated, and that the whole process, including tendering procedures, was very inefficient.

Over many years, contractors had responded to client concerns by developing alternative forms of contracting. Design and build put the main contractor in charge of everything, including design. Management contracting involved a specialist managing contractor employed by the client coordinating design and construction independently. These approaches were generally clearer, simpler, and better coordinated than the traditional one, and they had been used more and more often since the 1960s, especially for big private sector projects. However the traditional method was still used widely. The new methods generally increased the power of main contractors at the expense of architects, who often found this hard to cope with. But for clients matters were simpler and less troublesome with only one party to deal with, even if they cost more than the traditional method. In the 1980s some architects had responded by managing the specialist subcontractor trades directly, without a main contractor. Yet the design-build divide remained, only closer to the point of production than before, and use of the new system died out. Another, more successful, alternative was the architect's 'integrated practice' containing all the professional disciplines. However it was very expensive except for large architectural practices and it still did nothing to alter the design-build divide.

A third alternative was to enter the competition between builders and surveyors to become the group most widely recognized as 'project managers'. Project management means the management of *all* aspects of a project from conception to completion, and much more than simply managing projects. It took several forms and was not new, but it was different in that the role of design team leader, traditionally the architect's, no longer automatically is, and is very often not. This notion of project management owes much to the historic dissatisfaction with UK architects' lack of financial, costing and construction management skills. Architects were widely seen as too concerned with aesthetics and too little with practicalities. Builders and surveyors were increasingly outflanking them by working as and becoming project managers. In a cost conscious era quantity surveyors were increasingly inheriting the mantle of project managers especially, but far from only, on design and build contracts. Contractors and surveyors tended to talk a common language of materials, prices and costing, and of the architect as 'artist' or 'academic'. Clients, surveyors and contractors often seemed to be colluding to marginalize architects. In many cases, too, clients were effectively part of the team, forcing themselves in to ensure that their requirements were met.

For Bresnen, political ideology, deregulation, changing economic and social attitudes and above all economic change, had combined since the 1970s to alter, dramatically, the relative positions of architects, surveyors, builders and other parties in the industry. Architects had lost out and contractors and quantity surveyors had gained. Architects had lost their monopoly on project management but still managed many projects. They were still often slow to respond to calls to improve their project management abilities, to be more like architects on the Continent, for example. They seemed increasingly unlikely to be able to do so, and it looked as if they might retract into more and more of a 'pure design' role. In general the management of the industry appears to have been becoming much less unique, much more hard headedly commercial and efficient, less remotely and traditionally professional, yet much more effective in responding to client or customer needs.

The last chapter, one which was not presented at the 1993 conference but invited later, is by Peter Armstrong. There is a direct link between it and Ackroyd's and Lawrenson's chapter. Both discuss the way in which in the years after 1945,

27

management thinking and practices from the USA have apparently been somewhat injudiciously applied in the UK context. But whereas the former chapter is concerned with the effects of this in industry, Armstrong's focus is on management education.

Armstrong starts by noting how blind UK government, businesses and education had generally become to the possibility that their assumptions about 'the nature of management and the education appropriate for it' might be flawed and their apparent correctness contradicted by foreign and past UK experiences. Employer discontent about the MBA had been dismissed by the 'management education lobby... as symptomatic of a backwoods disbelief in management education *per se*'. Partly because of the activities of this lobby and partly because of changes in corporate structure, British ideas as to what management is had changed over time. In particular, management education's historic although not actually productive links with engineering had largely been destroyed, with very questionable outcomes likely for UK industry. UK management education was increasingly distanced from productive activities and increasingly motivated by the career ambitions of those providing and receiving it. It influenced business decision making in ways which reflected such narrow personal priorities. For over thirty years applied economics, psychology and sociology and such 'skills and techniques' as those of operational research and strategic planning, and an appreciation of the main functional specialisms, had been accepted as the basis of management education by most of its providers, recipients and paymasters. Employers' criticisms of the products as being overly ambitious and afraid of getting their hands dirty had been rejected almost out of hand by management educators as products of dilettantes or 'diehard...Luddites'. However a minority of employers were seriously concerned about the content of management education, and many employers harboured at least some suspicions.

Armstrong explores the history of UK management education to try to understand how it lost its early more technical, practical, emphasis. In the early days engineering was regarded as integral to management but more recently, 'enterprise management' thinkers felt that trained managers should be developed to run whole businesses, and saw engineering either as an irrelevance, or as a hindrance to management education and development. Before the Second World War the UK management movement was small in scale but influential in the long run because it spread the idea that management could be taught. Taylorite industrial engineering and early cost accounting influenced the first UK management education syllabuses. The professional engineering institutions were very influential on UK management education until well into the 1950s. Commercial, economic and financial subjects were neglected until after the Second World War. Finance, for example, was seen as a matter for owners, not managers. This lack of financial and commercial, and of economic and other social scientific content was first discussed around 1930. 'Broader' concepts of business and management education, also including 'human' and employment aspects were increasingly advocated in the 1930s, and Fayol's universalist notion of generally applicable management functions and principles was also starting to take hold then. From the 1930s L. F. Urwick took both Taylor's and Fayol's thought and expanded them into a general conception of management and managerial capitalism.

Indeed Urwick had tried to develop an abstract, general, body of knowledge for professional management from the 1920s onwards, although his thinking began to crystallize seriously after World War Two. He had considerable knowledge of US management education and practice which helped him to be very influential in the UK. He led the postwar Anglo-American Council on Productivity team which reported on American management education. He had already helped, during World War Two, to establish the Administrative Staff College at Henley-on-Thames. He chaired the Ministry of Education committee which designed the UK's first national system of management education. At first the engineering institutions and engineering content dominated the relevant syllabuses, although Urwick wanted far more emphasis on the 'people' side of management. Thus he (mis)defined engineering as excluding the human element, as being (only) concerned with 'things'. His influence helped UK management education to divorce itself from its engineering origins.

Urwick's Certificate and Diploma schemes for the study of management were taught in relatively low status institutions and were unsuccessful, with only 1,550 qualifications being awarded in fifteen years. But in 1960 the Diploma in Management Studies (DMS) came in. It was not especially successful, except compared with what had gone before. It did help to pave the way, for better or worse, for the rise, especially in the 1980s, of the US style MBA. The DMS usually covered economics, sociology, psychology, accounting, statistics, the main functional specialisms, operational research, and general management principles and practices. But the production engineering and work study elements of the Urwick syllabus were lost, partly because of the generally declining influence of the professional engineering institutions. Influential management educators increasingly stigmatized engineers as being narrow and lacking in business acumen, thus acting out part of a much wider self-fulfilling prophecy of a minority, but a very significant minority, of UK engineers as glorified clerks (cf. Glover and Kelly, 1987, Chapter 6). In the early 1960s influential advocates of the MBA were very active and drew heavily on their own and widespread faith in the USA as an example. In 1964 London and Manchester Business Schools were established after industrialists had contributed £5 million to an appeal. Aston, Warwick and Bradford Universities followed after a second appeal in 1969. Employers' criticisms of their products as academic, arrogant and afraid to get their hands dirty, were countered by the argument that as the USA was richer than the UK and had more business schools, the American model must be right. The pattern followed in the UK involved its advocates ignoring the USA's strong industrial engineering tradition of management education: the US business school model was the one that was followed.

In fact US undergraduate business degrees were far more common than postgraduate ones, and unlike the equivalent UK situation, American engineering degrees had a great deal of management content. The value and relevance of all this was ignored although manufacturing and engineering experience and qualifications appeared to have influenced the USA's twentieth century economic success far more than its business courses. Postgraduate business school education had begun in the USA in 1881 with an emphasis on economics and accounting, and it increasingly oriented itself towards general management, also including courses in law, marketing, finance and statistics. Case studies of decision making began to be taught at Harvard Business School in the 1920s. The approach to management was a top-down one, unlike that of the USA's engineering schools. Management education becomes more and more abstract, and from the 1920s onwards the division of labour between the USA's business schools and its engineering schools was very clear. Management was increasingly perceived as an abstract and general expertise all across the USA.

The development of MBA courses in the UK neglected the engineering and industrial engineering strengths of US education. The typical UK MBA covered social sciences, quantitative subjects and methods, marketing, finance, HRM, strategic management, operations, international business, and entrepreneurship. The last three tended to be optional more often than the rest. Manufacturing and construction-related courses were marginalized, or even dropped. So engineering and production were slowly excluded; finance and accounting, economics, marketing, HRM and law increasingly replaced or sidelined them. Design of products and the supervision of labour were excluded almost entirely. Management became thought of as being *above* specialization, *of* specialists, not something *within* their work. It was defined as an abstract and universally applicable practice. It was all about the control of people. Such a conception was of great value to 'management consultants and job hopping senior executives'. A 'gridlock of vested interests' was increasingly in control of the future. It neither depended immediately on UK industrial performance, nor did it normally acknowledge the fact that in Germany and Japan management was significantly less detached from what was being managed.

Conclusion

Armstrong's trenchant and important account of UK management education adds, along with Dingley's chapter, historical depth to our understanding of the current state of UK management. It suggests that to depict the quality and practice of UK management in the early to mid 1990s as seriously catching up with that of the world's most economically successful countries may be very premature. However there is a positive side to Armstrong's account insofar as the story that he tells *is* one of expanding educational provision, and of expansion taking place in a context in which it is the quality rather than the number of engineers which is a significant part of what matters. Also it is arguably what individuals do with their business and management and other technical knowledge which is ultimately important, rather than just the nature of the knowledge itself. Our own experiences in university teaching and research tell us that business and management education and research are slowly becoming more reflexive, practical and self-critical, more concerned with the interweaving of knowledge and action, and *both* more specific to the needs of particular students, occupations, employers and sectors of employment *and* more theoretically informed.

We would suggest that like Armstrong's, virtually all of the chapters in this book can be read both pessimistically and optimistically. Rather than explain why now, we invite readers to turn to the chapters and to explore their arguments and evidence in detail. We consider the implications of all of the chapters for understanding how UK management is developing, and in what directions, and why, in Chapter Thirteen.

References

Abbott, A. (1988), *The system of professions: an essay on the division of expert labour*, University of Chicago Press, Chicago and London.

Ackroyd, S. (1994), 'Professions, their Organisations and Change in Britain: Some Private and Public Sector Similarities and their Consequences', Paper to ESRC Seminar, 'Professions in Late Modernity', University of Lancaster, 30 June 1994.

Albert, M. (1993), *Capitalism versus Capitalism*, Whurr, London.

Anthony, P. (1986), *The Foundation of Management*, Tavistock, London.

Armstrong, P. J. (1984), 'Competition between the organizational professions and the evolution of management control strategies' in Thompson, K. (ed.), *Work, Employment and Unemployment*, Open University Press, pp. 97-120, Milton Keynes.

Armstrong, P. J. (1986), 'Management Control Strategies and Inter-professional Competition', in *Managing the Labour Process*, Knights, D. and Wilmott, H., (eds), Gower, Aldershot.

Armstrong, P. J. (1987), 'Engineers, Managers and Trust', *Work, Employment and Society*, Vol. 1, (4), pp. 421-40.

Armstrong, P. J. (1989), 'Management, Labour Process and Agency', *Work, Employment and Society*, Vol. 3, pp. 307-322.

Child, J. (1972), 'Organizational Structure, Environment and Performance: the Role of Strategic Choice', *Sociology*, Vol. 6, pp. 1-22.

Clegg, S. (1989), *Frameworks of Power*, Sage, London.

Durkheim, E. (1933), *The Division of Labour in Society*, Free Press, Glencoe, Illinois.

Durkheim, E. (1957), *Professional Ethics and Civic Morals*, Routledge, London.

Durkheim, E. (1970), *Suicide*, Routledge, London.

Ehrenreich, B. and Ehrenreich, J. (1977), 'The Professional-Managerial Class', *Radical America*, Vol. 11, March-April, pp. 7-31.

Finniston, H. M. (1980), *Engineering our Future: Report of the Committee of Inquiry into the Engineering Profession*, Cmnd. 7794, HMSO, London.

Fores, M., Glover, I. and Rey, L. (1976), 'Management versus *Technik*: A Note on the Work of Executives', Department of Industry (mimeo), London.

Fores, M., Glover, I. and Lawrence, P. (1991), 'Professionalism and rationality: a study in misapprehension', *Sociology*, Vol. 25, pp. 79-100.

Glover, I. A. (1977), *Managerial Work: A Review of the Evidence*, Department of Industry/The City University, London.

Glover, I. A. (1985), 'How the West was Lost? decline of Engineering and Manufacturing in Britain and the United States?, *Higher Education Review*, Vol. 17, 3, pp. 3-34.

Glover, I. A. (1992), "'But westward look, the land is bright'? Reflections on what is to be learnt from British management eduction and practice", *Journal of Strategic Change*, Vol. 1, 6, Nov-Dec 1992, pp. 319-332.

Glover, I. A. (1995), 'Professions at Home and Abroad: Now and in the Future', paper presented to the ESRC/Cardiff Business School Seminar Series on Professions in Late Modernity, Imperial College, University of London, 26 June 1995.

Glover, I. A. and Kelly, M. P. (1987), *Engineers in Britain: A Sociological Study of the Engineering Dimension*, Allen and Unwin, London.

Glover, I. and Kelly, M. (1993), 'Engineering Better Management' in Payne, G. and Cross, M. (eds), *Sociology in Action: Applications and Opportunities for the 1990s*, Macmillan, Basingstoke.

Glover, I. A. and Martin, (1986), 'Managerial Work: an Empirical and Cultural Contradiction in Terms?', 1986 Annual Conference of the British Sociological Association, Loughborough.

Glover, I. A. and Chia, R. (1995), 'Seven Dialectics of Modernism', Paper presented to the Second International Conference on Professions and Management, Stirling, 1995.

Granick, D. (1962), *The European Executive*, Weidenfeld and Nicholson, London.

Hampden-Turner, C. and Trompenaars, A. (1994), *The Seven Cultures of Capitalism*, Piatkus, London.

Handy, C., Gordon, C., Gow, I. and Randlesome, C. (1988), *Making Managers*, Pitman, Oxford.

Hartmann, H. (1963), *Amerikanische Firmen in Deutschland: Beobachtungen über Kontakte and Kontraste zwischen Industriegesellschaften*, Cologne and Opladen.

Jordan, G. (1992), *Engineers and Professional Self-Regulation: From the Finniston Committee to the Engineering Council*, OUP, Oxford.

Lane, C. (1989), *Management and Labour in Europe: The Industrial Enterprise in Germany, Britain and France*, Edward Elgar, Aldershot.

Lawrence, P A. (1980), *Managers and Management in West Germany*, Croom Helm, London.

Leggatt, T. (1978), 'Managers in Industry: their Background and Education', *Sociological Review*, Vol. 26, 1978, pp. 807-825.

Locke, R R. (1984), *The End of the Practical Man: Entrepreneurship and Higher Education in Germany, France and Great Britain 1880-1940*, Jai Press, Greenwich, Connecticut.

Locke, R.R. (1989), *Management and Higher Education since 1940*, CUP, Cambridge.

Marx, K. (1867), *Das Kapital*, Vol. 1, Hamburg, Published in English in 1976 as *Capital*, Penguin, Harmondsworth.

Maurice, M. (1972), 'Propos sur las Sociologie des Professions', *Sociologie du Travail*, Vol. 13, pp. 213-225.

Piore, M. J. and Sabel, C. F. (1984), *The Second Industrial Divide*, Basic Books, New York.

Reader, W J. (1966), *Professional Men: The Rise of the Professional Classes in Nineteenth Century England*, Weidenfeld and Nicholson, London.

Reed, M. J. and Anthony, P. (1992), 'Professionalizing Management and Managing Professionalization: British Management in the 1980s', *Journal of Management Studies*, Vol. 29, 5, pp. 591-613.

Sorge, A. (1979), 'Engineers in Management: A study of the British, French and German traditions', *Journal of General Management*, Vol. 5, pp. 46-57.

Sorge, A. (1994), 'The Reform of Technical Education and Training in Great Britain: a Comparison of Institutional Learning in Europe, *European Journal of Vocational Training*, Vol. 3, pp. 58-68.

Sorge, A. and Warner, M. (1986), *Comparative Factory Management: an Anglo-German Comparison of Manufacturing, Management and Manpower*, Gower, Aldershot.

Tsoukas, H. (1994), 'Refining Common Sense: Types of Knowledge in Management Studies', *Journal of Management Studies*, Vol. 31, 6, pp. 761-780.

Veblen, T. (1921), *The Engineers and the Price System*, Viking, New York.

Weber, M. (1923), *Wirtschaftgeschichte*, Drucker and Humboldt, Berlin, published in English in 1981, as *General Economic History*, Transaction, New Brunswick.

Wentworth, D. and Glover, I. (1996), 'The Sectoral and the Dialectical in the Formation of Entrepreneurs and Small Business Success: Evidence from a Small Scale Study of SMEs in Scotland and from the Study of Comparative Management and Managerial Work', to appear in Scott, M. G., Rosa, P. and Klandt, H. (eds), *Educating Entrepreneurs for Wealth Creation*, Avebury, Aldershot.

Whitley, R. D. (1989), 'The Nature of Managerial Tasks and Skills: Their Distinguishing Characteristics and Organization', *Journal of Management Studies*, Vol. 26, pp. 209-224.

Wilkinson, R. (1964), *The Prefects: British Leadership and the Public School Tradition*, OUP, Oxford.

Part II

CONTEXT

2 Through a glass darkly: towards a characterization of British management

Peter Lawrence

Introduction

There is a joke in Israel about the three academics who went there to study Israeli society. The first stayed four years; now he is back in the USA judiciously considering a follow up visit before daring to put pen to paper. The second academic stayed a year, went home and wrote an article. The third came for two weeks and is now on chapter eight of his book!

In part this story is a celebration of Israeli impetuosity and improvisation. But it also raises the issue of the paralysing effect of over-familiarity, debilitation through detail, and the related fear that any attempted generalisation will do injustice to some disparate fact or wayward circumstance. The problem is acute for anyone who tries to write broadly about their own country: one has had so much multifarious experience that it is difficult to see patterns, difficult indeed to believe that there are any.

Very much aware of the problem we have tried to 'crack it', to get some purchase on what might be different or distinctive about British management by exploiting a knowledge of management in other countries. Rather than ask what is British management like, we have posed the question: what would a Dutch person, German, Swede, or Saudi Arabian think? What then would seem to be different and interesting about those who manage in the sceptred isle? A bonus of this approach is that the more countries one takes as *point de repère*, the more contrasts are generated. This in turn prompts the question of what might be the most fruitful comparator country. In developing these ideas we have used, at least implicitly, several countries in this way, but it is a comparison between Britain and the USA which has been most profitable. It is because the two cultures actually share some business values and aspirations that the American contrast is helpful in illuminating some 'middle-range' British features.

Before 'setting sail' it is only fair to say that this is an exercise in broad brush stroke characterization, in bold generalisation, and the views proffered are not held to be always and everywhere true. Neither is it for the most part a question of black and white contrasts, but rather a matter of relative emphasis, variable priority and difference of degree.

So with these qualifications, what is British management like? We would like to suggest that possible answers might include the following:

Generalism

It is possible to position the management cultures of different countries on a generalism versus specialism continuum. The generalist approach views management as a generalizable activity, the practice of which calls for certain general qualities which may then be effectively deployed in a variety of contexts: functional, hierarchical, and branch of industry based. The USA is clearly an exemplar of this approach, and American managers like to think they can 'manage anything!', moving from purchasing to PR, forklift trucks to agri-business. Alternatively management may be viewed in specialist terms, every management job distinct by content, the emphasis on differential selection of managers by content rather than level of education, together with accrued experience and contextually specific know how. German management is like this with its valorisation of specialism, especially technical specialism, traditional distrust of managerial generalisation, the absence of an indigenous word for manager and the conviction that life's uncertainties may best be contained by experts authoritatively deciding on the basis of relevant and specific knowledge. On this generalist specialist continuum British management is undoubtedly generalist in its orientation:

in terms of self-image where British managers eschew any specialist label but delight in calling themselves 'good all-rounders'

in terms of a cultural glitch which equates specialism with limitation; consider that Winston Churchill's wartime quip that scientists should be 'on tap, but not on top' invariably evokes a nod of approbation from worldly powerholders

and in the very positive sense that recruitment tends to be in terms of character and social skills (Nichols, 1977) qualities that are independent of the context in which they are deployed.

38

Structural generalism

This generalist predilection has also given rise to what one might call 'structural generalism' whereby companies are broken down into profit centres or other units thereby shortening the hierarchy in the first instance but adding to the layers of *general* management at the top. As a wit once put it 'In Britain enterprise management has become the specialism of the generalists'.

Mobility

Clearly there is a rough relationship between generalism and specialism as outlined above and attitudes to manager mobility, primarily in the sense of mobility between employing organizations but with a secondary connotation of mobility between functions (sales, manufacturing, personnel, and so on). It should be emphasized that the reference here is to attitudes to mobility (the facts concerning the mobility of managers between companies being notoriously difficult to come by). Typically there is a positive relationship between generalism and (attitudes to) mobility, and this is certainly the case for Britain, though there are some 'mixed' or 'deviant' cases as the following table suggests:

Table 2.1
Generalism and mobility in management

Clear cut cases	*Generalism*	*Mobility*
USA	+	+
Canada	+	+
Britain	+	+
Germany	-	-
Mixed cases		
France	+	-
Netherlands	±	-
Sweden	±	-
Saudi Arabia	+	-
Israel	+	-

To take the classification a step further, it is also interesting to note the basis of British generalism. This is not primarily a matter of professionalism plus energy as in the USA, or of educated cleverness plus *savoir faire* as in France, or a diffuse ethic of social responsibility and network involvement as in Saudi Arabia. In

Britain the emphasis again tends to be on character, personality, and judgement, and upon social and political skills.

Paramountcy of leadership

British culture valorises leaders and so does British management. This is doubtless rational in a country that has had so many 'firsts':

> national integration (before the Norman conquest)
> industrial revolution
> parliamentary democracy

as well as having won so many wars (and had an Empire bigger than anyone else's!).

Leadership in other management cultures tends to be more programmable. In France industrial leaders are the cleverest and most urbane who passed the most examinations (in their younger days) and went to the best *grandes écoles*. In the USA the business leaders are those who have crossed professionalism with energy and drive. In Sweden the leaders are the manifestly competent, in a quiet way, who were not afraid of responsibility. But in Britain the leader is always a little bit special, more independent of the basis of legitimation. This leadership is a matter of character with a touch of charisma, flair with a touch of breeding. It is transformational rather than transactional leadership, about the embodiment of states of being rather than the mastering of means. The leader (not the system) is a focus for loyalty, is deemed to make a difference, will be a model to which juniors may aspire.

Interactive informality

In popular exchanges about the behaviour of managers in different countries a lot of play is made over the contrast between formal and informal styles. We would like to suggest while it is quite easy, a simple observational act, to characterise the interactive style as formal or informal, it is sometimes more difficult to say what is thereby connotated. Consider a few examples:

> Israel: here managers have a distinctly informal style, especially in the sense of their behaviour towards one another, and to their seniors, this being characterized by a marked lack of deference. Clearly this is rooted in the Israeli hostility to authority, especially gentile authority, which has usually meant oppression; this is the spirit of individual resistance to a hostile world and the power of others that is caught so well in Primo Levi's novel *If not now, when?* (Levi, 1987).

American management is very informal in the interactive sense with the accessibility of individuals, directness of speech, and studied casualness of deportment and manners. Yet all this depends upon, or at least is facilitated by, the systems and procedures that function to exercise an impersonal means of control to the advantage of those who are senior. Behind the insistent informality the power structure is intact and differences in emoluments and organizational privilege are substantial. This is a far cry from the prototypical country of Scandinavia, namely:

Sweden: among managers in this country there is a high level of interactive informality and a marked lack of deference. Importantly, these betoken the deep commitment of Swedish society to egalitarian values. The Swedish language is a little treasury of expressions along the lines of *en man är lika god som en an* (a man is just as good as the next man), proclaiming the virtues of equality and personal modesty. Swedish managers are mild mannered and reasonable. Unlike their American counterparts they do not parade decisiveness or forcefulness.

So what of British management? Certainly the style is at least superficially informal: the use of Christian names (across ranks) is normal, it is jackets off in the office, lots of swearing, and no particular attachment to behaviour that is dignified in a formal way. Our company hierarchies are shorter than those of France, and we do not call anyone Herr Doktor or Mr Director. One might infer from British practice in these matters the ethic that although it is fine for a gentleman to have rank, a gentleman does not pull rank. Even the famous English deference is sometimes blurred by *double-entendre* or subtly undermined by humour.

Yet it is rather more difficult to determine the meaning of the behaviour, beyond the thought that it perhaps reflects a long term exposure to American influence coupled with a national *penchant* for understatement. There is no reason to suppose that it indicates a Scandinavian style commitment to values of social equality. This semi-paradox can be given another twist by considering the case of Germany.

Anglo-Saxons delight in calling attention to the formality of German management and indeed this characterization is not without substance. Dress and deportment are formal, there is very little use of Christian names, not much joking around, and little swearing (one also sees far less alcohol in German companies than in British ones). The use of at least some titles is common, most noticeably the doctor title (many more German managers have a doctors degree than is the case in Britain or America) and interestingly the *Meister* (foreman) title.

So far so good, but the catch is that it is difficult to move from these observable formalities to more substantial behaviours that one might expect to be value connected. To put this matter briefly, the present writer has argued elsewhere (Lawrence, 1980) that German meeting behaviour is much more direct and much less deferential than in Britain, that there is a good deal of criticism upwards, and indeed that the phrase *konstruktive* Opposition (constructive opposition) is often bandied around as a set expression.

Informal system

Side by side with the notion of interactive informality is the idea of the informal system. The origins of this notion are to be found in the Roethlisberger and Dickson (1939) account of the Hawthorne experiments at the Western Electrical Company in Cicero, Illinois. These highlighted at worker level the existence of informal groupings, in-group behaviour, and informal task swapping, as well as informal norms on output and the response to company directives and supervision. This basic idea of an informal system at blue collar level was given a further thrust by Melvin Dalton's study (1959) of American managers, exhibiting a comparable range of informal adjustments, devious means to achieve both corporate and individual ends, cliques, cabals and power tactics.

Today the idea that there is an informal system that is parallel to the formal one is part of conventional OB wisdom, where the formal system is so to speak that which may be read off the organizational chart together with supporting procedures and job descriptions, and the informal system is the totality of creative departures therefrom.

The point to emphasise is that the informal system is an Anglo-Saxon concept. It has been inspired by studies in English speaking countries and these seem to provide the best empirical manifestation. To toy for a moment with some counter examples, while such an informal system clearly exists in companies in Israel there is scarcely any formal system against which it may be set off (Lawrence, 1990)! Or again the informal system seemed to the present writer to be much less in evidence in Sweden (Lawrence and Spybey, 1986) and conspicuously absent in Germany (Lawrence, 1980) where gentle British cynicism is often confounded by the fact that what is formally ordained is what is actually happening.

So in terms of our attempted characterization of British management one can typically speak of the existence of an informal system. This is a distinguishing characteristic, but it is not an exclusive one. It is certainly shared with the USA, and with some non-Anglo-Saxon countries such as the Netherlands though it is less to be taken for granted outside the English speaking world.

Transactional informality

Again it may be helpful to extend the simple and over used notion of informality by considering the variable propensity of organizations in different countries/cultures to define issues, move things forward, select, solve problems and settle issues through interpersonal contacts and coalitions. Now it is difficult to formulate this, but the argument would go something like this. In British companies:

> the hierarchy is less important than in France; the functional specialisation is less important than in Germany; the systems and SOPS (standard operating procedures) are less important than in the USA

so at least on a relative *faute de mieux* basis the intuitive, interpersonal, judgemental elements in doing and deciding loom larger.

The point may be illustrated with regard to business strategy, supported by a British-American contrast. When one interviews American executives about their jobs they put strategy in the foreground. It is paraded as a key part of the job; strategy formulation is done consciously, purposefully, openly, and so far as possible systematically. British executives make much less of strategy in accounts of their work (and seldom mentioned it at all before the 1980s), and still often speak of it a little shyly as though too much talk of strategy would sound pretentious or self important. One has the impression that strategy is something Americans work on, and the British think about sometimes in traffic jams on the M25.

The same contrast is observable when it comes to the communication of strategy. The American conviction is that strategy must be communicated, lucidly and forcefully, in order to be effective. Indeed the word that is often used by Americans in this context is cascaded (cf. French *cascade* = waterfall), where strategy is said to be cascaded down. In Britain there does not seem to be this same insistence on communication: the strategy formulation will be more intuitive, shared among mutually trusting power holders, but further communication may well be selective - a matter of choice.

Management versus technik

From the time in the 1970s when the wider world began to take an interest in management in West Germany the question of the relative importance of management and *Technik* was raised. What is more it is possible to make out a case for Germany to the effect that *Technik* dominates management, with reference to:

> the specialist orientation already discussed

> the persistent prevalence on engineers among the ranks of top management (members of the *Vorstand*, or executive board)

> the relative high status of the technical departments and of the production function

the Germans' own claims to lead on design, quality, delivery and reliability

The basic point to be argued here as part of a characterization of British management is that in this culture the reverse is true, and management firmly dominates *Technik*. In positive terms this follows from the generalist orientation together with the emphasis on leadership, character, and judgement based on personal responsibility rather than on the constraint of systems.

Attitude to conflict

Both attitudes to conflict and the reason for these attitudes vary across management cultures, though there is some convergence on a qualified acceptance of conflict. Consider a few examples:

Italy: the André Laurent studies (1986) show a strong rejection of conflict as threatening to both organizational order and individual authority.

France: the same source shows a similar though less marked hostility to conflict, though practitioner testimonies suggest that intellectualized disagreement in French companies is acceptable.

Germany: conflict and criticism are acceptable as suggested earlier; serious issues are at stake, error must not go uncorrected!

Sweden: conflict in the form of reasoned disagreement will not threaten organisational order, and may advance the matter in hand.

USA: conflict is normal and desirable, it will bring the toughest to the front (where they ought to be) and ensure that the best proposals get the resources.

Israel: conflict is the natural state of man; if you are not arguing with someone you are probably dead.

But it is probably the British attitude that is most distinctive, with its traditional view of conflict as disruptive and ungentlemanly. Conflict in management betokens a failure of the organization to integrate, a failure of leaders to lead. Consensus is prized for reasons of both organizational purpose ('all pulling in the same direction') and interpersonal harmony.

System versus discretion

It is the United States that is the land of management systems *par excellence*: systems of financial planning, or of budgetary control, of performance appraisal, costing, personnel selection, job evaluation, investment appraisal, market share analysis, and so on. The prevalence, and quality, of the system is a testimony to the American commitment to efficiency, and perhaps they also express the American desire to make achievement possible for everyone - apply the system and you will get this much right. It is also noticeable that American managers tend to have a high regard for the credibility and efficacy of the systems they operate, seeing them as constituting, in the words of Alvin Gouldner (1954) a kind of representative bureaucracy. And for that matter, in the author's experience, non-Americans working for American companies are also typically persuaded of the rightness of these systems. When we speak of American management as being professional in an exemplary way, a lot of what we mean by the professional accolade has to do with the systems and Standard Operating Procedures (SOPs).

Now clearly there is no black and white contrast here, but one does not find the same enthusiasm for systems in British companies. They may be there, but are less likely to be the object of corporate affection and esteem. After all, what merit is there in operating systems? If you get it wrong, you must be an ass, if you get it right, well, all you did was implement a system someone else devised - it might have been a creative act for them but it is just a bit of demeaning conformity for you.

In place of the primacy of systems the British are more likely to esteem discretion - the right to decide in an area that has not been systematized. After all discretion calls for character, leadership, judgement rather than for well trained conformity. The attraction of discretion is precisely that it is unprogrammable, opaque, and cannot be controlled. A monument to the gentleman amateur rather than to the well-trained organization man. One might express it by saying that a feature of British management is a desire not to submerge the individual in the programme.

Principle and pragmatism

There is not much principle in British management, in the sense that it is not doctrinaire, practitioners do not see themselves as applying the tenets of management science, there is no appeal to a set of higher order principles. Professionalism and training are fine, but they only take you so far. And cleverness has not got much to do with it (and is best left to foreigners). The orientation is pragmatic, unpretentious. The supreme value is common sense. The emphasis is on implementation rather than design, on 'selling' something workable to people who are going to have to live with it rather than upon a rationality driven perfection. The golden rule will take you further than mathematical modelling.

This down to earth orientation, which is all about people practice outcomes, is not an exclusive feature of British management but it is a characteristic one. Simplicity, not sophistication, is the hallmark of those who get it right.

45

There is a literature on management style/decision making mode that presumes a dimension running from individual-authoritarian-discrete at one end to democratic participative consensual at the other. Individuals, companies, even cultures may be graded in terms of this dimension. So that, for example, Harold Geneen of ITT is more authoritarian than say Lee Iococa of Chrysler, or Japan is more consensual than the USA. We would like to suggest that this conventional dimension is not especially helpful in 'getting at' the nature of decision making/compliance in British management.

In the British context the appeal to doctrine, principle, system, authority, or to the dictates of expertise are relatively weak. The appeal to acceptability, social integration, expectation, political convenience and common sense are relatively strong. Compliance is neither system-engendered not a dictate of higher authority: it is engineered. In terms of Etzioni's once famous typology (1961) much compliance in British management is social-normative. It is, that is to say, the product of the mild manipulation of social acceptance and group integration, in which the superior's approbation crossed with promotion prospects are gently 'coat-trailed'. The message to the individual is: do it this way, be like us, win approval; appeals to formal authority are kept in the background.

A *laughing matter*

Britain may not be the only country in the world that has a sense of humour, but it is the only one that has sought to raise humour to the level of a national characteristic. No one else feels it to be a source of national identity. We would like to argue that this British obsession with humour also informs the practice of management, and here again a comparison with the USA is helpful!

The interesting thing is that Americans clearly have a sense of humour. It shows not only in popular entertainment, from comics to sit-coms, but also in the tradition of humorous writing, from Mark Twain to Joseph Heller. But there is little humour in American management. Individuals make wisecracks to punch home their points or scare off the opposition, and there is in the author's experience often some joking about baseball scores at the start of meetings, but little else. Business is too serious a matter to be the context for humour.

Yet by common observation humour is a thread running through interaction in Britain, inside companies as well as in the wider society. What is more it has been argued recently (Barsoux, 1993) that humour in British management is not simply a cultural 'add-on', but that it performs certain functions including:

the reduction of tension
building rapport on first meeting
demonstrating social acceptability
building sub-group solidarity (via in-jokes, or a particular humour style)

coping with stress
ameliorating failure
asking questions/making comments that would not otherwise be acceptable
trying out *outré* ideas
cloaking criticism upwards that would otherwise violate deference norms

and so on.

Again these humour functions are not unknown in other cultures but Britain must surely be distinctive in the frequency with which recourse is made to them.

An uncertain conclusion

Much of what has been offered in this paper is the product of the authors' own research and experience in other countries. But we would like to end by taking a key idea from that most distinguished writer on cultural difference, Geert Hofstede (1980). One of Hofstede's four dimensions is uncertainty avoidance, or put it in a positive form, tolerance for ambiguity. That is to say that national cultures vary significantly in the degree to which they can tolerate uncertainty. Of the four dimensions, this is the one that arguably distinguishes Britain most from other modern societies. For Britain demonstrates a high tolerance for ambiguity: this tolerance is somewhat higher than that demonstrated by the Americans in Hofstede's substantial sample, definitely higher than that of the Germans, and massively higher than that of the French. Does this tell us anything about British management practice?

Well the Hofstede finding on ambiguity tolerance is certainly consistent with some of the other features canvassed here. The relative lack of emphasis on formal hierarchy, systems, and specialism (expert authority) all relate to high ambiguity tolerance in the sense that these things all serve to reduce uncertainty. Or to formulate in a positive way tolerance for ambiguity relates to an emphasis on persuading rather than ordering, leading rather than determining, and to an emphasis on discretion rather than systems.

There is another interesting connection, namely between ambiguity tolerance and the use and nature of the English language. Consider that in Britain:

precision is not a virtue as in French
explicitness is not a virtue as in German
directness is not a virtue as in American

and all these ends are beautifully served by the English language, a vehicle *sans pareil* for the expression of the oblique, the indirect, the conditional may-be and the down right vague. Our strength is 'fudging', and one can fudge a lot better in English than in French!

Finally we would like to suggest that there is just a hint of a philosophic position in the British tolerance for ambiguity. The case would go like this. An individual confronts the world, and tries to make sense of it. This is a natural and sensible response, it is part of the human condition. Yet there are some things that are unknowable, some events that are unpredictable, some occurrences that are random, and much that is the product of human ingenuity rather than of law-like behaviour. There is arguably a gain in psychological energy in recognising this, a certain freedom in not struggling to anticipate every consequence.

After all, if Michelangelo had known it was going to take seven years, would he ever have started to paint the roof of the Sistine Chapel?

References

Barsoux, J. L. (1993), *Funny Business: Humour, Management and Business Culture*, Cassell, London.

Dalton, M. (1959), *Men Who Manage*, Wiley, New York.

Etzioni, A. (1961), *A Comparative Analysis of Complex Organizations*, The Free Press, Glencoe, Illinois.

Gouldner, A. (1954), *Patterns of Industrial Democracy*, The Free Press, Glencoe, Illinois.

Hofstede, G. (1980), *Culture's Consequences*, Sage, Beverley Hills and London.

Laurent, A. (1986), 'The Cross Cultural Puzzle of International Human Resource Management', *Human Resource Management*, Vol. 25, No. 1, pp. 91-102.

Lawrence, P. (1980), *Managers & Management in West Germany*, Croom Helm, London.

Lawrence, P. (1990), *Management in the Land of Israel*, Stanley Thornes, Cheltenham.

Lawrence, P. and Spybey, T. (1986), *Management & Society in Sweden*, Routledge, London.

Levi, P. (1987), *If Not Now, When?*, Sphere Books, London.

Nichols, T. (1977), *Living with Capitalism*, Routledge and Kegan Paul, London.

Roethlisberger, F. J. and Dickson, W. J. (1939), *Management and the Worker*, Harvard University Press, Cambridge, Mass.

3 The limitations of America's *Pax Oeconomica*: Germany and Japan after World War II

Robert Locke

Introduction

In drafting this paper's title I have consciously chosen to be perverse. This is true because most people who discuss the postwar world stress the significance of American hegemony in bringing about the recovery of Europe and Japan and their subsequent economic development. There is some debate about the importance of the Marshall Plan to Europe's recovery. Alan Milward (1984), for example, asserts that Western Europe was on the way to recovery before the Marshall Plan took effect and would have recovered, no doubt, without it. Others, especially but not exclusively Americans, maintain that generous American aid was indeed a very important material catalyst for that recovery. Nobody seems to argue, however, about the significance of American capitalism, in the systemic sense, in the postwar world. Triumphant in 1945, it became the system writ large for the subsequent economic prosperity of the free world.

Here I wish to take a different tack. I want to extend our time horizons. If we assume that America led the world economically and managerially after World War Two, we cannot assume this to be the case today. I mean that the reputation of American business and American management has clearly declined. Moreover, this loss of reputation did not just happen, it has been occurring progressively over the past thirty years. It would seem in fact that the period of unblemished American hegemony was really rather short, say not running much beyond 1960. The obvious question, then, is what happened? I shall not argue that Americans stopped after 1960 doing the things they did very well before but that the source of American decline is traceable to the very period of hegemony, the late 1940s and 1950s. I shall, moreover, concentrate on Germany and Japan in the analysis. The argument is that subsequent American decline stemmed from the successful

49

resistance of the Germans and Japanese during the immediate postwar period to the American way of doing things, organizationally and managerially. It will be presented under four rubrics: 1) an explanation of The American Way of Doing Things, Managerially and Organizationally; 2) an examination of German dissent, Codetermination; 3) an examination of Japanese dissent, Collective Consciousness; and 4) an evaluation of the long term effects of the three systems from the perspective of comparative efficiency.

The American way of doing things, managerially and organizationally

Since it constitutes the principal focus of the paper, it is best to begin with a description of the American managerial model from which the deviation occurred. It consisted of two major components, shop floor and corporate management.

Shop floor

Evaluating the American contribution to shop floor management, Joseph A. Litterer (1961, p. 467) wrote in 1961 that about 1900:

> the skill and knowledge of Europeans...was the equal and sometimes the superior of that of Americans. The difference was in how this technical knowledge and skill was used. The European manufacturer used it to make a product. The American manufacturer used it to make a process for making a product. A high class machinist in Europe could be found setting up a semiautomatic machine for less skilled labor to operate and to make this product, or he might be engaged in making the semiautomatic machine with which to make a product. The literature of the time frequently mentioned that American machines and tools were superior to the European. This, however, should be understood to reflect not a difference in abilities as much as a difference in the thinking of European and American management. One appreciated the importance of, and understood how to obtain, the advantage from machinery; the other did not.

This quotation raises several points. First, and of major importance, the American shop floor innovations should not be confused with applied science. The Germans as much as the Americans have the distinction of introducing scientific knowledge into engineering. During the nineteenth century we get the growth of the German technical *Hochschulen* and with them the development of what the Germans call *Technik*, the unique blend of knowledge and skill which constitutes their chief contribution to modern engineering.[1] *Technik* did not replace the vaunted German apprenticeship system which trained German labour to high skill levels. *Technik* amalgamated the skill of apprenticeship with the knowledge dimension of science, thereby enabling the Germans to lead in the era of science-based technological

50

change. American higher technical education, too, participated in this 'scientific' revolution. Hence Americans as well as Germans broke significantly from the exclusively on-the-job educational routines characteristic of British engineering in the heyday of the practical man, the First Industrial Revolution (1780-1850). But the shop floor innovations described in the quotation were managerial, not scientific and German manufacturing firms did not pioneer their adoption. In Germany the skilled workers continued to make the product, a product creation process, however, in which a scientific knowledge as well as a skill component now had a place. The change the quote describes was American.

The American systems 'revolution' led to the 'revolution' in scientific management, usually referred to in Europe as Taylorism. When system replaced artisanal skill in production, the cost bureau, the time and motion study people, the quality control group, in fact, factory managers replaced foremen as king in the workshop, the foreman being reduced to little more than a conduit through which managerial ideas were translated into action. This American systems revolution and the 'scientific management' accompanying it brought the separation of thought (management) from doing (labour) in the workshop, a separation that is one aspect of classic Taylorist shop floor routine. As workers lost control over the conception and execution of work, considerable deskilling occurred, the result of the shift from a factory in which the skilled worker made the product to one in which the production engineer and his staff designed the production systems and the semiautomatic machines that low skilled operators used to make the product.[2]

The corporate revolution

Taylorism enabled American industry to produce good-quality, if relatively unsophisticated, products at low prices. It also called into being the corporate restructuring of American firms that has been described so thoroughly in the work of Alfred D. Chandler, Jr. and the Chandlerians. The key event was the revolution at the corporate top. If Taylorism made mass production possible through methodically managed operations systems, an equally significant revolution also occurred at the corporate level in strategic management. This division in management functions between strategic management (in corporate headquarters), preoccupied with the question 'what business should we be in?' and operational management in the factories, preoccupied with the question 'how best can we run this business?' was expressed organizationally in the move from the U to the M form corporate structure.[3]

This corporate reform brought managerial needs that were quite distinct from those required by Taylorism. Top managers concentrated on the dynamics of money rather than product management. They needed staffs that could deal with corporate finance and marketing; they required managerial accountants who could keep watch on money flows through the various corporate divisions, for this information was much more vital to decision making in a strategic setting. And so we entered an era when comptrollers, financial experts, and accountants dominated, the engineer being increasingly ignored. While in the workshop the skilled worker lost control to the systems' manager, and in the big corporation the owner stockholder lost control at the top to the professional money manager. Throughout the corporation, power and control, from top through middle, gravitated to 'management'.

Americans, therefore, invented 'management' and with it the American way of doing business. Burck's article, (1957, p. 147) a veritable *paean* to American know how, expressed it admirably: 'The American way of doing business in an expanding market is the natural way of doing business,' in which American management is the key, 'flexible, unfettered by tradition, creative, expansion-minded, democratic in its relations with employees as well as customers'. Or, to use Hartmann's words, (1963, p. 149) 'managerialism' constitutes in the American mind a 'fourth production factor,' a 'strategic variable for the development of the firm'. As large firms integrated backward and forward, new managerial functions emerged, e.g. marketing, public relations, finance, etc. as part of a firm's expanding 'managerial team'. When more humane views replaced Taylorist notions of workers as 'shirkers', personnel departments formed to cope with the Human Relations movement's preoccupation with placing the right person in the right job (testing and interviewing) and with worker motivation. Creating employee harmony became as much management's concern as the layout of the factory floor. The revolutions in shop floor and corporate management produced America's managerial model. The 1945 version, however, contained two additional elements, big labour and big government. Both entered the American managerial equation when the Great Depression forced government to champion labour's cause. The chief legislative expression of this support, the Wagner Act, legally established labour's rights to organize, bargain collectively, and strike. But government help was not restricted to labour advocacy. The breakdown in the system, which was the Great Depression, spawned the Keynesian revolution, that brave attempt to macromanage the economy in order to eliminate the wide swings in the business cycle that occasioned intolerable levels of unemployment. Accordingly, the dynamics of American managerial capitalism expanded beyond the firm to bring about, what Maier (1987, p. 68) has called, the 'congruence of the managerial sphere within factory and society'.

This, then, was the management model, put together during the first few decades of the twentieth century, that America offered in affluent triumph to a prostrate world in 1945. Systems management on the shop floor assured high volume production and productivity, the innovations in corporate management provided big business with the flexibility that permitted a quick mobilization of financial, material, and human resources to unprecedented levels and to shift these resources to new needs and opportunities that arose in the future. Big government, for its part, macromanaged the economy monetarily and big labour through collective bargaining forced management to share the benefits of this very productive capitalist system with the workers. The workers in turn accepted the capitalists and the rewards they received from the system as the *quid pro quo* for the workers' own enjoyment of the abundance that the management operated system generated.

In 1945 Americans replied to European and Asian socialist musings about wealth redistribution from capitalist exploiters to worker producers with a gospel of productivity, attained through 'scientific management' of privately owned productive forces in free competitive markets from which all benefitted. Indeed, this is the model to which historians refer when discussing American's role in bringing about postwar recovery and development. Hogan (1987, p. 429) presents it most forthrightly as:

the keys to a neo-capitalism in Western Europe similar to the one that supposedly had led to a new era of economic growth and social stability in the United States. Through American aid, and particularly through the use of counterpart funds, Marshall Planners tried to underwrite industrial modernization projects, promote Keynesian strategies of aggregate economic management, overhaul antiquated systems of public administration, and encourage progressive tax policies, low-cost housing programs, and other measures of economic and social reform. Through production centres and productivity teams, they sought to build an alliance of labour, business, and professional leaders behind these reforms. And through the technical assistance program, of which the productivity campaign was a part, they hoped to transform distributive battles into the search for a shared abundance and political problems into technical ones that were soluble, they said, by adopting American engineering, production, and marketing techniques and American methods of labor-management teamwork.

Hogan's pen pointed this American system at two enemies, one, the obvious one, socialism, the other, no less serious, the sterile monopolistic, unproductive, nationalist circumscribed capitalist system that had predominated in Europe heretofore.

Since the Keynesian aspect of the New Deal synthesis, in which Marshall Planners sought to make American federalism an essential part of a European recovery programme, one that would fuse 'the separate economic sovereignties into an integrated market capped by supranational institutions of economic planning and administration' (Hogan, 1987, pp. 22-23) is well known, it is the micro implications of the quote that are of greater concern. Even though governments spent billions to ease the balance of payment crisis or to purchase machinery, equipment, and food, this money mattered less systemically than the relatively small funds devoted to the transfer of management methods and techniques. Through production centres and productivity teams the Marshall Planners intended to build an alliance of labour, business, and professional leaders in Europe, and through technical assistance to promote American methods of labour-management teamwork.

In the UK Sir Stafford Cripps, Chancellor of the Exchequer, and Paul Hoffman, former CEO of Studebaker, and head of the Marshall Plan's Economic Cooperation

Administration, quickly set up an Anglo-American Council on Productivity to tackle the management problem. The AACP, 'one of the largest experiments in adult education ever undertaken', between August 1948 and June 1952, sent 138 teams of managers, workers, and other specialists, 900 people in all, on visits to America. These visiting teams produced, during the peak year 1950-51, a report a week. In total over 600,000 copies of these reports were sold. They constitute a 'set of documents the likes of which, on such a scale and of such practical value, has never been seen in the history of international and cultural borrowing' (Carew, 1987).

Although teams from Continental countries started for America somewhat later, and initially on a more limited scale, by 1950 the Europeans had begun to overtake the British. Germany, for example, spend $1.3 million dollars (compared to the £1,000,000 budget of the AACP) mostly to finance trips; France by 1952 had sent 200 teams across the Atlantic (2,600 Frenchmen in all) and the reports they produced were made available to management, government, and labour groups at home. The transfer of American management expertise to Europe, moreover, did not come uniquely through Marshall Plan agencies. NATO brought a rapid expansion of military operational research in Europe, with the requisite international meetings of OR groups taking place on both sides of the Atlantic. Private agencies, the Ford Foundation in particular, got involved in European management education. Paul Hoffman moved from his job at the Marshall Plan's agency to become head of the Ford Foundation, bringing Marshall Plan personnel as well as management educational concerns with him. American corporations, expanding overseas, directly contributed to this export of managerialism.

American management influence writ large, then, is a rich and complicated subject after World War II. Since the tale is familiar and since the limitation of this influence is the focus, the theme of how 'America made the European Way' or the Japanese way to postwar prosperity can be dropped.[4] How the Germans and the Japanese made their own, sometimes American-opposed, way to prosperity is our story.

Codetermination in Germany

Everybody knows that a new managerial class rose to take over large American corporations circa 1940, thus effectively separating those who control the firm from those who own it. This 'managerialism' is one component of the New Deal synthesis. The despoliation of the stockholders that resulted, to the benefit of the new managerial elite, has had strict limits. Managers, who remained dependent juridically upon stockholders for their jobs, certainly had to see to it that company stock values and paid out dividends remained high, otherwise a stockholders' revolt could throw the professional managerial elite out.

The rise of unions and collective bargaining, on the other hand, did not particularly decrease stockholder control. Neither juridically nor in the popular

American imagination did employees become the firm. The laws on collective bargaining simply required management to recognize and bargain in good faith with the union, should its employees in free election choose to have one. The stockholders and the professional managers, which stockholders selected, were the 'firm', the employees and the union they selected to represent them were 'outsiders'. This automatically meant that the employees' and the firm's business were not synonymous. Even an old union warrior like George Meany recognized the divergent jurisdictions when he acknowledged that issues like production standards, location of plant, investment policy, new product development, new plant construction, reinvestment of profits, and new equity capital were not subject to collective bargaining. They were very important to the firm but they were not the workers' business.[5]

The separation of employees from the firm, both in terms of ownership (stockholders) and control (stockholders' elected professional management), although typical of large British and American private corporations, was not limited to them. *The Economist* noted in 1950 that nationalized industries did not belong to their workers either but to the nation. The government, representing the nation, was charged with selecting the management. Ultimately management was, therefore, responsible to the government and not to the workers. The dominant view in America and Britain in both private and nationalized firms has always been that employee control over management would lead to company inefficiency and ruin because the workers would put their interests first and that these interests would be incompatible, in the long run if not the short, with those of the firm's owners, whether private capitalists or national citizenry.

German debates about the relative merits of capitalist and national ownership resembled British more than American, for in 1945 many more Germans than Americans believed that capitalism was in its death throes. Hans Böckler, the leader of the German Union Federation (DGB), proclaimed its end in March 1946, which he avouched was a cause for rejoicing since the capitalists could not again betray the workers as they had in 1920-21 (Schmidt, 1970). Similar views, afoot in the German Socialist Party (the SPD), prompted delegates at the Party's first postwar rally (May 1946) to make the building of socialism their principal national task. German capitalists and their political representatives disagreed, but their closeness to the now defunct Third Reich made their views suspect. Hence, the socialization of basic industries appeared inevitable. The story of why the predicted demise of capitalism proved false (the German Economic Miracle and the successful selling of the privately owned social market economy to the West German electorate) is too familiar and too involved to repeat.

If the West Germans eventually sided with the Americans on the private ownership issue, the management control issue under capitalist ownership was another matter. It pitted German capitalists and socialists against Americans, British, and many West Europeans. And in American ranks labour union officials stood with members of corporate boards. George Meany articulated the typical American attitude towards labour's involvement in management: 'For the American

Federation of Labor I can say flatly that collective bargaining is not a means of seeking a voice in management, we do not want so-called codetermination....' (Meany, 1955, p. 93). It was precisely labour's legally sanctioned codetermination in management decision-making that Germans sought. Why? To answer the question requires a brief excursion into the relationship between state and civil society.

In the British and American world of the seventeenth and eighteenth centuries political theorists made the state an oppressor, in the sense that governments could only infringe arbitrarily on an individual's natural right to life, liberty, and property. The distrust of government, moreover, extended from the political sphere to the economic: a nation's growth should be left largely to market forces which through competition allocate resources efficiently, thereby promoting consumer interests and accommodating, through the diffusion of political and economic power, the right of everybody to entry into the economy. Competition is a democratic doctrine. There is, in short, as Hadley (1970, pp. 391-92) points out, room for an Adam Smith in the eighteenth century because there was a John Locke in the seventeenth.

The German idea of freedom has always puzzled Englishmen and Americans because it regards the state as an active guarantor of individual rights and liberties in both the economic and political spheres, rather than their enemy.[6] This perception of the state formed the mindset and shaped the political behaviour of governments and the parties at conflict with each other in the economic sphere of German civil society. It helps explain, therefore, the difference between the British and the American view and the German view of management.

German businessmen and industrialists have had much less faith than British or American in the economic efficacy of the competitive market. On the contrary, Germans have always sought not only the protection of the cartel but have done so expecting the state's cooperation, support and approval. And the state has willingly granted them. The state, moreover, assuming a corporate view of society, has not hesitated to interfere with the market in order to protect the 'legitimate' interest of the working classes. Bismarck's social insurance programme is the most famous early example of state interventions, but there were others, including, and of special interest here, the Law for the Protection of Labour (*Arbeiterschutzgesetz*) which the *Reichstag* passed on June 1, 1891.

The movement that culminated in this law, although rooted in medieval corporatism, began in the 1830s when, with profit sharing in mind, the necessity for workers to participate in management became clear. After their propagation in the Frankfurt Assembly of 1849, the ideas were taken up by the *Verein für Sozialpolitik* in the third quarter of the nineteenth century (specifically therein by Friedrich Naumann, Franz Hitze, and Friedrich Lange, who talked about the creation of a 'constitutional factory'). In 1890 Emperor William II incorporated this reformist idea into a speech calling for the creation within factories of bodies representing workers that would be empowered to defend their interests in negotiations with employers. The resultant Law for the Protection of Labour, which Lange sponsored in the *Reichstag*, granted workers joint consultation rights (*Mitberatungsrecht*) on social matters. This was not codetermination (*Mitbestimmung*) but it allowed for the organization of plant committees in all factories covered by the Industrial Code of 1869 if they had more than twenty employees. And it required management to issue and abide by shop regulations spelling out relations with workers, (Shuchman, 1957). No more caprice. German businessmen and industrialists, who strongly opposed worker encroachments on their managerial authority, begrudgingly accepted the Law for the Protection of Labour because it did not grant codetermination to workers. Indeed, it did not even make the establishment of plant committees mandatory.

Two points are of interest in this account:

1. the codetermination issue is deeply rooted in German history, and

2. the state, in the German tradition, has been implicated in this history.

This hardly means that the state was an advocate of codetermination. Its position on the subject depended on who controlled the state. For this reason it was inevitable perhaps that the constitutional crisis that beset Germany from 1914 to 1945 included the conflict in civil society between labour and management over codetermination.

German entrepreneurs have always tried to personify the relationship between leader and follower. Much of this relationship has been highly authoritarian, as befits a military state, but it has also been based on paternalistic concern for the welfare of the personnel (of the sort officers in the army have for the well being of the troops) and on a thorough knowledge of the skills employed at every level in office or workshop. Although not adverse to consulting employees on social matters, entrepreneurs did object to any restrictions on their authority. Hence the employers' associations that represented owners resisted codetermination. Inasmuch as the Imperial government and bureaucracy were also of an authoritarian bent, the 1891 Law was about all that could be achieved until the outbreak of the First World War.

The war altered the balance of forces within the country fundamentally. Employer concessions to codetermination increased in proportion to the weakness of the regime, its need for workers' support, and the employers' fear of the red spectre. By the end of 1916, when the Hindenburg-Ludendorff military dictatorship opted for the total mobilization of labour under the Auxiliary Service Act (*Hilfsdienstgesetz*), the generals felt the necessity to placate the workers for their sacrifices by creating permanent plant committees of blue and white collar workers. Employers refused to cooperate. However, as the regime collapsed, the employer's association leaned more towards granting workers a greater voice in management; by the revolutionary month of November 1918, employers, out of fear of Bolshevism, capitulated entirely. Unions and the employers' associations signed collective agreements which gave a firm's employees rights of co-

57

determination with management in social policy and the right to be consulted in personnel and economic decisions.

Because to the German mind private agreements, even between powerful corporate bodies like employer associations or trade union federations, lack authority, codetermination quickly assumed constitutional importance during the struggles over the Weimar Republic. Already in December 1918 a socialist dominated provisional government decreed that the agreement between trade union federation and employer association would become legally applicable throughout the Reich. The following July a socialist-liberal-progressive majority in the Constituent Assembly, wrote codetermination into the Weimar Constitution.[7]

When the ensuing Reichstag elections strengthened the conservatives, the legislation they passed failed to provide the promised employee empowerments. The law, *Betriegbsrätegesetz* (February 4, 1920), did allow for the creation of works councils in firms with twenty or more employees (and the election of a shop steward in those with five to twenty employees) that could act on social, personnel and economic questions. It also called for the workers to elect one to two members of the firm's Supervisory Board.[8] But with this concession the stockholders still dominated board selections, and in the works councils, although the law spoke of employee participation in social, personnel, and economic decision making, that participation was limited in personnel matters to consultation and, in economic areas to cooperating with management in the implementation of new work methods and wage rates. Trade unions disliked the law especially since it stopped them from participating in works council elections. An anti union measure, the law at best gave employees the right to be consulted (and ignored) but it conceded no codetermination in decision making.

This legislative defeat guaranteed that political fighting over codetermination would continue. Labour unions pressed for full worker participation not only in the governance of firms but in suprafirm economic organs. In the twelfth congress of German unions at Breslau in 1925 Rudolf Hilferding called for a hierarchic system of economic councils based on codetermination in which unions would formally participate. The congress established a commission to investigate the matter and formulate an action programme. This commission's work led to a book by Fritz Naphtali (1928), one of the unions' best theoreticians during Weimar period, which crystallized trade union thought on codetermination - *Wirtschaftsdemokratie - Ihr Wesen, Weg und Ziel* (Economic Democracy - Its Essence, Way and Goal).

The employers for their part retreated rapidly from tactical concessions made under the stress of collapse and chaos. In typical German fashion, moreover, they sought state help in their task. They did so within the conservative ranks of pro-Weimar bourgeois parties and by supporting anticodetermination Rightist political groups intent on the Republic's destruction. The employers' role in Hitler's rise to power cannot be covered. One thing is clear, however: the crushing of German socialism and free trade unionism did not displease employers fearful of codetermination. The Nazis dissolved the works councils and applied the

58

Führerprinzip (authoritarian principle) in the management of firms just as they did in the management of the National Socialist State. Total Nazi victory in the constitutional conflict, therefore, brought total defeat of codetermination in the economy. This was the burden of history German socialist and trade unionists inherited when they crawled from the rubble, left the concentration camps, or returned from exile after World War II. Otto Brenner, one of the postwar reformers, remembered that 'the union leaders during the recovery period..., at whose head stood Hans Böckler, first president of the German Union Federation *(Deutschen Gewerkschaftsbundes)*', had lived through the fall of the Weimar Republic and had participated in discussions about the concept of economic democracy at the time. The postwar leaders formed a living bridge with their knowledge and experience between the trade union ideas of the 1920s and the social programmes that the united trade union movement advocated after the collapse of Nazi Germany. Obviously, they had scores to settle, not only with the Nazis but with the business and industrial leadership which had supported them. They wanted both excluded from power. But their programmes drew on the past. Ludwig Rosenberg, another postwar codetermination activist, remembered that 'many reflections, numerous proposals, and not a few of [their] impulses...found their origins in Naphtali's book. The postwar claims for economic democracy as a public control of monopoly market organizations, on the one hand, and, on the other, the break up of entrepreneurial structures [was] - as Naphtali and his friends formulated it... - as much an old as a contemporary goal' (Schmidt, 1970, p. 62).

If the free trade unions took up codetermination where they had left off in 1933, the issue had become, because of the Nazi experience, not just theirs alone. Even private property advocates believed after the war that something had to be done to give workers a voice in management. The Christian churches and the Christian trade unions went on record for codetermination. So did the Christian Democratic Union, Adenauer's party, in its Ahlener party day program which, with Adenauer himself expressing approval, spoke out in favour of codetermination (Shuchman, 1957, p. 101). Between 1947 and 1950 eight of the newly constituted states *(Länder)*in West Germany passed works council legislation which went far beyond that of Weimar. Works councils were given codecision right on social matters; in personnel 'they were granted rights of participation which ranged from joint-consultation to the right of veto'; and, in the all important economic area they were granted rights of codecision in basic matters that vitally affected the future of enterprises, such as 'expansion, consolidation, and shutdowns, and joint consultation in such matters as the purchase and sale of equipment, changes in production methods, determination of accounting procedures and sales policies' (Shuchman, 1957, p. 110). The laws also stipulated that works councils elect one to two members of supervisory boards. Hence the state laws not only restored empowerments claimed during Weimar; they expanded them, for the first time, so that economic decisions became part of works council purview.

But what of the Americans? If, after all, most Germans were keen about creating some sort of codetermination in 1945, it was largely beside the point. Totally defeated, the government and fate of Germany were in the hands of the occupiers. Without their approval Germans could do nothing. And, Soviets aside, the American were the major partner in the occupation. This was particularly true after the creation of the bizone (1947), which amalgamated the American with the British zone, wherein the bulk of West German heavy industry resided. Americans, with their faith in capitalist free enterprise, and Germans, with their statist traditions and belief in codetermination, were bound to clash.

German historians have handled the US reaction to codetermination accordingly, i.e. as champions of free enterprise and cold war anticommunism, Americans have opposed it. Actually, the American response was more complex, especially before the Cold War really set in. In 1946 the US State Department, under Secretary James Byrnes, did not oppose codetermination. After all, America's closest ally, Great Britain, was doing even worse; rushing headlong into socialism. When the British Foreign Secretary, Ernest Bevin, following Labour's nationalization of major industries, announced (October 23, 1946) that the UK favoured nationalizing German industries, too, Byrnes answered (December 17, 1946) that the US had no objections to the British plans. People in America also recognized that what might be ill advised for their country could, considering German history, fit German conditions. Meany (1955, p. 93) reasoned, for example, that, although not for America, 'codetermination in Germany had some logic as a means of maintaining economic democracy'. Americans thought that the German industrialists' penchant to rely on the state for political and economic protection (e.g. by fascist oppression of trade unionists and socialists and by state supported cartel building) had to be curbed. To do this often meant supporting policies that clashed with American 'principles.' Consequently Americans agreed at Potsdam that big business collaborators would lose control over their firms.

To some extent, too, American and German conceptions about the state's relationship with civil society provoked misunderstandings about codetermination. Germans want, Müller (1987, p. 53) specified in her history of the subject, 'a legal foundation for practical activity'. But Englishmen and Americans do not. When the Allied Control Commission issued Law 22, April 10 1946, regulating works councils, it reflected Anglo-American ideas: it was brief (13 short articles) and it did not even make the organization of work councils in firms obligatory. Workers and managers were free, through collective bargaining, to set up, without interference from the state, whatever arrangements they wanted, including no works council at all, to Americans a perfectly sensible arrangement. To the Germans this simply meant that the British and Americans were blocking the formation of work councils i.e. a serious law would have made them obligatory and have regulated their operation in considerable detail. This dispute with Americans, therefore, was rooted in different ideas of freedom.

Still, the American view of codetermination should not be misrepresented. When George Marshall replaced Byrnes as Secretary of State, Bevin also tried to get his support for British nationalization plans in Germany. Marshall answered that he would leave the matter to the military administration on the scene, a response tantamount to refusal because that military administration, from General Lucius Clay down, represented very conservative American circles. Not only did it fight communists but, when recruiting personnel for the reconstructed German administration, ignored trade unionists and socialists who were themselves anticommunists. The policy resulted in a German civil service with personnel of a conservative economic bent. The military authorities, moreover, opposed German codetermination. Initially, General Clay could not control events in the Ruhr, where British military authorities approved the codetermination deal in the steel industry, struck between German trade unions and management. But when the German state governments in his own zone wrote codetermination provisions into their constitutions, Clay first rejected them, then reluctantly accepted the constitutions with economic codetermination stricken from the texts. Clay's veto provoked widespread protests throughout the American zone.[9] He justified the action on constitutional grounds, stating that decisions about economic codetermination should not be made by state (Land) governments; their importance required the approval of the German people living in a sovereign German national state. Since General Robertson, the British military governor and a former executive of The Dunlop Tyre Company concurred, the British blocked economic codetermination legislation in their zone as well. Germans distrusted Clay's constitutional arguments, viewing them as a rearguard action, to delay codetermination until, with the recovery of capitalism, it could be defeated or at least tamed.

Clay's obstructionism, therefore, postponed a showdown until the creation of the German Federal Republic. That showdown, which resulted in the Codetermination Law for the Iron and Steel Industry of 1951 and the law on works councils a year later, vindicated Clay's delaying tactic, if it were his tactic, for proponents of codetermination did not achieve as much then as they would most certainly have done three or four years earlier. It is true that the 1951 law provided for parity (50 per cent elected by workers, 50 per cent by stockholders) in the selection of supervisory boards (*Aufsichtsräte*), with a neutral group choosing a 'thirteenth man' who constituted a swing vote if stockholder and employee board members voted their constituents' interests. The law also provided for the employee elected members of the Supervisory Board to choose a personnel director, to join the commercial and technical directors, on corporate Managing Boards (*Vorstand*). Since managing boards make decisions collectively, the Personnel Director has real authority in running the company.

The 1951 law only applied to coal and steel firms. When codetermination advocates tried to extend its provisions to all business and industrial firms, they failed. The 1952 law permitted employees to elect just a third of the members of the Supervisory Board in non steel and coal companies and it ignored the provision of the 1951 law that let employees' representatives on supervisory boards choose the Personnel Director on the Managing Board. The stockholders clearly commanded both boards. Moreover, the 1952 law restricted works councils to consultation not codecision making on personnel and economic matters.

61

Cold war politics modulated American reaction to the debate and passage of the 1951 Law. John McCloy, the American High Commissioner, tried to take a hands off attitude on codetermination, although he forced events by pressuring Adenauer to address the codetermination issue in order to fulfil Clay's promise to so act when a sovereign German state existed. Still, McCloy was not indifferent to this legislation. Although recognizing that it was for Germans to decide about codetermination, he told German trade unionists not to be surprised when Americans refused to invest in companies comanaged by workers, a not too subtle pressure against adoption.[10] Private American business representatives criticized codetermination openly. Getting wind of the German project, the National Association of Manufacturers sent a delegation to Europe led by Eldridge Haines to lobby against the *Bundestag* bill. Gordon Michler, head of the German Committee of the National Foreign Trade Council of the United States, joined the transatlantic trekkers to speak against codetermination. And in America a representative of the National Association of Manufacturers wrote an open letter to the German Council in New York, published in the *New York Times*, warning that Americans would not invest in German industry if the codetermination law passed.

Occasionally the protests proclaimed that codetermination was, to use the words of a *New York Times* (1951, April 12, p. 32-33) editorial, a 'new socialism in the relations between capitalism and labor'. But usually they employed less extreme language, pointing out that codetermination robbed stockholders of their rights of control. The argument was somewhat disingenuous, inasmuch as the stockholders had already lost control to the new management, but it was, in any event, certainly true that codetermination would challenge the control of an exclusively stockholder elected professional management. The Americans proclaimed that worker involvement in management would bring inefficiency. One commentator, Gilbert Burck (1954, pp. 250), stated in *Fortune* after the bill passed, that German 'labor managed to hang what may turn out to be a millstone on the necks of management, consumers, and itself. When management and labour go to bed with each other, it is usually the consumer who gets raped'. Codetermination, he continued, was the worst possible approach to making the economy more dynamic because it would lead to 'crippled national productivity, a retarded standard of living, and cartels' (p. 220). Burck even appealed to American labour leaders for support. He quoted two on German codetermination, one saying it was 'the worse approach to trade unionism I ever saw', the other, after meeting a labour elected member of a Supervisory Board, who in his opinion had taken on the air of management, 'how can a guy like that represent labour?'.[11] The reports about American labour's attitude towards codetermination were true. Robert Bowie, one of the Marshall Plan people, observed during a retrospective on The Marshall Plan, that American labour opposed codetermination and urged German labour to assume a proper union attitude: to represent workers in collective bargaining in opposition to, and not in partnership with, management (Hoffmann and Maier, 1984). Despite the understanding comment Meany made about the appropriateness of codetermination in Germany, American labour, determined to preserve its adversarial relationship with management, really did not like it very much.

After the *Bundestag* failed to pass a strong bill in 1952 American anxieties decreased. Even so Americans were not happy with the limited codetermination practices in vogue. The unhappiness increased when the SPD-FDP (Social Democratic, Free Democratic) coalition government, under Chancellor Helmut Schmidt, put through another codetermination law in the mid 1970s. Although the new law preserved stockholder supremacy in supervisory board selections, it extended the number of members elected by the employees, thereby shifting more in labour's favour (50 per cent employee, 50 percent stockholder elected Supervisory Boards, with the all important pivotal 'thirteenth' man elected by stockholders). Thus, the German labour management relations that emerged during postwar recovery and expansion could hardly be called an American import foisted on them by Marshall Planners. Americans certainly fought hard to put their ideas into effect; sometimes with great success since forces opposing codetermination within Germany strengthened after recovery. But the Germans, drawing upon their own deep rooted codetermination traditions, resisted these forces enough to create a managerial system that deviated markedly from the American.

The key points of difference are two. One is the German desire to provide a legal base for 'practical activity,' the American to eliminate state interference in just those practical activities of civil society. The differences are expressed in current German codetermination laws, which spell out empowerment, and in American collective bargaining legislation, which makes the state only a formal referee in a fight the substantive outcome of which is uniquely the business of management and labour.

The second difference is over the nature of management labour relations. American reformers chastized German 'management' in this regard. They accused it of making no more effort to understand the workers than German trade unions did management. Thomas H. Carroll of Ford Foundation, and Thomas L. Norton, of New York University, after a research study in the mid 1950s sponsored by the US and West German governments, recommended that a new national institute for executive development be established in Berlin, to help, by learning from the Americans, repair the 'enormous [defects] in human relations in German firms, some of the biggest of which do not even have personnel departments' (Burck, 1957, p. 146).

Americans, seeking to make management the 'fourth' factor of production, cultivated in firm and society the dogma of management through management development programmes and business schools wherein management was taught as a general codified form of knowledge. For their part, the German entrepreneurs fostered, less through 'knowledge' than intuition and '*Kniffe*' (knowing the ropes), job competence and individual responsibility in, and a sense of personal relations between, themselves and their underlings. While Americans stressed managerial functions, ever adding new layers to the 'managerial team', German entrepreneurs let it be known, by making personnel, sales, advertising, and public relations, staff

63

rather than line positions, that people in these positions were not 'key players' in the organization. When a technical director, member of the managing board of a firm with 8,500 employees, interviews every new job applicant personally, he is making a statement about leadership style. He, not the Personnel Department, is involved with the personnel.

In short, German entrepreneurs rejected American 'managerialism' ('God save us from the professional managers,' Hartmann (1963, p. 113) reports one commenting) and within it, Human Relations Management particularly (it was a tool of impersonal manipulation). 'What do the Americans have in their human and public relations?' asked a German business leader rhetorically. 'They have precisely no relations. Workers and entrepreneurs only work for dollars. By contrast, here we can move our people at a fast pace (*Husarenritte*). Here we have real contact between superior and subordinate. This might seem a bit patriarchal at times. But our people want to know those at the top personally' (p. 173). Considering the workers' struggle for codetermination, this entrepreneur's view of employer employee relations is a bit romanticized. But it constituted no less a rejection of American thinking. Hartmann observed that '[American Human Relations Management] had become the fashionable import in the early 1950s, ...[after which] this bull market turned into a bear, so that today one sees this programme only as a typical and scarcely exportable product of American economic culture'. American management training programmes in the firm as well as extramurally and the specific techniques of human relations management developed in the US Hartmann concluded, 'are spoken of [in Germany] no more today (p. 197)'.[12]

Human Relations Management, a creation of an American managerialism extremely jealous of its control prerogatives, proved to be no more compatible with German labour's view of codetermination than with the German entrepreneurs' ideas about leadership. Hartmann (1963, p. 172) highlights the difference: '[American] human relations tries to deprive subordinates of influence in the decision process - accordingly in comparison with the German situation, it cannot be emphasized enough, that by influence only the right to suggest is meant, in no way, however, codetermination and certainly no legally recognized voting rights on grounds of equality'.

Whereas German workers, and above all trade unionists, sought to establish labour management relations on the basis of legally prescribed codetermination, Germans entrepreneurs tried, in a no less un-American way, to personify the relationship between leadership and followers. The synthesis that took place in West Germany fused German entrepreneurial traditions in personal leadership with trade union striving towards codetermination. Worker participation in management decision and control is not a uniquely German phenomenon. But the Germans are the acknowledged pioneers in a movement that in the 1970s and 1980s gained world recognition. It would appear, therefore, that, if anything, German generated codetermination had a greater international influence in the postwar world than any management labour relations model generated by the American so-called, and

64

highly idealized, New Deal Synthesis.

Japanese collective consciousness

In Japanese economic history two salient factors have conditioned development: *First*, Japan in the seventeenth and eighteenth centuries did not participate in the Western movement subsumed under the heading 'the Enlightenment'. Eleanor Hadley in her excellent work *Antitrust in Japan* explains the significance of this fact: a 'feudal' society plunging into economic modernization without having undergone the political and social upheavals that happened in the West before the age of intense industrialization:

> Japan's early capitalists did not stand for any injection of fresh thinking into the hierarchical institution of the 'house,' and externally expected to operate as superiors and inferiors, as those favoured and not favoured.... It was a paternalistic hierarchy of people taught to think in terms of superiors and inferiors. As for external relations among businesses, there were no voices to suggest that all should have an equal chance, that businesses should be treated equally. In other words, there was no Adam Smith, for there was no John Locke. There was no public policy of competition, for competition is a democratic doctrine. Competition radically asserts, 'let all compete and may the best man win'. Among Japan's bureaucrats, as among Japan's political leadership, the ideology was that of superior and inferior. It should surprise no one that Mitsui, Mitsubishi, Sumitomo, and Yasuda were the superiors of Japan's business world (Hadley, 1970, pp. 34, 35).

There is a considerable literature about cultural heritage determining Japanese management belief and behaviour. 'In Japan,' Janet Hunter (1989, p. 79) points out, 'the relationship of the individual to other individuals and to society at large is still governed by his or her membership of various groups. ...These groups are the key to the moulding of the individual's identity'.[13] The basic group in traditional Japanese vertical-oriented society was the *mura*, the village and this *mura* like sense of loyalty, the argument runs, has been transferred to the modern firm.[14] As Nakane Chie notes:

> The group, based on the work place, has indeed a very similar function and role to that of the *mura*, the traditional rural village community. A man becomes secure through tightly knit communal activities. In return, he must always adjust himself to group demands and accept the group consciousness, even though it might seem unreasonable both in content and method of presentation (Chie, 1972).

Hadley (1970, pp. 391-91) moreover, has stressed the effect which the presence or absence of an 'Enlightenment' tradition had on conceptions of macroeconomic

65

reality. She observes:

> The low esteem in which the market mechanism is held and the absence of fear of abuse of power are but facets of the different orientation to political economy that one finds in Japan. Inasmuch as in Japanese conservative opinion the market mechanism is regarded as incapable of providing direction to the economy, no importance is attached, from this point of view, to market form. And inasmuch as efficiency is uncritically associated with larger and larger firm size, there tends to be the view that the higher the market concentration the greater the effective use of resources. In Japanese conservative opinion it is the government which steers, with producers the vital agents.... In the liberal tradition of the West a nation's growth can be left largely to market forces. The government's role...is seen as primarily that of promoting through the use of monetary and fiscal policy an environment in which business can operate and prosper. Because different market structures are regarded as producing different results, market reform is important. In the liberal view, competitive markets are to be preferred to concentrated markets on a number of counts: (i) allocation of resources and efficiency of production; (ii) consumer responsiveness; (iii) diffusion of power; (iv) accommodation of the 'right to entry'.

These quotes indicate, then, that the Japanese started industrialization with very different ideas from American ones about an individual's place in his or her firm, and the position the firm should hold in the hierarchy of enterprise. Hadley called the Western view 'liberal' which in the topsy-turvy world of today would be called 'conservative'. But in a 'classical' political sense she is undoubtedly right because traditional liberal philosophy set individualist against feudal values. Or as the French novelist, Stendahl wrote in *Lucien Leuwen*, the principal issue that divides society in our time (he is writing in the 1820s) is 'rank' versus 'merit'.

Second, the other factor that conditioned Japanese industrialization is that it occurred late and made, therefore, relatively high technological knowledge and skill demands, demands that the country was ill prepared to meet because of its very isolation from the West. The words knowledge and skill are used advisedly. Since the Japanese were behind, they did not need, nor could they have provided, like the Germans (with their scientific-research tradition, their *Hochschulen*), the creative scientists that could lead the world into a new technological era. They needed to copy and perfect the technology that the West had already invented. The Japanese *dirigiste* government accordingly, when it set about reforming higher education, stressed engineering instead of science. The Japanese engineers, moreover, acquired a special brand of education quite different from engineering education in the West. Professor Ken'ichi Yasumuro (1993, pp. 89-90) notes that these Japanese pioneers quickly learned that both formal and tacit knowledge are essential to manufacturing: 'Theories could be taught in higher educational institutes, and machines could be imported from Western countries. Foreign advisers and teachers usually lacked practical knowledge, because a strict division

66

of labour between the engineer and the skilled workers was already established in Western societies. They could not instruct the Japanese how to operate the machines....'

For successful technology transfer, Japanese engineers not only had to learn formal engineering that the Western engineer possessed but he had to spend time in the Western shop acquiring the 'non-verbal knowledge and technical skills' that Japanese labour did not possess and then on return to teach them to Japanese workers.

This 'feudal' outlook, projected into the late industrializing state, inevitably affected the evolution of Japanese management labour relations. Yasumuro pinpointed one effect. The necessity for the Japanese engineer to teach craft skills promoted the well known closeness between Japanese engineers and skilled craftsmen in the plant. Technical need, not a mystical belief in togetherness, cemented the working union in Japanese factories between engineers and skilled labour. Tough minded historians dislike talk about harmony in the plant. Andrew Gordon (1985, p. 413) noted that 'the relationships of industrial production [in Japan] most resembled those in the West at the outset'. Bitter strife and strikes characterized labour management relations in large Japanese firms during the period of intense industrialization (1890-1940). Such an articulation makes short shrift of the idea that *wa* (harmony) was always the relational pattern within Japanese firms. In Gordon's work we find ourselves on the familiar Western ground of conflict of interest and exploitation.

From a purely human psychological point of view there does seem to be something absurd about Japanese or any national history and society being peopled by cheerful, hard working, conflict free groups. Yet there is also no reason why harmony and conflict are mutually incompatible historical themes or why conflict and its results must always be expressed the same way. The discussion of German conflict showed that it took a different form from American, with different results, and the same argument applies to Japan.

Andrew Gordon himself emphasizes that, despite the commonality of conflict, the Japanese labour experience differed from the West in two ways. First, it was unique in that Japanese workers never developed strong industry wide or horizontally connected trade unions. Labour unions in Japan grew up firm centred. This was never the case in Great Britain, America, or despite its tribal traditions, even in Germany. The growth of working class consciousness during industrialization, especially under the impact of Marxism, certainly disproved the conservative claim that German firms were, in contradistinction to those in Western Europe and America, communities (*Gemeinschaften*). German workers, unlike Japanese, organized strong industrial unions, not company unions and, as noted in the case of codetermination, collective bargaining has taken place for a long time between union and employer federations. The sense of community that exists within the firm is expressed not in the unions but in the works councils. Indeed, one Japanese scholar states that the closest equivalent to the Japanese union is not the German union but the works councils.[15] Whereas German firms through works councils have a sense of community that is missing in America and present in Japan, in the trade unions they have a class solidarity that is present in Europe but absent in Japan.[16]

Second, Japanese labour management tradition is also unique, and this is a natural corollary to enterprise unionism, because workers have always sought status within the firm - to be accepted as regular employees like the white collar salaried staff rather than to identify themselves, in a class conscious sense, with other workers. Conflict was not thereby avoided. But the conflict took place in status not class terms. As Shinji Sugayama observes in a paper on "Business Education, Training, and the Emergence of the 'Japanese Employment System'":

> An examination of labour disputes in the course of Japan's industrial revolution indicates that workers' anger over status discrimination lay at the heart of many of these incidents. The labour movement in Japan was thus a movement aimed at the elevation of the status of workers rather than one built on class consciousness. For the Japanese labour movement, staff employees - treated by the company as 'regular' members of the enterprise community - constituted the 'reference group,' the model for the workers' status aspirations (Sugayama, in eds. Kawabe and Daito, 1993).

These two management labour relation peculiarities (enterprise unionism and vertical group status consciousness) have coloured the interaction between Japanese management and labour throughout industrialization. It is not possible to describe how the ebb and flow of power relationships worked themselves out before the end of the Great Pacific War. For anybody interested in that story, Andrew Gordon's book offers good and essential reading. But the eccentricities in the Japanese management labour heritage needed to be identified in order to be able to elucidate the nature of postwar Japanese dissent. For, if Japan faced the same reconstruction nightmare as the Germans, if the same Cold War considerations came into play during the recovery, if Americans set similar policy goals in Japan to those in Europe (to defeat the redistributive, zero sum class conflict Marxist challenge, by offering the dynamic, people of plenty, cooperative worker management model of capitalism), the Japanese no more followed American ideas when developing postwar management labour relations than did the Germans. What emerged from the defeat was a synthesis between the old and the new, but it was, like the German synthesis, the result of Japanese historical experiences not American, or German.

Before looking at the Japanese synthesis and to clarify its nature, another point should be made about German and Japanese traditions: They have produced very different legal outlooks. William Gould (1984, p. xiv) calculated that in Japan there are 15,000 lawyers compared to 500,000 in the US, a country with only twice the population. America indisputably, is the country where legalism is supreme. In Germany, where people like everything spelled out by the state in a law or regulation, the participation of the legal profession in corporate affairs is, if more regulative than trial oriented, more on a par with America than Japan. Perhaps greater class conscious inspires so much legalism. Law is uniformity and uniformity applies well to horizontal class relationships based on distrust. Whatever the reason, in Japan labour management relationships take place more 'informally' than 'formally'. Hence it is not possible when looking at the history of this relationship to follow the same sort of German legislative paper trail. There is no law on codetermination that empowers white collar and blue collar employees to elect a specified number of company board members, no laws that spell out in detail union jurisdiction within firms. If Japanese employee participation is not like American neither can it be grasped in a German legalistic way.

Nonetheless, the law does offers an insight into Japanese dissent. In Germany where codetermination battles were fought out in the Reichstag and the national political area, Americans could see what was afoot and they could apply the sort of pressure that has been catalogued here. In Japan, on the other hand, legal custom masked Japanese deviation from the American New Deal synthesis model. Two examples reveal how this took place.

When the Americans arrived in 1945, they set about reforming Japanese education. They wanted democracy, so the occupiers replaced prewar elitist education with American style public grammar and high school forms. They also reformed higher education along American lines. The same thing happened in labour law. The Japanese were allowed to draft legislation which was then submitted to the American occupation authorities for approval. Consequently, Gould (1984, p. xiv) wrote, 'Japan and the United States have labor laws that resemble one another and in some respects, appear identical'. Consequently, too, it is not surprising to find American conceptions of labour management relations legally established in Japan. Like American, Japanese law excludes supervisors from union membership, thereby accenting the adversarial relationship between labour and management, and American ideas about 'managerialism'. Japanese law, like American, provides for unfair labour practices and for agencies (labour relations commissions), like the American National Labour Relations Board, to adjudicate disputes. Both examples, and others that could be cited, smack more of a Japanese compliance with imported American values than a German codetermination defiance. But it is all very misleading.

If the Japanese accepted American educational forms and democratic goals, they infused them with a set of values very different from American ones. Joseph Adams, an American student who taught in Japan, explains the contrasting emphasis quite simply: individual versus group consciousness. In the Japanese schools group consciousness is nurtured primarily in three synergistic ways: by teaching methodologies, extra class group interaction, and moral instruction. The first (methodologies) involves group work in classroom (e.g. special students are mixed with slow learners whose performance they help raise to the group pace; discipline is administered not individually, by, as in America, sending students to the 'office,' but by letting the group decide and administer 'punishment'). The second (extra class interaction work) includes a range of extra class activities of

69

a pleasant (sports, arts) and an 'unpleasant' (food service and cleanup, in which, teacher, pupils, and administration staff all pitch in) variety. And the third (moral education), re-instituted after the war particularly at the urging of the Japanese Employers' Association (Nikeiren), fosters cooperative, family, and community values. 'Moderation' (Setsudo), Adams relates, 'not asserting yourself too much in group relations', is the chief value taught. And it is taught by experience as well as precept. "Regardless of students preferences, (they) are supposed to do the work their group is assigned to do, not out of preference, but out of an understanding of their 'duty' and the 'importance of the job'".[17] Nothing shows the extent to which a society's assumptions about what constitutes proper or desired, as opposed to actual, behaviour than the way a society tries to educate its young. Despite the American form, therefore, Japan's postwar reconstructed education system differed profoundly from the American. Consequently, after high school, American young people and Japanese carry into the work force dissimilar value systems (Adams, 1993).

The gap between American labour law and Japanese behaviour is equally startling. Although forbidden, supervisors in firms do belong to labour unions and the adversarial conflict resolution style the law sets up is mostly avoided. In the United States, Gould (1984, p. 15) explains, 'the case load of the National Labor Relations Board, which has responsibility for unfair labor practice, has become a major labor law problem (40,000 cases a year), but in Japan (the number of cases brought before labor relation commissions) is minuscule'. Even though Japanese law makes arbitration available to employees and employers, it is rarely used. The Japanese prefer joint consultation groups where informality and behind the scenes discussions take place. American trade unionists consider joint consultation to be a direct attack on the principle of collective bargaining, but collective bargaining in America and Japan does not mean the same thing. Issues like dismissals, discipline, transfers, which in America are often dealt with through collective bargaining are usually worked out in Japan by management, in consultation with unions or a majority of the workers in nonunion plants, and then promulgated by management as the firm's 'rules of employment'. If Japanese 'management' were like American this procedure would reflect managerial dominance. But the degree to which management and employees are interlaced within the Japanese firm makes 'consultation' a much more effective process, from the employees' viewpoint, than in America. Law and social practice vary considerably in Japan but this bothers not the Japanese, like it would the German, because 'the very precision of the law is alien to the Japanese (mind)' (Gould, p. xv). Law must yield to human custom.

Enough has been said, to intimate that the development of postwar Japanese management labour relations would follow a unique path. Gordon describes the occupation in terms of a protoclass struggle between aggressive Japanese labour unions, formed into national industrial federations, and a discouraged management. The unions, the more militant of which opted for socialism, demanded living wages, a voice in management, and launched coordinated strikes to obtain them. Management, as in Germany, started making concessions everywhere. The

Americans, then, fearing communism, cooperated with conservative Japanese government and corporate management to purge the unions of reds and halt communism. It is the same scenario as in the West. And the *dénouement* described by American historians like Gordon or Japanese Marxists is familiar: Japanese management, with American support, defeated the workers, thereby assuring a capitalist dominated postwar Japan.

But then, lo and behold, just as in Germany, what emerges in Japan in the aftermath does not resemble American management labour relations. There is much grousing about how the workers had to withdraw early postwar gains - how 'temporary' workers and women are not covered by the Japanese Employment System, how small firms deny their workers equal rights - and, as in German codetermination, this retreat is undoubtedly true. But in the settlement that emerged in the 1950s, to use the words of Professor Gordon, (1985, p. 411) hardly a friend of Japanese capitalists, "(managers) conceded (to worker) the status of 'employee,' the respect and security of a monthly wage, and the right to use all facilities to an expanding pool of workers. And they worked out an implicit system of job security and livelihood wages acceptable to most employees".

This settlement should not, however, be depicted in terms of management's gains or losses. The evidence suggests that applying American terms to Japan leads, again as in the German case, to serious misunderstanding. 'Management' is American; to use the word is akin to saying to the unwary that 'Managerialism,' in the sense used in this paper, won in Japan. But as there was no 'management' in Japan neither was their 'labour' in the American sense; and no American style management labour relations.

Top corporate Japanese leaders are certainly not like American ones, not in their relationship to stockholders. Whereas in American capitalism the 'outsiders' are allowed to engage in leveraged buyouts, hostile takeovers, and to claim, as major shareholders, a say on the board of directors of firm in which they play no organizational part, in Japan they are not. James Abbeglen and George Stalk (1985, p. 184) note:

> that Japanese companies...differ significantly from the Western pattern.... The essence of the Japanese company is the people who compose it. It does not, as in the American firm, belong to the stockholders and the managers they employ to control it, but it is under the control of the people who work in it, who play limited attention to stockholder's wishes. The company personnel, including directors, who are themselves life-time employees and executives of the company, are very much a part of the company. ....[P]ersonnel have a very real control over company decisions.[18]

Neither did 'management' seek to be in Japan as in America a 'fourth' productive factor, an estate onto itself distinct in education and training. In the US business schools grew up with management. Although it has not acquired the professional status of medicine or engineering, with prescribed degree requirements, the

71

enormous growth of graduate generalist business education, with the MBA at the forefront, lies behind the growth of American 'managerialist' consciousness. No such development occurred in Japan. There is undergraduate business education in universities; it is not, however, an education for management expertise but a general business education, namely the passing on of general knowledge about business systems, business firms, organizations, management, and some analytical methods plus elementary instruction in accounting and computer operations. If education is highly respected, management education is not.[19]

Management candidates are recruited into Japanese firms on the basis of suitability to company culture (will they fit in?) not management functional expertise. Once recruited, moreover, management specialties do not matter, people are moved about from job to job, department to department within the enterprise, so that they become company men, not occupational specialists. In unionized firms it is not uncommon for the manager to spend a stint as a union official before resuming a managerial career. Imagine senior corporate executives at General Motors or Ford having done time as officials in the UAW before returning to the corporate management ladder! While it would be perfectly acceptable for a Ford executive to have been at General Motors (not done in Japan), moving in and out of union management would be inconceivable. Surveys of major Japanese firms show that members of most Japanese corporate boards were union officials at one time.[20]

From the American perspective, this interrelation between union and company officials amounts to management control of docile workers. One observer of Japanese participative management claims that Japanese workers are happy remaining in basically a suggestive mode with respect to members of higher management (Lawler, 1986). But as Lillrank and Kano (1989, p. 127) observe, in light of the turbulent and often violent history of labour relations in Japan, there is no reason to believe that Japanese employees are basically docile and submissive. Japanese scholars, moreover, not only defend the enterprise union's willingness to look out after the interest of employees but its record in so doing.[21]

Nor has the 'management' side prospered unduly as it would have in American labour management relationships. Japanese managers have never been well paid. Under the prewar Zaibatsu, rewards were paltry and since the war, compared to the Americans, this has continued to be the case. A recent article notes, for example, that average pay ratios (income ratios) between the highest paid and the lowest in US firms are 110-160 to 1, in Japan 17-18 to 1, and in Germany 23-25 to 1.[22] In America, the private corporation is a wealth source that people have felt free to exploit and on occasion pillage for 'outside' advantage. Stockholders want high dividends, workers high wages, managers big rewards and emoluments. Society is rich and the abused corporation relatively poor. In this uneven exploitative process, top management has garnered a nearly disreputable share. In Japan, by contrast, the corporation, generally characterized, is rich and society relatively poor. Both labour and management serve the corporation and their interrelationship is conditioned accordingly. That relationship is different, therefore, in form and content from what is implied by 'labour' and 'management' in America.

Little of American 'managerialism,' moreover, is exhibited in Japanese leadership method and style. 'Classical American management,' in Philippe D'Iribarne's words, operates on the following behavioural principles:

to define precisely and explicitly the responsibilities of each person, formulate his/her objectives clearly, give the person freedom in the choice of methods for meeting objectives, evaluate the results carefully and reward or sanction the person according to his/her successes or failures (1989, p. 131).

These principles call for a management where a high degree of formalization, standardization, and centralization reigns, where managers possess good conflict resolution skills, 'good top down decision making abilities,' good problem solving, analytical skills, and a capacity to devise good externally imposed evaluation systems (Kagono et. al., 1981). This is Taylorism *par excellence*.

Japanese emphasize group harmony in schools, not because it is a cultural 'given', but a cultural 'goal.' In other words, it does not exist but has to be created and that is the job of management, in the school, and in the firm. Within the firm, leadership has a twofold task. It must run the business or factory well in terms of current operations (or technological capacity) and it must perceive and make the changes that are critical to the future of the firm (staying at the cutting edge of business and technology). In American managerialism managers conceive and control; in Japan all enterprise personnel get involved in both tasks as thinkers and doer. This necessitates an employee wearing two hats, that of the discipline person working diligently to uphold factory standards, that of the innovator preoccupied with improvement in product and work process. Everybody becomes an expert in both functions, so to speak, i.e. experts disappear.

Since to the Japanese, enterprise is community endeavour, they organize their work accordingly. Engineers make small groups the basis of workshop organization and activity. There are small groups, restricted to place, whose members interact with one another in the work process, small groups - teams - drawn from various departments to work together on a particular problem; small groups to deal with safety and working conditions, etc. Some groups work to perfect current practice. They work more in a Taylorist mode, since in every operation, the work has to be done, with performance maintained and costs contained. This requires group inspired and executed work to be performed and developed in relatively routine ways. But other groups get involved in continuous improvement which requires a mentality of subversion. The often 'informal,' 'spontaneous,' 'voluntary,' group, like the famous Quality Control Circle, cannot be contrived, or manipulated by regular operational management, if it is to be effective.

Japanese enterprise group dynamics succeeds not just because employees are involved but because the same employees participate in both the 'formal' operational group and the 'informal' questioning ones. Lillrank and Kano (1989, p. 127) explain that Japanese cultural traits permit Japanese employees to function simultaneously in parallel group structures that come into conflict with each other. In Japan:

> *honne* and *tatemae* are concepts used to describe one's true feelings as opposed to a facade. Although this distinction is by no means unfamiliar to Western cultures..., it is surprising how far this dualism is accepted in everyday Japanese life. To maintain a *tatemae* is perfectly acceptable and does not imply a shade of dishonesty. (It seems that the capacity of Japanese employees to accept management and yet oppose it can be explained by) an ability to operate in a multilayered social reality, where each layer has a life of its own.... (It) is one of the valid cultural explanations for why (well functioning parallel structures) have emerged and succeeded in Japan.

The leadership qualities required in Japanese 'organic' management are very different from those needed in 'classical' American management. Whereas in an American factory, in which a 'high degree of formalization, standardization, and centralization' exists, the management talents essential to success are, to repeat, good conflict resolution skills on the part of the boss, good individual top down decision making, good use of consultants brought in from the outside as trouble shooters, good externally imposed control systems, and good problem solving, analytical skills; in a Japanese firm, which lacks the formalized, standardized, externally imposed modes of work organization, good leadership requires group oriented consensus making, 'control by sharing of values and information,' the cultivation of 'relational skills,' and 'broad consultation before acting' (Kagona, p. 136).

Thus the human interrelationship that emerged in large Japanese corporations after the war did not follow American management labour patterns. The fact that Americans did not know the Japanese language and feared the industrial prowess of Japan not at all in the immediate postwar years, probably hid deviant forms of corporate behaviour from Americans. The famous Toyota production system, which started in the 1930s, was developing quite successfully by the end of the 1950s. But when Taichi Ohno, (quoted in Lillrank and Kano, p. 5) one of the developers, tried to discuss the system with Westerns 'few people took heed.' It was, to use his words again, '(a)fter the oil crisis, as Toyota's profits increased with each passing year from 1976 to 1978 and the gap between Toyota and other competitors grew, (that) people began to take notice'. A Japanese study mission, to take another example, provided the American Society for Quality Control with information about Japanese Quality Control Circles in 1965. Dr. Joseph Juran presented the idea in June 1966 to a larger Western audience at the Stockholm conference of the European Organization for Quality Control. It was considered 'too outlandish and unbelievable' (Alexanderson, 1978, p. 4).

The point, however, is not just that the Americans were a lot of arrogant ignoramuses. The ignorance was systemic, a product of the very deviation between the American and Japanese way of management. Because in Japan academic management schools (the academic wing of American managerialism) did not exist, there was very little academic involvement in the development of Japanese management practice. The lack of ties between university social science and industry in Japan meant that American academics could not be informed about Japanese managerial innovations through their contacts with Japanese universities. On the contrary, academics in Japan's neglected social sciences turned to the West to learn, thereby overlooking, for a some time, the really significant managerial events unfolding right in their own backyard. Higher education, consequently, offers one more example of how systemic difference itself, by promoting American ignorance about Japan, encouraged postwar divergence between American and Japanese organizational modes.

Efficiency

That Germany and Japan dissented from the American way of management is one point, that this dissent in the long run has resulted in business and industrial efficiency greater than America's is another. Perhaps the best known argument in defence of the second point stresses the effect that management systems have on corporate strategies. Because Japanese, German, and American management serves different masters (known as stockholders and stakeholders), the efficaciousness of planning and the execution of operations differ. The literature on planning emphasizes the importance of long term perspective to short, and market share strategies to short term profit maximization. Since enterprise well being takes precedence over the dividend demands of stockholders, the Japanese firm can pursue long term goals without worrying about maximizing profits and dividends in the short run. The only recent favourable judgement of American management is that it is good at dealing with crises when poor long term strategies bring American firms to ruin. Since there is no codetermination in American capitalism, the employees can be ignored when painful decisions are made involving plant closures and layoffs. Profitability for stockholders not job security for employees is determinant and American managers act freely and ruthlessly in this context (Kagono, 1981). But crisis management skills in downsizing do not seem, *ex post facto*, to offset American management's inability to achieve beneficial long term economic results.[23]

German managers, as well as Japanese, have usually been accorded high marks in the execution of strategy. During the early 1970s, when strategic planning became fashionable, the German entrepreneur was heavily criticized for a lack of expertise in this respect. But in the 1980s the best strategy was deemed to be to make a good quality product and the German system of internal promotion of plant experienced managers was found, like the Japanese, to be superior to the American one. The reputation of codetermination also grew.

75

Indeed, over the years the American complaint against codetermination changed. Predictions about the managerial incompetence of labour elected supervisors proved to be manifestly absurd . There were reports about managerial excellence achieved through codetermination. As the *New York Times* (Nov. 19, 1975) wrote:

> American companies regard labour union delegates in the boardroom as something of a heresy. The Germans argue that it works for efficiency and actually benefits management, since labour does not consider itself at war with business all the time.[24]

Americans, therefore, fell back on legalistic, property rights arguments against codetermination. Henry Ford II, vexed at the prospect of Ford 'stockholders' losing the right to appoint management boards and control policy in Germany, spoke out, at ceremonies commemorating the fiftieth year of Ford's German operations, against this infringement of property rights (New York Times, 1975). The US Chamber of Commerce in Germany, more specific and legalistic, claimed the law would 'violate the property right provisions of a 1954 German American Trade Treaty'. It was not so much bad experiences with codetermination in German branches of American firms that upset managers but the general principles involved. 'American executives are particularly worried about Germany's commitment to fifty-fifty worker participation on Supervisory Boards', *The Economist* reported (April 12, 1976), because '...if German workers get to elect half the boards of an American company, General Motors fears that the United Auto Workers' Union in America might decide that it is a good idea in Detroit, too'.[25]

In the 1980s an even more positive appreciation of codetermination emerged. Ray Marshall (1987, p. 3) President Carter's Secretary of Labour, underscored the importance of worker involvement in 'economic policy making' and 'workplace management decisions' in order to attain economic efficiency:

> Improved US economic performance and competitiveness require greater worker participation. ... Indeed, a major conclusion is that American business is losing its competitive position in the world economy at least in part because inadequate worker involvement has resulted in misguided and uncoordinated management and economic policies, which have placed our producers at a serious competitive disadvantage.

It is, then, specifically, the labour management relations that appeared in the New Deal synthesis that Marshall finds to be at fault, for American managerial capitalism, if it permitted collective bargaining, never accepted codetermination.

However, it was not so much that employee representatives on corporate boards made superior managers, as that they did not, compared to stockholder elected managers, make inferior ones. From an efficiency perspective, moreover, the most positive statement that can be made about codetermination in the boardroom is that it reduced labour strife and hence contributed to the remarkable labour peace characteristic of German industry, and with that to increased German productivity.

As reasonable as they are, arguments about the beneficial effects of codetermination in the boardroom on corporate strategy do not really come to grips with the subject of comparative enterprise efficiency. If workers' participation in Japanese and German industries reduced labour turmoil and strike actions, compared to America, unless the argument were that Japan has less strife than Germany, it could not explain why many Japanese factories are more efficient than German ones. Claims, moreover, that the Japanese Employment System allows Japanese management to take a long term, market share view, could be true, but the next step, the conclusion that this accounts for superior performance is a *non sequitur*, for Japanese firms in industries and businesses with lower productivity than their counterpart in the West have these same management strategies and systems.

To handle questions of comparative efficiency obviously requires a greater selectivity with regard to type of industries involved and greater depth of analysis in terms of organizational culture. Since it is really Japanese superiority in manufacturing that is at stake, the question of comparative efficiency can be reformulated: how is it that the Japanese have managed, in complex manufacturing industries where their superiority has been rapidly gained, is acknowledged, and is growing, to satisfy customer demand for quality products of great variety at low cost and what does this achievement have to do with labour management relations? To answer this question another has to be posed: what are the yardsticks to be employed in rendering judgements about efficiency?

In a recent publication, called *After Taylorism*, a labour sociologist noted how the concept of 'productivity' has undergone change because of new approaches to production. He observes that productivity measurement is as much a result of the production system itself as of some externally contrived standard (Veltz, 1989). 'Under Taylorism' he noted '(productivity is measured in terms of the) local optimization of human work in manufacturing' and this work is evaluated 'additively,' each isolated work unit considered in itself and added to the next to form a process (p. 6). This concept of 'productivity' measurement fitted well, the classical American concept of management defined by D'Iribarne, where each individual's duties were clearly demarcated and defined. The new idea of productivity, Veltz wrote, emphasizes 'the coherence and integration of the diverse steps in the cycle of production, intra and interenterprise'. The yardstick for measuring productivity had to be extended from the workplace, e.g. Taylor's famous time and motion studies, to the enterprise level.

This sociologist never uses the word 'Japan' when talking about this change. But the very things for which the Japanese have become famous in their manufacturing suit this new definition of 'productivity'. Take the Just-in-Time system of manufacturing, which avoids the necessity of accumulating inventory at each step in manufacturing. Efficiency, e.g. lower cost, is achieved under JIT by intra enterprise coordination or even interenterprise when outside suppliers are

77

concerned, not through isolated work station performance. Or take Kanban manufacturing at Toyota, where the people in the line must think of what is going on ahead of them and behind them as well as their own tasks. Or small group work, where tasks are assigned to groups not individuals and every individual within the group is expected to do all the jobs the groups is assigned. Professor Mashiko Aoki (1990, p. 5), using the example of the Japanese automobile industries, describes this enterprise wide view of productivity quite graphically:

> The central production planning office drafts quarterly and monthly production plans for each factory, based on its market demand forecasts, and present corresponding procurement plans to outside suppliers. These prior plans provide only a general guideline, however. The integrated production-delivery plan for a ten-day period is prepared by the commodity-flow office on the basis of orders from regional and overseas dealers. ...(T)he engineering office of each factory prepares a sequence of daily production schedules. These daily schedules are adjusted during production in response to actual orders transmitted to the factory through the on-line network system. Consequently, instead of the standardized long production runs characteristic of American factories, on the final assembly line...wagons, two-door hatchbacks, and four-door sedans with red, beige, and white bodies; with left-hand and right hand steering wheels; with a variety of transmission, engines, and options, roll one after the other along the line....

Aoki's comments illustrate the significance of intra enterprise coordination and the importance of information and communications to achieve productivity in this context. Indeed, although the implementation of small group work and JIT production systems predated the electronic information revolution, this revolution has enhanced the interactive enterprise nature of productivity. The on line, computer fed customer orders from dealers to the assembly line worker, that Aoki described, is a fine instance of the wedding achieved between different departments within the firm through information technology.

Professor Hajime Yamashine (1991) too, in his lectures on Japanese manufacturing has pointed out the importance to performance of intra firm communications. The close coordination needed between research, factory, and market for product development is obtained through group work. Group comprehensiveness is achieved by each product development team being composed of people from the many departments involved in the process (sales, research, production, design, etc.); group cohesion, the evocation of a sense of global responsibility within each individual rather than responsibility limited to the individual's functional input, by the fact that department representatives will have worked at and know the functions of others on the team (brought about by a company policy of rotating people regularly from job to job in different department).

Others have noticed how the new technology has broken down the Taylorist view of productivity in the workshop itself. Werner Fricke explained in 1986 that the new computer aided information technology ends distinctions between manager and managed because only those involved operationally in the networking systems can formulate the planning implications. In other words, the new technology fathers the concept that the workers are both the doers and the thinkers. Another German, this time from the Chemical industry, described the new work process invading his firm along similar lines:

> Where traditional work organization had limited flexibility and control systems eliminated individual responsibility, the new concept of production, in the chemical industry, requires more individual responsibility for quality as well as more thinking, with a corresponding information network, about how things hang together.... The self conscious worker of this new generation will be led less and less by an authoritarian style. It seems possible and is indeed desirable that cooperative leadership styles are to be expected from management (*Führungskraften*). This includes the planning tasks, which heretofore have been a sign of the bosses' authority. In the new production concept...central management will be restricted to general planning and goal setting, while the detail planning will be pushed backward to the production work level (Bouillon, 1987).

There is a striking similarity between this German's predictions in the late 1980s and the way factories actually began to work in Japan in the 1960s. Although the Japanese did not invent the electronic information technologies (the Americans mostly did), they rapidly adopted them and then used them to bring about increased productivity measured in terms of the 'coherence and integration of the diverse steps in the cycle of production....'.

Japanese superiority in product development and production has been the result. Research cited by the Ashridge Management Research Group (1990) suggested that whereas Western firms take 16 to 26 days over the sales, order and distribution cycle for a car, Japanese firms take 6 to 8 days. While Western firms take 14 to 30 days to manufacture a vehicle, Japanese firms take 2 to 4 days. And while Western companies spend 4 to 6 years on a new vehicle design and introduction, their Japanese competitors do it in two and a half to three years. The success within the factory proper is explained to a great extent by the remarkable superiority that Japanese firms have achieved in 'average setup time of exchanging dies' during manufacturing. While, one study shows, it took, Japanese plants in Japan 7.9 minutes to change dies, it required Japanese plants in the United States 21.4 minutes. Greater speed in changing dies allowed the Japanese firm to have more frequent setups (13.8 in two shifts in Japan, 9.0 in Japanese owned factories in the United States, 2.0 in American factories in the United States, and 1.83 in European factories), thereby permitting greater flexibility in manufacturing. These achievements can be attributed to a close and continuous study of the relationship between machine design and the die exchange process in Japanese companies (Yamashine, 1991).

Obviously, the Japanese Employment System that emerged during the first decade after the war fostered the production techniques from which the new view of productivity emerged. Payment by seniority and rank permitted employees to change jobs without the loss of pay and prestige involved in a wage system pegged on skill levels; status equality between blue and white collar workers favoured group cohesion and flexibility; job security gained through 'lifetime employment' left the firm free to introduce new technology without the opposition of a labour force fearful of job loss through its implementation.

The resounding success of Japanese industry led not just to the export of products but to the export of the productivity concept and the ideology of work on which it is based. Since Western social scientists strive, in their cultural context, to be 'scientific,' they have 'denationalized' the borrowed management labour models. The sociologists' work in *Après-Taylorism* exemplifies this avoidance of national cultural explanations. So does the Ashridge Management Research Group's (1990) survey of global human resource management. Firms, this survey reports, in many nations now talk about the whole organizational culture instead of the skill level of individual managers, for the 'mind set and outlook of managers is more important than formal structures and reporting lines [the heart of classical American managerialism] in bringing about a flexible, yet cohesive organization'. Quoting the management guru Kanter, the survey stressed the superiority of 'process over structure' because it is not how responsibilities are divided but how people pull together that counts. And it called for the creation of what Christopher A. Bartlett and Sumantra Ghoshal (1989) describe as 'transnational' organizations, with 'integrated networks which share decision making and where components, products, resources, information and people flow freely between the interdependent units...and dynamic integrative ways of taking decisions through using the commitment of every individual employees to the overall corporate agenda' are extant. The 'highly formalized and institutionalized central mechanisms (a clear attack on classical American management) of management have, it stresses, had to give way to 'cooption,' to consensus building with each individual understanding, sharing, and 'internalizing,' the company's purpose, values, and key strategies constituting the most effective means of coordination'. And the survey claims that survival today depends on the firm's 'basic strategy,' on 'its guiding principles of conduct' being 'widely shared' throughout its organization, wherein 'detailed information about everything' is provided for everybody. The whole organization is expected 'to think and act directly on thinking'. Flexibility but cohesiveness, process over structure, shared decision making, integrative thinking, consensus building, global responsibilities, collective motivation, the 'firm as a brain' - these are the buzz words used in the West to describe how the firm operating in fast moving interdependent markets must be managed. Their very existence in the vocabulary of Western managers and management experts indicates the extent to which dissent from the American labour management way resulted in industrial

80

efficiency in Japan.

But what of Germany's dissent, from the standpoint of the new definition of productivity? Joseph A. Limprecht and Robert H. Hayes explained the performance of German world class manufactures in 1982 in terms of the bottom-up personal leadership style of German executives, their knowledge of the shop floor, and the respect that they have, consequently, from the workers. The contrast they draw is with know nothing American management, with its delegation of authority, that produces ignorance of the shop floor in top American management echelons.[26] Personal leadership, however, is only one of the components that went into German labour management relations. The other was labour backed codetermination.

The fact that German academics and industrialists, after twenty five years of codetermination, talk German industry's need to adopt new work processes, does not speak well for the efficiency of the German systems at the plant level. Indeed, Werner Fricke (1986, p. 54) asserts that German codetermination currently is in a technologically induced crisis because of its inability to cope with the systems oriented work and management processes necessitated by the introduction, 'within the framework of computer-supported production, of new information and communication technology'. In other words, the German way of labour management relationship that evolved after the war is scarcely better able to compete with complex high technology Japanese manufacturing than the American. Why?

The answer is that German works councils, the codetermination units closest to the workplace, deal in wage and income policy making, job protection, the regulation of work conditions, protection against dismissals and the effects of rationalization. Over the years they have confronted these problems with much success from the workers standpoint. But 'questions of labour organization,' Fricke (p. 547) clarifies, 'manoeuvring room for workers groups and individuals as well as the shaping of work and technology (on the shop floor)' have even under codetermination been left to management to arrange, a management operating primarily on Taylorist principles. In sum, the employees in their work stations do not codetermine, their representatives in the various elected councils do. Suffering from the rigidifying effect of the legally restricted negotiating system established under German codetermination law, these councils are just as unresponsive to the needs of workers in the new technologies as traditional Taylorist forms of management. And yet, the success of the new technologies depends on the employee participating actively in the management of their exploitation. Because there is little codetermination in the workshop, Germans compete less efficiently in the new technologies with Japan.[27]

This chapter begins and ends as an essay in revisionism. Nobody would be so perverse as to claim that America did not play a major role in bringing about recovery. In 1945, with fifty percent of the world's manufacture and temporarily without significant industrial rivals, the US was the only country capable of assuming economic leadership. Nobody, moreover, would be so mean spirited as to say that the Americans did not respond - if out of self interest - generously with skill and treasure to the challenge of reconstruction. The Marshall Plan, but not just it alone, was indeed 'our finest hour'. Nor would anybody gainsay the contention that the American system was superior to and defeated communism. The problem arises with the claim that the American way of doing things had to be adopted by Germans and Japanese for them to recover and prosper under capitalism. The argument presented is not just that Germany and Japan resisted the American system but that their successful resistance led to flourishing organizational and managerial systems that have contributed to America's subsequent industrial decline.

Two points can be emphasized when discussing the dissent. One, which this essay has mostly ignored, is the American system of market driven, free enterprise capitalism, in which, despite Keynesianism, government's economic role is slight. The Japanese never subscribed in theory or practice to the idea that market forces were best able to allocate resources and assure efficiency of production and Japan's rise to economic power was not based on these precepts. The second point, the one explored, was management labour relations. These relationships in Germany and Japan after the war were not patterned on any American New Deal synthesis. Uniquely German and Japanese developments, they have managed, to the surprise and chagrin of many Americans today, to mobilize the hearts and skill of enterprise employees in these two countries much better and to greater economic effect than the conflict ridden system of labour relations of which Americans were so proud when the war came to an end.

Notes

1. For German engineering education see Locke (1984). The German idea of *Technik* I discuss in Locke (1989, pp. 77-80). The idea of *Technik* as opposed to the Anglo-American concept of applied science is also discussed at great length in the works of Michael Fores, Ian Glover and Peter Lawrence.

2. The classic study of Taylorism's effect on labour is Harry Braverman's *Labor and Monopoly Capital* (1974). Braverman writes that Lenin believed, as did also Clark Kerr and other American labour sociologists, that all modern industrial societies, capitalist or socialist, are subject to a 'scientific management' which of necessity divides the managers from the managed. But, Braverman avers, Lenin misunderstood Marx, i.e. it was not inevitable, as Lenin believed, that socialist societies borrow Taylorist modes of management and production (Braverman, pp. 10-14; see also Kerr et al., 1960). To Braverman it can be replied, that all societies, capitalist as well as socialist, can be subjected to organizational forms which diminish the division between manager and managed. Indeed, this essay demonstrates that it is not inevitable under 'capitalism' that Taylorist work-organization forms prevail.

3. U form = functionally organized and centralized management, M form = multidivisional, decentralized management in which the strategic function of headquarters is, unlike in the U form, organizationally separated from the operational management of the divisions.

4. Michael Hogan calls his concluding chapter 'America made the European Way,' an example of the 'the Americanization of macro and micro management' thesis.

5. See Meany (1955, p. 93 and pp. 272-79). Unions, moreover, did not deny, in the final analysis, the rights of management to discharge employees. They only insisted on a seniority principle in case of rehire. But they did consider job reclassification or reassignments union business and often wrote restrictions about them into collective bargaining agreements.

6. The classical discussion in English is Leonard Krieger (1957).

7. Article 165 of the constitution called for 'the equal participation of blue and white collar workers (*Arbeiter* and *Angestellten*) in the regulation of wages and working conditions as well as in the entire economic development of production forces' (Schmidt, 1970, p. 62).

8. In the German corporation there is a two-tier board system at the top, (1) the Supervisory Board (*Aufsichtsrat*) and (2) the Managing Board (*Vorstand*). The Supervisory Board has considerable power. It elects the Managing Board which runs the firm's daily operations. Moreover, the Supervisory Board's approval is necessary in all basic decisions effecting the firm (long term planning, layoffs, new plant and equipment, new capital equity issues, etc.). The works council (*Betriebsrat*) is a lower level committee elected by employees.

9. For example, Jack Raymond, New York Times correspondent in Germany reported: 'Hundreds of thousands of workers demonstrated in Hessen in a double-barrelled protest against high prices and the refusal of the US Military Government to accept ...measures passed by the State Parliament months ago. There appeared to be universal popular support for the demonstration. Newspaper editorials approved of the Trade Union League calling demonstrations...in at least 20 towns and cities. ...In Frankfurt 20,000 persons, probably the largest gathering since the war, packed the Roemerberg, the old city square.... [Max Bock, vice president of the Trade Unions League], called for lower prices and higher wages, price control and the right of workers to participate in management policies. ... The third of these points referred to the Works Council Law, which was adopted in the State Parliament by an overwhelming majority but requires the approval of General Lucius D. Clay....', *New York Times*, August 13, 1948.

10. It seems the other allies were less reticent about speaking out. The *New York Times*, March 21, 1951, p. ll:3, observed that the governments of France, Belgium, the Netherlands, and Luxembourg 'have protested strongly against...legislation on codetermination.... Tacit in the protests is the threat, openly voiced by some private concerns, that investment capital would be

withdrawn from the affected enterprises and the possibility for the fresh inflow of investment money, sorely needed by the West German economy, would be shattered. ...André François-Poncet, French High Commissioner, personally intervened... Representatives of the Belgian steel firm Arbed, ...declared that the Luxembourg industry believes the present draft for a codetermination law is equal to expropriation....'.

11. This is an interesting case of reverse snobbery because the man was criticized for not having the rough manners of the workers and for being almost indistinguishable from the other executives on the board.

12. Hartmann (1963) p. 197. Specific human relations management techniques mentioned are TWI (training within industry) American intrafirm communications methods, profit sharing inducements, entrepreneur trade union partnership ideas, and concepts of common risk sharing.

13. Hunter (1989, p. 79). An extensive international survey of managers done by David Wheatley and associates of the London consultancy Employment Conditions Abroad asked the question whether individual interest should prevail over group or group over individual. On a scale of 0 to 100 (100 being most individualist) of 14 nations rated, the US rated top with a score of 83 and the Japanese at the bottom, with a score of 23. The West Germans were rated among group consciousness countries, with a score of 51 (Dixon, 1989, p. 18).

14. Nakane Chie's well known work on Japanese society expresses this view most clearly (Chie, 1972).

15. Thus according to Shimbakuro, 'There is nothing to match Japan's trade unions except Germany's management consultation boards. If one were to seek a corresponding system in this country to Germany's workers' management participation through the management consultation board, it would have to be the workers management participation through labor unions' (Shimbakuro, 1982, p. 131).

16. Horizontal allegiance also exist to a greater extent on the left side of the management labour equation. The Germans have great respect for qualifications. They identify with their *Beruf* or calling and with the required academic qualifications. That is why degrees awarded become legally part of a person's name (*Dr-Ing. Schmidt, Dipl-Kauf. Braun*, etc.). Expertise and membership in horizontally connected specialist groups is a German hallmark. White collar workers (*Angestellten*), moreover, distinguish themselves clearly from blue collar workers. Each has their own union; each elects their own representatives to works councils; white collar employees would rather be classified as such and earn less money than earn more and be classified with blue collar worker (*Arbeiter*).

The difference between German and Japanese forms of social allegiance should not be exaggerated, especially when comparisons are made with the US. German works councils have strong firm loyalties. German leadership is personal and firm specific; descriptions of the sense of solidarity existing between top management and shop floor are not wrong. It is simply a matter of degree. Germans on a scale from one to ten, registering horizonal to vertical group loyalties, with Americans one and the Japanese ten would be rated five.

17. Joseph Adams related his experiences in a paper "Education For 'The New Model'", which was presented in Sociology 722, University of Hawaii at Manoa, Spring 1993.

18. Abbeglen and Stalk, 1985, p. 184.

19. Katsuyuki Nagaoka (1991) notes that there is 'only one small business school [in Japan] and that is not yet well known'.

20. Clark (1979, p. 109) notes: 'Of 313 major Japanese companies 74.1 percent had at least one executive director who once served as a labour union leader. The figure was 66.8 percent in 1968. In Japanese management, executive directors are the top day to day decision makers'. William B. Gould (1984, p. 5) writes 'The Japanese pattern of mobility between labour and management means that union presidents and other high officials are sometimes (though not often) graduates of the University of Tokyo and other leading Japanese universities. It also means that almost anyone who has worked for a Japanese company has been a member of a union at some point. It affects the style and attitude of trade unions in Japan by inhibiting militancy, providing expertise, and creating more contact and perhaps some egalitarianism between blue collar and white collar employees'.

21. Shirai (1983, p. 117).

22. *Honolulu Advertizer*, Feb. 11 1993. It is worth noting, too, the 'relatively narrow differential between blue collar and white collar salaries in Japan' (Shirai, 1983, p. 117).

23. An executive at Toyota corporation informed the author in the early 1990s that in general Japanese corporations reinvest 60% of profits and American 40% in new plant and equipment, one example of systems failure.

24. 'Bonn May Add to Labor's Say', *New York Times*, Nov. 19, 1975, p. 59:2.

25. p. 86. Robert T. Kuehne (1980, p. 108) in a work on codetermination echoed this sentiment: '[American business in Germany oppose it] not because of significant negative experiences with codetermination but because they fear that US unions might demand the same rights as their European counterparts'.

26. Limprecht and Hayes (1982, p. 138) observed that German 'first line supervisors...are skilled workers with long experience who usually enjoy the respect and confidence of their fellow workers'. German managers are known for their technical ability. 'The technical competence at all organizational levels makes possible a bond between management and the shop floor'.

27. We are not talking about the Swedish idea of semi autonomous work groups. They have not achieved the productivity levels of the Japanese (Breisig, 1990). Employee or union instigated semi autonomous work groups have been inspired by Western views of confrontational labour management relations. Fearful that management wishes to exploit the worker, the unions have sought to create the work processes the new technologies require, while protecting the

workers' welfare. Japanese 'management labour' relation works better because it combines, what are contradictions in Western eyes, Taylorist principles of work organization with employee group participation.

References

Abbeglen, J. and Stalk, G. (1985), *Kaisha: The Japanese Corporation*, Basic Books, New York.

Adams, J. (1993), "Education for 'The New Model'", paper presented in Sociology 722, University of Hawaii at Manoa.

Alexanderson, O. (1978), 'QC Circles in Scandinavia', *Quality Progress*, July, pp. 18-19.

Ashridge Management Research Group *(1990), The Quest for the International Manager: Survey of Global Human Resource Strategies*, Ashridge.

Aoki, M. (1990), 'Towards an Economic Model of the Japanese Firm', *Journal of Economic Literature*, Vol. 28, March, pp. 1-27.

Bartlett, C. A. and Ghoshal, S. (1989), *Managing Across Borders: The Transnational Solution*, Harvard Business School Press, Boston, Mass.

Bouillon, R. (1987), 'Liegen Chancen im Qualitats-Zirkel?', *Die Mitbestimmung*, 11/87, pp. 679-81, pp. 680-81.

Braverman, H. (1974), *Labor and Monopoly Capital: The Degradation of Work in the Twentieth Century*, Monthly Review Press, New York.

Breisig, T. (1990), *Its Team Time, Kleingruppenkonzept in Unternehmen*, Bund-Verlag, Cologne.

Burck, G. (1954a), 'Can Germany Go Capitalist?', *Fortune*, April, pp. 114-122, 247-52, p. 250.

Burck, G. (1954b), 'The German Business Mind,' *Fortune*, May, pp. 111-114, 219-220.

Burck, G. (1957), 'The Transformation of European Business', *Fortune*, November, 145-152.

Carew, A. (1987), *Labour Under the Marshall Plan: The politics of productivity and the marketing of management science*, Manchester University Press, Manchester.

Chie, N. (1972), *Japanese Society*, University of California Press, Berkeley and Los Angeles.

Clark, R. (1979), *The Japanese Company*, Yale University Press, New Haven, Connecticut.

Cohendet, P., Hollard, M., Malsch, T. and Veltz, P. (eds). (1989), *l'Après-Taylorisme*, Economica, Paris.

D'Iribarne, P. (1989), *La logique de l'honneur: Gestion des entreprises et traditions nationales*, Aux Editions du Seuil, Paris

Dixon, M. (1979), 'When International Relations Break Down', *The Financial Times*, Nov. 8, 1989, p. 8.

Fricke, W. (1986), 'New Technologies and German Codetermination', *Economic and Industrial Democracy*, 7:4, pp. 543-51.

Gordon, A. (1985), *the Evolution of Labor Relations in Japan*, Harvard University Press, Cambridge, Mass.

Gould, W. B. (1984), *Japan's Reshaping of American Labor Law*, MIT Press, Cambridge, Mass.

Hadley, E. M. (1970), *Antitrust in Japan*, Princeton University Press, Princeton, New Jersey.

Hartmann, H. (1963), *Amerikanische Firmen in Deutschland: Beobachtungen über Kontakte und Kontraste zwischen Industriegesellschaften*, Westdeutscher Verlag, Cologne and Opladen, Germany.

Hoffmann, S. and Maier, C. (1984), *The Marshall Plan: A Retrospective*, Westview Replica Editions, Boulder, Colorado.

Hogan, M. J. (1987), *The Marshall Plan: America, Britain, and the Reconstruction of Western Europe, 1947-1952*, CUP, Cambridge.

Hunter, J. F. (1989), *The Emergence of Modern Japan*, Longman, London.

Kagono, T., Nonaka, I., Okumura, A., Sakakibara, K., Komatsu, Y. and Sakashita, A. (1981), 'Mechanistic versus Organic Management Systems: A Comparative Study of Adaptive Patterns of US and Japanese Firms', *Annals of the School for Business Administration*, no. 25, Kobe University, Kobe, Japan.

Kawabe, N. and Daito, E. (1993), (eds), *Education and Training in the Development of Modern Corporations*, University of Tokyo Press, Tokyo.

Kerr, C., Dunlop, J. T., Harbison, F. and Myers, C. A. (1960), *Industrialism and Industrial Man*, Harvard University Press, Cambridge, Mass.

Krieger, L. (1957), *The German Idea of Freedom: History of a Political Tradition*, Beacon, Boston.

Kuehne, R. T. (1980), *Codetermination in Business: Workers' Representatives in the Board Room*, Praeger, New York.

Lawler, E. E. (1986), *High-Involvement Management: Participative Strategies for Improving Organization Performance*, Jossey-Bass, San Francisco.

Lillrank, P. and Kano, N. (1989), *Continuous Improvement - Quality Control Circles in Japanese Industry*, Center for Japanese Studies, Ann Arbor, Michigan.

Limprecht, J. A. and Hayes, R. H. (1982), 'Germany's World-Class Manufacturers', *Harvard Business Review*, Nov-Dec, 1982, pp. 137-145.

Litterer, J. A. (1961), 'Systematic Management: The Search for Order and Integration', *Business History Review*, xxxv Spring, pp. 450-473.

Locke, R. R. (1984), *The End of the Practical Man: Entrepreneurship in Higher Education in Germany, France and Great Britain, 1880-1940*, JAI Press, Greenwich, Conn.

Locke, R. R. (1989), *Management and Higher Education Since 1940*, CUP, Cambridge.

Maier, C. S. (1987), *In Search of Stability: Explorations in Historical Political Economy*, CUP, Cambridge.

Marshall, R. (1987), *Unheard Voices: Labor and Economic Policy in a Competitive World*, Basic Books, New York.

Meany, G. (1955), "What Labor Means by 'more'", *Fortune*, March, pp. 92-95 and pp. 272-279.

Milward, A. S. (1984), *The Reconstruction of Western Europe, 1945-1951*, Methuen, London.

Müller, G. (1987), *Mitbestimmung in der Nachkreigzeit: Britische Bezatsungsmacht-Untemehmer-Gewerkschaften*, Patrios-Schwann Verlag, Düsseldorf.

Nagaoka, K. (1991), 'Japanese Business Education', paper presented at the Anders Berch Synposium, Department of Business Administration, University of Uppsala, Sweden, 15 September 1991.

Naphtali, F. (1928), *Wirtschaftsdemokratie: Ihr Wesen, Weg und Ziel (Economic Democracy: its Essence, Way and Goal)*, BDG Verlag, Frankfurt am Main.

New York Times, (1975), 'Henry Ford Scorns Labor Role', November 19, p. 55-56 and p. 59:2.

New York Times, various issues (see text and Notes).

Raymond, J. (1948), *New York Times*, August 13, 1948, pp. 4-6.

Schmidt, E. (1970), *Die verhinderte Neuordnung 1945-1952*, Europäische Verlagsanstalt, Frankfurt am Main.

Shimabukuro, Y. (1982), *Consensus Management in Japanese Industry*, ISS Incorporated, Tokyo.

Shirai, T. (1983), 'A Theory of Enterprise Unionism', in (ed.), Shirai, T., *Contemporary Industrial Relations in Japan*, University of Wisconsin Press, Madison, Wisconsin.

Shuchman, A. (1957), *Codetermination: Labor's Middle Way in Germany*, Public Affairs Press, New York.

Sugayama, S. (1993), "Business Education, Training and the Emergence of the 'Japanese Employment System'", in (eds), Kawabe, N. and Daito, E., op cit.

Veltz, P. (1989), 'Introduction', in Cohendet, P., Hollard, M., Malsch, T. and Veltz, P. (eds), *l'Après-Taylorisme*, Economica, Paris.

Yamashine, H. (1991), 'Time and Innovation: The View from Japan', Stockton Lecture, London Business School, London.

Yasumuro, K. (1993), 'Engineers as functional alternatives to entrepreneurs in Japanese industrialisation', in Brown, J. and Rose, M. B. (eds), *Entrepreneurship, networks and modern business*, Manchester University Press, Manchester.

4 Modernity, manageability and the development of modern management

Paul Jeffcutt

Introduction

This chapter will examine the conditions of emergence and contemporary development of the theory and practice of Management as a constituent of modern society. Here we shall be concerned with Management as a realm of knowledge concerned with the organization of human progress, as well as with Management as an empirical practice in which complex organizations have become both vehicles of and harbingers of progress in modern society. Through this approach we shall examine both the workplace or the firm (i.e. the organization) as a significant constituent of the moral and economic order of modern society, and the professional territory of management as both the authority for and a set of techniques for intervening in (i.e. organizing) this moral and economic order.

The chapter argues that Management must be understood as an archetypal 'Human Science', given its central concern with the tension between order and disorder in the achievement of progress in modern society. Furthermore, Management in achieving pre-eminence as the primary Human Science of manageability, became canonized in terms of colonial processes of regulation and control both in and outside of complex organization (i.e. concerning both producers and consumers). Accordingly, the cross disciplinary development of Management, over the past century, has become dominated by the restless search for new styles or forms that could be consumed as ultimate answers to perennial quests for manageability. However, the chapter maintains that such attempted 'last words' are, by their very nature, always incomplete and unable to provide closure. Consequently, the development of Management has been characterized by the increasingly rapid accession and supersession of 'fads' in an apparently insatiable will to progress. The chapter concludes that despite the inevitability of their failure, such partial challenges to established boundaries and prioritizations can be understood as reorientations that open the potential for more significant change in our modern world.

Management as a human science

Inextricably interconnected with the emergence of modern society is the formation of what Foucault (1974) has described as 'a body of discourse that takes as its object man as an empirical entity' (p 344). This body of discourse, he argues, is constituted around three fundamental and interconnected spheres, the sciences of life, labour and language, which together are described as the 'Human Sciences'. The significance of these modern sciences, of which Management is an archetypal constituent, is their concern for praxis; the managing of the border between theorization and practice. In other words, the order of the Human Sciences is to intervene, and the interventions of the Human Sciences are to order, both their space and the surface between human beings and their 'world'.

The implications of this argument, that the emergence and development of modern society needs to be understood as being in symbiosis with the Human Sciences, are extensive and considerable. Indeed, this interconnection (i.e. between empirical positivities and realms of knowledge) in the process of modernization concerns transformations that have been experienced in different forms and in different phases over the past two hundred years on a truly worldwide scale. Accordingly, whilst this chapter is only seeking to pursue these arguments in respect of developments in the theory and practice of Management, we shall need to acknowledge their significance to the broad territory from which this theory and practice emerged (Jeffcutt, 1995).

On the one hand, these interconnections can be traced through emerging modern understandings of social progress articulated from moral philosophy and political economy to the developing disciplines of sociology and anthropology (Stocking 1987, Thompson et al., 1990). On the other hand, these interconnections are also evident in the formation of a moral and economic order in the 'advanced' societies of Western Europe through which the transitional mass of the rapidly expanding population were managed, both as a 'body' and in terms of their individual bodies (Stallybrass & White, 1986).

Consequently, the interconnections between modern society and the Human Sciences establish both the authority for and a set of techniques for intervening in the moral and economic order of society, understood as an organic, progressive but differentiated whole. We may thus understand the workplace or the firm (i.e. the organization) as an increasingly significant constituent of that moral and economic order, as well as an important site of intervention in that order. Indeed, it was the great institutions of modern society, from the arenas of government to those of the market, which emerged as both agencies of and harbingers of progress (i.e. following the 'grand theories' of Tylor and Spencer). Accordingly, complex

90

organizations by their very rationality and sophistication, embodied both progress over backwardness and the promise of the attainment of further heights of civilization. Indeed, such sociocultural hierarchies were echoed in practices of intervention (i.e. management), where self-control and social regulation enabled the cultivation of the progressive qualities of abstinence and foresight over the regressive qualities of instinct and impulse (Burrell, 1984).

This chapter will consider the modern field of Management to be distinguished by a dual focus, on the theorization of organizational analysis, as well as on the practice of managing and organizing. Iconographic as the starting point for the emergence of these twin activities is the work of the North American mechanical engineer and management consultant F. W. Taylor. In the light of our earlier discussion, 'scientific management' can be understood as a reforming and regulatory 'grand theory' through which an organization would become a 'mini-society' that was archetypally modern. The modern 'scientifically managed' organization would thus comprise a utopian moral and economic order in which management and workers would be functionally divided and specialized, whilst their interactions would be scientifically regulated and harmonized around efficiency, progress and reward. Scientific management thus offered a model of organizational progress through which the disorder of change could be managed and controlled to provide both mutual benefit, meaning productivity and profitability, and the harmonious recapturing of a more advanced order. However, the equity and reciprocal benefits of this 'great mental revolution' were not immediately apparent to the managements and workforces of the industrialized countries of the world in the early twentieth century. Accordingly, the 'one best way' of managing and organizing propounded by Taylor soon become modified, through the popularization of derivative 'efficiency systems', into variations that were contingent on the resistance of particular managements and, to a lesser extent, workforces.

Consequently, the significance of 'scientific management' is not as a point of origin for the theory and practice of Management, but rather as a prime channel of convergence which integrated pre-existing discourses and practices from the Human Sciences.[1] Hence, this chapter argues that 'scientific management' should be understood both as a conduit and an important platform of departure from which Management, formed through over a century of antecedent struggle in the modern interrelationship of human beings and their 'world', began to take on the shape and qualities that have been subsequently canonized as identifying its field, its discourse and its discipline (as both a mode and an object of understanding).

This territory of Management, between human beings and their 'world', becomes visibly delineated and described through the articulation of 'efficiency systems' that sought to improve labour productivity without compromising managerial structures of authority, such as the Bedaux system, popularized in Britain and Europe (Lash & Urry, 1987). These efficiency practices and discourses are properly connected under the rubric 'Taylorism'; since, on the one hand, such 'efficiency systems' can be considered as consolidations that are both distinct and derived from Taylor's work on 'scientific management', whilst on the other hand, such efficiency practices and discourses need to be considered as being inextricably interconnected with disciplinary discourses from the Human Sciences, focused on the progress of organized activity. It is this loose and contingent collection of discourses and practices of control and discipline that develop to become connected under the rubric 'Taylorism' which form and shape the explicit 'field' of Management.

The practices and discourses of 'Taylorism' thus represent a rationalization and a consolidation of 'scientific management'. The overarching philosophy of organizational progress was retained, in which the disorder of change would be scientifically managed and controlled to provide the stabilizing benefits of increased productivity and profitability. However, here we find that, on the one hand, managements have restored their rationality and regained control over disorder through technologies of work intensification, product standardization and accountability. Whilst, on the other hand workforces have likewise retained their demarcations and hierarchies through the consolidation of skilled worker's participation in the supervisory process (e.g. rate setting) to the disadvantage of the unskilled (i.e. female, migrant and black labour, Lash & Urry, 1987).

> Evolving beyond its technical and national origins, Taylorism became an important component of the philosophical outlook of modern industrial civilization, defining virtue as efficiency, establishing a new role for experts in production, and setting parameters for new patterns of social distribution ... A mental revolution that had been so deeply embedded in the structure of industrial society that it was a social philosophy that no longer could be casually abandoned (Merkle, 1980, p. 62).

Accordingly, it is appropriate to understand the Taylorising process of organizational change as indeed part of a great 'mental revolution'. Although these organizational changes should be perceived as a symptom of a wider and more far reaching revolution in both thought and practice, than had been advocated in Taylor's utopian proposals, which had begun to emerge over a hundred years earlier in the transition to modern society. As part of the process of the modern organization of capital (i.e. intensification, Lash & Urry, 1987) great institutions were developed in the industrialized countries of the world. These complex, formal organizations became the very vehicles of progress, both embodying superiorities that distanced them from their past and also promising further benefits from the harnessing of human beings and scientific potential into productive and profit-making capacities. Through such institutions, many controlled by dynastic families, the socioeconomic and the sociocultural orders of modern society became joined in the pursuit of progress (Marcus & Hall, 1992). As a consequence, organizations need to be understood as both sites and embodiments of the modern struggle for progress, as well as formations which comprise the dynamic moral and economic order of modern society. Accordingly, by the late nineteenth century the sociocultural evolution, that is, both the cultivation and the civilization, of the industrializing countries of the modern world, is expressed through their complex organizations.

Each institution has brought with its development demands, expectations, rules, standards. These are not mere embellishments of the forces which produced them, idle decorations of the scene. They are additional forces. They reconstruct. They open new avenues of endeavour and impose new labors. In short, they are civilization, culture, morality ... if one is going to live one must live a life of which these things form the substance. The only question having sense which can be asked is how we are going to use and be used by these things, not whether we are going to use them (Dewey, 1927 cited in Person, 1929, p. 112).

Interestingly, Management as an explicit articulation of the Human Sciences becomes formed approximately a century after the emergence of modern society, yet, during this hundred years, we have already argued that Management is already there in the disciplinary discourses and control practices of modern society, articulated through human sciences predominantly concerned with sociocultural evolution (see endnote 1). These partly visible and overlapping components converge and continue their development more collectively through the conduit of 'Taylorism'. With this visible integration of a loose collection of managerial and organizational discourses and practices, the territory of Management, as a Human Science of modern society, between human beings and their 'world', becomes visible, formatively delineated and described. Accordingly, pre-existing disciplinary discourses and control practices continued their part in the symbiotic process of evolving with, as well as managing and intervening in, the moral and economic order of modern society.

These twin processes, interconnecting the Human Sciences and Modern Society, articulate the formation of Management as both an arena of theory and practice. Unsurprisingly, in Management we encounter a very similar process to that which can be observed in the formation of Sociology and Social Anthropology as arenas of theory and practice. In both cases, 'grand theories', for example, the sociocultural evolution of society or a great mental revolution in organizations, became articulated through a mix of paternal and authoritarian management strategies in the modernization of a moral and economic order. Accordingly, the idea formed in the early twentieth century, of a 'well managed' organization as a rational, technical bureaucracy characterized by accountability and efficiency that operates in a mass market, is thus an embodiment of the idea of progress in society as well as being inseparable from practices of intervention (i.e. modernization) that are seeking to modify the moral and economic order towards these ends; both in terms of specific sites, such as organizations, and in society in general.

Consequently, Management from the early twentieth century becomes consolidated as a Human Science that is concerned with organizational progress in

93

the advance of industrial society. Moreover, this is a progress that is defined in terms that are common to the Human Sciences (as the regaining of the stability of an improved order from the dislocation and disorder of change) but articulated in respect of the specificities of productivity, accountability, consumption and profitability. Accordingly, organizations are conceptualized as rational-technical entities within an industrial society and Management undertakes a pragmatic, interventionist and consultancy oriented approach to its sites of interest. Hence, enabling this formation of a 'fresh' arena of the Human Sciences, on the one hand, is the growing significance of organized activity as both sites and managed embodiments of progress; whilst, on the other hand, is the convergence of pre-existing discourses and practices which regulated social organization, to become visibly interconnected around the integrative conduit of the 'sciences of management and organization'.

Accordingly, Management becomes an archetypal Human Science seeking to intervene in and to order the space and the surface between 'organizational man/woman' and his/her 'organizational world'. As a consequence of this formation, Management becomes canonized as the Human Science concerned with the colonial process of regulation and control of social order both in and outside of organization (i.e. both producers and consumers). As we have observed, this orientation is first explicitly articulated by the disciplinary discourses and practices of control we considered under the rubric 'Taylorism', and supported by a wide range of professionalization processes around the 'sciences of management and organization'.

Management and transformation

It is entirely appropriate that Management should explicitly emerge at the 'height' of modern society (Hassan, 1985), in the early twentieth century. Suffused by an intensity and diversity of experimentation, artists (e.g. Futurists, Vorticists), musicians (e.g. Stravinsky, Bartok) and writers (e.g. Joyce, Lawrence) sought to represent the dynamism of modern life, at the same time as innovation in transportation and communication (e.g. aircraft, motor vehicles, radio) intensified the transformation of human beings and their 'world' through simultaneity, movement and plurality. Not only was there an enormous and rapid increase in the volume of commodities, but a mature 'colonial' trading system also enabled the distribution and marketing of these raw materials, services and finished products on a worldwide basis. Accordingly, through processes of ordering and control based on rational calculation, Management became the 'visible hand' of intervention in the institutions of modern society through which progress would be both effectively pursued and reliably achieved. This 'visible hand' was effected and empowered by new professionals in their managing of complex organizations, interventions which sought to harness and integrate forces for change at the leading edge of the transformation of society.

The young factories!
They live heartily.
They smoke higher than the peal of the bells.
They are not afraid to hide the sun,
Because they create sun with their own machines.
Like a dog shaking itself on leaving the sea,
The foaming factory scatters around itself
Drops of energy which wake the city."
(Jules Romains, "L'Eglise", 1908; cited in Tate Gallery, 1991, p. 4).

The form in and through which Management became canonized was that of rational-technical organization or 'bureaucracy'. As we have been observing, this was the archetypal modern efficiency system of both theory and practice (Clegg, 1990). On the one hand, this form was understood as exhibiting both technical and sociocultural superiority over less capable forebears (i.e. as a more advanced form of organizational order, Lash & Urry, 1987). Whilst, on the other hand, this form promised a means of both consolidating gains that had been made and achieving continuing improvement in the moral and economic order of society (i.e. the process of modernization, Harvey, 1989). Furthermore, 'bureaucracy' was understood as the organizational vehicle of progress for both liberal capitalist society, that is, a non-discriminatory impartiality in the exercise of individual freedoms and responsibilities (Perrow, 1972) and communist society, meaning a productive system as the foundation of a workers' state, which would eliminate shortage, provide and distribute resources for all (Lenin, 1968). However, these particular promises of progress were only partially realized and at considerable human cost (Bauman, 1989, 1992).

To further develop our consideration of the 'management' of progress in modern society we now need to focus on tensions between construction and destruction that are inherent to this idea and experience of change. We have considered progress as the dynamic through which modern society would become transformed for the better, through an amalgam of constructive and destructive forces. On the one hand, progress would effect the destabilization of former continuities through the functional energy of division. On the other hand, progress would also effect the adaptive 'invisible hand' of reformation through which an improved order would be reconstructed. Indeed, as Williams (1958) considered, the transition to modern society was characterized by a strong sense of loss (as articulated in the nostalgia of Cobbett) and disputes over the direction of development (the romanticism of Coleridge). However, we observed the maturation of modern society to have become increasingly characterized by a self-confidence that the tensions of change could be effectively managed to ensure the developmental continuities of socio-cultural evolution. Accordingly, the Human Sciences exercized both regulation and reassurance in modern society through the articulation of progress over regress and optimism over nostalgia.

Although in the exercise of these disciplinary discourses and practices of control, the fear of the future remains powerfully there in the disorder that needs to be both contained and censored (i.e. managed). As we have considered, this fear is largely articulated in terms of the mass of society, focusing on both their individual bodies and the body of the population. Accordingly, the contamination of the mass both individually and collectively was sought to be contained as these cultural 'others' were harnessed, through paternal and authoritarian strategies, in the pursuit of progress. However, as Marx and Engels, observed so presciently, construction and destruction are each brought into tension through progress:

> Constant revolutionising of production, uninterrupted disturbance of all social conditions, everlasting uncertainty and agitation distinguish the bourgeois epoch from all earlier ones. All fixed, fast-frozen relations, with their train of ancient and venerable prejudices and opinions, are swept away, all newly formed ones become antiquated before they can ossify. All that is solid melts into air, all that is holy is profaned, and man is at last compelled to face with sober senses, his real conditions of life, and his relations with his kind (Marx & Engels, 1848, translation of 1888, pp. 45-46).

These tensions are further revealed through nineteenth century reinterpretations of the myth of Prometheus, classically articulated in the story of Frankenstein (Shelley, 1969). Science in its search for progress and the creation of a perfect order, creates instead a fallible and perverted order (a monster) which destroys its creators. In the Human Sciences, the pre-eminent interveners in the development of modern society, these tensions are necessarily articulated through an ambivalence towards the project of progress. On the one hand, facilitating sociocultural evolution as the agency of modernization; whilst, on the other hand, criticising the transformations of sociocultural change.

> From this foul drain the greatest stream of human industry flows out to fertilise the whole world. From this filthy sewer pure gold flows. Here humanity attains its most complete development and its most brutish; here civilization works its miracles, and civilized man is turned back almost into a savage (deTocqueville, 1835, on Manchester cited in Kumar, 1978, p. 64).

Such ambivalence in the early phase of transition to modern society was articulated by oppositions in the Human Sciences. On the one hand, we considered social theory which optimized the opportunities of the process of transition (e.g. Saint-Simon, Comte, Tylor, Spencer); whilst, on the other hand, we considered romantic and nostalgic reactions to such change (e.g. Cobbett, Carlyle, Coleridge). Of particular interest was social theory which sought to incorporate the tensions of this ambivalence to social change. Accordingly, the reforming work of Marx and Engels offered a far sighted critique of the process of modernization (i.e. the bourgeois revolution) allied to an alternative conception of social progress (i.e.

towards Advanced Communism). At the same time, the more paternal work of Arnold sought to manage the threat of the mass through the educational (i.e. civilising) activity of the State.

In the phase of 'high modernism' (i.e. the early twentieth century, Hassan 1985), with Management formed as an explicit and expert facilitator of progress (e.g. the theory and practice of 'Taylorism'), the critical voices of sociocultural change emerged from older arenas of the Human Sciences like Anthropology and Sociology. In this phase, the organization of the mass continued its pre-eminence as the representation of progress in modern society. Accordingly, the bureaucratic ordering of complexity, as practised in business enterprises and other institutions, becomes a persuasive model for the organization of the greater collectivities of modern society (e.g. the city). This interconnection, through communication technologies, of the complexity of social organization with the rationalization of systems of administration, is a site of both romantic regret and pessimistic observation.

They were nearing Chicago. Signs were everywhere numerous. Trains flashed by them. Across wide stretches of flat open prairie they could see lines of telegraph poles stalking across the fields toward the great city (Drieser, 1900 cited in Tallack, 1991, p. 4).

The relationships and affairs of the typical metropolitan usually are so varied and complex that without the strictest punctuality in promises and services the whole structure would break down into an inextricable chaos. Above all, this necessity is brought about by the aggregation of so many people with such differentiated interests, who must integrate their relations and activities into a highly complex organism (cited in Kumar, 1978, p. 71).

However, it is in the work of Weber and Durkheim, emerging in this period of 'high modernism', that the critique of the theory and practice of organization as the archetype for progress became most explicit. For Durkheim, the complex organizations of modern society became sites for the reconstruction of solidarity in a society that was being transformed through the process of modernization. Organizations were thus understood as articulating a collective moral and economic order that was formed through tensions between integration and regulation (Thompson et al., 1990). Accordingly, organizations needed to be approached as representations of a 'conscience collective' (i.e. a shared moral code, Gordon, 1991); in other words, as symbolic forms which articulate culture.

In a series of profound and probing discussions of education, politics, professional organization, morality and the law, Durkheim demonstrated that these modern spheres must be studied in terms of symbolic classifications. They are structured by tensions between the fields of the sacred and profane; their central social processes are ritualistic; their most significant structural dynamics concern the construction and destruction of social solidarities (Alexander, 1988, p. 3).

For Weber, the complex organizations of modern society were sites of rationalization whereby the uncertainty and disenchantment of modernization became managed and controlled. Accordingly, bureaucracy was both a response to and a reflection of the modern condition. On the one hand, the uncertainties and disenchantment of the modern world were made manageable through rational action; whilst on the other hand, the freedom to act was constrained by this imposition of an ethic of rational calculation. Under these circumstances, the modern world becomes manageable through the proliferation of bureaucratic organizations, but at the price of modernization. This was a bargain which empowered the construction of ever-expanding organizational 'iron cages' where individuals worked to meet the functional requirements of a system determined by objective, calculable rules for optimal performance.

> The iron cage is not only a prison but also a principle. As a principle it 'makes us free' to be modern. It makes us free because it is only through the purposefulness and goal directedness of organization that the uncertainties of disenchanted modernity could be coped with. In Weber's view it would be only false prophets who would insist otherwise. Rational calculation would limit uncertainty to a world which was, in principle, manageable. The freedom of modernity, experienced in the loss of entrapment within received meaning, is not something which is merely one-dimensional, something wholly positive. It is also something simultaneously experienced negatively - as a loss of freedom to organizational and rational constraint (Clegg, 1990, p. 33).

For both Durkheim and Weber, complex organizations articulate the modern condition, inscribing an order (i.e. 'solidarity' or 'rationality') through which the disorder (i.e. 'uncertainty', 'disenchantment', or 'anomie') that was implicit to this condition was made manageable. However, this was a manageability that was only achieved through loss, essentially the loss of individuality to the 'coercion' of community (Durkheim) or the 'iron cage' of bureaucracy (Weber). Indeed, it is clearly significant that these understandings emerged at a transitional stage in modern society when the 'invisible hand' of the market was becoming explicitly superseded by the 'visible hand' of management in the formation of social order. Consequently, it is the combination of these two forms of order ('solidarity' and 'rationality') that characterises the later twentieth century development of Management (Clegg, 1990) as well as the management of the centrally planned societies of both capitalist and communist nation states (Bauman, 1989, 1992).

98

Concluding discussion

Management can thus be understood as a thoroughly modern constituent of the Human Sciences; being characterized by the heterogeneity, division and disorder of the modern condition as well as being predicated upon the ordering and management of this very condition through its theory and practice. This fundamental tension is articulated in two complementary and contradictory foci of activity which together constitute the 'field' of Management.

On the one hand, we can observe an area of knowledge that is inevitably cross and multidisciplinary: where a theoretical field concerned with the analysis of organization has become relatively recently established (i.e. with the majority of its work having been conducted over the past 60 years), formed from theoretical foundations that were largely dominated by other Human Science disciplines (e.g. Anthropology, Economics, Politics, Psychology, Sociology) which developed earlier in the nineteenth century.

Whilst, on the other hand, we can observe an area of practice that is inevitably cross institutional and multicultural (in terms of place, size, sector, scale, scope, etc.): where a field of professional practice has become established, again largely over the past 60 years, which has sought to manage difference in the pursuit of progress, both across and within the diverse settings of organized activity. As have considered, such practices of managing and organizing were again formed on foundations of practice which emerged earlier in the regulation of modern society.

Consequently, Management, from its explicit 'high modern' formation at the turn of the century develops a plural structure that is both 'multidisciplinary' and 'multicultural'. On the one hand, this plurality reflects the functional areas of business enterprise, such as Marketing, Production and Accounting, the distinctive concerns of which have been sought to be integrated through the functional practice of managing. As we have observed, it was the rise of such complex organizations as 'high modern' sites of societal progress, to which the rise of Management has been symbiotically interconnected. On the other hand, this plurality reflects the Human Sciences, as Management becomes an arena of contestation and collaboration between already established disciplines which sought to pursue the broader issues of order/disorder and progress in modern society through organization (i.e. representing both a specific site of interest and an archetypal expression of the modern condition).

However, Management, in its canonization as an explicit arena of Human Science concerned with the organization of progress, became at the same time shadowed by an ambivalence to modern society. On the one hand, facilitating the modernization of efficiency systems and the extension of bureaucracy into organized life (e.g. Taylorism); whilst, on the other hand, both recognising and exposing the coercion, repression and provisionality that accompanies this search to extend progress through manageability (e.g. Weber, Durkheim). Accordingly, this ambivalence becomes articulated through both the forming and crossing of significant boundaries:

99

Complex organization as a site of tension between order and disorder in social change.

Management as both a practical science of managing and a theoretical science of manageability.

Management as a heterogeneous Human Science that is concerned with the development of functional arenas of complex organizations, as well as with organization as an embodiment and expression of change in modern society.

These interconnections are vital and sustaining, distinguishing Management as an activity that is both concerned with and constituted by modern boundaries and tensions. Accordingly, whilst Management is necessarily the theory and practice of organization both *in* and *of* modern society, these are difficult interconnections that have frequently been oversimplified in a search to reduce their ambivalence and ambiguity. The development of Management in the twentieth century can thus be characterized by moves which aim to separate and reduce the tensions that are constitutive of the theory and practice of organization (Locke, 1989; Hassard & Pym, 1990; Reed & Hughes, 1992). As we shall consider (Cooper, 1986, 1989), this selective focusing on 'order' (e.g. strategy and structure) is linked to a corresponding censorship of 'disorder' (e.g. provisionality and ambiguity). Furthermore, such tensions can be understood as endemic to modernity.

There is mode of vital experience - experience of space and time, of the self and others, of life's possibilities and perils - that is shared by men and women all over the world today. I will call this body of experience 'modernity'. To be modern is to find ourselves in an environment that promises adventure, power, joy, growth, transformation of ourselves and the world - and, at the same time, that threatens to destroy everything we have, everything we know, everything we are (Berman, 1983, p. 15).

This desire to create order from disorder permeates the modern world, and can be observed from late nineteenth century 'depth-models' of the person (e.g. conscious/subconscious, Freud) and society (e.g. superstructure/base, Marx), to late twentieth century syntheses of apparently incommensurable theoretical perspectives (e.g. images of organization, Morgan, 1986). Accordingly, whether exposing the dark underside of society for reform or expressing a liberating vision of the future, the aspiration of the cultural practices of modernism is to seek to attain a fresh and renewing order through the resolution of tensions that are vital to modernity (articulated so graphically by Baudelaire and Berman, see above). As we shall observe, these archetypally modern tensions between transformation and destruction have the promise of being resolved or overcome through strategies of innovation and experimentation.

With the essential truth of the world being understood as underlying and hidden, the essential focus of modernism becomes the revelation of that truth through rational processes of uncovering (Boyne & Rattansi, 1990). Here a complex surface that appears incoherent, contradictory and unstable (e.g. the symbolic world) is able to be understood, ordered and coordinated (i.e. rationalized) at theoretically submerged levels of unity (i.e. 'reality'). Accordingly, this characteristically modern belief in a harmonious and unified deep structure of reality privileges the processes by which that reality is knowable (i.e. intellectually and culturally penetrable), particularly privileging the authors of such penetrations. Modernism is thus focused on the process of interpretation and its problematics (Ryan, 1988), a process which entails a restless searching for new strategies that are more original or authentic in their revelation and expression of underlying structure. Correspondingly, modernity has been characterized by the institutionalization of such creative searching, both scientific and artistic, exemplified by the widespread establishment of institutional bases for such intellectual effort (i.e. municipal universities, galleries, theatres etc.), and the patronage of an associated avant-garde. Through the intellectual heroism of such a modernist vanguard', the tensions of disorder, ambiguity and disunity that were recognized as endemic to the condition of modernity, seemed to be able to be progressively resolved or overcome in the project of achieving order, meaning and unity. As we considered earlier, complex organizations and their associated professionals represented important vehicles of progress for modern society.

Over the past hundred years Management has thus exhibited the character of an archetypally 'high modern' field of activity (Reed, 1985; Clegg, 1990), where innovations and experimentations in the theory and practice of organization have been restlessly pursued, consumed and discarded (as 'fads') in an apparently insatiable will to progress. This process is exemplified, over the past decade, by the concerns of the Management avant-garde having become redefined from 'systems' and 'structures' to 'culture' and 'symbolism'. As part of this process of redefinition, the practice of organizational analysis became redescribed as a skill that was more 'artistic' and 'authorial' than 'technical' (e.g. 'connoisseurship', Turner, 1988) in its revelation of the qualities of organized activity. In this way, a newly empowered field of theory and practice (i.e. organizational interpretation) became able to offer a more persuasive means (i.e. microqualitative rather than macroquantitative) of revealing the order that was understood as lying beneath the apparent disorder of complex organization. Consequently, as I have argued elsewhere (Jeffcutt, 1993, 1994a, 1994b), the major focus of researchers and practitioners in organizational interpretation has been a search to manage disorder through the rationalization of the organizational irrational and the harmonization of the organizational dysfunctional. Accordingly, the major features of this 'turn' have been the articulation of visions of progress that are both nostalgic and utopian (e.g. heroic and romantic organizational narratives); the dispensation of persuasive strategies for remedying current deficiencies or obstacles to the achievement of such visions (e.g. charismatic turnaround, cultural regeneration), alongside the elevation of a particular avant-garde (i.e. the interpreters of organizational culture and symbolism) in Management. The quest of this reforming vanguard thus became the managing of uncertainty, a search to re-establish a manageable order from the disorder (i.e. fragmentation and incoherence in the theoretical and empirical base of Management) that earlier prophets and prophecies had been incapable of solving.

However, organizational interpretation has been but one of a series of recent 'fads' (Pascale 1990), representing an intensified quest for order through which the modernising momentum of Management has developed into a 'late modern' phase. Characterized by restless searching for metanarratives that will effect ever more novel forms of closure, 'late modern' Management presents a succession of 'last words' which promise to achieve the impossible (i.e. resolving the ambiguities of undecidability) through strategies which can only accomplish the mundane; the plausible redescription of hierarchies that inscribe particular relations of privilege and authority (i.e. power/knowledge). In this way aspiring meta narratives provide the leverage whereby existing elite forms may be superseded, but importantly also maintain the pre-conditions for their own subsequent supersession. For example, the persuasive supplanting of a formerly privileged modernist genre in Management (i.e. narratives of open systems/contingency) enabled the rise of a new avant-garde form (i.e. organizational interpretation), however, this did not necessarily coincide with the supersession of the former elite (Weick, 1985). Even so, the eminence of organizational interpretation remained short lived as it became rapidly challenged by aspiring metanarratives (e.g. re-engineering). Consequently, it is important to go on to consider this avant-garde process of 'reforming modernism' from a postmodern perspective.

The periodization 'postmodern' was first employed by the historian Toynbee (1954) to characterize the increasing instabilities of rapid social change during the twentieth century. Toynbee's analysis of the problems of social change, akin to the 'future shock' of Toffler (1971), is a clear precursor of Bell's (1974) prognosis of 'postindustrial' society. Such visions, and fears, about the nature and character of the functions and dysfunctions of intensive scientific and socio-economic change, presaged a proliferation of accounts that have articulated a fundamental shift in both the organization of society and the ways in which that organization is understood (Harvey, 1989; Lyotard, 1984). However, whilst such accounts are joined by their assertion of a breach between the modern and the postmodern, they also express widely differing articulations of this transition; in respect of both the nature of the threshold with modernity and the characteristics that symptomize the postmodern condition. Two broad positions can be identified here; firstly, accounts which can be designated 'late modern', where the postmodern condition becomes an extrapolation or extension of modernity (e.g. Bell, 1974, 1976; Harvey, 1989); secondly, accounts which can be designated 'postmodern', where postmodernity becomes a condition that both exceeds and moves beyond modernity (e.g. Lyotard, 1984, 1989; Baudrillard, 1988).

Having already examined the former position in Management, we shall now briefly consider the latter. Here, modern order is understood as a pursuit of privilege through the maintenance of hierarchies that seek authority through the censorship, suppression and proscription of other equally viable alternatives.

Consequently, with the postmodern being critically beyond the modern, postmodernism becomes characterized by the interrogation, disruption and overturning of such metanarratives. These positions can be clearly differentiated in terms of their management of the interrelationships between organization/text and author/representation (for further detail see Smart, 1992; Jeffcutt, 1994a, 1994b).

Consequently, modernist order may be understood as logocentric, privileging a heroic and rational voice that aspires to originality, purity and authenticity whilst censoring and suppressing the undecidable. It is this melee of contradictions, 'unity of disunity' (Berman, 1983), that manages order from incoherence through the suppression of difference, which postmodernism overturns and implodes. The strategy which postmodernism adopts in this process is that of recognising and articulating difference, a tactic of destabilization from the margin which is initially comparable to that of a late modern avant-garde seeking to reform a modern order. However, the significant difference here, between late modern reform and postmodern overturning, concerns the issue of undecidability. Postmodernism (like reforming modernism), in attempting to overturn a disciplinary and prejudicial order through the articulation of ambiguity and contradiction from the margin, is (unlike reforming modernism), not seeking to coordinate this difference into a fresh hierarchy through the articulation of a superior vision of progress. Postmodernism hence articulates a postmodern condition of undecidability and perpetual redefinition, rather than the nascence of the prioritizations of a fresh elite.

Accordingly, in the final analysis of this consideration of the development of Management in modern society we may draw three significant conclusions: importantly, each refer to contemporary debates in both the theory and practice of organization (e.g. Hassard & Parker, 1993; ESRC, 1994).

Firstly, that Management can be understood as a Human Science that is centrally concerned with the tension between order and disorder in society. Accordingly, it is both distinguished from and connected to other Human Sciences (e.g. Sociology, Social Anthropology) by its focal site of interest (i.e. the complex organizations of modern society) and its master concept (i.e. manageability) through which its interventions, in both theory and practice, are framed.

Secondly, we have considered the development of Management over the past century to be a field of activity canonized in the pursuit of progress and characterized by the restless search for new styles or forms that could be consumed as ultimate answers to perennial quests for manageability (Pascale, 1990; Huczynski, 1992). Although, as we observed through our discussion of organizational interpretation, such 'last words' would, by their very nature, always be incomplete and unable to provide closure. Accordingly, their destiny was inevitably to be discredited, discarded as inadequate 'fads' and superseded in Management's apparently insatiable will to progress.

Thirdly, despite the inevitability of the failure of the 'fads' of Management to deliver ultimate answers to perennial questions of order and disorder, such partial challenges to established boundaries and prioritizations can be understood as reorientations that open the potential for more significant change in our modern world. Indeed, such challenges emerge as a 'carnivalesque' force to challenge the 'canons' of Management; for example, over the past decade the eccentricities of the former backwater of organizational interpretation became rediscovered as the 'leading edge' of the theory and practice of organization. However, as I have also argued (Jeffcutt, 1993, 1994a, 1994b), the development of organizational interpretation in the Management mainstream has partially challenged, redescribed and extended the whole plethora of modern boundaries of which the theory and practice of organization is composed.

Importantly, we need to recognise that such openings can also enable the pursuit of the long overdue task of redescribing Management from a modern to a postmodern science of human practice. However, since symbolic inversion effects a redistribution as well as a retention of hierarchy, such overturning needs to be understood not as ultimate and complete (i.e. as an avant-garde process) but as a first step in a process of transformation that is both continuous and infinite, where boundaries implode and hierarchies 'metaphorize' (Cooper, 1989). Consequently, a process of postmodern overturning in Management will need to instil some life into the aridity of petrified texts, equally as well as, some text into the witlessness of instrumental life.

Notes

1. The four arenas of Management theory and practice which became explicit and interconnected through 'scientific management' have significant pre-histories through the nineteenth century: 'managing' (Chandler, 1977; Joyce, 1987), 'accounting' (Miller & O'Leary, 1987), 'occupational psychology' (Sanderson, 1987; Hoskin & Macve, 1988), 'marketing' (Goodall, 1986). Accordingly, these discourses and practices focusing on ordering and organizing can be understood as experiencing about a hundred years of dispersed and fragmented modern development prior to their consolidation and professionalized incorporation into the theory and practice of Management (see Jeffcutt, 1995).

References

Alexander, J. (ed.), (1988), *Durkheimian Sociology: Cultural Studies*, Cambridge University Press, Cambridge.
Baudrillard, J. (1988), *Selected Writings* in Poster, M. (ed.), 1988.
Bauman, Z. (1989), *Modernity and the Holocaust*, Polity, Oxford.
Bauman, Z. (1992), *Intimations of Postmodernity*, Routledge, London.
Bell, D. (1974), *The Coming of Post-Industrial Society*, Heinemann, London.

Bell, D. (1976), *The Cultural Contradictions of Capitalism*, Heinemann, London.

Berman, M. (1983), *All that is Solid Melts into Air*, Verso, London.

Boyne, R. and Rattansi, A. (eds), (1990), *Postmodernism and Society*, Macmillan, London.

Bryman, A. (ed.), (1988), *Doing Research in Organisations*, Routledge, London.

Burrell, G. (1984), 'Sex and Organizational Analysis', *Organization Studies*, Vol. 5, No. 2, pp. 97-118.

Chandler, A. (1977), *The Visible Hand*, Harvard Universtiy Press, Cambridge, Mass.

Clegg, S. (1990), *Modern Organisations*, Sage, London.

Cooper, R. (1986), 'Organisation/Disorganisation', *Social Science Information* Vol. 25, No. 2, pp. 299-335.

Cooper, R. (1989), 'Modernism, Post Modernism and Organizational Analysis No. 3', *Organization Studies*, Vol. 10, No. 4, pp. 479-502.

ESRC (1994), *Report of the Commission on Management Research*, Economic and Social Research Council, Swindon.

Foucault, M. (1974), *The Order of Things*, Tavistock, London.

Goodall, F. (1986), 'Marketing Consumer Products before 1914' in Davenport-Hines, R. (ed.), *Markets and Bagmen*, Gower, Aldershot.

Gordon, S. (1991), *The History and Philosophy of Social Science*, Routledge, London.

Harvey, D. (1989), *The Condition of Postmodernity*, Blackwell, Oxford.

Hassan, I. (1985), 'The Culture of Postmodernism', *Theory, Culture and Society*, Vol. 2, No. 3 pp. 119-131, Sage, London.

Hassard, J. and Pym, D. (eds), (1990), *The Theory and Philosophy of Organisations*, Routledge, London.

Hassard, J. and Parker, M. (eds), (1993), *Postmodernism and Organisations*, Sage, London.

Hoskin, K. and Macve, R. (1988), 'The Genesis of Accountability', *Accounting, Organisations and Society*, Vol. 13, No. 1, pp. 37-73.

Huczynski, A. (1992), *Management Gurus*, Routledge, London.

Jeffcutt, P. S. (1993), 'The Transition from Interpretation to Representation Organisation Studies', in Hassard, J. and Parker, M. (eds), *Postmodernism and Organisations*, Sage, London.

Jeffcutt, P. S. (1994a), 'The Interpretation of Organisation: A Contemporary Analysis and Critique', *The Journal of Management Studies*, Vol. 31, No. 4, pp. 225-250.

Jeffcutt, P. S. (1994b), 'From Interpretation to Representation in Organizational Analysis: Postmodernism, Ethnography and Organisational Symbolism', *Organization Studies*, Vol. 15, No. 2, pp. 245-278.

Jeffcutt, P. S. (1995), *The Management of Transition: Culture and Complex Organisation in Modern Society*, Sage (forthcoming), London.

Joyce, P. (ed.), (1987), *The Historical Meanings of Work*, CUP, Cambridge.

Kumar, K. (1978), *Prophecy and Progress*, Harmondsworth, Penguin.

Lash, S. and Urry, J. (1987), *The End of Organised Capitalism*, Polity, Oxford.

Lenin, V. (1968), 'The State and Revolution' in *Collected Works*, Progress Publishers, Moscow.

Locke, R. R. (1989), *Management and Higher Education since 1940*, CUP, Cambridge.

Lyotard, J. (1984), *The Postmodern Condition*, Manchester University Press, Manchester.

Lyotard, J. (1989), *The Inhuman*, Polity Press, Cambridge.

Marcus, G. and Hall, P. (1992), *Lives in Trust*, Westview Press, Boulder, Colorado.

Marx, K. and Engels, F. (1888), *The Manifesto of the Communist Party*, reproduced 1952, Progress Publishers, Moscow.

Meek, V. (1988), 'Organizational Culture: Origins and Weaknesses', *Organization Studies*, Vol. 9, No. 4, pp. 453-473.

Merkle, J. (1980), *Management and Ideology*, University of California Press, Berkeley.

Miller, P. and O'Leary, T. (1987),'Accounting and the Construction of the Governable Person', *Accounting, Organizations and Society*, Vol. 12, No. 3, pp. 235-265.

Morgan, G. (1986), *Images of Organization*, Sage, London.

Pascale, R. (1990), *Managing on the Edge*, Simon & Schuster, New York.

Perrow, C. (1972),*Complex Organizations*, Scott Foresman, Illinois.

Person, H. (ed.), (1929), *Scientific Management in American Industry*, Harper, New York.

Poster, M. (ed.), (1988), *Jean Baudrillard: Selected Writings*, Polity Press, Cambridge.

Reed, M. (1985), *Redirections in Organisational Analysis*, Tavistock, London.

Reed, M. and Hughes, M. (eds), (1992), *Rethinking Organisation*, Sage, London.

Ryan, M. (1988), 'Postmodern Politics', pp. 559-576 in Featherstone, M. (ed.), *Postmodernism*, Sage, London.

Sanderson, M. (1987), *Educational Opportunity*, Faber, London.

Shelley, M. (1969), *Frankenstein*, Oxford University Press, London.

Smart, B. (1992), *Modern Conditions, Postmodern Controversies*, Routledge, London.

Stallybrass, P. and White, A. (1986), *The Politics and Poetics of Transgression*, Methuen, London.

Stocking, G. (1987), *Victorian Anthropology*, Free Press, New York.

Tallack, D. (1991), *Twentieth Century America*, Longman, London.

Tate Gallery (1991), *Dynamism*, Exhibition Catalogue, Liverpool.

Thompson, M., Ellis, R., Wildavsky, A. (1990), *Cultural Theory*, Westview Press, Boulder.

Toffler, A. (1971), *Future Shock*, Pan, London.

Toynbee, A. (1954), *A Study of History*, OUP, London.

Turner, B. (1988), *Connoisseurship in the Study of Organisational Cultures*, pp. 108-122, in Bryman, A. (ed.), 1988.

Weick, K. (1985), 'The Significance of Corporate Culture', pp. 381-389, in Frost, P. et al., (eds), Organizational Culture, Sage, Beverly Hills.

Williams, R. (1958), *Culture and Society*, Chatto & Windus, London.

Wolff, K. (ed.), (1950), *The Sociology of Georg Simmel*, Free Press, New York.

5 The professional as a machine: the death of each day's life

Michael Fores

The idols of the market are the most troublesome of all, those namely which have entwined themselves round the understanding from the associations of words and names. For men imagine that their reason governs words, whilst, in fact, words re-act upon the understanding; and this has rendered philosophy and the sciences sophistical and in-active (Bacon 1620, book 1, aphorism 59).

Introduction: Dr James Mortimer, the Man of Science

Amongst the two or three principal criteria for identifying those people who should be classed as expressly 'professional' in the English speaking countries, and thus too as those people who should not be so classed, there has usually been one listed broadly thus:- 'A professional person has special access to a particular body of knowledge, vital for the effective operation of specialist work'. The specialist scientists and knowledgewrights of our species have been foremost amongst those who have insisted on (say) Name N being tagged securely to Item A, in aid of identification and subsequent understanding.[1] So when it has been claimed, by association with the criterion spelled out here, something along these lines that professional people are closer to a particular part of science than the majority of people are there is a general inclination to accept the claim whatever it may signify in detail. The scientists and other important people will not have got things wrong on such important matters, layfolk will be inclined to assume; so the whole affair of propagating 'the professions' must be legitimate. 'QED', as the scientists say, in their rather strange, private and Latinate phrase.

There is a major trouble over the specification of the thing(s) called 'science', to which this paper will turn later, especially in the latter of its two sections expressly about 'rationality'. But, on the main issue raised here, people will be generally inclined to accept the type of linkage which suggests that for the doctors, for example, when they are learning, and subsequently when they are 'practising' their activities and their 'specialisms', there has been Medical Science, deployed in their support. And for the lawyers, there has been much of their own special material, likewise articulated and 'logged' onto paper, in aid of the good operation of their specialist work.

There is a major problem of specification, because of an assumed singularity of the world and the universe about us, over the assertion of such separable bodies of knowledge as a Medical Science, which the Main Note on Science addresses below. But to illustrate the specific science/profession link raised here, it may be worth quoting from one of the Sherlock Holmes stories, written by a medical practitioner, and as if narrated by a fictional Dr Watson, another 'medical man'. Despite the fact that Holmes has always been celebrated for his 'deductions', also for his operation in a broadly scientific manner, it was a medical practitioner who was dubbed a 'man of science' by contrast. Holmes may have helped to set up, in the stories, what was called in chapter two of *A Study in Scarlet*, The Science of Deduction; but when Holmes had specialist dealings with a Dr Mortimer in *The Hound of the Baskervilles*, this question was put into the former's mind for answering 'What does Dr James Mortimer, the man of science, ask of Sherlock Holmes, the specialist in crime?'. Note the particular point at issue. However apparently scientific Sherlock Holmes may have been in the course of his work, the higher status of the doctoring trade had resulted in its being dubbed as one suited for 'men of science'. Mere detectives could not aspire to such high status!

The 'professional' person has been conceived thus generally in the English speaking lands in recent generations as someone with a special social cachet, as someone with standing in the local community, as someone who typically has certain tasks marked up, as being the exclusive preserve of members of named Profession P, and as someone with the special stance towards a branch of science in the general way sketched out above. So it is perhaps suitable to quote here from detective fiction, if only because the apparent paradox of the given title above, 'the professional as a machine', might be thought to require some detective work for an attempted solution. Indeed, both detectives and latterday scholars might perhaps hope to throw some light, as the saying goes, on how anyone might have been so apparently outlandish in viewing, as to try to associate the actions of such high-status people as the 'professionals' of the English speaking lands with the actions of machines.

It will be necessary to specify below what machines are, in order that an attempt at a solution can be made here, as openly as can be achieved to the issue just raised. (See, for instance, the section below entitled A Model). But here suffice it to say that, with their assumed close association with science, and with their presumed off-job preparation in being scientific in some way, expressly professional people in the English speaking countries are widely accepted as having been more rational actors than most human beings. Yet expressly rational

110

behaviour, in the sense that best choices for action can be readily calculated before that action has taken place, is an expressly machine characteristic. So here is the reason for having quoted from Shakespeare's *Macbeth* for the sub-title above:

> Methought I heard a voice cry, 'Sleep no more!
> Macbeth does murder sleep', the innocent sleep,
> Sleep that knits up the ravell'd sleave of care,
> The death of each day's life, sore labour's bath,
> Balm of hurt minds, great nature's second course,
> Chief nourisher in life's feast. (II, ii, 36)

The main issue to be addressed here, therefore, has been the murdering of a proper conception of the lively existence of the species, *Homo*, with the taking up of one of the most commonly heard rationales for adopting professional behaviour by human beings. That is the character of the dire crime which has to be investigated here.

A crime to be solved

For present purposes, a professional person has been, for a few generations at least in the English speaking countries, generally accepted to be what was indicated above. He or she is someone working in a relatively prestigious specialist occupation, the apologists for which have stressed a role of local service and the manipulation of accumulated knowledge. So members of the clergy, such as the present writer's father, being officially in England 'clerks in Holy Orders', have had their Theology; and they will have studied, in recent generations, at a place called a Theological College. The lawyers have had their statutes, their common law as interpreted on the record, their law books and the longstanding Law Faculties at universities, which are far older than most of the Arts and the Science Faculties where most university students congregate today. The medical practitioners, generally known outside academic places just as doctors, have had their bits and pieces of a wider body of science, which have sometimes been put together and tagged as Medical Science. See also the Note, on science, at the end, in which it is pointed out that such a term as medical science has no precise meaning at all, if only because of the singularity of the world around us. Statement X, claimed as a part of Pathology, is not thus prevented from being claimed as well as a part of Physics.

Now, switch back again to the particular criterion discussed above, concerning knowledge manipulation. Science is, and always has been, a type of knowledge, in the primary sense of the single idea. Most Westerners of recent generations have had sufficient personal familiarity with science, to be able to grasp many of its main features. Science is a body of tested knowledge, which has been assembled in a manner which has optimized the chances of what is called, in the

111

trade, its 'objectivity'. That is to say, although we have all been taught to celebrate something called Boyle's Law, most people realise that using Boyle's name here means that because this law is commonly applicable in nature, anyone might have articulated it in the first place; thus, it has been called Boyle's Law, not because he ever owned it, not because he discovered it somewhere where it already existed to be found, but because he was its original inventor.

As such, science is a constructed body of knowledge of the world about us, in whose construction the identity of individual human beings should have been excized, as much as possible, from influence. It has been in this general tradition, that any Scientific Statement S has been well-accepted to be the best available statement of a particular Time T, being one about identified and named characteristics of a named Item M. So science, in this sense of the idea, has been accepted as provisional knowledge about things carefully identified by such given names of things as Item M, and of the classes of things such as Class N, as encountered in the human surroundings. The thing(s) called 'science' has(have) often been manipulated and propagated in a special, and a protected way, as will by shown later in this paper. But for normal, profane items of the human surroundings, the usage of naming and identification sketched out here has generally operated. And Dr Conan Doyle's fictional Dr James Mortimer would have been a 'man of science', to the fictional Holmes, broadly in the manner set out. As a medical practitioner, for whose working mode 'practice' is the real thing of working, rather than preparing for working proper (as in piano playing), Mortimer would have been expected to have been able to act broadly in the fashion we all know from the old school laboratory, regarding a secure naming of things, probity in observation and so on.

The particular link, therefore, between science, professional people and their status, might be associated with a certain rigour and integrity adhering to science. Yet there is the crime to be solved, as this has been sketched out above. For all the puffing of the science link for these particular human beings, and for all the puffing of the calm headed rationality of those people touched by the thing(s) called 'science', we have to face a complete shambles of general conception about how specialist human beings operate. An example of this has been with the way in which the ill-named historians of technology, not only concerned with loggings of various types, have systematically neglected a proper treatment of technical skill (Fores, 1994b). How precisely has it been that reality has been slaughtered? Perhaps Macbeth succeeded in murdering sleep, as his conscience tore into his soul, after he had committed a foul murder. But here we have to investigate the death of active *Homo*, more of a notional slaughter.

A model

In my piece expressly on *Homo et Machina*, with both of them (an organism and a mechanism) primarily conceived as dynamic entities, there has been put out for general viewing by others, a very simple explanatory device which may be thought to have lain at the core of the piece (Fores, 1994a). Such exposition of the main thread of an argument has been set out fully in the revelatory and light-shining spirit of science, as this is conceived and outlined in the Note at end of this chapter. There may be ramifications from what is in the paper named here, regarding the way that many varieties of posh talk and writing in the latterday West have taken up the metaphors of the machinewrights. So we have seen and heard a lot about 'the structure' of this, the 'basis' of that and the 'causes' of the other, for ever as if the speaker or the writer knew exactly what had been going on. But the named piece, *Homo et Machina*, was put together, in the typical way of constructive *Homo*, to address some specific issues. One of the main ones made explicit was whether it is possible to learn anything general about active *Homo*, by examining and discerning what may be general about the actions of *Machina* - if, indeed, there has been anything so discernable?

To cut a longer story short, as set out there (Fores 1994a), *Machina* is, and always has been (as used by *Homo*, and not by the other animals, which are far less constructive than *Homo*), a device characterized more by its dynamics than its statics. Thus, what is common to machines, besides the fact that they are what the economists call 'scarce goods', valuable and tradeable things unlike science (cf. Main note), lies with their active operations as force and energy transmitters. An electronic computer is as much, by this criterion, a member of the type, *Machina*, as is a simple lever. But so, as well, was Marx's idea of a system, which he believed that the one he called the capitalist could be found playing with, this assumption being at the heart of the failure of *Capital* as a scientific enterprise, given the fact that active *Homo* had been assumed out of sight from the start (Fores et al., 1991, pp. 88-91).

To be sure, *Homo*, making use of ever more sophisticated members of the type, *Machina*, must have appeared increasingly more powerful, and increasingly more destructive too no doubt, to other animal species of the single planet, Earth. But, if a focus is put on what has been called 'the division of labour', where *Homo* and *Homo* have been concerned, a conclusion can be drawn for the matters addressed here. Centrally to the case argued out in the earlier piece (Fores, 1994a), there has to be recognized the relative predictability of machine dynamics. From a lever to a car engine, from a car engine to its own EMS (Engine Management System), *Homo* has devised, constructed, purchased and used *Machina* for what it can do predictably. That is, given its user has known the values of the inputs applied to *Machina*, which is not well considered as an organism. *Machina* is and always has been an affair with discernable design characteristics, so to cite a phrase used by engineers and other machinewrights, something made by people readily distinguished from scientists, by the character of their principal products from working efforts made. So, in the normal manner of action, while the machine-wrights make, and make use of, *Machina*; the scientists of the single species, *Homo*, have specialized in making 'logs' (bio-logy, socio-logy ...) of those things

113

they have 'observed'. (See the Note at the end on the special use of the word 'observation' regarding science, a point taken up in Fores and Porter 1993, where the self-styled Moderns have been characterized as bird watchers at a distance).

Given all this, in machine dynamics, as opposed to human dynamics, prediction and postdiction of actions tend to have been identical. Or, at least, when *Machina* is not 'down', its users can normally be very confident of how it will operate over the following period of time, provided the values of its inputs are known. So, the example of the simple lever is not a bad one to propose here, in order to try to put across the main point at issue.

Yet, in contrast with this case of what might be called Machinecraft, *Homo* alone, and *Homo* and *Machina* operating as if in harness together, have not typically faced a future in which the key items have been predictable. From crossing the road on your own, to operating and surviving in the poorly named organization with other members of the teeming species, *Homo*; from designing new types of *Machina*, to trying to run businesses or households; *Homo* has not been able to be successful in the dynamic terms hinted at here, without taking risks, and without finding ways to treat the relatively unknown. Just a few days of what is called participant observation in the looking-at-*Homo* trade would confirm on this matter. So it would confirm what everyone bar the 'wise' folk knew implicitly all the time.

Another paper (Fores, 1994a) argues this theme out more fully than can be set down here, with some examples given of how the knowledgewrights of the academy have overvalued the importance of formalized knowledge, after periods of change which they have recklessly misspecified as revolutions in the past. Ideas of the scientific revolution have generated, for instance, the unbelievable proposition that there has been a discernable scientific method (cf. Fores and Porter, 1993). A later section below here will pick up from this theme; but, for present purposes, a simple conclusion can be made explicit, and this is in the proper manner of putting up propositions for a broadly scientific test, by anyone who wishes to have a shot at them. Because *Homo* and *Machina* have had, over the years, to face together risky circumstances, and so they have had to deal with the relatively unknown at the specific time of action; and because *Machina* has been a specialist in the relatively predictable and unknown, in the terms of dynamics addressed here; *Homo* has, willy nilly, been the specialist in what *Machina* has not been good at. *Homo*, the more adaptable dynamic player in such dramas, has had to deal with the residual component of action shared with *Machina*, being that which is least easily logged, least easily written down onto paper, and articulated.

Accordingly, for all the battering from the scholars of the West, which the rationalizing human understanding (e.g. Bacon 1620, book 1, aphorism 48, on the Idols of the Tribe of *Homo*) has received to the contrary, *Homo* has been, and remains, the specialist, dynamic risk taker. *Homo* has remained the animal whose dynamic operations are typically impossible to log on to paper by outsiders. If, say the secrets of human skill were discernable in such a light-shining manner, these would have passed over from the arena of human competence into the arena of

114

machine competence; and real life *Homo* would be found doing something else. Here, then, in a few words, is the character of what has been discussed as the Articulation Trap in my piece, *Homo et Machina* (1994a, pp. 71-77). If you can explain at any time any dynamic function onto paper, the chances are that it will be slipping out of the area of human working competence.

Three modes of 'rationality'

There have been various ways in which human beings have sought to isolate, and to name, 'rational' conduct by human agency. For present purposes, three of these can be outlined here. Someone may be said to be 'rational', because he or she is not generally thought to be insane by those close by. Second, there is the rationality of conduct involved, when (say) pushy *Homo* A has advised *Homo* B to be rational. When taken out of code, this signifies, to B, 'do as I say, and don't answer back', or 'agree with me and do not try to reason why' (cf. Fores, 1994a, p. 73). Third, there is what may be taken here as being the strongest of the ideas of 'rationality' as put to use by Max Weber in his grasp of world history, human beings and *Herrschaft*/boss-ship have, allegedly, become more 'rational' over the years, because there has been an increased possibility for the calculation of alternative outcomes before action has taken place (e.g. Weber, 1923). For convenience here, these can be called RI ,RII and RIII modes of human rationality of conduct.

Regarding the RI type of human conduct, it may be worth thinking of both the village idiot and the exponents of witchcraft, of the days which many scholars call traditional. The English word idiot stems from a Greek root, implying privacy of behaviour. So the one called an idiot is thought to inhabit a private domain, unshared by others of our species. In this sense, irrationality of action implies a high degree of unpredictability of conduct, as indeed this might have been accepted to be associated with both the actions of the local witch, and that of God who moves in mysterious ways. Rational folk, in this RI sense of the idea, are broadly predictable people, in the sense that they are unlikely to try to poison you, if they invite you to a meal at home; they are unlikely to murder you in your bed; they are unlikely to turn you into a toad, on a whim of their own. To be sure, not all of human life is predictable, as has already been argued in the section above, A Model, but rational/RI conduct by *Homo* is conduct within predicted bounds of action.

Regarding the RII type of conduct, everyone knows the types of individual who, as the saying goes, tend to get their own way consistently. While working out the theme of the present paper, I was reading a detective story by Simenon, *Maigret and the Dosser*, in which one such figure was well sketched out. A polite, but strong minded and socially climbing, provincial lady had married a medical practitioner, who seemed to prefer to cure the sick to sharing her own social ends. A terrible thing for a doctor to want to do! So, almost inevitably, he had to go, even though the wife was a pious Roman Catholic who did not hold with divorce! It was he who had gone, first in flight to Africa, later to be someone attacked as he lived under the bridges of Paris, as what is known locally as a *clochard*. The daughter of the marriage, in contrast (whom the world might have called more resilient than her father), had 'escaped', as her interview with Maigret had had it, in a more conventional way, into marriage. That is, she had escaped from a local environment, in which one particular person's ideas, opinions and habits always just so happened regularly to prevail. 'Be rational', as advised by her mother, would be likely to have the status of a politely phrased command, with dissent an unexpected outcome. As already implied, almost everyone knows people of this type: some decide to leave home to avoid them! Advice here to be rational invariably means the opposite of what has been articulated; and this is rather as 'act naturally' tends to mean 'do as the culture indicates'.

The RIII type of human conduct and action is closer to an expressed scholarly ideal. And there are those commentators on the Grand Issues of human life, who, like Weber, have not bothered to examine active *Homo* in close detail, who have gone to town on paper about increased RIII conduct from *Homo* over time.

Here then is Weber, in a posthumous book, and a chapter expressly on The Rational State (1923, Chapter 29) which 'has existed only in the Western world' (p. 338). In some earlier types of regime: 'In reality everything is (was) based on the magical theory (of rule) ... Very different is the rational state in which alone modern capitalism can flourish. Its basis is an expert officialdom and rational law' (pp. 338, 339). As already suggested here, Marx had previously conceived what is now widely known as 'capitalism', as having been characterized by something working like a machine, that is, in the 'large scale industry', which took him about as many pages to describe in a chapter, as some writers use in a book on what is now given as 'the Industrial Revolution' (1887, Chapter 15, pp. 492-639). But Weber seems to have wanted to stress the calculability of living in such a machine system: 'What it (capitalism) requires is law which can be counted upon, like a machine; ritualistic-religious and magical considerations must be excluded' (pp. 342, 343). Note the specific use of the metaphor of a machine dynamics, concerning Weber's thesis of some sort of essential predictability of action in 'capitalism'.

Then, here is the focus of the last chapter of the same book, expressly on The Evolution of the Capitalistic Spirit: 'In the last resort the factor which produced capitalism is (was) the rational permanent enterprise, rational accounting, rational technology and rational law, but again not these alone. Necessary complementary factors were the rational spirit, the rationalization of the conduct of life in general, and a rationalistic economic ethic' (p. 354). Except that this sounds very much like a blueprint for a heaven for *Machina*, rather than some type of 'improved' condition for active *Homo*! The electronic computer, if it could think, speak and feel the culture around it, would surely love this vision of the calculability of all that is important. 'No need for that freaky type of human decision-making at all! Machines rule: OK?'.

116

Rationality, 'science' and the apathetic fallacy

Normally, in human speech and other types of interaction, it is assumed that single words are used to identify single things or single groups of things. (See also brief comment in the Introduction, and further comment in Note at end of this chapter). Thus, if a shepherd cries wolf enough times, hearers will imagine that he has just seen yet another sheep; and so the normal idea of a distinction made between sheep and wolves, which the scientists share with everyone else who uses language, will have seemed to disappear. Similarly, if, in any single language, both cats and courage are given the same name, 'courage', it is to be predicted that users of this particular language (say, Cattish) will have become convinced, with such usage, that cats must be particularly courageous animals. As Bacon had it, as he set up what he called the Idols of the Market, words, which human beings need for any discourse, have an active influence on the human understanding: 'words still manifestly force the understanding, throw everything into confusion, and lead mankind into vain and innumerable controversies and fallacies' (1620 book 1, aphorism 43; see also the quote at the head of this chapter). A message from the Lord Chancellor of England, who was a lawyer by training: 'Because words react on the human imagination, *Homo* should be extremely careful over labelling things' (free translation from Bacon's Latin prose).

Consider, now, two of the various things which have been named, tagged, and thus generally puffed about, as identified by English speakers as 'science' in recent generations. For convenience, in the present section only, these are called Science I (science as knowledge, SI) and Science II (science as a process, SII) separately. Separate names have been used here, in order to indicate separate things so named, in a simple scheme of classification devised in *History of Science* (Fores, 1983). And consider an attempt made by Singer, whom most people would tag as having been an Historian of Science, to answer this simple question, 'What is science?' at the outset of his book, *A Short History of Scientific Ideas to 1900*, as published by the Oxford University Press (1959). It is notable that precisely the same question was posed at the outset of an earlier version of the same book entitled, *A Short History of Science* (1941), from the same publisher; also that the answer, in each case, was set out in the first section of a piece of script, entitled *Introduction: Nature of the Scientific Process* (that is to say, the character of the Scientific Process, assumed to have been relatively unchanging, given the selected use of the word nature).

'In a sense', claimed the author of both books, 'the book is itself an answer' to the query posed (Singer 1959, p. 1; 1941, p. 1). But an answer to a question about precisely what? That is, given the condition of the scripts filed, shelved, and otherwise piled together as having something important in common, under the single, identifying tag, History of Science? On this book's first page, and perhaps with its author having been mindful of all those attempts at precise definition of terms, attempted in the school physics laboratory, Singer made an attempt to tie down his quarry. Critical, for example, to the parts of science called Physics

117

conventionally, has been the need never to confuse 'power' with 'energy', 'volts' with 'amps', and so on, as amplified in the Note at the end of this chapter.

For this particular, named and identified writer, Charles Singer, as published by the prestigious Oxford University Press: 'Science is often conceived as a body of knowledge (SI type, his stress). Reflection, however, will lead to the conclusion that this cannot be its true nature (character). History (the past) has repeatedly shown that a body of scientific knowledge that ceases to develop soon ceases to be science (SI type) at all. The science (SI) of one age has often become the nonsense of the next' (Singer 1959, p. 1; 1941, p. 1). The last statement is one which can easily be supported, concerning the claim made about changes in Science I and its forerunners over time. It can be checked easily from the many scholarly volumes given over to expounding the History of Science, as so indicated from the names on library shelves, in computer 'memories' and so on, in an era of much 'organization' of the various 'fields' of knowledge. Yet note, all the same, this strange effect in train, which the deviser of the Idols of the Market would have found intriguing in seeking to deny the SI (body of knowledge) sense of the idea of science, this particular, single author has been happy enough to use precisely that sense of the single identifying word in his own chosen formulation. "A cat cannot possibly be a mammal; but, for my purposes of defining cats, I shall assume that it is one. Today I shall be Charles Singer; but tomorrow I may decide to be somebody else, who has a completely different grasp of that elusive thing called 'science'".

How, then, did this specific, single, named author, Charles Singer, often named too as one of the pioneers in the West of a specific History of Science, seek to tie down 'the true nature' of the variety of 'science', which he had decided (somewhat imprecisely) to stress? The reasons given for his decision to opt for the Science II sense are as intriguing as the character of the decision itself. Just after in the passage given over to 'What is Science?', and at the start of a passage on 'Origins of the Scientific Tradition', which has treated those Stone Age cave-paintings that some other scholars might wish to claim as Art (and so part of my patch, please get off it), we can all read that: 'Anthropologists perceive germs of the scientific process in the rudest races of mankind'. So, with this author's idea of 'science' being associated with *Homo* perceiving order in the human milieu, an 'elusive' undertaking: 'Science then, is no static body of knowledge (SI type) but rather *an active process* (SII type, author's stress) that can be followed through the ages. ... and no body of doctrine which is not *growing* (author's stress), which is not actually *in the making* (his stress) can long retain the attributes of science (SI type)' (1941, p. 2; 1959, p. 2).

It is certainly the case that Science I, and its forerunner Natural Philosophy, have altered over the years, both by refutation and addition, given especially their character as provisional knowledge of parts of the universe (See Note at end). But Singer's implication has been, as indicated here, that, with the single identifying tag, 'science', not being useful for Science I (as specified here) because of its variability; Science II must have been less varying over the ages, to warrant his

118

choice of this sense for defining the 'nature' of 'science'. Yet this claim seems to deny both common sense - that *Homo*, being an animal capable of learning, will have altered any   conceivable modes of Science II over the years - and the indications from the subject area, the History of Science, which suggest that there have been major changes in the past, for an 'active process' engaged in by human beings trying to make sense of nature. (cf. Fores and Porter 1993, re Troy I and Troy II and their heterogeneous characters).

In a sentence, both of the things confusingly tagged as 'science', as treated here, Science I and Science II, have been subject to much alteration over the years, where they and any forebears have been concerned. Quite apart from this observable fact, from the character of what the historians may have been able to find out about all the various things they may have wanted to call 'science', *pace* Singer and his chosen definition of 'science', the subject area called the History of Science has been constrained to have been primarily about shifts in Science I and its forebears. Scientists and their antecedents have overwhelmingly published what they have found out about 'nature', and not what they may have speculated about (say) concerning how to study nature. Accordingly, Singer's first volume named here was written, in the main, as a history of Science I; all the while the author of *A Short History* (1941, 1959) of science had been straining to conceive his main subject matter of special concern in quite different terms (Science II, as identified here). *A Short History of Science* (Singer 1941), published by the Oxford Press, was never intended to be about the 'science' of its own definition. Few cooks could have devised such a tasty pickle! In the Physics laboratory of old at school, any diligent teacher would have reacted: 'Muddled thinking, Singer; start all over again'. Come back, Francis Bacon, all is forgiven! And please tell us, when you arrive, precisely what you meant, about how the Idols of the Market, concerning 'the commerce and association of men with each other' (1620 book 1, aphorism 43), have been the most tricky of them all.

Say that Science I, being a body of published knowledge, can be observed to have been fairly orderly in character, in the sense that one part of it has been constructed to fit reasonably well with other parts of the same single science. But this does not mean that Science II (a process of inquiry) need necessarily have shared this particular, orderly characteristic with Science I, a totally different thing! As Glover, Lawrence and I sought to argue, in our paper about the professions and rationality, a bee does not have to have been a particularly sweet type of animal, for it to be able to make honey (1991, pp. 91-94). Confusing aspects of a process and its own product goes some way towards misgrasping both, as the chapter on *Homo et Machina* has argued has become common for those seeking to model active *Homo*, when this animal has tried to get to grips with active *Homo*, the key components of skill have simply been neglected as having been too difficult to model on to paper. So writers on active *Homo* have become like mice caught in a trap, given their obsession with articulated statements made after light-shining episodes (Fores, 1994a, p. 46).

Certainly, it has been a part of a specific, Western and bourgeois upbringing, for most of us to assume that the Scientists have been particularly rational sorts of people. Those called Artists, by contrast, have tended to be celebrated for their expressly creative, and their imaginative, exploits. But why should some type of notional Science II, and/or some type of doing science, be expected to have been relatively devoid of a major, real life, creative and imaginative streak, given this single and observable feature of the whole tangled affair?. It is Science I, which is tested, not Science II. (See also Note at end). Yet here is Ziman, a professor of physics, asking exactly the same question as Singer did, 'What is science?', in a book expressly about *Public Knowledge: the Social Dimension of Science* (1968), published by the Cambridge University Press. And here are some similarly unfortunate effects for lay understanding, with a scholar's professed attempts to answer his own query posed, if only because 'the names of actual objects (have been used), but confused, badly defined, and hastily and irregularly abstracted from things' (Bacon 1620, book 1, aphorism 60). In more everyday terms of expression, the writers on science have simply scattered their favourite word around, seemingly with no discrimination at all.

While Ziman pointed to the difficulty involved in answering the particular query, 'what is science?', he has still insisted that 'Science has become a major part of the stock of our (Western) minds; its products are the furniture of our surroundings. We must accept it, as the good lady of the fable is said to have agreed to accept the Universe' (1968, p. 1). In other words, perhaps, 'Science is very important, whatever it turns out to be!' (my phrasing). But how, in all good sense, can this author's *Public Knowledge*, which turns out, not surprisingly (given his chosen book title) to have been his answer to the query posed, 'What is science?' (Chapter 1, title) have as its 'products'? Does this not smack of anthropomorphism? *Homo* produces things ... so something inert (Science I, defined as science in Ziman 1968, though not in Ziman 1978, see below), and something sitting quietly on paper or in computer 'memories', has seemed to have life breathed into it! Science lives! 'What did you have for breakfast today, Science? Do you like rock 'n roll music? Up and at them, Science! Show them what you can do!' So we seem to be back with the likes of Medieval beliefs, whereby inert stones had an active wish to be with Mother Earth! 'Go on, Stone! You can do it, if you really TRY!!'.

Here is part of the context into which this author, Ziman, has slotted his chosen grasp of the thing(s) called 'science':

Science is very clearly a conscious artefact of mankind ... with a definable scope and content ... The task of defining Poetry, say, whose subject matter is by common consent ineffable, must be self-defeating. Poetry has no rules, no method, no graduate schools, no logic: the bards are self-anointed and their spirit bloweth where it listeth. Science, by contrast, is rigorous, methodical, academic, logical and practical. The very facility that it gives us, of clear understanding, of seeing things sharply in focus, makes us feel that the instrument itself is very real and hard and definite. Surely we can state, in a few words, its essential nature (1968, p. 1).

Note the same use of 'nature' concerning a so-called 'natural science', as had been used by Singer, so to indicated science's character and to imply a consistency in something. 'What is the nature of nationality? Discuss.'

Yet it is the stuff of lack of 'definition', of a lack of 'logic', of a lack of 'method' of argument, 'clarity' of 'understanding' and so on, that this author should have elected to try to define the thing(s) called 'science' partly in terms of its 'objective' and its 'goal', these being features of human conduct, given his chosen grasp of the 'nature' of the thing as an inert body of knowledge:

> Science is not merely *published* [author's stress] knowledge or information [SI variety of science]. ... Its facts and theories must survive a period of critical study and testing by other competent and disinterested individuals, and must have been found so persuasive that they are almost universally accepted. The objective of Science [SII type] is not just to acquire information nor to utter all non-contradictory notions; its [S II's] goal is a *consensus* [his stress] of rational opinion over the widest possible field. ... this is the basic principle upon which Science is founded' (Ziman 1968, p. 9).

Science lives! It acts perhaps like a 'spirited' and 'lively' teenager, obsessed with that 'objective' in its life! Does it not seek to rule the world too, with its famous rigour, and all the rest of the puffery of the thing(s) called 'science'?.

Surely, it has not been so very 'basic', to anything but fairy tales, or to the worship of awesome things, for this author to have aimed to define science as knowledge in terms of the alleged goals of the executors of science as an activity! That which was an inert body of knowledge in 1968 (Ziman, CUP) has miraculously become a piece of acting human agency by a living thing in 1978 and 1991 (Ziman, CUP). The stone lives! 'Could do very much better, Ziman. See me. F. Bacon'.

Then, from the same author, and from the same famous academic press of the university where Bacon and Newton both had studied: '... the goal of science (SII type) is a consensus of rational opinion over the widest possible field' (Ziman 1978, p. 3, author's stress). For the John Ziman, and for the Cambridge University Press, to whom in 1968 science had been defined formally as a body of knowledge, by 1978 - abracadabra! - it had changed its form to something else, to become 'a complex human activity' (Ziman 1978, p. 1, as republished in paperback in 1991). Transformation!

Perhaps those people whom we call the scientists today, and their forebears, have sought such a consensus. But who is able to tell whether, or not, they have done this 'rationally' (in any conceivable sense of that idea), given that it is virtually impossible to climb into the minds of other people? And, anyway, the whole farrago of attempts made by the enthusiasts for the thing(s) called 'science' to tie it (them) down in profane definition, as they regularly seek to tie other things down, has smacked of propaganda and self-interest. In particular, and as suggested above, just because Science I (a body of published knowledge) may have been judged to be rational and orderly, this provides no good reason at all why the rest of us should have let ourselves be nudged, bullied, sweet-talked and generally persuaded into accepting the untestable character of the rationality of Science II (an activity or a process of action, quite a different thing). 'Science must be orderly and rational, because I say so as an orderly and rational person!'. 'How Greek we were in the lab today, my children', so the scientists claim, to stress their mobility of action (Fores 1984a, p. 76). This seems to be the measure of the claims made by the propagandists for 'science'; and, at this stage here, it is worth trying to draw some conclusion for the present piece of writing. Can all the shilly-shallying about the things(s) called 'science', from those people whom lay folk might imagine to know what they have been talking about, finally be instructive?

Take just the thing(s) called 'science' here. With precisely the same name commonly given to two identifiably different things, a process and its own main product, it would not be surprising if some of the characteristics of the one had appeared to have been visited rather recklessly onto the other. See also what was said above about cats and courage, and the strong words about the Idols of the Market from Francis Bacon, one of the great heroes of those who have sought to promote Science and Natural Philosophy.

Perhaps the most disturbing feature of the conceptual shambles discussed here, lies with an outcome of what might be called 'the anthropomorphic conception of science'. So the historians' Pathetic Fallacy has been strongly at work, with a human-like life seeming to have been breathed into Science I, in truth as inert as any of the bodies whose motions Newton sought to model and make sense of. 'The human understanding resembles not a dry light, but admits a tincture of the will and passions, which generate their own system accordingly; for man always believes more readily that which he prefers (Bacon 1620, book 1, aphorism 49, concerning the Idols of the Tribe, called *Homo* here). The discussants of 'science' seem to have 'preferred' an anthropomorphic conception of their beloved thing(s), which has rendered, willy nilly, human effort to seem to have been machine-like in its operation. Active *Homo*, the real life agent of much worldly change, has been caught up in the bookish machinations of the historians' Apathetic Fallacy, to have appeared to be lifeless.

Any conception of (say) Rational Man (one constructed by males mainly, in the event, with male behaviour mainly in the frame for commentary) has been constrained to make active *Homo* seem to be acting like a machine: this is a lesson which can be learnt from earlier sections here. The main reason for placing the present section into a piece of writing expressly on the 'professions', concerns the way in which the 'science'-link criterion has been made to operate, so as to help to stress a 'professional' distinction and separation of status and functions. Yet, on the ground, the more that these particular people have puffed themselves up, and been puffed up by others, as being 'scientific' sorts of human actors, the more they have been flirting with a calculative ideal of humanity, such as Max

122

Weber's, a dynamic ideal, which is more appropriate for the operations of electronic computers, levers and steam turbines than for human beings. Accordingly, the historians' Apathetic Fallacy is alive, well and prospering impressively in the suburbs and the university faculties of Anglo-Saxony. 'The professional clothed up, dusted off, and made to look like a machine. Discuss'.

Synthesis

It is now feasible to pick up the pieces here, these being potential components (things piled together) of a larger whole. So it is possible to try to stitch up a case, in the way that *Homo*, the constructor, is wont to do in a whole range of endeavours and activities. In the conclusion written for the collaborative piece in which Glover, Lawrence and I were involved, the point was put that a whole, systematic world view has been very suspect indeed, as this has found favour with a Western 'psycho-intellectual *Drang nach Ordnung*' (1991, pp. 96-98). The theme of the present paper might be said to represent an example of that general effect in operation, one which seems to have had its origins in Medieval Christendom (Fores and Porter, 1993). If status-seeking intentions had not intruded on the whole matter addressed in the present paper, it would be unthinkable that posh *Homo* would have wanted to deck himself out as a machine, this comment being made gender-specific purposely, since the present (male) writer believes that females would not have produced such an absurd farrago of rationalization on to paper and in print. As to the farrago itself, the strange, long running story of the professional decked out as a machine, has made it extremely difficult for official, paper-borne commentaries on (say) *Homo*-craft to be able to take full and proper account of the countless real life circumstances, in which *Homo* has to act skilfully and so very much unlike a machine.

Rationalizing *Homo* may have become obsessed with a use of the metaphors of the machinewrights, which have appeared to give *Homo* definite and certain opinions on complex matters. So we have had Weber apparently sure of the 'basis' of this, Marx apparently sure of the 'system' of his 'modern industry', Ziman discussing the 'essential nature' of the other, and a whole raft of similar boastings about regularity in the conditions of the human milieu. All manner of people, celebrated as having been particularly 'wise', and most of them being male, have appeared to be able to tell us of discernable order in this milieu. So the array of abstractions found on the printed page has nudged further and further away from any firm link made with anything that has ever occurred off the printed page to form a sort of bookish metaworld of human familiarity (Fores 1994b, p. 164). The rationales for the 'professional' people of Anglo-Saxony, and for their good conduct, have formed part of this mire of unreliable knowledge (cf. the title of Ziman 1978, republished in 1991).

Note

1   Science is a special type of knowledge, constructed by human agency about
what has been assumed, for three hundred years or so, to have been a single
world and a single universe around the species, *Homo*. As such, science is an
artifact of human ingenuity, and a body of recorded, tested and published
knowledge of aspects of the human surroundings, with the testing having been
involved with attempts by human agency to do this.   Scientists have
endeavoured to reconcile the results of human observation, with the abstractions
used in published scripts about identified, named and observed features of these
surroundings.   'Observation', in this sense, and as commonly used regarding
science, is a shorthand tag to indicate the use of all the human senses and aids
in that use. And it is with this effect, that acts of the scientists have often been
rationalized for their light shining exploits, in aid of the use of the single human
sense of sight.   So it should be apparent how vitally important for the whole
affair, has been a secure tagging of things 'observed', as raised expressly in the
Introduction to this chapter.   Thus, when Scientist M talks or writes of Item P
or Class Q,   Scientist N will have understood the precise subject matter
designated and indicated with the acts of naming performed.

Partly because hardly anyone nowadays believes Statement X of science to be
anything but provisional, the notion of a class of human activity engaged in
'scientific discovery' is absurd and extremely misleading for outsiders to what
may have been going on. In the first place, any abstraction about the human
surroundings (e.g. Newton's Laws of Motion), will have been inventive in the
first and crucial instance. Quite possibly, it took Newton two decades to work
out this piece of 'logging' about the world. But there is another way in which
it makes more sense to conceive science as having been invented than simply
'discovered'. According to the definition of science noted here, as a construct
of a type, the scientists have not sought (say) to 'discover aspects of God's
plan'.   They have, instead, sought to make statements, to be tested
subsequently, by other members of our species, as being as close as possible at
the particular time to a notional truth about the single universe. This, then, is
the manner of the operation of the 'objectivity' principle, which has concerned
the product of human effort (science as defined here, in the SI sense of a
section above, following the first meaning of the word in most dictionaries).
So, as with the human agency involved in making tables, soup, engines or
anything else, it has been a 'product', in the economists' sense, which has been
crucial, not a 'process'. It is in this, that any characteristics of science have to
be sought, and not in human activity, which is typically unplumbable (cf. the
section entitled A Model).

With science thus conceived, in would be recklessly inapt to try to tag a
process and a product by the same name 'science', as has been attempted in
some books about the thing(s) called 'science', as criticized above. The means
used by human actors in making and testing science are relatively unimportant

here, since all the main characteristics of science are to be sought in the constructed knowledge involved. Because this is knowledge of the single world and universe, any boundary proposed within science, say, between a notional Physics and a Medical Science, has no scientific or commonsense legitimacy. An animal, well classed within the group, Cat, is widely thus accepted to have been a non-Dog concurrently; but Statement X, claimed as a part of Physics, is not thus debarred from being treated in books called *Chemistry for Students*.

Science is just the body of the best formulated knowledge of the world at any time, with some of its special characteristics sketched out here. A further characteristic lies with the fact that, when Person A tells Person B about Statement X, X has not thereby left A's possession. Furthermore, there would be no good sense for scientists, as opposed to (say) machinewrights, seeking to sell the products of their working efforts (what they have decided they may 'know' about the single world around us). For, in their special trade, a product from work is not classed as 'a part of science', unless others have got at it for testing. Thus, it is important to note how science is of the type of what economists call 'public goods', which have no value *per se*. By contrast 'scarce goods' are those which can be owned by individuals; can be traded for a price; and have such a condition that, when a transaction has taken place between *Homo* A and *Homo* B, there has been an alteration in the stock of tradeable things in the possession of both.

References

Bacon, F. (1620), *Novum organum*, London.

Fores, M. (1983), "Science and the 'neolithic paradox'", *History of Science*, Vol. 22, pp. 141-163.

Fores, M. (1994a), '*Homo et machina*: of divided labour, revolutions and a history of marvels', *History of science*, Vol. 32, pp. 63-87.

Fores, M. (1994b), 'Hamlet without the prince: the strange death of technical skills in history', *History of Technology*, Vol. 16, pp. 160-183.

Fores, M., Glover, I. and Lawrence, P. (1991), 'Professionalism and rationality: a study in misapprehension', *Sociology*, Vol. 25 (1), pp.79-100.

Fores, M. and Porter, R. (1993), 'Modernity and apocalypse then', typescript, Wellcome Institute for the History of Medicine, London.

Marx, K. (1867), *Das Kapital*, Vol. 1, Hamburg, published in English in 1976 as *Capital*, Penguin, Harmondsworth.

Singer, C. (1941), *A Short History of Science*, Clarendon Press, Oxford.

Singer, C. (1959), *A Short History of Scientific Ideas to 1900*, Clarendon Press, Oxford.

Weber, M. (1923), *Wirtschaftsgeschichte*, Drucker and Humboldt, Berlin, published in English in 1981 as *General Economic History*, Transaction, New Brunswick.

Ziman, J. M. (1968), *Public knowledge*, CUP, Cambridge.
Ziman, J. M. (1978), *Reliable knowledge*, CUP, Cambridge. Republished as a CUP Canto paperback, 1991.

Acknowledgement

This chapter has been put together using the facilities of the Wellcome Institute for the History of Medicine in London; and I would like to thank Lyn Dobson and Samantha Anderson especially.

6 The limits of management: problems of the average car company

Karel Williams, Colin Haslam, Sukhdev Johal, John Williams and Andy Adcroft

Introduction

Professions are often viewed cynically; as G.B Shaw observed 'all professions are conspiracies against the public', and that aphorism continues a long literary tradition of disparagement. The newest profession of management is presented as different because it has real expertise which can promote the public good. This assumption is celebrated in a new literary genre, where authors such as Peters and Waterman or Womack, Jones and Roos vie with each other to acclaim successful management. Implicit in this are two key assumptions. First, there is a direct relation between good management practices and superior performance so that everyone can become excellent. Second, there is a political message about non-intervention because everything will be for the best if we let management get on with finding better ways of making and doing things.

Our own position is more radical. We have elsewhere dissected some of the confusions of *The Machine that Changed the World* (Williams et al., 1992a); and our historical work on Henry Ford's production of the Model T shows the extent to which the idea of mass production and lean production as successive eras rests on misleading stereotypes (Williams et al., 1992b and 1993c). Building on these foundations, this chapter argues the case for rejecting the concept of 'lean production' and demonstrates an alternative form of analysis. On the specifics of measurement, it disputes the size of the performance gap, challenges the preoccupation with physical productivity and reconceptualizes the problem by presenting a range of alternative measurements. In interpreting the causes of, and remedies for uncompetitiveness, it challenges the 'lean production' assumption that management is a privileged social actor which can always deliver cost reductions. More positively, it argues that American owned car companies have structural handicaps which are beyond management.

The article is organized into two main sections that deal separately with the intellectual problems of measuring the gap and identifying the causes of performance difference. Section one on measuring the gap, shows how and why the gap cannot be precisely measured using orthodox productivity measurement techniques and presents a multidimensional alternative analysis where the best to worst gaps are generally smaller than 2:1. It also argues that best to worst comparisons are fundamentally misleading because they obscure the point that most American and Japanese car assemblers are average performers which share common problems about cost recovery. Section two on the causes of performance difference begins by demonstrating that orthodox productivity measurement techniques do not identify the cause of performance differences which are often beyond management control. It then argues that the option of taking labour out is often not available and that the American owned assemblers suffer under the structural handicap of extra costs which arise from the distribution of employment, social charges, and exposure to cyclicality. Readers who are persuaded by these arguments can draw their own conclusions; the aim is not to replace one emphatic dogma with another. A third short concluding section does however present our understanding of the implications of the problem shift which is proposed in sections one and two; if the problems of the average (American) car company are beyond management, political intervention and regulation cannot be ruled out.

Measuring the gap

The Machine that Changed the World (Womack et al., 1990), like the various *Harbour Reports*, and the *Andersen Bench Marking Project Report* all encourage us to think about performance gaps in a stereotyped one dimensional way. The comparisons, league tables and quadrant diagrams encourage a basic dichotomy between good and bad sectors, companies and above all plants. The good and the bad are distinguished by one supposedly invariable characteristic; the good need a low labour input to assemble a vehicle or complete a given task whereas the bad need a high labour input for the same operation or task. This position is associated with claims about a large performance gap between Japanese and Western firms which is dramatized by best to worst comparisons, such as Krafcik's 2:1 comparison between General Motors (GM) Framingham and Takaoka. And it is garnished with the rhetoric of excellence; 'world class' is used no less than 79 times in the 20 page Andersen report. What needs questioning is this whole way of thinking about performance differences.

The business school academics and consultants who promote these measures have borrowed the techniques of comparative physical productivity analysis which were first used in applied economics in the late 1940s. Performance gap means differences in physical productivity at line and plant level which are measured using comparative ratios of (labour) input to physical output as in vehicles per employee or hours to assemble. The comparison is usually made in the form of net ratios which correct for differences in output characteristics and in the amount of work undertaken; this complication cannot be ignored when there are, for example, large differences both in the span of process operations undertaken by different assemblers and in the size and complexity of the vehicles produced. The process of correction involves moving from gross to net by correction that takes the form of cumulative subtraction. Step by step the calculation strips out the differences between the cases that are being compared and, on the bottom line, isolates the residual net difference in efficiency. The common sense case for adjusting gross ratios is overwhelming but the question is whether it is possible to construct valid like for like comparisons by correcting for the many differences in internal organization and external conditions.

Our position is that these cumulative correction techniques have never, and will never, produce a precise bottom line. This argument is fully developed in *Deconstructing Car Assembler Productivity* (Williams et al., 1994) and can be briefly summarized by presenting four strong reasons to doubt these techniques.

1. *The calculation quickly cumulates uncertainty because the individual adjustments at each step are not precise and independent.* The process of adjustment only works if each step adds a precise adjustment, but many of the adjustments are necessarily imprecise either because they take an observable difference, or because they involve imputed relations of variation which are beyond the realm of the observable. It is, for example, not possible to make a precise allowance for differences in product type and complexity; this variable can only be roughly proxied by taking a related variable such as weight or number of welds. Nor is it easy to disentangle and separately allow for conceptually distinct variables like hours worked and capacity utilization which are variably intertwined in different advanced economies.

2. *The individual adjustments, which are typically made for less than 5 or 6 differences, correct for an arbitrary sample of the infinite number of differences that separate individual cases.* If, for example, we correct for product type, hours worked, capacity utilization and span of operations, why not consider manufacturability, option content and model run? Those who have done such calculations know the list of corrections must be kept short; if the list is extended, overlapping imprecise corrections generate wildly implausible bottom lines. But, logically, the list of variables to be controlled stretches out beyond 5 or 6 towards infinity.

3. *Step by step correction makes the individual plant or company cases more alike at the expense of creating an increasingly implausible and bizarre counterfactual world.* For example, to correct for GM's capacity utilization, which averaged no better than 60 per cent in the late 1980s, requires the counterfactual assumption that GM can take a 70 per cent share of the

American car market or find vast new export markets in Japan or Europe.

4. *The bottom line result is ambiguous because it typically corrects for supply side differences but ignores the effects of variable market demand pressure which is a powerful pull-through influence on factory flow and labour utilization.* Market pressure cannot be ignored because there is no simple positive relation between productive excellence and the ability to sell product. For assemblers, the relation is mediated by product design, distribution and market maturity, while many component manufacturers face a derived demand which depends on the success of one or two assemblers.

These general problems are compounded in management discourse by the recent tendency to make comparisons across short spans of the productive process and an increasingly cavalier attitude to the business of adjustment. In recent management literature, the focus has been on comparisons of line productivity and final assembly factory productivity. The discussion of the early 1980s 'productivity miracle' at British Leyland (BL) showed that almost anything can be proved by selective citing of line productivity figures which may well not represent the company as a whole (Williams et al., 1986). Vehicles per employee comparisons for major plants or companies are more interesting. Even then, comparisons of individual assembly plants are not necessarily representative of company differences and are a poor guide to sectoral differences because final assembly typically accounts for only 15 per cent of the value of the vehicle.

We can understand more about the extent, variability and multidimensional nature of the performance gap by using three different comparative measures to register some relatively simple points. First, at a sectoral level the gap between the American and Japanese industries is best illustrated in terms of sectoral hours to build; this series shows us that the hours gap between the two national industries is, and for over 20 years has been, considerably less than 2:1. Second, there is considerably more variation in plant and company performance which can be approached by considering value added per employee on a company basis; this series gives a league table of companies which is instructive because it shows the limits of best to worst comparisons when most Japanese and American assemblers cluster around an average and change position over a decade. Finally, the complex and multidimensional character of any performance gap can be explored further by introducing cash flow per vehicle produced as a third performance measure; this series shows the limits of Japanolatry because, on this measure, average car companies in Japan as well as America have real problems.

The physical gap between the Japanese and American industries is best illustrated by calculating sectoral hours to build. Table 6.1 presents the results of a calculation of build hours per vehicle for the French, German, Japanese and American motor sectors. Sectoral hours to build are calculated by multiplying the number of employees in the national motor sector by average hours worked. Bosch (1992) and Lehndorff's study (1992) provide realistic estimates of hours

130

worked per year in several different national industries and act as a cross check. The health warning is that vehicle output always includes heavy trucks as well as passenger cars; but the importance of this difficulty should not be over estimated because in 1988 trucks over 3 tons accounted for only 2.5 per cent of Japanese vehicle output and trucks over 6 tons account for just 3 per cent of American vehicle output.

Table 6.1
Motor sector build hours per vehicle

	France	Germany	Japan	USA
1970	267	278	254	189
1971	257	270	224	162
1972	241	268	217	169
1973	238	266	203	167
1974	248	308	200	182
1975	292	279	176	174
1976	254	246	173	163
1977	251	258	158	165
1978	253	278	146	170
1979	241	294	147	179
1980	252	318	139	202
1981	260	271	138	204
1982	243	267	140	204
1983	225	262	139	163
1984	237	266	141	165
1985	220	258	139	155
1986	199	266	133	154
1987	175	255	132	173
1988	162	256	132	174
1989	n/a	286	132	170

Source: *Automotive News Market Databook*, Crain Publications Inc., *Yearbook of Labour Statistics*, International Labour Office, *Industrial Statistics Yearbook*, United Nations, all various years.

An interesting outcome is that it is possible to find a major national motor sector which currently *does* take twice as many hours as the Japanese to build a vehicle; in the latter half of the 1980s, the Germans took around 260 hours to build a vehicle against just over 130 hours in Japan. But, the physical gap between the Japanese and the American motor sectors was much smaller especially in years, like 1985 and 1986, when demand was brisk in America and the sector could build a vehicle in just over 150 hours; between 1983 and 1989, the American industry took between 12 and 32 per cent more hours than the Japanese. Because the hours gap is so much narrower than the exponents of lean production suggest, relative wage levels and structural differences become of considerable importance in determining the balance of competitive advantage between Japanese and American based producers. This important theme is highlighted in the second section of this chapter.

Table 6.1 is also instructive because it provides a time series perspective on differences which the existing management literature constructs in snapshot form. This is illuminating because, like all our other time series, it shows substantial changes in relative positions over the past twenty years. Management rhetoric about Japanese *kaizen*/continuous improvement is seriously misleading insofar as it implies or assumes that change takes the form of the Japanese sector opening up an increasing advantage over all the others. Against this, the table identifies one national sector (Germany), which has been stuck on high hours, managing no reduction on 246 hours over the past twenty years. The American industry illustrates the opposite case of a sector stuck on low hours because the Americans have managed no improvement on 160 hours over the past twenty years; cyclical fluctuations of demand are the main influence on build hours variation and the opening of Japanese transplant factories in America since 1983 has had no discernable effect. Stability in Germany and America is balanced by two cases of dramatic hours reduction; in the 1970s, the Japanese sector managed to halve its hours to build from an initial level of 254 hours and the French industry managed the same feat a decade later. Both industries have performed very strongly in recent years with the Japanese sector building increasingly sophisticated cars in the same hours and the French sector extracting further hours reductions; Renault has achieved a 25 per cent increase in vehicles per employee since 1988 (Williams et al., 1993b). The achievements of the French industry are real, but France is not Japan and it does not figure in the management literature.

Table 6.2
Company value added per employee in US $

	Honda	Nissan	Toyota	Chrysler	Ford	GM
1983	38,329	27,950	41,085	53,962	43,632	44,379
1984	40,452	26,284	41,816	43,386	49,815	44,369
1985	59,302	37,806	59,601	67,080	56,084	45,385
1986	83,533	47,580	71,339	69,939	60,743	42,709
1987	87,368	62,951	85,668	75,526	77,736	44,868
1988	84,227	63,329	90,663	65,312	86,484	53,738
1989	68,247	59,881	83,932	73,078	83,516	53,143
1990	73,661	65,179	103,794	68,107	76,142	44,307
1991	79,473	69,489	112,859	70,040	68,861	44,433

Source: *Consolidated Company Reports and Accounts*, various years.

Any national sector is of course an average of companies and plants which perform at different levels. On the whole, company performance comparisons are more interesting than plant analysis because every company is a collection of plants which perform differently because of differences in the saleability of their product lines which feeds through into variable capacity utilization. The 1992 Harbour Report league tables of assembly plant productivity are little more than translations of capacity utilization into a different language; in its ranking of 31 Big Three car assembly plants, on our calculations, the top quartile have an average utilization of 87 per cent and the bottom quartile an average utilization of 55 per cent. If we are concerned with company level differences in performance, the best single measure is value added per employee which uniquely takes account of company level differences in vertical integration. The adjustment is automatic because value added equals sales minus purchases of materials, components and services; companies which buy-in more have a lower value added to sales ratio. International comparisons of value added per employee require translation into a common currency and we have chosen to translate into US dollars. Variation in exchange rate does influence company ranking; but we would argue that in the table 6.2 comparison between Japanese and American companies, the exchange rate is less a source of bias and more a fact of life for Japanese companies which export components and finished cars to America and repatriate the proceeds. As long as cars are internationally traded, exchange rates are as relevant as factory efficiency in determining cash flow and profitability.

Here again we can begin by considering the snapshot for a recent year. The difference between best and worst in 1991 was indeed substantial, but in a cyclical peak year not 2 to 1. Toyota's value added per employee is 70 percent greater in 1988. The more illuminating observation concerns the broader distribution of performance which shows a strong tendency towards clustering around the average with Toyota as an outlier. Toyota is in a class of its own because c. 1990 it added $20,000 more per employee than its closest rival; on a company workforce of around 100,000 this translates into a lump sum advantage of $2 billion in one year. Most of the other assemblers, Japanese as well as American, were clustered in the range $60,000 to $87,000 per employee; the Japanese companies did not consistently occupy the upper positions in this central range; the worst performer was (unsurprisingly) GM but the next worst performance (in a cyclical peak year) was turned in by Nissan. From this point of view, we find it hard to see why 'Japanese' transplants or manufacturing techniques should transform American performance because the Japanese have only one super company Toyota; all their other assemblers do no better at adding value than their American counterparts.

As usual, the time series view changes the picture. It shows all the Japanese assemblers improving their position relative to the Americans during the 1980s; in 1983 the 3 Japanese assemblers occupied the bottom three positions and only Toyota was within sight of adding as much value as the American Big Three. Toyota has usually been the best of the Japanese companies; Honda's flash in the pan performance of the mid-1980s owed much to the exchange rate effects of its early shift into American transplant production. More recently, since 1988, Toyota turned its Japanese lead into a world supremacy not seen since Henry Ford at Highland Park. This lead can be attributed to the combined effects of Toyota's productive techniques and its strong domestic sales performance against companies like Nissan and Honda who, like the Americans, appear to be stuck on a value adding plateau. The two effects (techniques and market success) cannot be disentangled using a value added measure which shows market place ability to recover costs incurred in the factory. In this respect, the measure faithfully reflects the complexities and interconnections of the real world; and the implication is that where market space is limited it is not possible for all companies to be equally excellent. For the other Japanese assemblers, the road block problem is Toyota's dominance of the Japanese market where it sells 43 per cent of passenger cars. Their strategic response is not imitation of the techniques used by the super company but a shift into export sales and transplant production which is partly an attempt by the Japanese also rans to find market space elsewhere; the Japanese also rans must then suffer the effect of Yen appreciation which depresses their value added in a way which is beyond management.

The argument so far suggests that it would be useful to shift the focus of analysis on to the average assembler companies, Japanese as well as American. In considering the average car company the crucial issue is whether, at existing costs

134

and prices, they can recover their conversion costs in the market place and generate a surplus for product renewal to maintain or increase volume; cash flow from existing operations is the parameter which determines whether and how assemblers can stay in the business. To explore these additional issues, table 3 presents a simple analysis of cash flow which is calculated crudely by subtracting labour costs from value added; to put all the assembler companies on a near equal footing, we calculate cash flow per vehicle produced and express the results in US Dollars. The significant finding is that, whatever the differences between assemblers, they do not translate into financial advantage in terms of cash flow. Furthermore, average assemblers, Japanese as well as American, are mostly weak; the average assembler can recover its labour costs which account for a normal 70 per cent of value added but cannot steadily generate a substantial cash surplus over and above labour costs. This problem is likely to have knock on effects for the whole sector because component firms which supply cash hungry assemblers are unlikely to have fat margins on their OE contracts.

Table 6.3
Company cash flow per vehicle produced (US $)

	Honda	Nissan	Toyota	Chrysler	Ford	GM
1981	n/a	429	n/a	n/a	424	835
1982	n/a	430	n/a	574	697	921
1983	830	464	546	917	901	1,424
1984	1,025	395	558	455	1,033	1,294
1985	1,401	508	812	1,403	1,185	1,198
1986	1,917	604	970	1,452	1,327	1,084
1987	1,486	735	1,126	1,527	1,744	1,204
1988	1,552	931	1,140	1,307	1,984	1,677
1989	1,110	703	1,087	948	1,945	1,540
1990	1,220	790	1,312	936	1,574	699
1991	1,323	770	1,434	537	925	565

Note: Cash flow is defined as value added less labour's share.

Source: *Consolidated Company Report and Accounts*, various years.

The snapshot for 1991 shows an interesting dispersion of performance which needs some commentary and explanation. Two Japanese assemblers, Toyota and Honda, are strongly cash generative with cash of more than $1,300 per vehicle in 1991. So was one of the American Big Three because Ford managed approximately $1,000 per vehicle in 1991. The rest, (Nissan, Chrysler and GM) turn in much weaker performances with between $537 and $770 per vehicle. The immediate puzzle is why Toyota cannot turn its otherwise super performance into a cash gusher. Toyota does have a strong cash flow from the operations it undertakes in its own factories. This is a matter of simple arithmetic when labour's share of value added at Toyota is consistently below that of other car companies; Toyota's labour share of value added was 44 percent in 1991. But Toyota, like the other Japanese assemblers is much less vertically integrated than its American Big Three counterparts; as table 6 in the next section demonstrates, in recent years Toyota's value added to sales ratio averages 14-15 per cent against 19-20 per cent in the case of Nissan and Honda and 34-38 per cent in the case of the American Big Three. The problem is not that Toyota's vehicles do not generate cash but that a large part of the cash is generated inside Toyota's supplier network which does most of the work. It is hardly surprising that the upper tiers of this network are dedicated to supplying Toyota at prices which Toyota sets as it struggles against the consequences of vertical disintegration.

The time series again supplies a different, complementary perspective. The first interesting point is that the burden of vertical disintegration has been too much for Nissan; the Japanese home market boom of the late 1980s did no more than raise cash per vehicle to a cyclical peak of $931 in 1988 and the subsequent mild market downturn has damaged Nissan's cash flow and forced the company into operating losses. The news since then has been of Nissan's intention to postpone model replacement and rationalize componentry. In a broad historical perspective there is an obvious analogy between Nissan in Japan now and BMC/BLMC in Britain thirty years ago; like BMC, Nissan has high volume, substantial market share and an unusually wide model range whose regular replacement is problematic because the company only generates the cash for new models in unusually favourable market circumstances. Nissan's consolation of the early 1990s was that GM and Chrysler were even worse off. The problem of the American owned assemblers is that their cash flow fluctuates dramatically according to cyclical movements in a saturated and mature American market. In a good year all three American companies can realise more than $1,300 on each vehicle and the strongest of them, Ford realized nearly $2,000 at its peak in 1988; in a bad year the two weaker American companies (Chrysler and GM) realise a surplus over labour costs of $600 or less per vehicle and then have to borrow to cover the costs of model replacement. The regular alternation of cash on the upswing and debt on the downswing leaves all the American Big Three with a burden of short term debt: worst placed is GM; according to GM's 1991 report, the company's current debt was then $95 billion of which $51 billion was due within the year (GM Report and Accounts, 1991).

Causes of performance difference

In *The Machine that Changed the World* differences in performance are confidently attributed to one active cause, differences in management practice. 'lean production' is a cluster of management practices and the 1992 Andersen Report argues that these practices improve organization of the labour process in development, production and distribution and realise better materials flow inside and outside the assembly factory. Readers are assured that firms which adopt these practices will be rewarded with high performance; firms with poor performance have simply not made the right productive interventions. This position is broadly coherent with the more general *a priori* of the business school where management figures as a purposive social actor whose rational decision making or, more recently, commitment to excellence, brings success. What we want to do is question this model of cause and effect.

We can begin by observing that orthodox productivity measurement techniques do not identify the causes of observed differences in productivity. The procedure of cumulative subtraction leaves a residual, the bottom line productivity gap, which supposedly reflects the influence of an X variable whose presence/absence generates the difference. The X variable is identified by a process of addition which brings an external discourse to bear in a way that generates explanation or, more exactly, confirms what the discursively orthodox knew all along. *Deconstructing Car Assembler Productivity* (Williams et al., 1994) showed that engineers and accountants identify X as production techniques and management accounting; economists identify X as quantity or quality of factor inputs; and business school professors identify X as management practices. These confident identifications cannot all be correct and are all equally speculative. Attempts to vindicate particular identifications through empirical work on the covariation of different variables seldom vindicate the *a priori* identification of X. As we pointed out (Williams et al., 1992a) in our review of *The Machine that Changed the World* (Womack et al., 1990) Krafcik's results on the causes of productivity variation cannot be reconciled with the book's mono-causal assertive emphasis only on 'lean production'; Krafcik's research identified automation, manufacturability and 'lean production' as joint causes of high assembler productivity and there is no reason why 'mass producers' should not automate or produce more manufacturable products.

More fundamentally, we would question the whole model of management activity, the concept of the firm and the assumptions about management competence which underlie texts like *The Machine that Changed the World*. It needs to be noted that much management activity is cost increasing; the general law of capitalist management is that 'the number of suits expands to claim any surplus created in production'. The American Big Three carry a burden of staff employment in head office and in divisional functions like financial control. Similarly the extravagant system of home market distribution of Japanese firms incurs large staff costs. Table 6.4 illustrates this point by showing that Toyota employs 30,000 in distribution and Nissan with half Toyota's market share, employs no less than 81,000 in distribution; the reason is simply that Nissan (unlike Toyota) owns a large part of its (unsuccessful) dealer network. Nissan is sinking under the burden of unproductive white collar employment which is difficult to reduce without undermining an already weak home market performance.

Table 6.4
Comparison of manufacturing and sales employment in
Toyota and Nissan

	Toyota					Nissan			
	Motor Corp.		Motor Sales		Total employ-	Motor Corp.		Motor Sales		Total employ-
	No.	%	No.	%	ment	No.	%	No.	%	ment
1985	61,665	77	18,236	23	79,901	58,925	54	49,575	46	108,500
1991	72,900	71	29,523	29	102,423	56,873	41	81,453	59	138,326

Source: *Corporate Profiles*, various years.

Western business school analysts might argue that what the Americans and Europeans need is Japanese style production without the burden of unproductive Japanese distribution. But it is doubtful whether all or many Western firms can be redirected in this way: many of them are not unitary, controllable entities and management is often not capable of defining and executing new strategies. Many firms are divided on functional or geographic lines into competing or semi-independent centres of power. Thus GM figures as the textbook example of M-form organization but it does not have a single assembly division or central management group like Ford and Chrysler (Harbour 1992, p. 38). When eight different organizations manage GM assembly plants, it is hardly surprising that GM's downsizing is always too little and too late. Furthermore, in most firms, managers are generally concerned with the routine business of incremental decision-making in firms moving along well defined trajectories of possibilities. When that is not enough, management often does not innovate in the Schumpeterian sense but behaves like turkeys voting for Christmas. Thus, Mercedes Benz has discovered that it is a high cost producer of luxury cars; the company is now considering whether to build a car smaller than the existing 190/C class and has already decided to open an American factory which will produce a four wheel drive utility vehicle (*Financial Times*, 6 April 1993).

Even if management controls its own firm in a purposive way, all management must face the fact that bought-in materials and components, whose costs are largely beyond internal management control, account for a substantial part of total costs. This is a major constraint on the possibility of cost recovery and on value added productivity because value added equals sales minus purchases. In a typical Western manufacturing firm bought-in materials and components account for more than half the value of sales; the components typically come from smaller suppliers and the materials from outside the industrial sector in which the manufacturer operates. External costs in the motor sector are important because purchases from outside the auto sector account for a substantial proportion of the total cost of each car and because the conversion costs in the lower tiers of the supplier network cannot be managed by assemblers and upper tier suppliers. The availability of cheap high quality inputs from outside the auto sector is a crucial determinant of competitiveness. Table 6.5 estimates the relative importance of non-auto sector purchases in America and Japan by subtracting the average value added per vehicle realized in a national sector from the sales revenue per vehicle realized by the two largest domestic manufacturers (GM and Ford in the United States, Toyota and Nissan in Japan). In both countries, purchases from outside the auto sector account for an estimated 40 per cent of the sales revenue per vehicle realized by these companies.

Table 6.5
Non-auto sector purchases in Japan and America

	Major manufacturer sales revenue per vehicle col. i	Motor sector value added per vehicle col. ii	Imputed non-auto sector purchases per vehicle col. iii	Non-auto purchases as per cent of selling price col. iv
United States	12,142	7,471	4,671	39%
Japan	12,559	7,367	5,192	41%

Note: col. iii is calculated by subtracting col. ii from col.i.

Source: *Consolidated Company Report and Accounts*, various years, *Industrial Statistics Yearbook*, United Nations, various years.

If we now turn to consider costs within the car sector, the central point is that conversion costs in the lower tiers of the supplier network are always beyond the control of upper tier management. The Japanese assemblers do, of course, organise their upper tier suppliers into unitary *kieretsu* networks. But, as table 6 shows, these Japanese firms are substantially less vertically integrated than their Western counterparts; all these Japanese firms buy-in sub-assemblies and the most vertically disintegrated assembler, Toyota, subcontracts the final assembly of nearly half its vehicles.

Table 6.6
Value added/sales ratios for Japanese and American companies

	Honda	Nissan	Toyota	Chrysler	Ford	GM
1983	18%	17%	14%	40%	38%	37%
1987	21%	19%	13%	39%	38%	32%
1991	20%	20%	15%	29%	35%	32%

Source: *Consolidated Company Report and Accounts*, various years.

Toyota's value added accounts for only 14 per cent of the sales value of each car, against an average Western ratio of around 35 per cent. Even if Toyota controls its first and second tier suppliers, it gains little extra leverage over costs than the average Western firm which undertakes many more processes in its own factories. And Toyota's choice of a vertically disintegrated structure is itself significant; if Toyota's manufacturing techniques are so wonderful, why don't they do it all in-house? Henry Ford at Highland Park chose vertical integration and brought work in-house because he could produce parts at half the cost of outside suppliers, even though Ford workers had the highest wages and the shortest working hours in the industry (Williams et al., 1992b). Toyota lacks or cannot practice Henry's virtuoso technical ability, and instead Toyota chooses vertical disintegration which allows Toyota to exploit a steep wage gradient into the supplier network whose positive effects on costs partly compensate for the negative effects on cash.

Because management does not control many costs, conversion efficiency and cost recovery are powerfully influenced by a set of structural variables which have different values in various national economies and car producing regions. On the supply or cost incurring side, these variables include enduring conventions about wage levels and hours worked, national systems for allocating social charges like retirement costs to firms, and a pattern of supply side segmentation into differently sized firms with a definite wage gradient between large and small firms. On the cost recovery side, assemblers and their suppliers need a pricing structure and the market space to recover the costs incurred in production. In mature markets, where demand is cyclical, the pricing structure should allow a margin to cover the extra costs of capacity underutilization in demand troughs. Under a particular national settlement, indigenous firms can exploit/must suffer the values of different structural variables which are embedded in institutional structures and enforced by social actors like trade unions. It is now often easier to shift production or try and find market space elsewhere so as to exploit a different national or regional settlement.

Supply side structural variables have an obvious relevance to the competitiveness of national industries. This point can be illustrated by considering the structural burden on the German industry and the structural advantage of the Japanese. As tables 7 and 8 show, the German industry operates under the double disadvantage of short hours and a high mark up for social costs.

Table 6.7

Hours worked per employee in major assembler firms, 1990

	Honda	Nissan	Toyota	Ford Europe	GM Europe	VW
Hours worked	2,036	2,296	2,268	1,710	1,657	1,626

Source: *Bosch, 1990, Lehndorff, 1990.*

Table 6.8

Hourly wage costs in the automotive industry, 1991 (US $)

	Germany	Japan	US
Employer wage costs	26.95	20.52	21.24
Gross hourly earnings	15.59	15.70	15.41

Source: *VDA communication.*

The German union IG Metall has obtained a standard 35 hour working week for German workers whose Japanese counterparts worked a long day and a six day week before the present recession; as the Bosch and Lehndorff figures show, in 1990 the disparity in hours was such that a German firm like VW had to employ 1.5 workers to get the hours that Toyota could get from 1 worker. The burden of extra employees is particularly punishing because German firms produce under a

141

national settlement under which firms directly pay a large part of the costs of social security; as the VDA series shows the German industry pays a $15 hourly wage (broadly comparable with wages paid by major assemblers in America or Japan) but a massive 72 per cent social mark-up makes German employer wage costs per hour at least $5 higher.

Table 6.9 on wage gradient illustrates another set of supply side structural peculiarities which in this case give Japanese based firms an advantage over American and European based producers. The Japanese motor sector has a steep wage gradient between large and small firms and a large percentage of employment in small and medium firms; in 1988, no less than 26.5 per cent of total Japanese motor sector employment was in small establishments employing less than 100 workers and, on average these establishments paid wages which were just 56 per cent of those paid in large firms employing more than 1000. No other major national industry operates with this double structural advantage; all the rest either have a shallower wage gradient and/or a smaller proportion of employment in small firms. Thus Table 6.9 shows that although the American motor sector has a wage gradient as steep as in Japan, only 7.9 per cent of employment is in firms employing less than 100.

Table 6.9
Wage gradient and employment structure in the Japanese and American motor vehicle manufacturing sectors, 1988

	Japan		United States	
	Wage gradient	Share of employment	Wage gradient	Share of employment
1-99	56.4	26.5	51.5	7.9
100-499	72.4	20.3	59.3	18.0
500-999	86.2	12.6	68.3	9.7
1000+	100.0	40.6	100.0	64.0

Source: *Statistical Yearbook*, Japan, and *Bureau of the Census*, US.

The demand side variables influencing cost recovery are also important and diverse. One is relative prices; the Ludvigsen report (1992) demonstrates that retail prices for comparable or identical products are typically 25 per cent higher in Europe than in America or Japan. The German industry's nightmare is competition from the Japanese who can live with substantially lower prices than the Germans need to recover costs. In the case of the Big Two Japanese assemblers and the Big Three American assemblers, the relevant difference is in their home market bases. As table 6.10 shows, the American market is mature and shows a pattern of no sustained growth since the early 1970s combined with vicious cyclical fluctuations as volatile replacement demand is brought forward or postponed. By way of contrast the Japanese market has doubled in size since the early 1970s and shows a pattern of sustained but unsteady volume growth with fewer, weaker downturns. These Japanese home market characteristics provide the demand side basis for the techniques of productive intervention used by a firm like Toyota. If the basic objective is to improve flow so that less labour sticks to the product, that objective can only be attained when demand is brisk: flow cannot be sustained against market restriction. In Toyota's case stability of demand is equally important because it allows production smoothing which is the condition of possibility for instruments like *kanban*. In addition Toyota's high performance after 1985 owes much to its 45 per cent share of a 2 million increase in home market demand between 1985 and 1990.

Table 6.10
Car registrations and market cyclicality

	Japan		United States	
	Car registrations	Year on year %	Car registrations	Year on year %
1970	2,379,128		8,388,204	
1971	2,402,757	1.0	9,729,109	16.0
1972	2,627,087	9.3	9,834,295	1.1
1973	2,933,590	11.7	11,350,995	15.4
1974	2,286,795	-22.1	8,701,094	-23.4
1975	2,737,595	19.7	8,261,840	-5.1
1976	2,449,428	-10.5	9,751,485	18.0
1977	2,500,095	2.1	10,826,234	11.0
1978	2,856,710	14.3	10,946,104	1.1
1979	3,036,873	6.3	10,356,695	-5.4
1980	2,854,176	-6.0	8,760,937	-15.4
1981	2,866,695	0.4	8,443,919	-3.6
1982	3,038,272	6.0	7,754,342	-8.2
1983	3,135,610	3.2	8,924,186	15.1
1984	3,095,554	-1.3	10,128,729	13.5
1985	3,104,074	0.3	10,888,608	7.5
1986	3,146,023	1.4	11,139,842	2.3
1987	3,274,800	4.1	10,165,660	-8.8
1988	3,717,359	13.5	10,479,931	3.1
1989	4,403,745	18.5	9,852,617	-6.0
1990	5,102,660	15.9	9,159,629	-7.0
1991	4,868,000	-4.6	8,175,582	-10.7
1992	4,454,000	-8.5	8,210,627	0.4

Source: *Automotive News Market Databook*, various years, and *Company Corporate Profiles*, various years.

After all the qualifications have been stated and all the complexities have been laid out, the fact remains that reducing motor sector labour hours is potentially a powerful instrument of cost reduction which can transform the cost recovery position of a sector that takes out labour. Thus, the industry's most recent success story, the French reduction of sector build hours by some 100 hours since the early 1980s, takes around $2,000 out of each product and safeguards the French position within the West European industry as producers of small cheap cars which the Germans cannot produce profitably. But labour hours reduction is, as Tom Waits observed in a different context, 'not for everyone' because it depends on initial conditions which are often not satisfied and the reduction is ultimately self-limiting.

Work on Ford at Highland Park (Williams et al., 1992b and 1993c) and on the more recent achievements of the Japanese and French, suggests that there are two crucial preconditions which must be met before hours reduction can be achieved. The first is a large management prerogative over the labour process in factories where unions have little power; this condition is satisfied in all three cases and it is crucial for the Ford and Toyota style of productive intervention which depends on endless recomposition of the labour process. The second initial condition is the market: both Ford (Highland Park) and the Japanese operated with increasing market shares of growing markets and French firms like Renault have pulled the hours reduction trick with stable demand. The reduction in labour hours is ultimately self limiting because all successful car firms sooner or later encounter market limits. Thus Ford in the 1920s built the new Rouge factory which was then the most perfect conversion apparatus that the world had ever seen: but market limitations prevented Ford from exploiting Rouge's full potential. The other limit on hours reduction is technical because as long as car manufacture involves fabricating and assembling thousands of different parts into bodies, interiors and major mechanicals there is an apparently irreducible minimum of well over 100 motor sector labour hours in any car. Ford at Highland Park around 1915 like Toyota in the late 1980s was never able to build a car with a negligible labour content; on our calculations, in 1915 Ford took 123 internal hours to add value equal to 40 per cent of Model T selling price and more recently, if we exclude distribution employees, Toyota has taken 70 hours to add value equal to 15 per cent of the value of a much more complex car. A preoccupation with the imaginary system of 'lean production' obscures the basic point, that Henry Ford still stands as the master who established the possibilities, and limits, of hours reduction.

As neither precondition is satisfied in the case of the American Big Three, the recommendation to reduce hours by appropriating 'lean production' techniques is unlikely to be helpful. Both the American and Japanese national industries have been highly competitive on motor sector hours to build since the mid-1970s when, the Japanese reached parity with the Americans at around 170 hours (Table 6.1). More recently the Japanese sector has had a small hours advantage which varied between 16 and 42 hours, according to market conditions, between 1983 and 1988. But the unionized Big Three operating in a saturated and cyclical car market are unlikely to be able to close that gap by management action; downsizing GM might help by removing a burden of unproductive excess capacity but that would not produce a significant hours improvement if a narrower range of GM cars captured a smaller market share. If hours are effectively fixed beyond management control, the gap between the American and Japanese industries can be reinterpreted as a cost gap which is determined by structural variables that are beyond management. In many ways, this is only restating the obvious: as 150 +/- 20 motor sector build hours is around the irreducible minimum, the outcome of the contest, between two national sectors operating around this level, was always likely to depend on relative wages and other structural variables. And if we review the evidence, this is what we do find.

The structural sources of Japanese advantage do change over time. As Table 6.11 shows, in the first decade after the Japanese had achieved build hours parity, their relatively low wage levels were crucial. They were then absolutely unstoppable because their labour costs per hour in major assemblers were half or less those of the Americans and in small suppliers the ratio was even more favourable to the Japanese. Yen appreciation and rising real wages only slowly eroded the advantage of the low wage competitors: as late as 1985, according to VDA, the Japanese hourly cost was $11 against $23 in the US. Although wages in large Japanese assemblers have been close to American levels since 1990, the low wages paid by the sector's many smaller suppliers remain a potent source of advantage for the Japanese.

Table 6.11
Employer labour costs per hour in the US and Japanese motor sectors, 1980-91 in US $

	Japan	United States
1980	7.40	12.67
1985	11.15	22.65
1990	18.03	20.22
1991	20.52	21.24

Source: *VDA*, Frankfurt, 1992.

From an American perspective, we would now identify this as one of several major structural handicaps which have disadvantaged the American industry since the late 1980s. Table 6.12 presents the results of an illustrative calculation of the relative weight and importance of the three most important structural variables for one recent year.

146

Table 6.12
US motor sector structural cost handicaps per vehicle against
the Japanese motor sector, 1988

1 Extra American wage cost arising from an industry structure which displaces less employment into small firms paying lower wages	$543
2 Extra social charges arising from American requirement for extra workers because each American worker supplies 2,000 hours against 2,300 hours in Japan	$321
3 Cyclicality burden arising because fall in demand from cyclical peak of 1986 raises sector build hours by 20 hours per vehicle	$505

Source: VDA, *Statistical Yearbook of Japan*, *Industrial Statistics Yearbook*, SMMT, *International Financial Statistics Yearbook*, various years.

This calculation does not have an additive bottom line. That would be misleading when the relative importance of the variables shifts from year to year with changes in the market and capacity utilization and when an exhaustive structural analysis of all the differences can never be made. But we cannot help observing that in an average year like 1988 these three structural variables together account for nearly $1,400. In the same year, after allowing for wage gradient and the distribution of employment between differently sized firms in the two economies, we estimate that the American motor sector had an actual internal labour cost per vehicle which was some $1500 higher than the Japanese sector's internal labour cost per vehicle. Thus, arithmetically at least, the three structural handicaps account for almost all of the observed difference in labour cost per vehicle.

This kind of comparison of national sectors is illuminating but incomplete when the American industry now includes many Japanese owned transplants as well as American owned factories: in 1991 transplant assembly plants produced 1,500,000 cars with a target capacity of 2,500,000 vehicles by 1994. The transplants are significant because they represent a form of internal competition which avoids many of the structural handicaps which afflict the Big Three's long established American plants. As new entrants with young workforces and no retirees, the transplants avoid many of the social costs which the Big Three must pay: according to Candace Howes, the hourly wage of $15 is the same in the transplants and the

Big Three, but employer labour costs per hour are $22.50 in Big Three plants against $17.50 in the transplants (Howes, 1991). As minor players with low market shares, the transplants are often able to avoid the worst effects of market downturn which always hurts major players with large market shares. And because the transplants are branch assembly operations operating under a free trade regime, they can access cheap parts from the low wage supplier networks in Japan. The University of Michigan Transportation Research Institute (UMTRI) study of the Honda Accord showed that 38 per cent of the value of the car came directly from Japan and most of the rest came from transplant component suppliers whose propensity to import is high (McAlinden et al., 1991, pp. 64-71). While the Japanese transplant auto sector had an overall import to sales ratio of 48 per cent (Williams et al., 1992d). It is not necessary for the transplant plants to be superproductive because their structural characteristics give them a large advantage over their American owned competitors.

Finally, we would observe that the American Big Three are challenged because they have fewer defensive and offensive options than their Japanese counterparts. The Japanese can save costs by reducing their broad model ranges and lengthening their short model lives; the Americans, especially GM which is too big, cannot take this option without risking market share and, whilst Chrysler, which is too small, has the additional problem that every new model must be a winner. The Japanese can obtain cheap components from small Japanese suppliers while they slowly develop low wage Asian alternatives; low wage Mexico is half a continent away from the traditional Big Three plants in Michigan. Japanese companies together export half their output and can increase sales of components at the same time as they send higher value added cars to America and Europe; Big Three exports from American factories are negligible and will remain so when they have no distribution in Japan and any GM or Ford exports to Europe would cut across the interests of their local manufacturing operations. Japanese companies operate in an environment where financial institutions have modest expectations of short run profit and approach restructuring in a constructive way; whereas GM and Ford must rely on size to protect them from the financial engineers who buy and sell assets.

Living without lean production

In much productivity discourse there is a tension between the two roles of diagnosis and prescription; those who study productivity both measure the gap and act as agents of change. As management discourse increasingly appropriates productivity measurement, the tension has come to be resolved in favour of enthusiastic promotion of change because business school gurus and management consultants make their living by telling other people what to do. And in the world of 'the executive summary', measurement itself functions as a rhetoric of change. Thus, in Andersen's benchmarking report, the first recommendation is 'find out how far behind world class you are...' and the second recommendation is 'Use the resulting crisis to commit the firm to closing the gap....' (Andersen 1992, p. 5).

Western car companies are generally eager to use orthodox measures opportunistically in this way; the huge success of the 'lean production' concept represents a case of academic supply meeting an insatiable industrial demand. Within these companies, the measures and the concepts serve to establish the necessity for change. They are often used in bad faith by management which knows that Japan is not the answer. One assembler tells us privately that its gap against Japanese best practice is 20-80 percent 'depending on the measure and the year'. The same firm organises conferences where it publicly endorses 2:1 as an effective way of persuading managers and workers to accept the objective of competitiveness and the instrument of changes in organization and working practice.

Against this background, like Auden's poet living in 'a low dishonest decade', all we can do is warn that it is better to live without the illusion of 'lean production' which suits some car company managers but will not save struggling car companies. We have tried to establish this point by laying out a range of evidence and argument that allows readers to draw their own conclusions. The first section showed that productivity gap thinking misspecifies the extent and nature of the gap; and the second section argued that it grossly overestimates the capacity of management to deliver gap closing performance improvements.

Obviously caution should be applied to generalising from one case. However, the case does suggest two key conclusions:

1. Most companies are simply average, mainly because most cannot create or locate the market space to become 'excellent' like Toyota.

2. Often structural forces thwart the best efforts of management in a way which are beyond management. The outcome of competition is often determined by these forces.

The would be profession of management often lives by rhetorical illusion and myth. The limits of management have obvious implication for policy when many problems are beyond (company) management. Furthermore, insofar as competition is distorted by structural variables, public intervention to create a level field is entirely justifiable. Industries which seek redress against unmanageable structural disadvantage need not apologise for their existence and demands; trade unionists who see their national social settlement threatened by low wage, non-union competition should take the lead in pressing the case for regulation. This paper has concentrated on exploring the gap between the negative (cynical) image of the profession and the positive (uncritical) image of management, on analysis rather than solutions, diagnosis rather than prescription; it has not aimed to open the discussion about possible and necessary forms of intervention. It has served its purpose if it forces a problem shift and thereby establishes the case for action directed against real problems.

References

Adcroft, A., Cutler, T., Haslam, C., Williams, J. and Williams, K. (1991), 'Hanson and ICI: The Consequences of Financial Engineering', *University of East London Occasional Papers on Business, Economy and Society*, No. 2.

Andersen Consulting (1992), *Bench Marking Project Report*, Andersen Consulting, London.

Automotive News (1990), *1990 Market Databook*, Crain Communicator Inc., Detroit, USA.

Bosch, G. (1992), 'Working Time and Operating Hours in the Japanese Automobile Industry', Gelsenkirchen: Institut Arbeit und Technik.

Company Report and Accounts, various years.

Datastream International, Company accounts.

Financial Times, news reports, various dates as cited.

Harbour and Associates (1992), *The Harbour Report: Competitive Assessment of the North American Automotive Industry 1989-1992*, Harbour and Associates, Troy, Michigan, USA.

Howes, C. (1991), cited in *US-Mexico Trade: Pulling Together or Pulling Apart?* Office for Technology Assessment, Washington DC.

International Labour Office, *Yearbook of Labour Statistics*, various years, Geneva, Switzerland.

JAMA, *Motor Vehicles Statistics of Japan*, various years, Tokyo.

Japan Statistics Yearbook, various years, Prime Minister's Office, Tokyo.

Krafcik, J. (1986), 'Learning from NUMMI', *International Motor Vehicle Project Working Paper*, MIT, September.

Krafcik, J. (1988), 'A methodology for assembly plant performance determination', *IMVP Research Affiliates*, MIT, October.

Krafcik, J. (1989), 'Explaining high performance manufacturing', *IMVP International Policy Forum*, MIT, May.

Lehndorff, S. (1992), 'Operating time and working time in the European car industry', Gelsenkirchen: Institut Arbeit und Technik.

Ludvigsen & Associates, (1992) *Report on European Car Prices*, Ludvigsen and Associates, London.

McAlinden, S. P., Andrea, D. J., Flynn, M. S. and Smith, B. C. (1991), 'The US-Japan Automotive Bilateral 1994 Trade Deficit', *Transportation Research Institute*, Ann Arbor, University of Michigan.

Organization for Economic Cooperation and Development (various years), *Industrial Structure Statistics Yearbook*, Paris.

United Nations, *Yearbook of Industrial Statistics*, various years, New York.

US Department of Commerce, various years, *Foreign Direct Investment in the United States-Operations of US Affiliates of Foreign Companies*, various years, US Department of Commerce, Washington DC.

US Department of Labor, various years, *Employment and Earnings*, Bureau of Labor Statistics, Washington DC.

Verband der Automobilindustrie, Fax Communication, 1992, Frankfurt.

Williams, K., Haslam, C. and Williams, J., (1986), *The Breakdown of Austin Rover*, Berg, Oxford.

Williams, K., Haslam, C. and Williams, J., (1989), 'Why Take the Stocks Out?, *International Journal of Operations and Production Management*, Vol. 9, No. 8, pp. 91-105.

Williams, J., Haslam, C. and Williams, K. (1990), 'Bad Work Practices and Good Management Practices: The Consequences of the Extension of Managerial Control in British and Japanese Manufacturing since 1950', *Business History Review*,Vol. 64, No. 4, pp. 657-688, Winter.

Williams, K., Haslam, C. and Williams, J., (1991), 'How far from Japan: a case study of Japanese press shop practice and management calculation', *Critical Perspectives on Accounting*, Vol. 2, No. 2, pp. 145-169.

Williams, K., Haslam, C., Williams, J., Cutler, T., Adcroft, A.and Johal, S. (1992a), 'Against Lean Production', *Economy and Society*, Vol. 21, No. 3, pp. 321-54, August.

Williams, K., Haslam, C. and Williams, J. (1992b), 'Ford versus 'Fordism': The beginning of Mass Production?', *Work, Employment and Society*, Vol. 6, No. 4, pp. 517-555, December.

Williams, K., Haslam, C. and Johal, S. (1992c), '*Tout Va Bien*?: An analysis of Renault-Volvo cars and the French Car Industry', Paper presented to senior managers of Renault, November (University of East London, mimeo).

Williams, K., Haslam, C., Williams, J., Adcroft, A. and Johal, S. (1992d), 'Factories or Warehouses: Japanese Manufacturing Foreign Direct Investment in Britain and the United States', *University of East London Occasional Papers on Business Economy and Society*, No. 6.

Williams, K. Haslam, C. (1992e), 'Lean Production', *Die Mitbestimmung*, pp. 39-43, April.

Williams, K. and Haslam, C. with Adcroft, A., Johal, S., Thompson, P., Wallace, T. and Williams, J. (1993a), 'Leyland-DAF: A good deal gone bad?' *University of East London Occasional Papers on Business, Economy and Society*, No. 11.

Williams, K., Haslam, C., Williams, J., Adcroft, A. and Johal, S. (1993b), 'Japanese Manufacturing Transplants: The case for regulation' *University of Birmingham Occasional Papers on Industrial Strategy*, UK.

Williams, K., Haslam, C. and Williams, J. with Adcroft, A. and Johal, S. (1993c), 'The Myth of the Line' *Business History*, Vol. 35, No. 3. pp. 67-85, July.

Williams, K., Haslam, C. and Johal, S. (1993d) 'Machiavelli not MIT: The causes and Consequences of Volvo's Failure', Mimeo, University of East London.

Williams, K., Haslam, C., Williams, J. and Johal, S. (1994), 'Deconstructing Car Assembler Productivity', *International Journal of Production Economics*, July.

Womack, J., Jones, D. and Roos, D. (1990) *The Machine that Changed the World*, Rawson Associates, New York.

Part III

EVIDENCE

7 Durkheim, professionals and moral integration

James Dingley

Introduction

In the area of business and management morality has recently started to attract an increasing amount of attention from academics as an important influence on organizational activities. However this is usually defined in a rather limited way as business ethics or corporate responsibility. Such a limited view of morality often tends to reduce its discussion down to rather restricted debates of a legalistic or public relations type of exercise, where moral concerns are reduced down to just another factor to be weighed in the balance and assessed in the same light as any other factor of production. In other words they become a means to an end rather than an end in themselves, so that ethics are something to be manipulated and calculated but are not seen as a natural extension of a pre-existing moral order or community that should command our uncritical deference.

However, the essence of morality is that it is of an obligatory nature that implies that there is a core of behaviour which is of itself good and which carries a sense of sacredness about it. Transgression of such behaviour has an implication of automatic sanctions that are beyond appeal or calculation. There has been relatively little written about this view of morality in recent management or organizational literature and thinking, for it implies the idea of an organization as some kind of moral community, an idea that would tend to conflict with the predominant concept of organizations as primarily economic and rationally efficient and consequently bound by laws of economic rationality that preclude non-economic, i.e. moral, consideration. In other words the market economy model rules; the model established by Adam Smith, David Ricardo, J. S.Mill, Jeremy Bentham and recently reiterated by the likes of von Hayek and Milton Friedman is still the underlying way in which we perceive organizational activity, if not all human behaviour.

The market model, by stressing the concept of economic laws has two implications of immediate concern. First, it tends to isolate economic activity off from other areas of human behaviour as being somehow different and thus subject to different standards and interpretation. Second, it tends to imply that economic behaviour is determined because it is subject to laws that are seen as pre-existing and impersonal. Why we behave economically is not seen as problematic, only how. This one dimensional view is then further reinforced by behavioural scientists who uncritically accept the market economics paradigm by only ever addressing the problem of organizational behaviour within the confines of that paradigm and who similarly utilize a paradigm premised upon scientific laws of human behaviour. Why we should behave in a particular way is rarely posed as a relevant question, only how.

Such a simplistic view of man is a relatively modern phenomenon, even at work, and has its roots not just in the philosophy of science that sees behaviour as fixed in a set of unproblematic laws but also in the rise of a concomitant moral philosophy, i.e. utilitarianism. Utilitarianism combined with the idea of universal laws of economics to mount a number of attacks, in the eighteenth century, against aristocratic privilege (Lux, 1990), and the most famous of these was mounted by Adam Smith, who held a chair in moral philosophy. As Lux observes, the man credited with the founding of modern market economics was a moral philosopher concerned primarily to make a moral point about the rights of non-aristocrats in a world dominated by aristocratic privilege. Smith wrote during the age of enlightenment and at the time of the first stirrings of modern political democracy and he should really be read alongside Tom Paine and *The Rights of Man*.

Morality was thus a key factor in the establishment of market economics. There was a desire to establish a new moral community in which certain moral precepts would be enshrined as inalienable and pre-existing rights and which would give rise to a new order based on Liberté, Egalité and Fraternité. It was to this end that utilitarian philosophy was developed (Lux 1990, Chapters 2 and 3).

A moral community was no new concept. It was at the heart of all organized economic activity prior to the eighteenth century, in the guilds and the professions. These organizations now came under attack as being atrophied and corrupt, as a thinly veiled pretence behind which vested interests and privilege sheltered, which had ceased to carry out their moral regulatory role. They were originally established as moral communities specifically to exercise a moral regulation over their members and to act for the wider good (what we would now call society at large) and thus justify their existence. As they were seen to be no longer performing this function their existence and rights were increasingly questioned, and in an age of democracy it was logical to seek the transference of oligarchic privilege and regulation to the people so that they could not only control their own destinies but could also enter into the wider moral community of society and participate in the *polis*.

Utilitarianism was a system of moral philosophy that was designed to facilitate this change from an oligarchic and now corrupted system of guild and professional control to a democratic order of popular control through the market. However, it was later argued by Durkheim that the very nature of utilitarianism actually undermines the notion of moral community that was originally addressed by the utilitarians so that moral regulation so necessary both to success and happiness in human affairs is lost. To retrieve this lost sense of moral regulation he advocated a rediscovery and reapplication of the principles of medieval guild and professional organization in an amended form to the organization of modern industrial society so as to achieve a moral reintegration that will give a renewed sense of purpose and wellbeing.

Utilitarianism

This is the moral philosophy that has dominated the English speaking world and pervaded its behavioural sciences since the eighteenth century. It is most commonly associated with the works of Bentham and Mill, the economics of Smith and the sociology of Spencer. Its guiding principle is that people are fundamentally driven or motivated by self interest and this is in turn defined as the maximising of pleasure and the avoidance of pain. People are assumed to be self-seeking individuals who in an open market with no external constraints will know what goods and services have the greatest utility value for them in the pursuit of their maximising their pleasure as they know best. Therefore people should be freed from all constraints likely to limit their pursuit of pleasure (Etzioni 1988, Chapter 2).

Pleasure becomes defined as a moral good. Mabbott (1966 p. 15-16) summarises the utilitarian position as follows. Good is defined as a means to an end. Good only succeeds when it leads to pleasure. Bad only succeeds when it leads to pain. The pursuit of individual - for who else knows better their own self-interest/pleasure than the individual concerned? - happiness thus takes on a moral dimension. A good society thus becomes defined as one in which the greatest number of individuals are left free to pursue their own self-interest. This in turn became conflated with Smith's invisible hand, whereby when everyone pursued their own self-interest, this would ultimately lead to the greatest good for the greatest number.

Self-interest in a free market and the pursuit of happiness thus become moral imperatives as well as vehicles from which to attack the protected and vested interests of mercantalist corporations, guilds and professions, as they appear to hinder individual activity and self-interest.

This in turn led to a redefinition of society and the social order. The old Augustinian view of a transcendent order in which the people were placed (e.g. as portrayed in Pope's *Essay on Man*) and worked out their allotted roles was now replaced by a view of society as an atomistic collection of individuals whereby

157

order was maintained by people entering freely into contracts of a mutually advantageous and binding nature. Contracts could, of course, be renegotiated, or, when they had run their course, simply not renewed and new alternative ones be entered into. This was morally good because it left people free to pursue their own self-interest and reduced to a minimum any state or other outside interference. This was thought of as a self-regulating, self-adjusting mechanism of regulation that was in itself good and therefore a moral basis for order in society. The old Hobbesian problem of order is thus solved by dispensing with Leviathan; Humankind's own self-interest serves to regulate the whole.

This view of society is most clearly spelt out in the sociology of Spencer, and it was with an attack on Spencer and his utilitarian sociology that Durkheim commenced his own work and that led him to an interest in the corporations of medieval Europe that had exercized a regulatory function over economic activities, i.e. the guilds and professions.

Guild and professional organization

Whilst the origins of the guilds and professions were quite distinct in their organizational form and functions they were quite similar in other respects, and, as was common with most medieval institutions, although they had economic roles they also had explicitly moral and religious roles. An essential feature of medieval life would have been the assumption that all three were inextricably bound up together. Thus a church was not just a place of worship. It was also a meeting place, a place of refuge and a storage place for produce and farm implements. No economic activity would have taken place without the previous sanction and blessing of the church and the successful conclusion of any venture was equally a matter of religious obligation e.g. the Harvest Festival. Not only the activity itself but also the internal division of labour and inner operations would have been subject to religious sanction.

The professions actually originated in the church in the eleventh century as branches of ecclesiastical learning (originally law and physics) which they professed to God. They thus professed to the highest moral authority of all. They were based in the collegiate organization of the church and therefor susceptible to the oversight and regulation of their collegiate religious orders and fellow professors.

Their calling (as in being called to the bar) was therefore to a higher moral order. Indeed they were actually seen as an extension of the moral regulatory system of the church, and agents of God's will. Hence an early distinction grew up between professions and other occupations (to become organized into guilds) that still exists today. Ideally the professions professed to God and sought his will in human affairs and therefore did not represent clients. Consequently they were not retained directly by a client, nor were they paid by a client so that they would be free of any temptation e.g. monetary inducements, that would detract from their primary

158

calling of professing God's will. Thus we see a distinction between barristers and solicitors. A client retains a solicitor who then engages a barrister. The role of the barrister is not to represent the client but to interpret the law and to argue and debate the law in court. It is only the solicitor who represents the client, and the barrister is there to represent the law as it may be interpreted as God's will.

Thus barristers originally lived in religious communities and, later, inns of court that provided for them so that they could be freed from worldly concerns. Equally the same applied in medicine, which was grouped into three strata and specialisms; physicians, surgeons and apothecaries. Physicians were the elite who were originally founded in religious hospitals and foundations and later in (royal) colleges which were well endowed and provided their members with rich livings. In this setting surgeons and apothecaries could then consult them. The same applied to academics who lived in their colleges and universities, religiously sanctioned and protected, so that they might be free to profess their knowledge and learning direct to God and obeying his authority without worldly interests corrupting their calling.

Originally the professions existed totally within the church as religious foundations and only during the Renaissance period did they emerge as separate and independent bodies in their own colleges. But it was this concept of worldly disinterest and of professing to an higher moral authority that was the key to their prestige and autonomy. They professed to God not Mammon; it was also this that enabled them to recruit from the younger sons of the aristocracy and gentry (a living without having to engage in trade) and ensured their further high standing. Gentlemen do not work; professionals, by not accepting payment, as such, were deemed not to be engaged in trade and were consequently able to retain their image as gentlemen. That gentlemen could be trusted was implicit in the concept because they deferred to a higher authority; tradesmen could not because they deferred directly to Mammon and were susceptible to worldly influences. Thus, even as late as 1958 the Royal College of Surgeons, in their submission to the Pilkington Royal Commission on medical education could argue:

There has always been a nucleus in medical schools of students from cultured homes.....This nucleus has been responsible for the continued high social prestige of the profession as a whole and for the maintenance of medicine as a learned profession. Medicine would lose immeasurably if the proportion of such students were to be reduced in favour of the precocious children who qualify for subsidies from the Local Authorities and the State purely on examination results (Pilkington, 1958).

The modern usage of the term professional has come to be derived from the Weberian concept of technical competence and expertise, but this is a popular lay misconception. Whilst it now involves concepts of competence and expertise this merely reinforces the idea of trust i.e. they should be technically able, but it is actually built on a much more fundamental concept of trust because they defer to

159

an higher transcendental moral authority. It is this that is the core of professional autonomy and organization, the fact that they have a moral function (Dingley 1977, Chapter 3).

The moral function was designed to attach them to God, but the moral regulation was via their colleagues. By being grouped together in colleges they were thus open to the scrutiny of their colleagues and dependent on their approval to retain their livings as well as the formal sanction of ecclesiastic authority. As more professionals emerged and started to practice outside of the collegiate environment so the moral precepts came to be increasingly standardized and codified into codes of ethical conduct which are, today, still seen as central to the concept of a profession. The collegiate nature of professions is also identified in their communal organization which stresses an organic (as in Burns and Stalker, 1961) mode of self-regulation, where all members are deemed to be equal and share the responsibility for regulating each other according to the established ethical code as a community.

Moral authority lies in the community's responsibility to regulate its members because they are seen as deferring to an higher authority on which they are in turn dependent; and it is their ability to live up to that ideal that is the key to their continued prestige and position.

Whereas professions were established with reference to professing a body of knowledge and learning to the highest moral authority of all, God, the guilds were founded in trade and with a definite orientation toward Mammon. They were trade organizations whose prime purpose was the regulation and protection of trade: 'To this end the guilds organized autonomous producers into a system of industrial regulation to the common interest' (Dingley 1977, p. 2).

All production of goods and practice of crafts were restricted to guild members which in turn meant subjection to an elaborate system of controls covering the scale and methods of production, conditions of work, the quantity and quality of goods produced and the price of sale. Any knowledge of markets, methods of production and so on was expected to be shared, and the independence, wellbeing and equality of all craftsmen was expected to be placed before the interests of any individual. The community interest was deemed to exceed that of any individual thereby making internal regulation into a moral imperative to preserve the communal integrity of the whole.

It was equally seen as inherent in their function and interests to guard the consumer against fears of exploitation and shoddy workmanship, therefore, not only was trade regulated but:

> Entry to a craft was normally restricted to those of free birth and to those above political, social and moral suspicion, it being the custom for a guild to investigate the character of an aspiring member on the assumption that good character would be an indication of good work. The good character of its members was also regarded as important to the good repute of the guild as a whole, in gaining public trust and confidence not only for its trade but in

160

respect of its civic responsibilities and aspirations (Dingley 1977, p. 2).

A guild, once established, was regarded as a legal trading entity and that implied both an economic and a moral role. The moral role was quite explicit and specifically aimed at curtailing practices that were seen as injurious either to the guild or to the customer, an external regulation specifically to limit the pursuit of economic self-interest. Guilds were also expected to carry out a wider range of civic and political responsibilities e.g. policing, assessing tax returns and so on, and therefore they had to be seen as publicly responsible.

The guilds were thus seen as moral communities with an highly specific moral regulatory function. They were there to ensure an inner harmony between members by regulating all relationships between them and preventing any sense of unfair trading advantage arising. They were also there to act as moral regulators on behalf of the public, to protect their interests as well. One aspect of this was very long apprenticeships that not only aimed at a thorough technical training but was also concerned to develop a moral character and ethical outlook in a craftsman: 'it aimed at moulding a youth into a good citizen and a good Christian as well as a good workman' (Southgate 1962, p. 30). The maintenance of an high moral profile was deemed to be in the best interest of both client and trader.

Guild members were encouraged to think of each other as part of a fraternity who should watch over each others' affairs and assist each other in both commercial and non-commercial matters and both through the guild and individually. To this end great emphasis was placed on organizing feasts and social events and also on regular church attendance at which all were expected to attend. Religion was another important aspect of guild life. Most of the important events in a guild's calendar were preceded by a religious service and any new venture had to seek religious sanction. The church was the final arbiter in guild affairs.

Guilds were organized internally on a communal basis. All members were entitled to participate in their affairs at open meetings held regularly, and officers were elected and officials appointed for specific tasks. A guild was, like a profession, deemed to be a community of self-regulating equals.

After medieval times professions and guilds declined and had their original ideals corrupted, although the professions found a new lease of life after the industrial revolution in organizing the new occupational groups. However, they both displayed similar organic types of structure that emphasized communal involvement and responsibility and they equally recognized a moral role and function as central to their existence. Their decline in late medieval times was directly related to their loss of a sense of moral purpose, when the privileges they had accrued as a result of their moral authority started to be abused and perverted for solely mercenary advantages.

The guilds in particular had three specific roles, economic, moral and political (Dingley 1977, p. 3), which were seen as self-supporting and inextricably bound up; and although there were economic and political factors behind their demise the

161

loss of a sense of moral purpose was an important factor. Whilst with the professions it was with the rediscovery of a sense of moral purpose, as expressed formally in their ethical codes and informally with their ideals of gentlemanly conduct, that they were able to re-establish themselves after the industrial revolution. The Victorian idea of a gentleman, a public school education and the new professions went together (Dingley 1977, Chapter 3).

Durkheim and moral order

The primary concern of Durkheim's sociology is morality. Order in society is a problem of social solidarity. But social solidarity is a completely moral phenomenon (Durkheim 1933, p. 64). Order and solidarity are questions of limiting human passions and of thereby controlling behaviour so that we all act in harmony with each other. Only in this way can we achieve those forms necessary that make social life possible, and the means by which we do this is the development of a system of moral regulation that curtails our potentially limitless passions and desires:

> Human passions stop only before a moral power they respect. If all authority of this kind is wanting, the law of the strongest prevails, and latent or active, the state of war is necessarily chronic (Durkheim 1933, p. 3).

It is the nature of this moral authority that is his main concern in all his main works but is most clearly addressed in his first major work 'The Division of Labour in Society' which opens with a general attack on utilitarianism in general and Spencer's sociology in particular.

Durkheim starts with an explicit attack on Spencer (Durkheim 1933, Chapter 7) who sees social solidarity as a product of spontaneous cooperation resulting from contracts freely entered into that express the (economic) self-interest of the relevant parties. The contracts bind people to mutually agreed activities and in turn these bind people to each other, which creates an order and cohesion that produces a sense of solidarity amongst people and thereby gives us society. Society, according to Spencer, is thus a product of spontaneous cooperation built on the pursuit of economic self-interest and self-adjusting according to that interest. Any outside interference not only distorts that but may even lead to disharmony and loss of solidarity.

Durkheim ridicules this utilitarian view of society. First, he argues, what is to keep us to such contracts? If self-interest is the determinant of behaviour (and morality) it is as likely to be in our interest to break a contract. Next, from whence does this spontaneous behaviour arise? Durkheim goes to great length to show that most social behaviour is not spontaneous, that it is socially derived and that economic behaviour is not something apart from other forms of behaviour; and he actually argues that it is derived from a pre-existing social relationship.

However, he also attacks Spencer on the deeper level of what actually constitutes self-interest and the idea implied in it of the pursuit and maximising of happiness and the avoidance of pain. As Durkheim points out, if the pleasure principle was the primary driving force in human affairs we would never have progress for it invariably involves pain and distress and only a small minority usually have any vested interest in change. Progress is invariably painful.

Self-interest and the pursuit of pleasure is also criticized at a much deeper level, as being self-destructive, stress producing and painful. Our wants and needs are potentially endless and can never be satisfied and the more we pursue them the more we become aware of this, consequently the less satisfied we are and the more unhappy we become. What we really require is some limit on our wants and passions. Self-interest is just ungoverned passion that is actually very destructive because it is blind to anything other than its own immediate gratification, irrespective of costs either long or short term:

Alas what wonder, man's superior art
Unchecked may rise and climb from part to part,
But when his own great work is but begun
What reason weaves by passion is undone.
(Pope 1966, Essay on Man, Epistle 2)

Augustinian poets, Hobbesian political theorists and Kantian philosophy all understood the point that Durkheim took up i.e. some constraint is necessary for our own good. Freedom is a discipline, for without some restraint we merely become slaves to our passions and lose any sense of purpose or direction, we become unhappy and destroy ourselves (this is the basis of anomic suicide which he identified in *Suicide*) and explains his statement 'Human passions stop only before a moral power they respect' (Durkheim 1933 p. 3). It was morality that provided the constraint and discipline needed and it was with the nature of that morality that he was pre-eminently concerned.

Durkheim proceeds from the assumption that people are social beings and not individuals, and the idea that people are primarily social animals implies a moral imperative in the social. Thus good is a reference to the social or collective. What is good for the collective is good for individuals and this invariably involves a denial of individual self interest, so that to be social is to be moral and to be moral is to be social. What maintains the sense of solidarity that binds the collective together is good, for the collective is the source of individual being and welfare. It is the source of conscious life.

Two related concepts are used to build this theory; *conscience collective*, i.e. a sense of communal being, a common collective set of sentiments by which a community thinks of itself in a common way, and; social solidarity, i.e., the extent to which members of a community feel solidarity with each other and think and act in a solidary manner through their utilization of the *conscience collective*. It was with the development of these ideas that his first major work *The Division of*

Labour in Society was concerned. Solidarity was the product of a *conscience collective* that was strong enough to bind people together and restrain their desires and passions to within the bounds of collective sentiments. These sentiments give us an idea of our role and place in the collective, they give us guidelines as to how we should behave and what are reasonable expectations given our position and visa vie others. Hence they limit, control and direct our behaviour, giving us a consequent sense of ease and well-being, a feeling of social integration and harmony with our fellow humans that, because we are social and not individual, makes us feel good about and within ourselves. Because we are of society we only have a sense of well-being when we are properly integrated into it and our passions restrained.

In his analysis of suicide this is at the heart of his concept of anomic suicide (Durkheim, 1970) where suicide rates are highest amongst people who have had radical alterations in their social situations. Thus not only do the very unsuccessful who have fallen down the social ladder display an high propensity to suicide but so do people who are very successful, finding themselves suddenly thrust into a social milieu that they do not comprehend and leaving them feeling lost and helpless. Their success comes to feel empty and meaningless as does life itself.

In *Division of Labour in Society* he first develops the concept of anomie to explain problems of disorder and conflict in industrial society, and in doing this he also develops his equation that to be moral is to be social and vice versa. To be moral and social was one and the same thing, and this is also the root of his attack on Spencer and the utilitarians who equate individual self-interest with morality.

At work, as in any other social sphere, we need a sense of moral regulation to constrain our endless and disparate economic wants. We need a moral force to bind us to our fellow workers to give us a sense of social solidarity and to generate a *conscience collective* so that we can think and act in harmony. This moral force is a social phenomenon, it is a reference to the social that is good and provides us with a sense of a pre-existing obligation to something greater than the individual before which we must defer, (here Durkheim borrows heavily from Kantian philosophy), and the only force greater than the individual is society. However, it is the social that utilitarianism rejects by raising the individual and self-interest to be the ultimate source of good, of morality.

Utilitarianism, it is claimed, merely leads to ungoverned passion that leads to chaos and disorder. Although a force may arise temporarily that can impose an arbitrary order, it is short lived because it lacks any moral authority beyond its ability to impose physically its will. Once that is lost it collapses. Utilitarianism is incapable of satisfying the basic human needs of affiliation and belonging that are essential to our being. It further encourages us down that self-destructive path. Individual welfare is not to be found outside of social constraints but in being intimately bound up with them:

For wit's false mirror held up nature's light,
Showed erring pride whatever is is right;

That reason, passion answer one great aim
That true self love and social are the same.
(Pope 1966, Essay on Man, Epistle 4).

It was not just the philosophy of utilitarianism but its conjunction with the economic division of labour in modern society that disrupted the moral regulation of Humankind. If the source of morality lies in the social, unless you socialise and come regularly into contact with your fellow humans it is very difficult to develop a sense of collective consciousness and empathy with them that will allow you to build up a sense of solidarity with them. This is the fundamental foundation of morality, i.e. you can't be social with people you don't meet. From this point you can't be moral either and the source of regulation disappears and chaos emerges.

The legacy of Durkheim

In the study of organization and management Durkheim has often had a much greater influence than is appreciated. Burns and Stalker's models of mechanistic and organic structures are a simple organizational application of Durkheim's mechanistic and organic forms of social solidarity. But they look simply at social structures and patterns of interaction, not at the idea of a moral community with a sense of social solidarity.

Another example is the work of Elton Mayo (Dingley, 1992) whose human relations philosophy and ideas of social man and anomie build on Durkheim quite explicitly. Yet in none of his works will you find any reference to the concept of morality (morale is the closest that he comes to it). This is especially surprising given the extensive references to Durkheim and the avowed indebtedness to him. A third example is found in the work of Rensis Likert (1961) and his linking pin model which is a simple restatement of Durkheim's ideas about overlapping occupational groups.

He was also used extensively in industrial relations research by such writers as Fox and Flanders (1969) to provide a model from which to analyze and suggest reforms to the UK industrial relations system.

That he should be referred to so often is hardly surprising. He was specifically concerned to address the problems of modern industrial societies and keen to suggest practical solutions. But what is surprising is that the central concern of his sociology i.e. morality, should be ignored. Morality was the one superior force capable of restraining people and ameliorating their passions so that they would cooperate to their mutual benefit. Without reference to morality attempts at management and organization were just empty psychological and social manipulation that failed because that is precisely all they are. Durkheim was very clear on this and addressed the question very clearly both in his discussions of occupational groups (in *The Division of Labour in Society*) and in his thoughts on professional ethics (in *Professional Ethics and Civic Morals*).

Perhaps one reason for this neglect of morality when borrowing from Durkheim may lie in the way that he tied it in with his theory of religion and God. People with 'practical' concerns maybe think that this disbars such concepts from use in the 'real' economic world. If so they only display their own limitations.

Durkheim's sociology is actually built around a trinity (even holy) of three interrelated concepts that constitute a whole: the social, the moral, and the religious which he sees as one and the same, and leads him to a materialistic interpretation of God. God is merely the idealized type of a society that is held by a society of itself, it is then externalized as an abstract entity that acts back on society, both as a collective and as individual members, through religion as morality. The superior being, the moral force in front of which man has to defer, is actually none other than man himself, as a collective (the only force greater than man) that emerges out of our interactions together, we create God out of social intercourse. Here he uses a kind of early systems concept of the whole being greater than the sum of the component parts in direct opposition to the utilitarian ideas of Spencer or Margaret Thatcher. Hence the vital importance of the social. It is both God and morality: and religion is not apart from everyday life but a product of it acting as a restraint upon our destructive passions.

Back to the professions and guilds

It was precisely these religious/moral questions that both the guilds and the professions understood and addressed in their heyday and were so important to their success, and which neglected helped lead to their demise. Both involved not just the active participation of religion but the deliberate fostering of a sense of morality and moral obligation likewise to their fellow members and to their clients/customers. Even utilitarianism and Adam Smith started with an avowedly moral purpose.

The moral purpose of both is addressed explicitly in their reference, overtly, to religious regulation and in professing to God; transgression here would have been regarded as a sin and open to sanction e.g. expulsion from the guild and the inability to maintain one's livelihood, apart from possible damnation in the after-life. But morality is addressed not just in the formal sense of regulatory mechanisms sanctioned by the church but in the Durkheimian concept of religion i.e. as a social community and social interaction. They were *conscience collectives* that produced their own social solidarity and ideal which through constant interaction they were forced to confront on a regular basis and live up to. Also, given the small and intimate nature of medieval society, they would be forced into close and continual contact with other guilds and professions with whom they had to deal as well as with their clients and customers.

The medieval corporation actually appeared in the individual's life as the superior force to which he had to submit, not just in the technical sense but in the moral/religious sense, it was God.

166

Consequently it was to these medieval corporations that Durkheim looked to find inspiration to overcome the problems of anomie that he saw as critical concerns in modern industrial society. To recreate a social framework within which a proper feeling of social solidarity could emerge, a *conscience collective* that offered a moral regulatory system capable of binding individuals to a common good was needed. What he advocated was a system whereby all those involved in a common industry are joined together into a common occupational group e.g. workers, managers and directors that he calls professions, because of the emphasis on ethics, but that he clearly sees all this as the modern equivalent of the guild:

> The name in history of this professional group is the guild and this is held to have been bound up with our political ancient regime and therefore as not being able to survive it (Durkheim 1957, p. 17).

What is stressed is not just the need for moral regulation but that such regulation must be of those people being regulated and not some alien and imposed regulation if it is to have any real or lasting impact; its authority must lie in itself, which is what occurred in the professions and guilds. To do this you must build upon groups that have a spontaneous set of common interests that naturally bind them together and have a community of shared sentiments based on regular interaction. You cannot be moral where you have no social interaction. People with the same trade but in different industries spread throughout a modern national economy have little such interaction or interest and are thus not in a position to develop any moral framework. It is only those with whom we come into regular daily contact that are likely to affect us. It is workers, managers and directors within an enterprise who have a direct common interest, yet who the pursuit of self-interest sets against each other.

In looking at the guilds what Durkheim saw was a system whereby apprentice, journeyman and master craftsman were all bound in a common occupational grouping that emphasized a sense of moral obligation and duty to each other and limited destructive economic self-interest by regulating relationships between them and allowing harmonious cooperation. This is what is lacking in modern industrial society:

> Some hazy generalizations on the loyalty and devotion owed by staff and workmen to those employing them; some phrases on the moderation the employer should use in his economic dominance; some reproach for any too overtly unfair competition... (Durkheim 1957, p. 9, 10).

This is the cause of much of the conflict and strife in the economy, that directors should have a clearly developed idea of their obligations to their staff, that managers have a duty to workers as well as to shareholders and workers likewise. In practical terms directors who give themselves massive pay rises whilst insisting on pay restraint for their workers (no matter how well argued in market economics

167

terms) or making large numbers of them redundant are the source of the very conflict they so decry and imposes such costs against them. Wherein lies the common cause or moral purpose to bind them? However, this can only come about when they are in close social contact around a community of genuinely common interests where people can identify a common good for themselves. This was the lesson of the guilds and professional ethics.

Conclusion

Recent interest in the idea of organizational culture shows an emerging realization that there is a real social side to economic activity that is apart from psychological needs. However, it is likely to be driven down to the same sort of manipulative level unless the wider social and moral context of economic activity is taken into account. The need for a wider context into which to place economic activity is crucial, not only to regulate it but also to direct it, if we are to have economic prosperity and happiness.

To do this we require to rediscover a sense of obligation to a greater good than our selfish ends, and this is only possible in a social context.

References

Burns, T. and Stalker, G. (1961), *The Management of Innovation*, Tavistock, London.

Dingley, J. C. (1977), 'To The Exclusion of The Ill-educated and Unworthy', MA Thesis, University of Leeds.

Dingley, J. C. (1992), 'Durkheim, Social Man and Elton Mayo', paper presented to the British Academy of Management Annual Conference, University of Bradford.

Durkheim, E. (1933), *The Division of Labour in Society*, Free Press, New York.

Durkheim, E. (1957), *Professional Ethics and Civic Morals*, Routledge, London.

Durkheim, E. (1970), *Suicide*, Routledge, London.

Etzioni, A. (1987), 'Toward a Kantian Socio-Economics', *Review of Socio-Economics*, Vol. 45, Part 1, pp. 37-47.

Etzioni, A. (1988), *The Moral Dimension; Toward a New Economics*, Free Press, New York.

Etzioni, A. (1989), 'Toward Deontological Social Sciences', *Philosophy of the Social Sciences*, Vol. 19, pp. 143-156.

Etzioni, A. (1991), 'Too Many Rights, Too Few Responsibilities', *Society*, Vol. 28, Part 2, pp. 41-48.

Fox, A. and Flanders, A. A. (1969), Reform of Collective Bargaining: From Donovan to Durkheim, *British Journal of Industrial Relations*, 7, 2, pp. 151-180.

Hearn, F. (1985), 'Durkheim's Political Sociology: Corporatism, State Autonomy and Democracy', *Social Research*, Vol. 52, No. 1, pp. 151-177.

Hobbes, T. (1968), *Leviathan*, Penguin, Harmondsworth.

Likert, R. (1961), *New Patterns of Management*, McGraw-Hill, New York.

Lukes, S. (1973), *Emile Durkheim*, Penguin, Harmondsworth.

Lux, K. (1990), *Adam Smith's Mistake*, Shambhala, Boston.

Mabbott, J. (1966), *An Introduction to Ethics*, Hutchinson, London.

Mayo, E. (1947), *The Political Problems of an Industrial Civilization*, Harvard University Press, Cambridge, Mass.

Mayo, E. (1949), *The Social Problems of an Industrial Civilization*, Routledge, London.

Mayo, E. (1993), *The Human Problems of an Industrial Civilization*, Macmillan, London..

Pilkington, (1958), *Royal Commission on Medical Education*, HMSO, London.

Pope, A. (1966), *Collected Works*, Oxford University Press, Oxford.

Southgate, G. (1962), English Economic History, Dent, London.

8 Manufacturing decline and the division of labour in Britain: the case of vehicles

Stephen Ackroyd and Dave Lawrenson

Introduction

This chapter is concerned with the extent to which manufacturing decline in the UK is a failure of management and, in particular, the absence of appropriate expertise and competence amongst managerial groups. A single cause or reductionist explanation of manufacturing decline is not, of course, being sought. Numerous factors are implicated in manufacturing decline: the structure of economic institutions, the supply of capital for investment, the role of the state (or the lack of it), the organization and outlook of labour, the competition between different professional groups as well as the capacity of management, to name but a few of the emphases in the literature. (For a useful, if somewhat inconclusive, recent summary of the literature see Coates, 1994). The issue is now not so much what the influential factors are, so much as how they interact, and how that interaction has developed. What is needed are intellectually satisfying models of the connections between influences, and the isolation of the significant variations in effect at particular times and places. To this end, we have been considering the British vehicle manufacturing sector in the present century. At the centre of our interest in this paper is the division of labour in the vehicle industry, and particularly the role of manufacturing management. We are concerned to develop an understanding of this, in a way that will be relevant to both theoretical discussions and further research.

This large 'case' has been chosen for two reasons. The first is that vehicle industry is an integral part of the industrial sector in steepest decline. What has been variously termed 'industrial decline' (Hirst and Zeitlin, 1990); 'manufacturing decline' (Ackroyd and Whitaker, 1990) and 'manufacturing failure' (Williams, Williams and Haslam, 1990) is uneven. In some sectors of manufacturing considerable strength remains in the British economy. Clearly, Britain is still quite strong in chemicals, and pharmaceuticals, in foods and much retail related manufacture. In addition, but of more questionable significance, Britain is the home base for some of the largest diversified manufacturing conglomerates in the world (Hanson, BTR, BAT, etc). Britain has manufacturing firms of all these types capitalized at around £10 billion, and at least thirty capitalized at more than £1 billion. Many of these large British manufacturing firms are rapidly moving into world operations, by placing more and more of their capacity overseas and increasingly operating on a global scale. Only from the point of view of domestic manufacturing employment and the UK domestic economy is this manufacturing failure. The point which needs to be made is that manufacturing failure is concentrated in consumer durable and capital goods manufacturing. These are the sectors where falling employment and the decline of capacity are obvious. These are the areas where there is the starkest contrast between Britain and Germany and Japan. Not only are very large and successful British firms rare in consumer durable and capital goods manufacturing, but Britain is deficient in firms of medium size of all sorts. In manufacturing there is nothing approximating the strength in depth of the small and medium engineering firms found in major industrial competitor nations (Lane, 1991). Hence, it is engineering and consumer durable manufacture which must be the critical areas of interest when it comes to the consideration of manufacturing decline.

Secondly the vehicle sector has been selected for particular attention in this chapter because of its importance in contemporary debate. Because of the popularity of ideas like Fordism, and its perceived theoretical importance, the vehicles sector is of particular interest at present. Indeed, emphasis on Fordism has caused much debate in this area to be conducted with this sort of industry centrally in mind, and has led many commentators to take the automobile industry specifically as being paradigmatic for manufacture. The work of analysts from a variety of schools is converging on the consideration of automobile manufacture within the general vehicles sector. Whatever theoretical starting point analysts adopt it seems - neo-liberal, neo-Schumpeterian, or neo-Marxist - automobile manufacture is taken to be very important. Writers have argued in terms of this type of manufacture being the basis of the mode of production in late capitalism, as being central to the technical innovations of the fourth Krondratieff, or simply basic to the industrial infrastructure of a modern industrial state. By contrast, we make few theoretical assumptions. The aim in this chapter is to use an approach influenced by the work of Max Weber, in which the distinctive outlooks and activities of specific occupational groups and the patterns of interaction in which they are implicated are identified and described.

Once vehicle production in this country is examined in an empirically serious way, findings are thrown up that have considerable conceptual relevance. One of our key findings, for example, is that there are many differences in the ways that vehicle manufacturing has developed in Britain from the pattern of classic 'Fordism'. By contrast with the experience of the USA, and to a lesser extent some

172

other European countries, large scale automobile production in Britain does not represent a distinct break with earlier systems of production. If we mean by Fordism the development of very large, vertically and horizontally integrated manufacturing facilities utilising very large numbers of unskilled workers on the lines of North American Ford, there was nothing remotely on that scale ever developed in Britain. The largest car manufacturers in Britain, Morris in the 1920s and Austin in the later 1930s, never had more than 20,000 total employees (which was the figure for Austin in 1935). U.S. Ford surpassed 20,000 employees in 1916, before its main production site was moved from Highland Park to River Rouge. In 1935, Ford employed 80,000 people in car production at River Rouge alone. Similarly in terms of output, even the highest production from a single firm - Austin in 1938 - no firm in Britain ever produced one tenth of the number of units as Ford. Perhaps the most compelling comparison is that, in the 1930s, Ford's River Rouge complex produced five times more units than all the car producers in Britain put together. It is true that the largest British firms in the vehicles sector were and are amongst the largest in terms of employment, but they were anything but integrated. Smaller producers were often more integrated than larger ones. For all car and lorry makers, their major component suppliers were larger then they were. In 1935, Dunlop was the thirteenth largest firm in terms of employment and Lucas seventeenth, whilst the largest car maker (Austin) was twenty eighth. At no time between the wars did any volume manufacturer of cars and lorries produce its own vehicle bodies.

In these ways the automobile production displays many important features that do not fit readily with expectations generated by contemporary discussions. Another important point to make is that, both at the time and more recently, the main justification for the lack of integration between assemblers and suppliers in engineering, and in the continued use of skilled and semi-skilled labour as opposed to the uniformly unskilled labour that the models of Taylorism/Fordism suggest, was in terms of the benefits of flexibility that these features of organization supposedly conferred. There are in fact many ways in which vehicle manufacture in this country for much of the century had many points of similarity with the model of flexible specialization in manufacturing proposed by Piore and Sabel (1984) with strongly connected networks of specialized firms sometimes in dense concentrations in particular regions. Our research certainly corroborates the conclusion of McKinley and Zeitlin (1986) in their discussion of British Engineering 1880 - 1939 in these respects. Writing of the inter-war industry they write:

> Rather than a wholesale movement towards direct control over the labour process, British car makers developed a variety of production regimes in which flexibility and maximising effort through tightly controlled piecework systems were key features. Within this framework, management willingly ceded a high degree of autonomy to production workers to maximise flexibility...

If these interpretations are correct, their importance can hardly be exaggerated. The British route to post-Fordism could not have been more direct. As will be argued in this paper it never was Fordist in the first place, and industry was organized in a way that should have made it eminently suited to the supposed conditions and markets of the contemporary world. If this is so, it makes the failure of British manufacturing in capital goods and consumer durables difficult to understand.

Despite the broad themes to which our research is relevant, our aims in this paper are quite modest. The main aim is to produce an account of organization and management of the British vehicles sector in a historically and temporally limited frame, to examine its development and to assess what it reveals about the matrix of factors that have produced the selective version of manufacturing decline seen in Britain.

Continuities in British vehicle production

In Britain there has been a great deal of historical continuity in the methods used in the production of all kinds of vehicles. The emergence of relatively large scale car manufacture does not, as in the USA, represent a major watershed in the development of production methods. The methods used and developed in car production in Britain were not greatly dissimilar, for example, to those in use in the nineteenth century for the production of stream locomotives and railway rolling stock. The same techniques were also applied to the aircraft industry. Methods of production involving the same procedures in the utilization of labour, the same kinds of managerial roles and relationships were carried over from one production activity to the next. This system of production we shall call 'craft flow' production. Although in car manufacture there were some extensive developments of this system of production and its associated organising roles, large scale car production in this country was organized in essentially the same as way in other areas of production. Nor was the system rapidly found to be unviable in car production. On the contrary it survived in a recognisable form until well into the postwar period. In aircraft manufacture craft flow production methods and organizational roles have been preserved in a recognisable form until the present time.

There are some obvious reasons why automobile manufacture in this country did not develop on Fordist lines. Fordism can be seen, at least in part, as a response to the problems of mass production in the absence of an adequate supply of skilled labour. In addition, Fordism prospered with the development of mass consumption of cars. By contrast with this, in Britain, before the start of relatively large scale vehicle production, the manufacture of engineering products was well-developed. Traditionally this had taken place using high proportions of relatively skilled labour. Engineers formed one of the first effective trade unions, the Amalgamated Society (formed in 1850) being a prime example of the so-called 'new model' unions of skilled workers. Management as it developed, neither felt the need, nor ever seriously undertook (before 1960 or so), the use of unskilled labour for many core production tasks in engineering-based manufacture. We shall argue, on the contrary, that methods were developed which involved continuing the traditional utilization of labour, or something very like it. The use of a high proportion of skilled (and organized) workers within surprisingly flexible production systems was retained. In addition, also, mass production did not develop because of the failure of substantial markets to emerge. Even in car production, the U.K market remained relatively small, with the product being defined as a luxury item.

That there are continuities in the vehicle sector in Britain, broadly defined to include a spectrum of vehicles from railway locomotives and rolling stock through cars and commercial vehicles to planes of various kinds, can be relatively easily established from the examination of the organization of the companies producing these products. There are many similarities in the details of organization and management, in such things as employment practices, labour utilization and patterns of management recruitment and training in different branches of vehicle production. There is also compelling evidence for the thesis of continuity of methods of production in the fact that there was a sharing of a pool of senior personnel between these different areas of vehicle production throughout the first half of the century. As we will suggest, senior engineers, that is key personnel who were trained in very similar ways, moved between railway, car and aircraft production firms quite extensively. Because of its importance to our argument about the division of labour amongst British management and particularly for developments in the 1950s and 1960s, it is necessary to analyze this system of production in some detail.

Origins and development of craft flow production

The emergence of craft flow production can be understood by contrasting it with earlier production methods applied to complex engineering products. Originally, production and assembly were carried out in one location by one gang of workers. This system we term 'static build', and was organized utilising craft skills. It was assumed that each product would require many skills and, partly because of this, would be able to incorporate variations. As a matter of routine, not only would new products incorporate improvements accumulated from learning from previous production, but there would be scope for customer specification as well. In this way, because of the ability of the workforce to apply general principles of craft to new situations, companies could produce a wide range of products. Subsequent development of production introduced significant variations on this. Static build had some obvious deficiencies. In addition to dependency on skilled labour, which we shall argue was not a key deficiency, static build suffered from low throughput and inefficiency. It was difficult to use both production labour and supporting component supply services efficiently. The demand on different kinds of labour

175

was periodic because of the relatively long production cycle involved in static building. The production cycle also placed periodicity on the demand for work from component supply shops. At times, labour and machines in support functions were idle, at other times they were over-stretched and incapable of supplying.

Early developments of static build involved the emergence of team forms of working, in which craftsmen and less skilled mates and assistants worked together. Another important development was for parts of a complex product to be made separately, and the final item then to be assembled from subunits and assemblies. By dividing the work into sections, and moving it between gangs, it was possible to increase the number of teams working and to reduce the time necessary to produce or overhaul a vehicle. This was also achieved without altering skill requirements at the core of production very considerably. The sectionalising of assembly meant that the amount of variation between peaks and troughs in requirements for supplies was evened out because the task cycles of each section were less than for the whole of a vehicle. In such a system, of course, it was an essential aspect of engineering design that it take cognisance of the need for team working and sectionalization. However, the system also allocated considerable informal responsibility to decentralized teams of workers within the production process for organizing themselves. There were at least two dimensions of this: first for the allocation of work within teams and, second, for coordinating production with other teams. It is important to recognise the extent of informal cooperation for the coordination of production.

In the railway engineering industry a locomotive, carriage or wagon for repair would enter the shop on a track, and the track or line would be divided up into a number of work locations where specific operations were performed, for example, dis-assembly, repair of the frame, wheel replacement and so on. At preordained times, a locomotive, carriage or wagon would be moved to the next stage, eventually leaving the erecting shop repaired or built. The number of stages varied depending on the size of the shop and the volume of throughput. At Crewe, the system, locally named the 'belt system', had eight stages. During the last five stages of this locomotives were wheeled and connected to the locomotive in front by a steel cable which, at a given time, dragged the line of locos to the next stage (Fowler, 1929, p. 62; Reed, 1982, p. 164). Beames describes the system as follows:

> The method of processing the repair of locomotives is representative of the principle, now employed throughout the works, of moving the work to the man rather than the man to the work. The locomotive is moved down the shop in the eight successive stages. At each stage the appropriate components are added by men expert in their particular work, and the duration of the working time in each shop is regulated to 7 hours 50 minutes. By this means, an engine is stripped and given a heavy repair in 12 days, as compared with 30 to 40 days generally occupied on such work (Beames, 1928, p. 254).

For locomotives the construction and repair of boilers took the greatest amount of time. Therefore the repair of a boiler dictated the time taken for an overhaul. Boiler repair and frame repair were divided and allocated to different shops. More men were allocated to boiler repair than under the previous single location system and the boilers were not necessarily refitted to the same frame. Another variation allowable was the dissociation of the original parts of a locomotive. For every frame being repaired there could be more than one boiler being repaired. This meant that when the frame was overhauled a boiler was ready for final assembly at the same time. The time taken to repair all of the locomotives was reduced dramatically. These ideas and procedures were applied in other sectors of vehicle production at the time. Their key advantages were: a rational approach to manning and the more continuous use of labour and machinery. Component flows became more voluminous and complicated with this development and required some managerial attention. But, by taking control of component flows management ensured that vehicle production and repair was not halted because of lack of stock. In all industries progress departments emerged to control the flows of components (Lemon, 1930; Lewchuk, 1987, p. 163)

As the foregoing description reveals this mode of vehicle construction typically would necessitate the movement of the developing product between gangs of workers. Such movements were mainly cooperatively coordinated by groups of workers under the general control of senior engineers. A disaggregated production system like this involving the movement of subassemblies and volume material flows can be confused with mass production using conveyors and automated flow lines. Craft flow production was, in fact, compatible with limited use of such technologies. In some of its forms in the car industry, limited use of flow line technologies was made. But the point to note in all craft flow production, is that the productive process is coordinated by the design activities of engineers and cooperative action between semi-autonomous gangs of workers and not primarily by technology. The craft flow system certainly predated automobile production, being applied in a modified form to both volume car production and aircraft manufacture.

Craft flow production in automobile manufacture

Lewchuk has recently argued that the British motor industry entailed a distinctive 'British system of mass production'. Whilst this involves a welcome recognition of the uniqueness of British production methods there is a problem with an implied similarity between British and American procedures. Although British industry went through periodic rationalizations, at the end of the interwar period there were still some thirty important and largely independent car producers. Even for the five or so larger producers it is debatable whether the British ever had a system of mass as opposed to volume production. Lewchuk's description of the 'British system of Mass Production' agrees at many points with our description of craft flow production, but arguably his appreciation of the British system is mitigated by his implicit comparisons with the American industry and his concentration on the volume producers among the British manufacturers. Even for these companies, however, Lewchuck notes some obvious features of craft flow production. He argues that the system adopted at Austin was 'flow production without direct control over labour' (Lewchuk, 1987, p. 178).

Lewchuck also acknowledges clearly that management in the British motor industry was aware of the distinctiveness of their system. Frank Woollard, manager of Morris Motors is quoted as describing the system as being:

> not aimed at attacking enormous quantities, but ... an endeavour to secure continuous flow so that a relatively small plant can meet the greatest overseas plants on fairly level terms (Lewchuk, 1987 p. 169).

At Morris it is well known that work was produced in sections by large numbers of sub-contractors and then later assembled (Tolliday, 1992, p. 38). This sectionalization was also applied to production within the Morris organization. For example, front and back axles were assembled at separate locations within the Cowley plant and then brought to the production line (Ware, 1976). Tolliday argues that the practice at Morris was fundamentally different from Ford, because:

> the separate operations at each stage still needed time and attention by individual workers for efficient completion (Tolliday, 1992, p. 33).

Lewchuk confirms this perspective and describes how even when flow production had been introduced into the Morris engine plant, hand fitting was not eliminated (Lewchuk, 1987, p. 168). That the systems in the car industry are similar to those used in the railway engineering industry is not purely chance. As shall be shown, many of the managers in the motor industry were trained in the railway workshops. For example, Lewchuk speculates that the system of flow production at Morris engines was inspired by F. Woollard's (the plant manager) experience of craft flow production when an apprentice at Eastleigh railway workshops.

While generalizations are problematic, it is possible to see different kinds of craft flow production in the automobile industry in the inter war period. In small firms craft domination of production was retained in a simple form. Lewchuck gives the example of the early Daimler Company where for a long period management lacked any significant engineering expertise and could not control or coordinate production. The production methods themselves, however functioned using informal coordination. As Lewchuk revealingly suggests, the management were 'forced to rely on shop floor workers to perform these functions'. In larger firms there was more extensive use of semi-skilled labour. In Austin and Morris, the number of fully skilled men in final assembly operations was kept to a minimum for reasons of cost-limitation. In these firms, perhaps a majority of production operations were undertaken by workers classed as semi-skilled. This is evidence

178

that can be used to give some credence to the idea that cost limitation was imposed through deskilling. But deskilling was clearly not a central policy in the development of large scale manufacture as it was in the USA. Large numbers of skilled men continued to be employed in British factories in jobs central to production processes. Many areas in sub-assembly operations such as engine assembly and power-train production, not to mention machining and component manufacturing, continued to be organized around skilled labour. Indeed, in many areas, production was also coordinated by skilled workers in the manner that has been described for craft flow production generally. If skilled workers were not utilized in some new operations, such development was typically introduced with the consent of established skilled groups in the industry. Expansion of production using dilutee labour was undertaken on the tacit agreement that reduction in the scale of operations would produce a reversion to the exclusive use of skilled labour. In short, skilled work may have been diluted in these firms, but it was not progressively moved to the periphery of operations. On the other hand, this sort of accommodation of semi-skilled workers did limit technological integration of some operations in plants otherwise dominated by craft flow production.

Senior engineers in this automobile industry, in which we can include both William Morris and Herbert Austin, were usually well aware that they were not adopting Ford's methods because of their relatively low capitalization and reliance on skilled workers. As in other areas of vehicle production, British management was concerned with ensuring that the production process could produce a range of different products as well as numbers. This was achieved efficiently in car production, as in other kinds of vehicle production, by the use of craft flow production. It was this system that allowed all parts of the production process to be coordinated with each other. It was this which ensured, within limits, that machines, work in progress, raw materials and labour were not standing idle. The division of the work in this fashion required knowledge of the production process and this was acquired through the apprentice system, which, as we shall see, extended to include very senior personnel.

Craft flow production in aircraft manufacture

Craft flow production was also utilized in the aircraft industry. In this industry the major development during the interwar period in production techniques was the development of the 'split constructional method' (Robinson, 1949, p. 46). This is another name for craft flow production utilising sectionalization. Workers were required to build the parts of the aircraft separately and there was little specification of work tasks. Each section was allocated to a different group of workers and was only brought together at final assembly. Again the system utilized the skills and the capacity for organization of the workforce. Thus, in this branch of manufacture too, the work was organized on a craft flow basis. Robinson, who was works manager at Handley Page, one of the major airframe producers between the wars and during World War II, was quite explicit in his rejection of Fordism:

> methods which are suitable for long runs of continuous production, where the basic design of the vehicle to be made is only slowly changing, are quite unsuitable for the production of the smaller numbers that are called for in aircraft manufacture (Robinson, 1949, p. 40).

He was also clear on why it was necessary to adopt the craft flow production, thus in words that echo Woollard's:

> (The) Basic problem of aircraft production (is) to manufacture an article by methods capable of rapid expansion for large and efficient production, at the same time flexible enough for changes in design to be introduced rapidly (Robinson, 1949, p. 40).

Robinson saw the ability to man tasks evenly as the chief advantage of sectionalization. He wrote:

> ...labour is more evenly distributed with the maximum efficiency, tending to greater output and the maximum number of men can be engaged on an aircraft at a given time (Robinson, 1949, p. 42).

Close managerial knowledge of the production process was considered vital to the production of airframes. Robinson argued that the chief aim was to ensure that the greatest number of 'components' should be worked at the same time. In order to achieve this the engineer needed to undertake close investigations, to see in what way assembly man-hours could be reduced. Hence, in the airframe industry, efficiency was seen as being achievable by the development of sectionalization, and this required managerial knowledge of the production process. In the nineteenth century, craft training had enabled management to control a craft workforce by sharing an intimate knowledge of the nature and pace of work. In the interwar period, the need for efficiency led to the development of the craft flow system on the basis of this managerial craft knowledge of the production process. In the production of aeroplanes, as elsewhere with craft flow production, craft workers are coordinated by craft trained managers.

The premium apprenticeship system and craft flow production

Craft flow production has its origins in the training the engineers received. Large numbers of senior British engineers, from earliest times to after 1940 or so, received a large part of their training on the shopfloor. Those destined for management did not serve as trade apprentices but as premium apprentices or

180

pupils. All trainees learnt about industry by working with and for craftsmen but here the similarities end. Trade apprentices learnt one craft only, premium apprentices and pupils, the future engineers, worked with craftsmen in all the major trades. The form that the premium apprenticeship took is described by D. R. Adams, training supervisor of Blackburn, one of the leading airframe manufacturers of the interwar period. Aeronautical engineers, he suggested:

> ..served two years full time in the shops under exactly the same conditions of work and discipline as the ordinary trade apprentice, with the exception that they were given experience in a number of essential shops. They were not expected to be skilled at any particular trade, but to know what was made in any particular department and to learn the 'feel' of materials and tools, and, what was of equal importance, to get to know their fellow men in the shop (Adams, 1943, p. 359).

The same pattern was followed in the railway industry. The contrast between trade and premium apprenticeships can be studied in a couple of papers given by Edgar Larkin to the Institute of Locomotive Engineers (Larkin, 1934). The pupil system offered a similar training with a greater emphasis upon technical training. A number of other features distinguished the training of engineers from that of trade apprentices; a period in the drawing office, the necessity for formal qualifications (usually matriculation), often family connections to managers of the firm and the ability to pay a large sum of money in the form of a premium (often equivalent to several years wages) (Bond, 1975; Larkin, 1934, 1979; Mountford, 1980). Not surprisingly this meant that the engineers tended to be recruited from the middle classes. The system of premium apprenticeship was the normal form of engineering training for managers in railway engineering and aircraft manufacture (Anon, 1943, p. 339), and was widespread in the car industry, for example, at Morris, Bristol, Rolls Royce, Wolseley and Standard (PEP, 1949, p. 49; Edgerton, 1991, p. 56; Harvey-Bailey, 1985, p. 23; King, 1989, p. 139, 118; Richardson, 1977, p. 101).

The engineers in the vehicle sector shared a common training heritage. Indeed King has noted the large number of major figures in the management of the interwar British motor industry who were railway premium apprentices (King, 1989). A few names will have to suffice as examples: Herbert Austin, Henry Royce, W. O. Bentley, Owen Clegg (works manager at Rover), F. Woollard, L. Pomeroy (Managing Director of Daimler and later General Manager of DeHavilland), Henry Morgan (founder of Morgan cars). The railways were not the only source of apprenticeships, for example, Leonard Lord, works manager of Cowley and later Managing Director of Austin, followed public school with an apprenticeship at Vickers. Englebach, Lord's predecessor at Austin, followed public school with an apprenticeship at Armstrong-Whitworth. Any brief examination of the background of management in the motor industry reveals that it is dominated by men who had served premium apprenticeships. In the aircraft industry

McKinnon Wood argued that most of the higher staff came from the car industry (Wood, 1935, p. 10). Roy Fedden, the driving force behind Bristol aero engines, and Ernest Hives, Managing Director of Rolls Royce, were both premium apprentices in the car industry (Edgerton, 1991, p. 56; Harvey-Bailey, 1985, p. 5). Again, a number of key figures in the aircraft industry were trained in the railway workshops. Royce has already been mentioned, A.V. Roe, founder of AVRO and Saunders-Roe, two of the major aircraft companies of the interwar period, was a premium apprentice at Horwich railway workshops (Anon, 1948, p. 118). There are also a number of other figures who followed a similar route. The traffic was not all one way. Healey, the founder of the sports car firm and a former technical director of Triumph, had been a pupil at Sopwith (an early aircraft producer out of whose ashes Hawker developed) (King, 1989). What is clear is that in this sector the premium apprenticeship was central to management training.

Nature and consequences of craft flow production

Thus it is clear that the craft flow system rested on direct managerial knowledge of the production process. Premium apprenticeship gave management extensive knowledge of the production process which enabled them to control production which retained craft skills. Hence not only in the last century but during much of the present one, managerial control in vehicle production rested on knowing what work was necessary and what was a reasonable pace of work. That is why prospective managers were trained in what were termed the 'essential shops'. Indeed, in the engineering trades, in the absence of much in the way of higher education in either engineering or management in Britain, the premium apprenticeship was a major source of management expertise.

It cannot be too strongly emphasized as well that this production system did not destroy worker discretion but, to a considerable extent, depended on it. Skills remained central to the production. Production, even when sectionalized, was organized around teams of workers at the centre of which were skilled operatives. In fact, the craft flow system required high degrees of both specialization and teamworking in production. Worker autonomy extended to the task of dividing work between themselves, coordinating productive activities between different skills, and between workers with different levels of skill. Also involved were high levels of coordination of production between teams of workers engaged in different aspects of the production process. The differentiation of labour according to competency was thus a central element of craft flow production and characterized craft flow production at all levels, from senior engineers managing production down to the shop floor. The preservation of worker discretion was an essential feature of craft flow production. It enabled the British vehicle industry to retain its ability to respond flexibly to variations in demand.

Despite their significant differences from mass production manufacturing principles, British methods of vehicle manufacture were able to expand when required. Sometimes the increases in production achieved were dramatic. For example, Morris increased engine production at the same plant from 2,000 to 60,000 per year in the space of a few years (Lewchuk, 1987, p. 170). On the LMS, the productivity of locomotive overhaul increased by 400 per cent in the late 1920s (Fowler, 1929). Craft flow production was also particularly appropriate for incorporating product changes whilst expanding, so that new marks were regularly produced. Perhaps the most compelling example here concerns the greatly expanded production during World War II. This was effective not only because of the greatly increased scale of production, but because it incorporated necessary design changes on a continuous basis. Thus, not only cars but a range of different military vehicles of all sorts were produced in large numbers. Aircraft production was expanded smoothly also, despite the developed form of craft flow production in that sector, in which sections of the product were sometimes made at dispersed sites. The Spitfire fighter aircraft, for example, which was a technically complex product by any standard, went through more than twenty distinct marks, and many more minor variations during the war period and usually kept abreast with or ahead of the improving enemy technology. After the war, in a similar fashion, British Rail modernization initiated in 1955, combined the use of diesel and electric traction, whilst continuing with steam locomotives in service. The railway workshops, therefore, built and repaired steam, diesel and electric locomotives, each type of locomotive varying widely in basic technology.

It is true that the capacity to expand production smoothly was not without limit. Above certain thresholds in output there were bottlenecks to production, at which the traditional system of craft coordination of production could no longer cope. At these points, significant improvements in integration of production were required. In large volume car plants, significant coordination of production was introduced by the limited use of flow line technology to supplement craft coordination. Similar problems were dealt with in railway rolling stock and aircraft production in the 1950s. They were solved by the development and application of new managerial techniques. Large productivity increases were gained in railway engineering and aerospace during the late 1950s and early 1960s with the adoption of the operational research technique of network analysis (Hudson, 1969). By and large, however, the craft flow system worked remarkably well, producing a wide variety of goods in surprisingly large volumes.

Supposed inherent deficiencies of craft flow production cannot readily explain the post-World War II problems of British manufacturing. Not only were the difficulties and bottlenecks in production that were occasionally encountered soluble for vehicle production, the quality and variety that the method of production made possible was more and more relevant to increasingly sophisticated consumer markets. Paradoxically however, in car and railway manufacturing the craft flow system of production was only retained for a relatively short time after World War II. Instead we see dramatic modernization and rationalization of production. At precisely the point at which the demand for mass produced consumer durables was beginning to weaken, and the associated Fordist production

183

principles becoming obsolete, there are a series of disastrous attempts to rationalise areas of vehicle manufacture in this country on a mass production pattern.

Why British management should have abandoned craft flow production on the eve of the decline of the appropriateness of mass production methods is a complex question. One line of argument that definitely can be rejected is the idea that the craft flow system carried the seeds of its breakdown. Lewchuk argues in this way that the amount of discretion left to the workforce meant that during the postwar period they had learnt to use this to their advantage and to overturn management prerogatives (Lewchuk, 1987, p. 183). This supposedly led to the identification of the need to rationalise production along American lines. We disagree and suggest instead that the industrial relations difficulties which Lewchuk sees as leading management to adopt Fordism, we think are the product of the attempt to impose Fordism. It is true that the attempted rationalization of the vehicle industry, which was undertaken in the postwar period, involved breaking the traditional patterns of utilization of craft skill as well as introducing a new way of organising production. Rationalization therefore helped to provoke the radicalization of workforces and the development of organized resistance of workers to avert deskilling. But this occurred after the engineers had already been pushed out of the control of their organizations, and the traditional system of management by craft trained engineers had broken down. Hence, we argue instead that it was not problems of the division of labour between engineers and workers in production that were the basic problem, but prior problems of the division of labour amongst groups of managers, which led to the abandonment of the craft flow system.

What happened in the large scale manufacture of vehicles in the 1950s and 1960s were two things, both of which are in their own ways precursors of tendencies that have affected all consumer durable and capital goods manufacture in this country. Either there was the simple withdrawal of capital from involvement in the production of complex products and/or there was amalgamation with other producers of similar weakness and vulnerability in terms of capital investment. The significant weakness in investment by comparison with other countries in the postwar period has been shown for all manufacturing sectors (Ackroyd and Whitaker, 1990). This tendency was marked in vehicles manufacturing. We may note some examples of the different effects. First, there was simple withdrawal of capital to such a point that the company concerned was not viable. This was the fate of the Singer Motor Company, employing 8,000 workers in 1935, and among the 100 largest employers at that time, Singer remained a significant producer of vehicles only until the Second World War. By contrast, the Standard Motor Company was also starved of capital after the Second World War, but survived in some form following its amalgamation with Triumph in 1945. Such weakening of investment would not have been possible in technologically coordinated production systems.

There were also, of course, massive amalgamations of vehicle producing firms in the 1950s and 1960s. The larger groups that were formed often did not have better long term prospects than those of the producers that comprised them.

184

Progressive amalgamations of production capacity in the 1960s produced companies that, in terms of general measures of scale such as the total capitalization and the total numbers of employees, were of comparable size to Continental and smaller American producers. Moreover, in some cases, the best known of which being the British Motor Corporation/British Motor Holdings/ British Leyland Group, significant efforts were made to reorganize and rationalize production thoroughly, moving decisively away from craft flow production towards an under-capitalized British version of mass production. It is an interesting and little known footnote in the history of world car manufacture, that before rationalization Morris, an important constituent Company of the BMC group, had its methods of production avidly copied by the nascent Japanese car industry after World War II, when Morris Minor cars were manufactured under licence in Japan. On the railways, Beeching consciously attempted to rationalise rolling stock production and repair by the imposition of Taylorism, which previously had largely been absent, and novel forms of management accounting. He also chose to ignore many of the production recommendations of his engineering staff. Perhaps because of the rapidly increasing technical sophistication of the products, amalgamation between firms in the aircraft industry did not also involve so much rationalization of production methods and deskilling, although a similar tendency for capital withdrawal as in the car trade was also present in this sector.

Amalgamation was an inappropriate and ineffective solution to an underlying problem which was present in British vehicle manufacturing companies using the craft flow system. This is the problem of the strategic management of companies.

The fate of the engineers in management

In their essentials, the initial problems of vehicle manufacturing in this country are not difficult to characterize. The markets for these products were basically relatively small and internally differentiated. In the market for family cars, where there was some potential for volume sales, the total market was small by comparison with the USA. In the family car market, the profusion of marques and models suggests even that part of the market was characterized by high degrees of segmentation. Differentiation and variety continued to be important selling points (Maxcy and Silberston, 1959; Church, 1994). Because of the relative smallness of markets in general, returns to capital invested in these industries were limited also. Production was relatively labour extensive rather than capital intensive. But the key point to note is that the markets for vehicles were anything but stable, being subject to considerable fluctuations with the trade cycle. For most branches of vehicle production the underlying trend of demand during the present century was upward; but, superimposed on this, there were regular downturns in demand requiring reductions in activity. As relatively large and costly products, purchases of vehicles would be postponed in adverse trading conditions. This feature of the markets for vehicles ensured a continuing need for both expansion and, periodically, contraction of productive capacity.

As we have seen, craft flow production could and did respond well to expansion of demand by reaching new productivity targets. While sharp upswings in demand could usually be met by increased production, they did sometimes produce managerial problems. Under the craft flow system, variable costs (made up mainly of materials and labour) are a high proportion of total costs, so that increases in production would lead to greatly increased costs which took some time to convert into sales revenue. Vehicle producers could suffer acutely from what we would identify today as cash flow problems, even in the upswing of the trade cycle. The history of the British vehicle industry between 1920 and 1960 reveals that many basically sound companies (in terms of the qualities of their products and their ability to innovate) periodically experienced cash flow problems. With surprising regularity, bankers were called upon to assist companies; and their involvement was typically very costly. Then as now, the tolerance of British bankers for long term involvement in companies is low, and the quality of their insight into the long term prospects for specialized manufacturers is questionable. However, recurrent crises in companies were seen, in some ways correctly, as problems of existing management. Typically engineer-managers were blamed for a lack of general managerial foresight or acumen. Expedients undertaken to solve managerial problems in the wake of crisis often involved the reduction of the executive powers and responsibilities of engineers (especially on the boards of companies) and the increased influence of financiers and accountants. For example, despite the acknowledged genius of Herbert Austin, the engineer who originated the Austin Seven, one of the few vehicles to break through into very large sales between the wars, he was removed from executive responsibility for his own Company in the 1920s, as a response to a cash flow crisis. In this sort of way the engineer manager ceded power and authority to the accountant on the boards of companies.

In a different way the contractions of markets that periodically occurred in the vehicle industry also contributed to this trend. Again basically because of the cost structure of the industry, effective cost reduction in the downturn would necessarily involve shedding labour. For a number of reasons this was accomplished only with difficulty, and was something that engineers were often reluctant to undertake. Failure to shed labour might lead to crises of profitability. But shedding labour too readily would both lead to the alienation of a key productive resource, on whose willing cooperation production depended, and lead to difficulties in building up production again once trading conditions changed. What has been labelled labour hoarding, in essence a failure to shed skilled labour despite lack of work, was common practice during periods when the production sequences of models were inadequately coordinated. Such practices could also, however, cut deeply into profitability; and indeed could also contribute to financial crisis, with similar results to the cash flow crises already described. But whether provoked by temporary cash flow problems or problems of profitablity, the results for companies would often be the same - that of removing engineers from the control of companies and their replacement by accountants or non-specialists.

186

Practical control by engineers, not only of production but of what passed for strategic management, was a reality for much vehicle manufacture in Britain between the wars. For much of that time, also, the majority of production had been undertaken in a relatively large number of specialized manufacturing companies which were, apart from periodic problems, profitable. After 1950 or so, the tendency for limiting the levels of new investment becomes increasingly noticeable; that is, voluntary restriction of investment. There was also a series of amalgamations between companies. Cutting back on investment and making amalgamations were both undertaken as a response to periodic problems of profitability. Whilst amalgamations may have staved off immediate difficulties, they did not solve the underlying problems of the industry. With a few exceptions, mostly in aircraft manufacture, rationalizations and amalgamations cannot be regarded as having been successful in the longer term. But whether internal reorganization or reorganization through amalgamation, was selected as the remedy to the problems of vehicle producers, changes in the composition of boards of directors, many of them removing engineers from the highest levels of decision-making, were a common accompaniment of change. The progressive exclusion from strategic control of the companies in which they organized production, helps to explain the origins of the defensive professionalism of British production engineers (Child et al., 1983). It is also a fact of great importance for the future of this branch of British industry.

The fact that accountants and other non-engineers found a decisive role in the management of companies as a result of the supposed managerial incompetence of engineers, tended to establish and perpetuate an exclusive division of labour amongst senior managers. Accountancy - and financial expertise generally - was defined as the antidote to the failure of management based on engineering, promoting the view that accountancy rather than engineering was a more reliable basis for executive decisions. Hence, engineering considerations were increasingly not addressed when the future of companies was considered, and strategic decisions were taken on considerations of the likely rate of return on assets already committed to production. Recruitment to senior management tended to be in terms of general commercial expertise and/or accountancy experience. Hence, from this time, it becomes necessary for engineers seeking careers in higher management to shed their professional identity and frames of reference. However, for this very reason, it is doubtful whether the general management that typically emerged in vehicle manufacturing companies was really qualified to diagnose the basic problems of the industry, and to make appropriate decisions as to what needed to be done. Certainly, accountancy is only a system of recording and rational calculation, lacking the general concepts and value commitments which would qualify it as a general system of strategic analysis. In short, accountancy is not (without qualification and addition) an adequate basis for insightful strategic management. The tendency for engineers to be excluded from strategic management and the emergence of a general management function in which both financial and management accountants played roles, has had some debilitating long-term effects on this branch of manufacturing.

Some theoretical conclusions

Much of what has been set out here as constituting the problems of vehicle manufacture in this country has been partially recognized in other writings commentating on British manufacturing and its problems.

Peter Armstrong has written about manufacturing in ways that have direct relevance. Armstrong argues that the division of labour between groups within management will be decided by the effectiveness with which they develop and control resources. Among the resources of managerial groups are professional techniques which allow the effective control of enterprises. By developing such things as ways of disciplining of labour, techniques for the coordination of activities or the limitation of waste, managerial groups simultaneously make contributions to the control of organizations and to securing their professional standing in management hierarchies. Groups which develop effective techniques can be seen to mount what Armstrong labels collective mobility projects, by pursuing (more or less self-consciously) policies of self-promotion based on their exclusive provision of effective expertise. Armstrong is quite clear that, in his view, collective mobility projects are structurally contained, and only successful to the extent that they facilitate capital accumulation. Within these assumptions he argues that the mobility of production engineers is limited because they have attempted to found their general expertise on techniques that could be and were to be appropriated by other groups. He gives two examples that are relevant in this context. Firstly, there is the engineer's control of workers through job content analysis and deskilling of jobs (Armstrong, 1984). According to Armstrong, engineers in this country originated and pioneered the development of these techniques following the lead of Taylor and others in the USA. However, these techniques were not made integral to engineering expertise but were detached and appropriated by a new group of specialist functionaries and consultants (work study engineers). The second example was the way in which production engineers pioneered the development of the basic techniques of cost accountancy. Again these techniques were appropriated by another group - the already powerful profession of accountancy (Armstrong, 1987b; see also Armstrong, 1987a).

We agree with Armstrong that the effective control of a broad spectrum of activities was not retained successfully by British engineers, which explains their lack of a strategic role in manufacturing enterprises. Moreover, the exclusion of production managers from strategic control of enterprises is explained by their failure to compete successfully with other groups within management. However, we suggest some crucial differences of emphasis. It was the inability of engineers to deal very effectively with some short-term problems arising from the character of the market for their products which led them to be excluded by other managerial groups from the dominant coalition of managers within companies. On the basis of our case material, it is clear that the engineers did not apply a Tayloristic type of job content analysis in any but the most marginal ways, because these techniques attacked craft organization of tasks which were the basis of the craft flow production system. It is hardly surprising therefore that these techniques were applied, if they were applied, by other groups than production engineers. There is more to support Armstrong's second idea. It is entirely understandable that engineers, faced with the production problems we have described, such high inventory and labour costs and cyclical demand, would develop the first principles of cost accounting. On the other hand, these procedures were difficult to integrate with other ideas about organization also held by this occupation. Clearly there was greater affinity of these ideas with established accounting procedures, and, for this reason, it was relatively easy for accountants to appropriate these techniques. The problem is that Armstrong does not provide reasons why the engineers were not able to defend themselves from other groups within management, while our approach does so more adequately. What is also missing from Armstrong's account is any sense that different arrangements for the division of labour between managerial groups will be different in terms of their consequences. In our view it is not the case that different ways of organizing the division of labour are equally functional.

Winston Higgins and Stuart Clegg have clearly grasped the point that different forms of the managerial division of labour may vary greatly in their effects on the overall effectiveness of management. They have argued in a valuable paper (1988) that competing modes of enterprise calculation (which are rational considered separately) need not combine in complementary ways. In this suggestion the authors are repeating the orthodox Weberian point that the increasing employment of rational systems of thought need not produce an increase in general or substantive rationality. Indeed, these authors argue that competing systems of rational thinking within enterprises are implicated in the decline of manufacturing in Britain and some other countries such as the United States and Australia. In their paper, Higgins and Clegg veer between a number of possible ways in which forms of calculation may contradict each other. However, they do suggest that the new forms of profit centred thinking which have arisen in American and British publicly quoted companies under the auspices of financial accountants, contradict and submerge considerations of investment planning and R&D, which are based on much longer time cycles. This, we suggest, is similar to our explanation of the effects of the managerial division of labour in British vehicle production. In our view, neither the expertise of production managers nor that of accountants and financiers were entirely adequate to solving the problems of manufacturing in this sector. However, by being unable to deal with short run financial problems (which they had little competency to solve), engineers effectively excluded themselves from strategic management, and so from being able to contribute to the solution of strategic issues (to which their expertise was relevant). At the same time, because of their ability to solve these same short-term but pressing financial problems, accountants were promoted to control of strategic management (for which their expertise was not appropriate). These very different systems of calculation could not be combined in the absence of some over-arching framework of assumptions and values, leading at best to inconsistency in the rules used to organise manufacturing activities, and at worst to the subordination of production to a narrow accountancy regime. What was manifestly needed was a more general framework of thought within which the different priorities of engineers and accountants might be effectively reconciled. This was absent.

In the writings of Karel Williams and his collaborators, the idea that there are typical contradictions in the British mode of manufacturing has also been given some consideration. Their project has been to expose the peculiarities of the British form of enterprise calculation (Williams et al., 1983). It is clear that, considered as a system of roles, there are some recurrent structural contradictions in British management. It is this that helps to explain why, as this team suggest in a recent paper:

> The British management problem is that, within their areas of discretion, British managers consistently take poor decisions about the priority of different problems and execute their strategies in a way that is generally inept (Williams et al., 1983, p. 89).

We agree with this, but think Williams and his team are insufficiently aware of how this ineptitude arises or how it constitutes a problem. Clearly it would be a mistake to think of British managers as being wilfully stupid and so failing to adopt obvious solutions to problems. It would be wrong to think that they have somehow deliberately failed to make investments and wilfully wound down their industries. The problems of British management in the case examined here are system failures, in that the system of roles that developed in British management was simply inappropriate to the tasks that were being faced. The case study materials on which this essay is based suggest that the theory of management is deficient if it does not take into account the possibility of critical failures in systems of management that are induced by unfortunate historical contingencies but which have no automatic solution. What is appropriate to do can appear differently to different parties, but, more than this, the consequences of the interaction between parties with different conceptions of the way forward need not be particularly constructive.

References

Ackroyd, S and A Whitaker, (1990), 'Manufacturing Decline and the organizations of manufacture in Britain' in *Restructuring for Economic Flexibility,* Stewart, P. Garrahan, P. and Crowther, S. (eds), Avebury, Aldershot.

Adams, D. R. (1943), 'The Education and Training of Aeronautical Engineers', *Journal of the Royal Aeronautical Society*, Vol. 47, pp. 318-375.

Anon, (1943), 'The Education and Training of Aeronautical Engineers', *Journal of the Royal Aeronautical Society*, Vol. 48, October 1943, pp. 318-75.

Anon, (1948), *Who's Who in Aviation*, Political and Economic Planning, London.

Anon, (1949), *Motor Vehicles*, Political and Economic Planning, London.

Armstrong, P. (1984), 'Competition Between the Organizational Professions and the Evolution of Management Control Strategies', in *Work, Employment and Unemployment*, Thompson, K. (ed.), Open University Press, Milton Keynes.

Armstrong, P. (1986), 'Management Control Strategies and Inter-professional Competition' in *Managing the Labour Process*, Knights, D. and Wilmott, H., (eds), Gower, Aldershot.

Armstrong, P. (1987a), 'Engineers Management and Trust', *Work Employment and Society*, Vol. 4, (2), pp. 421-40.

Armstrong, P. (1987b), 'The Rise of Accounting Controls in British Capitalist Enterprises', *Accounting Organizations and Society*, Vol. 12, (5), pp. 415-436.

Beames, H. P. M. 'The Reorganisation of the Crewe Locomotive Works', *Proceedings of the Institution of Mechanical Engineers*, Vol. 114, March, pp. 245-263.

Bellon, B. (1990), *Mercedes In Peace and War: German Automobile Workers, 1903-1945*, Columbia University Press, New York.

Bond, R. (1953), 'The Organization and Control of Locomotive Repairs', *Journal of the Institute of Locomotive Engineers*, Vol. 232, pp. 175-213.

Bond, R. (1975), *A Lifetime with Locos,* Goose, Cambridge.

Brown, C. J. F. and Sheriff, T. (1978), 'De-industrialization: a background paper' in *De-industrialization*, (ed.), Blackaby, F. , Heinneman, London.

Chandler, A. (1977), *The Visible Hand,* Harvard University Press, Cambridge, Mass.

Child, J. (1972), 'Organizational Structure, Environment and Performance: The Role of Strategic Choice', *Sociology*, Vol. 6, (1), pp. 1-22.

Child, J., Fores, M., Glover, I. and Lawrence, P. (1983), 'A price to pay? Professionalism and Work Organization in Britain and Germany', *Sociology*, Vol. 17, (1), pp. 63-78.

Church, R., (1994), *The Rise and Fall of the British Motor Industry*, Macmillan, London.

Coates, D. (1994), *The Question of UK Decline*, Harvester-Wheatsheaf, Hemel Hempstead.

Edgerton, D. (1991), *England and the Aeroplane*, Macmillan, London.

Forrester, D. A. (1977), *Schmalenbach and After*, Strathclyde Convergencies, Glasgow.

Fowler, H. Sir (1929), 'Locomotive Repairs', *Journal of the Institute of Transport*, Vol. 11, pp. 59-89.

Gispen, K. (1989) *New Profession, Old Order*, CUP, Cambridge.

Glover, I. and Kelly, M. (1987), *Engineers in Britain*, Unwin Hyman, London.

Handley Page Ltd. (1947), 'Technical Training at Handley Page', Internal Company Document.

Harvey-Bailey, A. (1985), *Rolls-Royce: Hives the Quiet Tiger*, Sir Henry Royce Memorial Foundation, Paulersbury, Northants.

Higgins, W. and Clegg, S. (1988), 'Enterprise Calculation and Manufacturing Decline', *Organization Studies*, Vol. 9, (1), pp. 69-90.

Hirst, P. and Zeitlin, J. (1989a), 'Flexible Specialisation and the Competitive Failure of UK Manufacturing', *Political Quarterly*, Vol. 62, (2), pp. 164-178.

Hirst, P. and Zeitlin, J. (1989b), *Reversing Industrial Decline*, Basil Blackwell, Oxford.

Hudson, C. (1969), 'The Use of Computers in the Production of Locomotive Repair Schedules', *Journal of the Institute of Locomotive Engineers*, Vol. 53, pp. 167-177.

Ingham, G. (1984), *Capitalism Divided?*, Macmillan, London.

King, P. (1989), *The Motor Men*, Quiller, London.

Landes, D. (1969), *The Unbound Prometheus*, CUP, Cambridge.

Lane, C. (1988), 'Industrial Change in Europe: The Pursuit of Flexible Specialisation in Britain and West Germany', *Work Employment and Society*, Vol. 2, (2), pp. 140-168.

Lane, C. (1991), 'Vocational Training and New Production Concepts in Germany', *Industrial Relations Journal*, Vol 21/4, pp. 247-259.

Larkin, E. (1934), 'The Progressive System of Workshop Training and the Embryo Locomotive Engineer', *Journal of the Institute of Locomotive Engineers*, Vol. 124, pp. 218-252.

Larkin, E. (1979), *Memoirs of a Railway Engineer*, Mechanical Engineering Press, London.

Lash, S. and Urry, J. (1988), *The End of Organised Capitalism*, Polity, Oxford.

Lemon, E. (1930), 'Railway Amalgamation and Its Effects on the LMSR Workshops', *Journal of the Institute of Transport*.

Lewchuk, W. (1987), *American Technology and the British Motor Vehicle Industry*, CUP, Cambridge.

Littler, C. (1982), *The Development of the Labour Process in Capitalist Societies*, Gower, Aldershot.

Littler, C. R. and Salaman, G. (1984), *Class at Work: The Design, Allocation and Control of Jobs*, Batsford, London.

Lumley, R., (1992), 'Business Education and Employment Relations: The Case of Germany', *Industrial Relations Journal*, Vol. 23/4, pp. 284-292.

Maxcy, G. and Silberston, A. (1959), *The Motor Industry*, George Allen and Unwin, London.

McKinlay, A. and Zeitlin, J. (1986), 'The Meanings of Organizational Prerogative: Industrial Relations and the Organization of Work in British Engineering, 1880-1939', *Business History*, Vol. 31/2, pp. 32-47.

McKinnon-Wood, R. (1935), *Aircraft Manufacture: A Description of the Industry and Proposals for its Socialisation*, New Fabian Research Bureau, London.

Mountford, E. R. (1980), *Swindon Reminiscences*, D. Bradford Barton, Truro.

Oliver, N. and Wilkinson, B. (1992), *The Japanisation of British Industry*, Basil Blackwell, Oxford.

Pollard, S. (1965), *The Genesis of British Management*, Penguin, Harmondsworth.

Political and Economic Planning (PEP), (1949), *Motor Vehicles*, Political and Economic Planning, London.

Rabinach, A. (1981), *The Human Motor: Energy, Fatigue and the Origins of Modernity*, Basic Books, New York.

Reed, B. (1982), *Crewe Locomotive works and Its Men*, David and Charles, London.

Richardson, K. (1977), *The British Motor Industry 1896-1939*, Macmillan, London.

Robinson, D. C. (1949), 'Some Developments in Aircraft Production', *Journal of the Royal Aeronautical Society*, Vol. 53, January, pp. 36-66.

Smith, C. (1990), 'Review Article: How are Engineers Formed?', *Work Employment and Society*, Vol. 3, (4), pp. 451-470.

Sohn-Rethel, A. (1987), *The Economy and Class Structure of German Fascism*, Free Association Books, London.

Tolliday, S. (1992), 'Management and Labour in Britain 1896-1939', in *Between Fordism and Flexibility*, Tolliday, S. and Zeitlin, J. (eds), Berg., Oxford.

Trebilcock, C. (1981), *The Industrialization of the Continental Powers*, Longman, London.

Ware, M. E. (1976), *Making of the Motor Car 1895-1930*, Moorlands, Ashbourne.

Weber, Max 1968 *Economy and Society*, Free Press, New York.

Williams, K., Williams, J. and Haslam, C. (1989), 'Facing up to Manufacturing Failure', in *Reversing Industrial Decline*, Hirst, P. and Zeitlin, J. (eds), Basil Blackwell, Oxford.

Williams, K. et al., (1990), 'The Hollowing Out of British Manufacturing and Its Implications for Policy', *Economy and Society*, Vol. 19, (4), pp. 456-470.

Williams, K., Williams, J. and Thomas, D. (1983), *Why Are the British Bad at Manufacturing?*, Routledge, London.

Wood, R. M. (1935), *Aircraft Manufacture: Description of the Industry and Proposals for the Socialisation*, New Fabian Research Bureau, London.

9 New public management and professions

Ian Kirkpatrick, Richard Whipp and
Annette Davies

Introduction

In recent years there has been a surge of interest in the emergence of so-called 'New Public Management' (NPM) (Hood, 1991; Stewart and Walsh, 1992; Ferlie, 1994; Dunleavy and Hood, 1994). Often the concept of NPM is used to describe the range of changes and upheavals, brought about by successive conservative governments, in the organization and management of the public sector (Dunleavy and Hood, 1994). One of the main issues raised by these writers is the impact of NPM on professional occupations which dominate the public sector in employment terms. These groups, it is argued, are now increasingly subservient to the *diktats* of all powerful management. Moreover, the legitimacy of their privileged role has also been challenged by a powerful 'New Right' intellectual critique which: 'questioned and substantially damaged the credibility of the two basic instruments of collectivist welfare policy - bureaucracy and professionals. They are billed as self interested, self-serving, inefficient and ineffective' (Wilding, 1992, p. 202). According to Crompton, the right of professional experts to 'monopolistic, or oligopolistic protection' (Crompton, 1990, p. 158) has, as a consequence of this critique, been substantially undermined.

Given these claims, a key question concerns the extent to which relations between professions and management have changed. Has there been a marked shift in the balance of power between the two? Alternatively, it could be argued that the impact of recent developments has been exaggerated. For some observers, despite the sustained ideological assault on professions over the last decade, NPM has not transformed professional-management relations substantially. They point to the uneven development of NPM and the way certain professions have successfully incorporated or resisted managerial imperatives (Ackroyd, 1994).

The aim of this chapter is to contribute to this debate about the impact of NPM on public sector professions. We ask whether there has been a weakening of professional power and influence *vis-a-vis* management, some kind of accommodation, or both? To illustrate our arguments, we will refer to the experiences of two well organized professional occupations - Consultants and Academic Librarians - in Health and Higher Education respectively. These groups reveal markedly different management-profession relations and different responses to NPM.

Before considering these cases, it is useful to rehearse briefly the role of professions in the public sector prior to NPM. In particular, one should consider the nature of relations between professions and bureaucracy. Subsequent sections review the debate over NPM, looking both at real developments and normative claims. As numerous accounts of NPM reveal, it is not clear whether the phenomenon represents a coherent project, linked to a set of actual changes in managerial roles, or a more diffuse phenomenon with numerous contradictory variants (Harrow and Wilcocks, 1990; Ferlie, 1994). In this chapter we argue against attempts to think of NPM as a coherent set of practices and normative ideas. Rather we believe that the NPM concept embraces a number of different elements, although two, the 'executive' and 'market' dimensions, have been dominant. These dimensions are similar to Ferlie's (1994) first two expressions of NPM and loosely correspond to broader macroshifts in government policy towards the public sector. Following this, we will describe how NPM has, or might, alter relations between professions and management.

Professions in the public sector

The public sector has traditionally been a prime site for the development of professions. The postwar expansion of the welfare state saw the incorporation of powerful 'liberal' professions (such as clinicians) and a proliferation of new 'public service' professions in Social Care, Education, Local Government and Health. Most of these services are still heavily dominated by professions in employment terms. In the NHS, for example, almost half of those employed claim professional status (Harrison and Pollitt, 1994). Many occupations have consciously modelled themselves on the medical profession, forming their own extra-organizational collegiate associations, and achieving degrees of market closure through a monopoly over the formal accreditation of expertise. Even the most peripheral groups, with the state's backing, have achieved impressive levels of external closure (Cousins, 1987, pp. 91-113). In the workplace, professional self-regulation and autonomy were upheld partly by claims of cognitive indeterminacy and to be working in the client's best interests.

Generally speaking, professions acted as the intermediaries of state welfare policy. To do so they were allowed considerable operational and to some extent, 'strategic autonomy', which amounted to deciding service priorities and, in some instances such as Health, resource allocation issues. At the same time however 'public service' professions were 'organizationally encapsulated', dependent on bureaucratic structures which ensured a vertical division of labour between themselves and other subordinate occupations. This same bureaucratic structure also minimized conflict between professions by imposing a horizontal division of labour between different functional specialisms.

Professions and bureaucracy

It is often assumed that the interests of public service professions and bureaucracy are diametrically opposed. Many sociologists have talked about conflicts which are inevitable, 'in-built' and usually submerged (Child, 1982). Kornhauser (1962), for example described this as a conflict between 'professional autonomy versus integration of professional activity in organizations' (Kornhauser, 1962, p. 215). Whereas bureaucracy demanded conformity to impersonal rules and hierarchial authority, the inclination of professions was to resist such control and demand autonomy. Professions resisted incorporation by claiming that task indeterminacy and client needs required self-regulation and freedom from external constraints. Their power was also supported by abstract knowledge (acquired through formal education) which was used as a resource to project the 'appearance' of cognitive superiority. Professional work, it was argued, could not be standardized or controlled through bureaucratic rules and routines, nor could it be evaluated by non-experts (Raelin, 1985).

These assumptions, although useful at one level do need to be qualified in the context of the public sector. As Larson (1977) argues, the assumption of an inbuilt conflict between professions and bureaucracy is often overstated. Such notions are based on unrealistic comparisons between the mythical status of 'free' liberal professions (medicine and law) and the reality of professional incorporation in modern organizations. This view ignores what Larson describes as the 'underlying structural affinities between profession and bureaucracy' (1977, p. 199). Indeed, most professions have some link with bureaucracy - even if it is only through the University. As mentioned above, public service professions have been particularly dependent on bureaucratic structures which acted as the 'matrices of their occupational specializations' (op. cit. p. 188). In these contexts, both professions and managers shared common career objectives - of career advancement through the formal hierarchy - and both relied on impersonal authority structures to assert their dominance over clients (Larson, 1977). Given this, one should not necessarily assume that the interests of professions and bureaucracy are opposed. There exist both sources of accommodation and common interest as well as conflict.

The accommodation between public service professions and bureaucracy was greatly enhanced by the realtive weakness of management (or 'administration'). Even where large numbers of administrators worked alongside professionals, the emphasis was often on the passive model of 'administered professions'. The job of the administrator was simply to support professional decisions about the nature and quantity of service provision. The NHS, for example, was characterized by a kind of 'consensus' management approach (Klein, 1983; Harrison et al., 1992). Administrators lacked power or the authority to challenge directly the interests of powerful professional groups (especially Clinicians) and were able only to maintain administrative frameworks around them (Freidson, 1970). Much of the time, open confrontations - over resources and rules - were avoided using various informal accommodation strategies (Goss, 1963). Another aspect of consensus was the shared 'custodial orientation' of professions and administrators; many of the latter were themselves exprofessionals (Ackroyd et al., 1989). Management, where it existed as a separate occupational grouping of any significance, was weak relative to the power and status of professional decision makers. Emphasis was on a conciliatory role; public service professions, not managers, were the key agents of state welfare policy.

The emergence of NPM

The advent of a Conservative administration in 1979 heralded a radical shift in government policy towards the public sector. This centred on a rejection of the Keynsian welfare state consensus which had dominated British politics since the Second World War (Gamble, 1988; Hall, 1988). Informed by a neo-Liberal intellectual critique, conservative governments embarked upon a project of transforming the state's role in the provision of welfare services (Kirkpatrick and Martinez-Lucio, 1995). Demands for fiscal retrenchment (which had emerged in the late 1970s) were coupled with the desire to re-commodify and radically change the way in which the public services were organized (Cousins, 1987). This project was however uneven and disjointed. In particular, two broad phases of its development can be identified.

The first phase lasted from 1979 until the late 1980s. During this period, government reforms concentrated on privatization and the imposition of tight controls over public spending. Emphasis was on economy, top down financial control, accountability and the use of performance indicators and external audits (Carter, 1991). The second phase began in the late 1980s and involved a shift in priorities: restructuring those parts of the public sector which could not be privatized, along market lines. The objective of this restructuring was to transform the state's role in the delivery of welfare services to one of 'steering' as opposed to 'rowing' (Osbourne and Gaebler, 1992). Specifically, it involved creating new arrangements through which the planning of services was separated from their actual delivery. This meant breaking up vertically integrated hierarchies and replacing them with a nexus of contracts negotiated through a 'quasi-market' of (public, private and voluntary) providers. A depoliticization of welfare services was also envisaged, so that their delivery become a managerial task, separate from the political job of planning, allocating resources and deciding overall priorities.

The creation of purchaser provider functions in the National Health service, Compulsory Competitive Tendering in Local Government and an increasingly mixed economy of social care (widening the role of private and voluntary agents) are well documented examples of this. Such policies were overlaid and legitimated by a rhetoric of quality improvement, consumer rights and diffuse notions of 'excellence' and cultural change (Harrison and Pollitt, 1994).

Although conservative governments emphasized managerial reform throughout, the nature and style of management which was practiced altered as the project unfolded. Broadly speaking, we argue that an 'executive' dimension of NPM developed in tandem with the first phase of government reforms. Priorities of fiscal control, efficiency and accountability called for a stronger, more 'rational', line management. In the late 1980s, however, the second phase of the government's reform project saw the development of a 'market oriented' version of NPM. Here the emphasis was on a more decentralized approach towards management. Indirect control, as opposed to top down control through hierarchies, would be achieved through contracts which allowed managers greater 'freedom within boundaries' (Hoggett, 1991, 1994). In this second phase, NPM also adopts a rhetoric of quality improvement and cultural change. The role of management is seen as developing service specifications, negotiating contracts and monitoring performance (Wilson, 1993).

Overall the two phases of the conservative government's reforms rested on different normative ideas about management roles, objectives and styles. The two phases also implied contrasting institutional environments for management, one characterized by vertically integrated hierarchies (top down control) and the other, by decentralized networks or quasi-markets (remote control).

Although these broad generalizations are useful, they require qualification. Two issues in particular need clarification. Firstly, one must take into account the uneven development of structural and managerial changes across the public sector. Quasi-markets and contracting arrangements have, for example, developed a lot further in the NHS and Local Government than in Higher Education. Secondly, there are also considerable gaps between the prescriptions of NPM and management practices. These issues can not be resolved in this chapter but must be borne in mind when attempting to describe changes in management-profession relations.

New public management

As far as conservative governments were concerned, the key agent of their reforms was to be a stronger and more assertive new public management (Hood, 1991; Gunn, 1988). Only by establishing the authority of managers over professionals and other recalcitrant interests could the state effectively drive through its reforms (Stewart and Walsh, 1992). In this section the aim is to map out the resulting two dimensions of NPM: the 'executive' and 'market'. Each dimension loosely corresponds to the broader phases of conservative government policy described above. Both also represent a distinct shift away from the model of passive 'administrative' management.

The first concerns the 'executive' dimension of NPM. This was typified by the Financial Management Initiative in the Civil Service and Griffiths reforms (1983) in the NHS. The object of these (and other) initiatives was to empower the management of public services in order to achieve control over expenditure and perhaps also improve efficiency. Usually this meant setting up management boards in hospitals, local authority housing departments and schools, and devolving budgetary responsibility to managers of cost centres (Ackroyd and Soothill, 1994). At the same time, management was held accountable for ensuring the value-for-money of services which were extensively monitored through batteries of performance indicators (Ferlie, 1994).

The new management was based on the ideological assumption that public sector bureaucracies were inherently inefficient and wasteful. Strong management, modelled on the private sector, had to be established, it was argued, to overcome these deficiencies. According to Aucoin (1990):

> The very term 'management' is one that derives from private sector experience, denoting as it does a concern for the use of resources to achieve results in contrast to the presumed focus of 'administration' as the adherence to formalized processes and procedures. Public sector bureaucrats, in this comparison, are perceived essentially as administrators, and thus are considered inferior to their private sector equivalents who 'manage' their organizations (p. 118).

The model of 'passive administration' was then to be replaced with proactive 'management' which would assert its 'right to manage' and unilateral prerogative to establish organizational goals and objectives. For some, this executive dimension of New Public Management was essentially a carbon copy of 'neo-Taylorist' management (Pollitt, 1990a). That is, it emphasized top down 'command and control' through established hierarchies (Ferlie, 1994), objective setting and cost minimisation.

Executive NPM developed unevenly across the public sector. The most important area was the NHS where a general management hierarchy was established. In other sectors, for example, Education and Social Services, the emphasis was more on improving the 'management' of services by professional staff, rather than recruiting a new management 'cadre' to run them (Ackroyd and Soothill, 1994).

The second strand of new public management, what we term the 'market' dimension, developed from the 'executive', but adopted a more diverse set of ideological claims. Management, in this context, was no longer strictly about command and control through a formal hierarchy. The emphasis instead was on designing service specifications, negotiating contracts and finding new ways to influence and direct the behaviour of providers. This required a wider range of

200

skills, beyond those of the cost controlling executive (Appelby et al., 1990; Wilson, 1993). Management objectives had to be achieved in an environment where operational decisions are decentralized and strategic (resource based) decisions, highly centralized (Hoggett, 1991).

A further aspect of this 'market' dimension of NPM was the rhetoric of cultural change, service 'quality' and notions of the 'sovereign consumer' (Keat and Abercrombie, 1991; Du Gay and Salaman, 1992). Public managers, the argument went, were accountable to the individual consumers of services and responsible for ensuring that prescribed standards of quality were met. According to Pollitt (1988):

> Successfully to address the consumer dimension requires not merely the acquisition of techniques but also the repeated proclamation of a new management philosophy with a view, eventually to an actual shift in organizational cultures (p.121).

Cultural change was thought necessary in some cases to overcome the 'dysfunctions' of bureaucracy, making it more open and responsive to the perceived 'needs' of internal and external 'customers' (Du Gay, 1994). Such arguments were associated with techniques such as Total Quality Management, internal marketing, Customer Care and Human Resource Management.

New public management and professions

The task of describing the changing relationship between professions and management in the public sector is bound to be extremely difficult given the characteristics of NPM presented here and its uneven development. This section considers how relations between professions and managers have changed as a result of NPM. We also suggest that the nature of these relations under executive and market dimensions of NPM will be different. Some examples are provided, although these mainly concern executive NPM. Given the more recent emergence of 'market' NPM it is less clear how this will impact on professional roles in practice.

The first point to make is that all versions of NPM were informed by New Right thinking which stressed the wastefulness and self-interested nature of public sector professionalism (Burrage, 1992). Anti professionalism was then an important element of the ideology of NPM although, as Ackroyd and Soothill (1994) suggest, it may not be the case that professionals were the main targets of government reforms. It is likely that instead professions were 'encountered merely as impediments to the development of rationalized managerial control' so that reforms were 'pro-managerial rather than anti-professional'.

When applied in practice, a more assertive brand of 'executive' management did provoke negative reactions from professions. As mentioned, executive management

201

represented a move away from the model of passive administration to one which stressed exclusive 'managerial' control over objective setting and resource allocation. By the same token management was to be held more accountable for the outcomes reinforced by performance-related-pay and fixed term contracts. In principle, this kind of management must in some ways interfere with professional objectives of self-regulation and autonomy. According to Lee and Piper (1988):

> Controls other than self-controls are needed to protect the organization from the potential profligacy of professionals and their occasionally myopic belief in their own and their professions' overriding importance (p.124).

Under executive NPM, public services were to be provided through the agency of managers. Professional expertise had to be 'on tap' rather than 'on top' (Pollitt, 1990a).

One might logically expect, under executive NPM, for there to be greater managerial intervention in resource decision making issues surrounding professional work, accompanied by challenges to the legitimacy of professional self-regulation. In some cases, attempts were made to impose bureaucratic controls on professions, standardizing their work and closely monitoring performance (Davies and Kirkpatrick, 1995b). Indeed, with growing pressure in the 1980s to control costs, some professional activities did come under closer scrutiny, for example, in the NHS following the Resource Management Initiative and clinical audits (Harrison and Pollitt, 1994).

The extent to which conflict between professions and management actually intensified varied according to a number of factors. Of central importance was the power base of professions and how far their expert knowledge was technically susceptible to measurement, routinization and reskilling. Much also depended on managerial resources and willingness to challenge professions head on. There was, for example, far greater accommodation, between managers and powerful professions such as clinicians than was the case with other less organized groups (Pollitt et al., 1991; Harrison et al., 1992). Another variable determining levels of conflict was whether executive management was imposed via a managerial cadre, or through the profession itself. Ackroyd and Soothill (1994) suggest that the nature of conflict varied greatly as a result of this. NPM had far less impact in contexts where 'management' was introduced through the professions, as in Higher Education, than was the case in organizations were a separate management cadre was established (as in the NHS).

So far, we have concentrated on the likely impact of executive management on professions. It is far less clear however how the second, 'market', dimension of NPM will effect profession-management relations. Here there is potential both for heightened conflict and ideological accommodation.

There is now evidence to suggest that the reorganization of public services around contracts and quasi-markets is starting to intensify pressures on managers to control costs and ensure value for money (Bennett and Ferlie, 1994; Deakin and Walsh,

1994). This is especially the case where contract specifications and performance standards are being extensively monitored by purchasing authorities. Pressure to secure contracts and meet specifications may force professionals themselves to address 'managerial' concerns as they too become absorbed with objectives of securing efficiency and value for money. In some sectors this is already leading to changes in the culture of provider organizations and to an environment characterized by low trust and declining lateral, or collegiate, relations between purchasers and providers (Charlesworth et al., 1994).

Closely linked to these developments is the rhetoric of quality improvement. In some instances, management, under pressure to secure or retain contracts, has started to employ a rhetoric of quality to legitimate new interventions into professional work domains. In doing so the aim is to ensure professional compliance with managerial objectives (Pollitt, 1990b). Management may, for example, use notions of transparency and consumer responsiveness to justify attacks on professional self-regulation (Walsh, 1991). As Pfeffer and Coote argue:

> Managers will no longer administer services within the policies and budgets laid down by a particular authority; instead they will organize the delivery of contracted services, within quality and quantity specifications to one of a number of clients...the influence of managers has greatly increased. One of the main effects of the changes has been to begin to limit the power of the 'caring' professionals (1991, p.12).

The 'market' dimension of NPM could therefore mean intensified pressures on managers to interfere in professional work. It also provides them with a stock of ideological resources, such as the rhetoric of quality improvement, which they can use against professions to undermine the legitimacy of their claims for self-regulation and autonomy.

However, given its more diverse ideological content, the market dimension of NPM could also create new opportunities for accommodation and integration between professions and management. The rhetoric of 'excellence', for example, implies flat structures, team working and greater freedom and empowerment for staff who possess shared cultural orientations. As Hoggett suggests:

> some aspects of the rhetoric of the new management - those which emphasize team working, encourage initiative, speak about harnessing human resources - are in many ways congruent with more traditional 'collegiate' forms of professional organization (1991, p. 255).

Under the market dimension of NPM, therefore, the emphasis may not be on making professions subservient to line management. It could instead involve finding new ways of incorporating professions into managerial priorities and relying increasingly on indirect or 'cultural' control. Professions then retain operational autonomy within a more regulated environment in which the overall priorities are set according to managerial concerns.

Taking our argument as a whole, new public management can be understood in terms of two dimensions: the 'executive' and the 'market'. These dimensions have a differential effect on the outcomes of professional-management relations. The former may increase the pressure on managers to control the costs of professional work within existing bureaucratic, or only partially decentralized, organizations. The 'market' dimension of NPM however suggests a wider variety of outcomes. Conflict may be intensified as providers are placed under pressure to perform and meet contract specifications. Management also has a wider stock of ideological resources which it can draw upon and use to challenge the power of professions. At the same time though, there are aspects of the ideology of 'market' NPM which point towards accommodation or integration between professions and management.

Admittedly, this is an early and very broad picture of NPM and its likely impact on professions. The reality is bound to be more complex as the relationship between professions and management works itself out differently in each situation. The outcomes of change are likely to be manifold. Accordingly the aim of the next section is to look at the experiences of two well established professions in the face of NPM. The two cases are also indicative examples of different structural relations between professions and management; they are suggestive of the divergent experience of groups across the public sector. Whereas in Health (Consultants), NPM has been introduced via a separate managerial occupations, in Higher Education (Academic Librarians) it has been promoted through the ranks of the profession itself.

NHS consultants

Recent work on the NHS has tended to confirm the capacity of consultants to withstand the threats to their professional strength. Research suggests that in broad terms this may well hold for the present, but that the forces contained within the process of market driven change promise greater challenges in the future (Kitchener and Whipp, 1995).

This section draws on a study conducted in 1991-93 of the introduction of market relations in the NHS in England and Wales. The research involved comparative analysis of hospital units attempting to cope with increased market pressure. Four sites were chosen for intensive integration using interviews, observation and a range of primary and secondary sources. The four hospitals had been experiencing common market pressures from the mid-1980s, starting with income generation schemes through to the internal market process, and Trust status.

The key finding of the project, taken together with the results of other work, is that the position of consultants is highly dependent on the parallel shifts in the roles of other groups in the NHS. The impact of both 'executive' and 'market' management initiatives has been a reorientation of not only top and line managers, but various support staff alongside the adjustment of the clinicians (for a more detailed account see Whittington et al., 1994, p. 833 especially Fig. 2). Consideration of each level will make the nature of the combined and uneven impact of the internal market apparent. Conflict and accommodation continues to coexist in the relations between clinicians and hospital management.

Management in the NHS has previously relied on a dual structure with hospital medical committees relatively autonomous from the earlier administrative or general management structures of the 1980s (Harrison, 1988). To a large extent doctors managed themselves in a way similar to other scientific professionals elsewhere. Following the 'Working for Patients' reforms, hospitals now combine general and medical management. Management boards bring together senior professional staff and non-medical staff. Consultants were thereby drawn into developing a strategic awareness at unit level. The language of portfolio management found a natural place amongst boards who increasingly saw hospitals as businesses with policies developed by the market. Although apparently threatening to professional logics, such boards were often made up of senior clinicians (around 50 per cent). Membership meant that consultants were intimately involved in the development of the hospital's first strategic plans.

A similar benefit for senior clinicians is seen in the changes around line management. Hitherto, financial responsibility equated with containing costs in relation to the emerging budgetary system of the 1980s. Medical heads had little authority though to police colleagues' expenditure. The changes of the last two years have bought a shift in internal control mechanisms, from a rules based approach to a more decentralized, market based system. Line managers became responsible for revenues and costs, more in line with business management. The keynote for medical staff has been the way clinical directors are often senior clinicians who now take comprehensive responsibility for their specialities. Although not necessarily advocates of the ideology behind the reforms many senior medical staff eagerly took the opportunity for using business management techniques, frequently spurred by the promise of new sources of revenue.

While it is still early in the process of developing market relations, the clinician's role has been extended. In taking on the role of 'part time marketeers' (Gummerson, 1991) certain doctors find themselves highly valued by GPs or District Health Authorities. As one non-medical manager observed: 'GPs will not relate to an accountant or planning manager...they are going to relate to the people they are referred to'. However, simultaneously, the new market relations have brought about a levelling of the conventional hierarchies within departments, as in the case of nurse managers becoming central in the creation of business plans. The same has also been true for certain support staff in the NHS. The variability in the pattern of relations among clinicians and management has been reinforced by the requirements of the quasi-market. Paradoxically, as consultants insisted on the practical difficulties in marketing a professional health care service, and the production of appropriate financial information, so the role of financial staff has been strengthened. As specialist marketing departments fail to emerge, so 'contract managers' have taken on the negotiation of costs and volumes with Health

Authority customers.

Although the position of consultants would appear to be the stronger of the two professional groups considered in this chapter, the situation contains some fundamental threats. Two problems stand out from the process of introducing markets in the NHS: the tension between centralization and decentralization, and the potential conflict between the market and professional practices.

The evidence thus far seems to suggest that maintaining coherence in the development of market relations in the NHS will be difficult. The tension will be between maintaining a 'corporate' strategy with the need to extend market based internal controls. Put simply, decentralization would undermine corporate coherence with the result that the relative autonomy of certain professional areas will be constricted in order to ensure a more consistent presence in the market (cf. Colling and Ferner, 1992). One general manager for example, was worried at the prospect of clinical directors approaching the same GP fundholders and was trying therefore to instigate closer controls of senior clinicians. It is ironic that market relations first appeared to offer a return to professional independence under the guise of empowerment and local responsibility, and yet subsequently has forced managers to reassert control.

The second threat to consultants' position stems from the implicit conflict between markets and professional practices. The tension between market criteria and professional standards is well known. However, in hospitals there appear to be a number of difficulties for clinicians which will have to be resolved. The pressure for out-patient treatment, as opposed to in-patient care, has led to a reduction in the number of beds. Consequently consultants stand to lose the opportunities for continuous patient observation and research work. Equally competitive relations between doctors in a region could well inhibit the former exchange of information between professionals. Interestingly, senior managers in hospitals (many of whom share some of the consultants' ideals) may have a key role to play in the fate of clinicians as they discharge their responsibility of balancing market demands and professional standards. In many respects, therefore, hospital consultants are not examples of a simple resistance to the market based phase of the NPM. It is more accurate to conclude that they exhibit many of features which have produced the uneven, and often unintended, set of professional-management relations seen elsewhere in the public sector.

Academic librarians

Although traditionally less well organized than Consultants, Academic Librarians have been relatively successful in achieving market closure. Since the early 1960s 'Robbins' expansion of higher education, the overall institutional position of professional librarians has remained relatively stable (Rodger, 1988). Despite fears of gradual deprofessionalization, this general fact has remained true in the 1980s and 1990s. However, and within this situation, the specific impact of NPM on

Librarians has been considerable. Notions of improving the 'management' of libraries acted as the driving force behind changes in professional roles and major reassessments of the way services were provided. Management was also associated with an increased differentiation of professional roles, between senior staff who took on management type jobs and junior staff who were subjected to heightened bureaucratic controls and work intensification (Davies and Kirkpatrick, 1995b).

Libraries were traditionally managed by a Librarian accountable to a University Library Committee and Senate. The post-Jarratt period saw a shift, in many institutions, towards making the library service an independent cost centre, turning the Librarian unto an accountable budget holder (Burrows, 1987). In the mid 1980s, some of the larger university libraries established new management structures, turning individual sub-units such as technical services into independent cost centres. Greater emphasis was put on hierarchical chains of command, emphasising superior-subordinate relationships over and above notions of collegiate equality between professional staffs on different grades.

New accounting regimes, lines of command and the greater scope for 'managerial' discretion, represented a clear shift away from older practices. Previously, only the Librarian and his/her immediate colleagues had responsibility for resources. Other staff, sometimes even those on senior academic related grades, possessed little or no 'managerial' (or administrative) responsibility. Professional staff typically spent the bulk of their time moving around between various backroom (cataloguing and classification) and front end (user enquiry) tasks. Experienced Librarians were sometimes allowed considerable autonomy to develop their own subject expertise, almost irrespective of wider resource implications. Despite a considerable overlap of professional and non-professional roles in practice, a sharp division of labour between the two continues to be formally upheld (Goode, 1961).

Calls from within the profession for greater emphasis on 'management' gained momentum in the early 1980s following substantial cuts in library budgets, coupled with rising book and journal inflation (Rodger, 1988). Such pressures revealed: 'a significant mismatch between professional strategy and belief on the one hand, and reality on the other' (Thompson, 1991, p. 1). No longer could academic librarians afford to ignore the costs and resource implications of their work. Like the rest of the University sector they were forced to look for more efficient ways of managing limited resources and, as Line (1986) puts it, 'scrutinizing every activity in terms of cost effectiveness'.

Managerial concerns entered into library work first and foremost as a means of controlling costs and of maintaining (or even increasing) levels of service without additional resources. One approach to this was to abandon the objective of achieving self-sufficiency in collections, opting instead for a self-renewing or a 'cafeteria' library policy.

Another response was to scrutinize the costs of professional work itself. According to Roberts (1991), during the 1980s, 'claims to professionality have been challenged and found wanting' (ibid, 450). Increasingly, cost conscious library managers queried the need for highly qualified academic-related staffs who seemed to be performing the same tasks as clerical assistants and junior, para-professionals. New information technologies, which effectively commodified core professional tasks such as cataloguing, were effectively harnessed by library managers at this time. One implication was that jobs which once demanded (and in some institutions still do) considerable professional expertise, were increasingly delegated to lower paid clerical and para-professional staffs (Gunson, 1990; Prince and Burton, 1988). These changes have weakened the power, status and autonomy of professional librarians. In particular they have signified a widening gulf between senior professionals, who define themselves as 'managers', and junior professionals whose work has been standardized and intensified (Kirkpatrick and Davies, 1994).

Changes in the external environment of universities, such as the introduction of selectivity based funding, also affected librarians (Pollitt, 1990c; Booth et al., 1992). In most institutions, all support services, including the library, were scrutinized by university administrators who raised questions about their value for money and 'quality' (Lines, 1989). To demonstrate their effectiveness Libraries were forced to collect performance indicators and participate in service level agreements with specific user groups (Davies and Kirkpatrick, 1995a). Some professionals were also required to develop liaison roles, spending more time outside the library in academic departments, gathering information about 'customer' needs and negotiating levels of service.

The combined impact of all these changes on professional librarians has been considerable. Some argue that librarianship can no longer claim professional status in the traditional sense but must focus instead on developing an information specialist role (Cronin and Davenport, 1988). Others regret the decline in professional 'competence' and the rise of a library management which seems to have embraced 'meretricious values of unenlightened cost accountancy' (Roberts, 1991). What is clear is that NPM has posed both threats and opportunities for professional librarians. As for threats, the demand for efficiency gains led to cuts in services and personnel; it also raised questions about the role of professional librarians. New technology, which increased user turnover and deskilled core professional tasks, was used to pursue these efficiency objectives. As a result, many junior professional staff have been drawn into lower paid routine work, subjected to various bureaucratic controls and to work intensification. In contrast, for some senior librarians, management has created new opportunities. These staff now control budgets and have much greater leeway over internal decision making.

Discussion

One must be extremely cautious when attempting to generalize about the impact of NPM on professions across the whole public sector. The two examples discussed above serve to illustrate how complex the issues are. Sub groups, even within the same profession may experience and respond to change in quite different ways (as seen in the NHS and university librarians' occupational groupings). There is also likely to be considerable variation in outcomes depending on the organizational context and the resources available to different professions to resist change, a subject which we have not had adequate time to do justice to in this chapter. Accommodation and conflict continue to coexist.

Despite these problems, it is possible to make a number of limited generalizations about the impact of NPM on public service professions. In particular, two key issues emerge, relating to the degree of incorporation of professionals into managerial or wider organizational concerns, and the extent to which there has been accommodation (or integration) between professions and the New Public Management.

Firstly, how far have the two professions discussed above suffered a decline in their traditional power and autonomy as a result of NPM? In the sociological literature this loss of autonomy is usually referred to as the 'proletarianization' thesis (Derber, 1982; Boreham, 1983; Murphy, 1990). A strong version of this thesis would see the effect of increased management control as leading to the commodification of professional work, bringing it within the control of formal bureaucratic rules and procedures. This results in substantial deskilling, a loss of autonomy and decline into para-professional status. Far less serious, 'ideological' proletarianization, however, implies that professions retain control over core tasks but lose autonomy to determine overall organizational goals (Derber, 1982). Here, planning and decision making is taken over by management and separated from task implementation, leading to the incorporation, or 'bureaucratization' of professions in modern organizations (Reed, 1992).

Looking at our two cases, one could argue that Academic Librarians have suffered a decline in their workplace autonomy. Many of their technical skills have become redundant, numbers have fallen and there has been far greater pressure on them to work within tight cost constraints and focus professional activities more closely according to objectives of efficiency. These changes were not brought about exclusively by the emergence of NPM (new technology played an important role) but they were driven by managerial objectives of improving efficiency.

NHS Consultants, as one might expect, have held on to their traditional autonomy over clinical practice - few managers are either willing or able to interfere in this area. At the same time however, their unassailable power to determine organizational goals, irrespective of managerial objectives, has now been challenged effectively. As the case material demonstrates, the effect of the new internal market in health has been to draw consultants into a variety of strategic and resource decision making processes. These imply a form of incorporation and increasingly, subordination to managerial interests. In this respect, the experience of Librarians is closer to the strong proletarianization thesis, while that of Consultants is closer to the ideological version.

Just as there has been conflict between professions and management, there are new forms of accommodation emerging. Some professions may have suffered a decline in their power of self-regulation, but this is not to say that they have been unsuccessful in acquiring new sources of influence. In some cases, there is a possibility of there being a positive gain whereby professionals succumb to managerial controls in exchange for increased cultural status and power. With Academic Librarians, for example, such accommodation between profession and management means that senior professionals themselves develop an increasingly active role as managers of resources, while junior staff work within highly specified job descriptions and concentrate on providing front end user services. This may also be the case for Consultants, although with them accommodation implied new alliances being struck between practicing professionals and line managers. It is worth noting how this accommodation mirrors, in key respects, the common interests which have always been present between profession and bureaucracy in the British public sector.

In both cases, an important way in which professionals have been incorporated into managerial concerns is through their increased accountability for resources (as cost centre budget holders). This, as mentioned above, may imply a loss of traditional autonomy, but could also have the unintended consequence of empowering the professional - offering greater freedom to make operational decisions about resources within overall strategic constraints. This kind of power may be used in a benign way, implying a trade-off whereby the professional accepts some involvement in managerial decision making regarding resource allocation, in return for limited discretion to build into the process a number of 'professional' concerns. This could mean balancing the objectives of efficiency and service 'rationing' with those of meeting client 'needs' (however defined). According to Harrison et al. for example:

> doctors...may be obliged to enter management in order to preserve their privileges (or limit their loss) and to prevent or neutralize the impact of those changes which particularly concern them (Harrison et al., 1992, p. 103).

In academic libraries, it has also been suggested that NPM could offer a way of empowering individual professionals and improving professional services. As Line (1990) suggests, "'Management' should be seen not as antipathetic to scholarship and professional knowledge, but as using them on behalf of the service" (ibid., p. 261). Of course, managing budgets may also be highly demoralizing (especially if those budgets are in decline in real terms). At the same time however, it does mean that the profession retains some control, within boundaries, over service priorities. Some professional input does then go into decisions about how the money is spent, albeit decisions about how to manage altered standards.

Finally, with incorporation there is also the possibility of a new elite 'professional managerial class' emerging. Stifled within their existing career structures and seeing little future in continuing in traditional professional roles, many professionals may seek to join the ranks of management and extend their jurisdiction over it, using the language of managerialism and the 'enterprise' as a cultural resource to improve their position. As Pollitt (1990a) suggests, there exist many 'constituencies...to which a more managerial approach is likely to bring enhanced career prospects and power' (Pollitt, 1990a). Just as managers may be forced to interfere more in professional work, so might professions (especially senior staff) decide to take over management. This process could reinforce - and perhaps even increase - the power and cultural status of the professional. To complement his/her certified expert knowledge the 'professional/manager' would also be able lay claim to his/her managerial accountability as an additional source of legitimacy and justification for acting on the consumer's behalf. Such a scenario has been described by Burris (1989), who suggests that professional/bureaucratic conflicts are now being transcended by an emerging form of 'technocratic control'. This implies a new organizational order in which experts trade in some of their traditional autonomy and develop integrated expert/managerial roles. The next few years will reveal whether these predictions are valid in the public sector context.

References

Abbott, A. (1988), *The System of Professions*, University of Chicago Press, Chicago.

Ackroyd, S. (1994), 'Professions, Their Organization and Change in Britain: Some Private and Public Sector Similarities and their Consequences', paper presented at the ESRC Seminar 'Professions in Late Modernity', University of Lancaster, 30th June.

Ackroyd, S., Hughes, J. A. and Soothill, K. (1989), 'Public services and their management', *Journal of Management Studies*, 26, 6, pp. 603-619.

Ackroyd, S. and Soothill, K. (1994), 'The New Management and the Professionals: Assessing the Impact on Public Services', paper presented at the Employment Research Unit Conference, 'The Contract State', Cardiff Business School, 27-28th September.

Aucoin, P. (1990), 'Administrative Reform in Public Management: Paradigms, Principles, Paradoxes and Pendulums', *Governance*, 3, 2, pp. 115-137.

Appelby, J., Robbinson, R., Ranade, W., Little, V. and Salter, J. (1990), 'The use of markets in the health service: the NHS reforms and managed competition', *Public Money and Management*, Winter, pp. 27-33.

Bennett, C. and Ferlie, E. (1994), 'Management by Contract - Rhetoric or Reality?' paper presented at the Employment Research Unit Conference, 'The Contract State', Cardiff Business School, 27-28th September.

Blunden-Ellis, J. (1987), 'Services Marketing and the Academic Library', *British Journal of Academic Librarianship* 2, 3.

Booth, Clive, and Roper, B. (1992), 'A new framework for quality', *Higher Education Quarterly* 46, 3, pp. 227-212.

Boreham, P. (1983), 'Indetermination: Professional knowledge, organization and control', *Sociological Review*, 31, pp. 293-318.

Burrage, M. (1992), 'Mrs Thatcher against deep structures: the ideology, impact and ironies of her eleven year confrontation with the professions', Working Paper 92-11, Institute of Government Studies, University of California, Berkeley.

Burris, B.H. (1989), 'Technocratic Organization and Control', *Organization Studies,* 10, 1, pp. 1-22.

Burrows, T. (1987), 'Funding and Governance of British University Libraries', *British Journal of Academic Librarianship,* 2, 3.

Carter, Neil. (1991), 'Learning to measure performance: the use of indicators in organizations', *Public Administration,* 69, pp 85-101.

Charlesworth, J., Clarke, J. and Cochrane, A. (1994), 'Tangled Webs? Managing Local Mixed Economies of Care', paper presented at the Employment Research Unit Conference, 'The Contract State', Cardiff Business School, 27-28th September.

Child, John. (1982), 'Professionals in the corporate world: values, interests and control', in *The International Yearbook of Organization Studies 1981,* Dunkerley, D. and Salaman, G. (editors), Routledge, London.

The Citizens' Charter: Raising the Standard, 1991, London, HMSO (Cmnd 1599).

Colling, T, and Ferner, A. (1992), 'The limits of autonomy: devolution, line managers and industrial relations in privatized companies', *Journal of Management Studies.* 29, 2, pp 209-227.

Cousins, C. (1987), *Controlling Social Welfare,* Wheatsheaf, Sussex.

Crompton, R. (1990), 'Professions in the current context', *Work Employment and Society,* Special edition 'A decade of change?'', pp 147-166.

Cronin, B, and Davenport, E. (1988), *Post-Professionalism: Transforming the Information Heartland,* Taylor Graham, London.

Davies, A., and Kirkpatrick, I. (forthcoming - 1995a), 'Face to face with the sovereign consumer: service quality and the changing role of professional librarians', *Sociological Review.*

Davies, A. and Kirkpatrick, I. (1995b), 'Performance indicators, bureaucratic control and the decline of professional autonomy: the case of academic librarians', in Kirkpatrick and Martinez Lucio (eds), *The Politics of Quality: Management of Change in the UK public Sector,* Routledge, London.

Deakin, N. and Walsh, K. (1994), 'The Enabling State: The Role of Markets and Contracts' paper presented at the Employment Research Unit Conference, 'The Contract State', Cardiff Business School, 27-28th September.

Derber, C. (1982), *Professionals as Workers: Mental Labour in Advanced Capitalism,* G.K. Hall & Co, Boston.

Du Gay, P, and Salaman. G. (1992), 'The cult(ure) of the customer', *Journal of Management Studies.* 29, 5, pp. 615-634.

Du Gay, P. (1994), "'Businessing' Bureaucracy: entrepreneurial government and public management", paper presented at the Employment Research Unit conference, 'The Contract State', Cardiff Business School, September 27-28th.

Dunleavy, P. and Hood, C. (1994), 'From Old Public Administration to New Public Management', *Public Money and Management*, July-September, pp. 9-16.

Enright, B.J. (1990), 'Concepts of stock: comprehensive vs. selective', in *Academic Library Management*, Line, M.B. (ed.), Library Association, London.

Ferlie, E. (1994), "Characterizing the 'New Public Management'", paper presented at the annual conference of the British Academy of Management, University of Lancaster, September 12-14th.

Freidson, E. (1970), *Professional Dominance: The Social Structure of Medical Care*, Aldine, London.

Gamble, A. (1988), *The Free Economy and the Strong State*, Macmillan, London.

Goode, W.J. (1961), 'The Librarian: from occupation to profession', *Library Quarterly*, 31, pp. 306-20.

Goss, M.E.W. (1963), 'Patterns of bureaucracy among hospital staff physicians', in *The Hospital in Modern Society*, Freidson, E. (ed.), Macmillan, Ontario.

Gummerson, E. (1991), 'Marketing-orientation revisited: the crucial role of the part-time marketeer', *European Journal of Marketing*, 25, 2, pp 60-75.

Gunn, L. (1988), 'Public management: a third approach?', *Public Money and Management* 8, 2, pp 21-5.

Gunson, N. (1990), 'Will sophisticated computer systems replace professional librarians or complement their skills?', *Computer Systems and Librarians* Nov/Dec, pp. 303-311.

Hall, S. (1988), *The Hard Road to Renewal*, Verso, London.

Harrison, S. (1988), *Managing the National Health Service: Shifting the Frontier?*, Chapman Hall, London.

Harrison, S., Hunter, D., Marnoch, G., and Pollitt, C. (1992), *Just Managing: Power and Culture in the National Health Service*, Macmillan, London.

Harrison, S., and Pollitt, C. (1994), *Controlling Health Professionals*, Open University Press, Buckingham.

Harrow, J. and Willcocks, L. (1990), 'Public services management: activities, initiatives and limits to learning', *Journal of Management Studies*, 27, 3, pp. 281-304.

Hoggett, P. (1991), 'A New Managerialism in the Public Sector?', *Policy and Politics*, Vol. 19, (4), pp. 243-56.

Hoggett, P. (1994), 'New Modes of Control in the Public Sector', paper presented at the Employment Research Unit Conference, 'The Contract State', Cardiff Business School, 27-28th September.

Hood, C. (1991), 'A public management for all seasons?', *Public Administration* Vol. 69, pp. 3-19.

Johnson, T. J. (1972), *Professions and Power*, Macmillan, London.

Keat, R. and Abercrombie, N. (eds), (1991), *Enterprise Culture*, Routledge, London.

Kirkpatrick, I. and Davies, A. (1994), 'Professional Knowledge work in transition: The case of Academic Librarians', paper presented at the annual conference of the British Academy of Management, University of Lancaster, September 12-14th.

Kirkpatrick, I. and Martinez Lucio, M. (eds), (1995), *The Politics of Quality: Management of Change in the UK Public Sector*, Routledge, London.

Kitchener, M. and Whipp, R. (1995), 'Change, continuity and confusion in the reformed National Health Service', in Kirkpatrick, I. and Martinez-Lucio, M. (eds), *Politics of Quality*, op cit.

Klein, R. (1983), *The Politics of the National Health Service*, Longman, London.

Kornhauser, W. (1962), *Scientists in Industry*, University of California Press, Berkeley.

Larson, M. S. (1977), *The Rise of Professionalism*, University of California Press, Berkeley.

Larson, M. S. (1990), 'In the matter of experts and professions', in *The Formation of Professionals*, Torstendahl. R, and Burrage. M. (eds), Sage, London.

Lee, R. and Piper, J. (1988), 'Organizational control, differing perspectives: the management of universities', *Financial Accounting and Management*, Vol. 4, (2), pp. 113-28.

Line, M. (1986), 'The survival of academic libraries in hard times: reactions to pressures, rational and irrational', *British Journal of Academic Librarianship*, 1, 1, pp. 1-12.

Line, M. (1990), 'Current issues in academic libraries', in Line, M. (ed.), *Academic Library Management*, Library Association, London.

Lines, L. (1989), 'Performance measurement in academic libraries - a university perspective', *British Journal of Academic Librarianship*, Vol. 4, 2, pp. 111-126.

Mann, P. (1990), 'University expansion, library contraction', *Library Association Record*, 92, 2, pp. 115-117.

McNulty, T., Whipp, R., Whittington, R. and Kitchener, M. (1992), 'Managing marketing change in professional service contexts', Paper given at the Cardiff Business School Employment Research Unit conference, September.

Murphy, R. (1990), 'Proletarianization or bureaucratization: the fall of the professional', in Tordenstahl, R. and Burrage, M. (eds), *The Formation of Professions*, Sage, London.

Osborne, D. and Gaebler, T. (1992), *Reinventing Government: How the Entrepreneurial Spirit is Transforming the Public Sector*, Addison-Welsey, Reading.

Pfeffer, N, and Coote, A. (1991), *Is Quality Good for You? A Critical Review of Quality Assurance in Welfare Services*, Social Policy Paper No. 5, Institute for Public Policy Research, London.

Pollitt, C. (1988), 'Consumerism and beyond', (Editorial), *Public Administration* Vol. 66, pp. 121-4.

Pollitt, C. (1990a), *Managerialism and the Public Services: The Anglo-American Experience,* Basil Blackwell, Oxford.

Pollitt, C. (1990b), 'Doing business in the temple? Managers and quality assurance in the public services', *Public Administration,* Vol. 68, pp. 435-452.

Pollitt, C. (1990c), 'Measuring University performance: never mind the quality, never mind the width?', *Higher Education Quarterly,* Vol. 44, 1, pp. 60-81.

Pollitt, C., Harrison, S., Hunter, D. J. and Marnoch, G. (1991), 'General management in the NHS: the initial impact 1983-88', *Public Administration,* Vol. 69, pp. 61-83.

Prince, B., and Burton, R. F. (1988), 'Changing dimensions in academic library structures: the impact of information technology', *British Journal of Librarianship,* 3, 2.

Raelin, J. A. (1985), 'The basis for the professional's resistance to managerial control', *Human Resource Management,* Vol. 24, 2, pp 147-76.

Raelin, J. A. (1991), *The Clash of Cultures: Managers Managing Professionals,* Harvard Business School Press, Boston.

Reed, M. I. (1992) 'Experts, professions and organizations in late modernity', paper given at the Cardiff Business School *Employment Research Unit* conference, September.

Roberts, N. (1991), 'A profession in crisis', *Library Association Record,* 93, 7.

Rodger, E. M. (1988), 'Progress in documentation: British university libraries 1977-87: some observations on the challenges of declining resources', *Journal of Documentation,* 44, 4.

Stewart, J. and Walsh, K. (1992), 'Change in the management of public services'. *Public Administration,* Vol. 70, pp. 499-518.

Thompson, J. (1991), *Redirection in Academic Library Management,* Library Association, London.

Walsh, K. (1991), 'Quality and the public services', Public Administration, 69, pp. 503-514.

Walsh, K. (1995), 'Quality Through Markets: The New Public Service Management', in Wilmott, H. and Wilkinson, A. (eds), *Making Quality Critical,* Routledge, London..

Whittington, R., McNulty, T. and Whipp, R. (1994), 'Market-driven change in professional services: problems and processes, *Journal of Management Studies,* 31, 6, pp. 829-846.

Wilding, P. (1992), 'The British Welfare State: Thatcherism's enduring legacy', *Policy and Politics,* Vol. 20, 2, pp. 201-11.

Wilson, D. J. (1993), 'Turning drama into a crisis: Perspectives on contemporary Local Government', *Public Policy and Administration,* Vol. 8, 1, Spring, pp. 30-45.

10 Can there be a valid future for human resource management?

Ian Glover and Jerry Hallier

Introduction

It is often assumed that Human Resources Management (HRM) has replaced, is replacing, or will replace personnel management in most or many employing units. HRM is usually differentiated from personnel management by the use of such terms as strategic, integrated, proactive and individualistic. Thus the creative development of the work of top job holders and of line managers at all levels, is seen as normally being crucial for organizational survival and success in both the short and the long term.

Whereas personnel management expertise is seen as being the property of personnel specialists, HRM is seen as being a matter for virtually all managers, with human resource (HR) or personnel specialists having no exclusive jurisdiction over any part of it. HRM is relatively proactive and personnel management relatively reactive insofar as the former is meant to anticipate and avoid employment related problems, whereas the latter is much more often seen as addressing them after they have arisen. Finally HRM is individualistic in that it is concerned with securing the commitment of employees to the pursuit of organizational or managerial visions and missions, at the expense if necessary of their occupational and other collective interests.

Our aim in this chapter is to ask whether this approach to managing people can have a useful and honourable future. We ask this question against a background of thought and evidence on the origins and nature of HRM which cast doubts on its integrity, and of data on the extent to which it is put into practice which suggest that it is more apparent than real. We go on to consider, along with our own, a mixture of moral, political and practical doubts which others have expressed. In the discussion and concluding section of the paper we emphasize the importance

217

of historical, ethical and cross-cultural knowledge for understanding HRM reasonably comprehensively and for pointing the way towards a useful future for it.

Issues

To answer the questions posed by our title we need to consider further what HRM means, to account for our use of the working definitions of it in the first paragraph of our introduction. To develop our understanding of its meaning we need to consider its origins, and to consider its future we also need to think about its present condition, its context and any trends, recent, current and possible future, which may be affecting or which may affect its development.

There can be little doubt that HRM is a notion with varied meanings. Many of the debates about its meanings consider the extent to which it is different from 'traditional' personnel management (Guest, 1987, 1989, 1991; Sisson, 1989a, 1989b; Timperley and Sisson, 1989; Brewster and Smith, 1990; Keenoy, 1990; Legge, 1989, Torrington, 1989; Boxall, 1992; Glover, 1992b; Guest and Hoque, 1993; Storey, 1995). Sisson (1989a) offers an important hint about reasons for and the nature of the ambiguity surrounding HRM when he compares international differences in personnel management in the USA, Japan, West Germany and Britain. Aspects of personnel management considered in the course of his comparison include industrial relations and collective bargaining; employee commitment; training, development and appraisal; the uses of external and internal labour markets; remuneration policies and systems; manpower planning and its relationships with business strategies. The nature and importance of each of these in each of the countries is usually quite different, suggesting that personnel management has a wide range of meanings internationally.

Sisson (1989b) went on to consider how several academic representatives of personnel management such as Armstrong (1987), Torrington and Hall (1987) and Fowler (1987) had expressed severe misgivings about HRM, mainly because of its variable meanings and what this implied for the stability of personnel management and employment practice. For example Guest (1987) had shown how the term HRM might simply be used to give personnel specialists more status or how the adoption of certain HRM style management and employment practices could have threatening implications for their role. In North America the adoption of HRM employment strategies had largely come to mean avoidance of dealings with trade unions whereas in other contexts it could mean greater emphasis on employee development, motivation, involvement and commitment. There was a general tendency for HRM approaches to follow the largely American 'excellence' literature in viewing 'people as the most important resource[s]' of organizations, and for them to be interested above all in the attitudes of all concerned to work and employment. Much of the ambiguity which had dogged both personnel and HRM was associated with the strongly prescriptive tradition of both and of management writings in general. This tradition had led some personnel management academics to see HRM as a threat, but others saw it as an opportunity. HRM could be seen as a threat in the 1980s because the role of the 'caring' personnel professional was vulnerable to the aggression of 'macho' management in a tough political and economic climate. Yet it could also offer opportunities, because of its interest in business strategy, organization structure and flexible and dynamic employment policies for the erstwhile personnel manager to become 'a fully accepted member of the management team with a shared responsibility for general management' at the workplace level, and at 'company level' it [could] mean the personnel manager 'assuming the role of the internal consultant' (Sisson, 1989b, p. 37). Timperley and Sisson (1989), in a discussion of the issue of whether manpower planning was being replaced by HR planning, insofar as employers' attempts to match the supply of employees to their demand for them was becoming more integrated with corporate planning, less mathematical and more socially and politically sophisticated, and hence more strategic, argued that commercial pressures did favour such a trend. This was because rapid and unpredictable market changes and nearly universal availability of finance, hardware and markets was both increasingly making accurate manpower forecasting impossible and putting a premium on highly flexible and proactive HR policies. Such arguments obviously lent credibility to the notion that HRM style thinking has strongly prescriptive and wishful tendencies.

Two other reasons for thinking that HRM means all things to all people are as follows. First, as Blyton and Turnbull (1992a) and others have noted, it was established to some extent in the USA before it began, largely in the 1980s, to make inroads in Britain. Yet the evidence on its existence in either country suggests that both its prevalence and its impact have been quite small (Guest, 1992a; Sisson, 1994). More specifically, there is a good deal of evidence of re-labelling of job titles and some activities, of large scale use of the term HRM in business and other sectors, and in education for business and management, of considerable growth in writing and research in the area, and of the teaching of it, albeit with much of the relevant material taken from personnel management courses.

Second, because part of its origins have been in personnel management, HRM has inherited a long tradition of masking its intentions behind dissimulating language (Legge, 1989). Personnel specialists and managers have a long tradition in the UK and the USA of claiming to lack coercive power while actually enjoying at least some along with a great deal of influence (see, for example, Watson, 1977, on the UK, and Ritzer and Harrison, 1970, on the USA). They have not only enjoyed power in their own areas of jurisdiction and expertise such as collective bargaining, recruitment and training. They have exerted all kinds of influence over staffing at most levels of organizations, and over a wide range of other significant matters, and they have done so over decades in which there has been considerable ambiguity about the basis of managerial authority (cf. Anthony, 1977). The early origins of some personnel management in concern for employee welfare and the proselytising Human Relations antecedents of much academic thinking about personnel management have lent an air of legitimacy to personnel and, later, HRM policies, however 'soft' or 'hard' they have been (Legge, 1989). Beginning with the work of industrial psychologists and others concerned with human factors in the early part of this century, and especially from the Second World War and into the 1980s, personnel and HRM's professional and academic representatives have claimed a certain amount of professional and organizational freedom and status by reference to their knowledge of relevant areas of social science and law. However this pursuit of professionalism appears to have been something of a front behind which personnel specialists seek, often successfully, to establish themselves as parts of management teams (Paterson, Martin and Glover, 1988; Paterson, 1996).

From a management standpoint the difference between personnel and HRM is that the latter has more overtly strategic ambitions which can be harnessed from time to time as 'one of a series of approaches management may take to secure the levels of compliance and cooperation it requires; different sets of circumstances will influence the adoption of one approach over others, while changing circumstances will encourage a shift from one to another and possibly, the creation of new practices and approaches' (Blyton and Turnbull, 1992a, p. 13). Such different approaches can include ones which lie largely outside the immediate ambit of HRM, in strategic management or in often specialist functional and professional concerns such as those of accounting, operations, or marketing and sales. The emphasis on flexibility in the rhetoric and practice of HRM is useful to managements for justifying their choices between its 'soft' and 'hard' forms (Blyton and Morris, 1992). The soft ones favour employee development involving the learning of broader ranges of skills to enhance functional flexibility. The hard ones favour variations in the volume of and the rewards given to labour to help match fluctuations in demand, thereby enhancing numerical and financial flexibility. The pursuit of these kinds of flexibility can highlight the tensions and ambiguities virtually always present in the process of management. For example numerical flexibility is normally a threat to employee commitment and the quality of output, and the pursuit of functional flexibility tends to conflict with organizational cohesion (Child, 1984). By asserting the notion of 'the human resource' as a strategic matter, one which personnel specialists only tended to argue sporadically, both management and HRM specialists hope and expect to enhance their power and their ability to control others.

Third, the very considerable ambiguity apparent in the use of language about 'management education' and so called management competence also adds to the air of politically useful vagueness surrounding HRM. The fact that there are certain 'strategic' abilities such as handling uncertainty which top job holders - among most others ! - need in virtually all organizations is undeniable. However their inherently multidimensional character and inevitably contingent practice has only too easily helped to generate confusion and obfuscation when attempts to identify, list, classify, enhance and apply them have been made (cf. Boyatzis, 1982). The term management education, which refers to a number of disciplines and areas of study which variously include and draw on and overlap with the study of HRM, is often confusingly expanded to include undergraduate and other largely pre-experience courses in business subjects and sometimes even more specialized vocational disciplines, including engineering ones.

In Britain the two professional associations which have been more prominent than others in the development of generalist management thought have been the (formerly British) Institute of Management and to a smaller extent, the retitled Institute of Personnel and Development (IPD). The latter has been a significant focus and repository of knowledge about the 'soft' aspects of management in a society in which many employers have manifested arms' length attitudes towards technical expertise and employee training and development, and in which, too, there has until recently been significant public neglect of most kinds of specialist vocational education and training. The sometimes rapid, diverse and often rather chaotic expansion of education and training of the kinds aimed at wealth creation since the 1950s has undoubtedly added to widespread confusion of specialist, if not always overall, purposes. Along with this, the ongoing historic conflict between the 'tough' versus 'caring' elements of middle class attitudes to employment and work have meant that there has been a fertile climate for the development and use of such politically useful weapons as HRM.

Evidence on the practice of HRM

There have been a number of studies in recent years which have been concerned, in various ways, with the extent of and to ways in which HRM is put into practice by British employers. One of the most important, possibly the most important, of these was that produced by Storey (1992). Because this is at least as comprehensive as any other it is considered first here, and in more detail than the other studies which we review in this section.

Storey's research was conducted between 1986 and 1988 and his findings are thus at least nine years old. They are slightly older than the average of the findings discussed below and this should be borne in mind. Storey obtained his main data from 15 'core' large, heavily unionized, typically divisionalized multisite organizations in the UK. He also obtained data from a further 25 smaller 'panel' private and public sector organizations. Most of the data came from line or general managers, rather than from personnel specialists, union activists or rank and file employees. This is significant because, first, HRM is generally defined as a line driven phenomenon. Second, it is significant because Storey's account tends to play down or ignore the views of two kinds of expert: those in personnel or HRM, and those who are 'human resources' as such. The 'core' organisations tended to exemplify standard British approaches to industrial relations. The 'panel' ones were smaller, often much, and were chosen for their innovative HRM reputations, and were the subjects of reactively perfunctory investigations. Thus most were only visited once, while the 'core' ones were visited several times with feedback workshops being held at Warwick University.

Storey admitted to doing little to examine the real, structural, behaviourial and attitudinal impact of relevant HRM style changes, as opposed to managers' accounts of them. However we would re-emphasize the point that Storey did ask his interviewees, mainly comprising 'some 350 line managers' in the 'core' organizations, about the practice and ramifications of virtually all aspects of HRM.

The main findings, which Storey and the authors of his book's foreword take to be indications of 'how human resource management works in practice and how work in Britain was re-organized during the 1980s' (Sisson, Edwards and Hyman, 1992:XI), were as follows. Managements reported substantial if rather diverse types and levels of concern with 'the moulding of a more tractable employee stock' (Storey, 1992, p. 77), which tended to coexist with traditional approaches to personnel and industrial relations management. Numerous specific HRM style initiatives are reported, along with much less in the way of institutional and long term change. Yet HRM did seem to perform useful symbolic functions for many line managers and there seemed to be much agreement on what to do, if not on how to do it. Changes often seemed to be imposed in an integrated, systemic and top down way, and provided evidence of growing use of HRM. Yet the account's details might also be made to suggest that these changes mixed the adoption of management fads and techniques, pragmatic ideas and changes and responses to external threats.

The book explores the roles of line and personnel managers in handling 'human resources'. Most HRM initiatives were line driven. Most personnel specialists were still 'regulators.... attached to the proceduralist symbolic realm' (p. 187), products of British management's pragmatic opportunism. Senior and middle managers spoke of devolving authority, greater innovativeness and flexibility, the customer orientation, and so on. The human resource implications of these had been taken up more often by line managers than by personnel specialists. There seemed to be little demise of middle managers, especially in production: instead jobs had become more responsible and generalist, after growing into 'manufacturing manager' and even 'business manager' roles.

However an apparently enthusiastic atmosphere amongst these kinds of people did not itself equal integrated and truly strategic HRM. Much more change in recruitment, selection, training, development and other practices, and in the behaviour of subordinates, would have been needed for that to be the case. Similarly, while employers were trying to replace traditional supervisors with more capable and dynamic 'first line managers', the results were varied and often rather unimpressive. Social and technical factors tended to make traditional HRM practices persist and to cloud HRM style developments with ambivalence.

Nor was there much evidence of great change in industrial relations. Existing procedures had generally been maintained, although decentralization of bargaining was common and productivity increases were secured without bargaining. Unions were often marginalized, but there was no dramatic change from pluralist to unitarist employee relations. Management attitudes towards unions tended to be cool if not overtly hostile, and rather neglectful. Little fundamental seemed to have changed in this regard since the 1960s and even earlier. However there was evidence of a more useful and confident stance towards industrial relations than had existed before the mid-1980s, and growing involvement of top and line managers in HRM issues. Even so, 'the hard part' of HRM, making it work over time, had yet to come. Changes of rhetoric and style were more apparent than those of substance: terms like image, chimerical, symbolic, legitimatory, reassuring and rite of renewal appear regularly in Storey's account. Yet there *was* evidence of more integrated and flexible management level work, and of unions being faced with a choice of getting involved or getting sidelined.

Storey was careful to avoid suggesting that HRM was being established widely. Nonetheless he did imply that events were and are moving in the general direction of HRM. Indeed some very large generalizations are made on the basis of relatively small numbers of interviews (averaging about 20 in organizations the size of Austin Rover, Bradford Metropolitan Council, ICI, Massey Ferguson, the NHS and Whitbread Breweries). He may have given too much credence to the enthusiasm of the main beneficiaries of managerial renewal. This focus is virtually always on management and managers, at least on those who were not victims of 'downsizing'.

In theory HRM is concerned with individual commitment, development and performance, yet individual employees, HRM's subjects, are almost entirely absent from the study. Advocates of HRM and of updated HRM style personnel practices both profess to be strategically oriented and to treat all employees in the same ways, emphasizing top down culture change and commitment, and in doing so they tend to ignore the individual differences which traditional personnel policies regard as important. So line managers in Storey's study had taken on more responsibility for such functional specialist personnel practices as recruitment, appraisal and training, when all relevant research suggests that they do such things rather badly. Therefore when they were asked how well they were doing these things and when they replied enthusiastically, it almost certainly did not mean that some sort of positive sea change was starting. Unfortunately the book does tend to suggest that it was.

Throughout the book the information is given that everything has changed and yet everything is the same as before. This does not only occur in the accounts of the dual approach to industrial relations of individualized contracts, pay and assessment, employee involvement and culture change, along with old style collectivist procedures. This dualism pervades much of the book, including the sections on the roles of personnel specialists and line managers. A great deal of the evidence offered is of managerial talk of new dawnings, of vision and mission statements and so on, yet much less evidence of long term fundamental changes in attitudes, behaviour or structures is provided. Many of the behaviourial changes that are reported could be nothing more than products of external threats and/or fashion, and some of the attitudinal ones could be interpreted as *post hoc* rationalization. Many of the book's empirical data are too dependent for their analysis on the recent HRM literature and would have benefitted from being

223

considered from comparative and historical perspectives. Moreover, in a book devoted to understanding how the 'human resource' is managed, too little attention is paid to the nature and the experiences of that 'resource'. Nevertheless the book does offer, apart from a useful review of much of the relevant literature, a good deal of suggestive evidence on the rhetoric and to a smaller degree the practice of HRM in Britain in the mid-late 1980s.

The theme of rhetoric fronting often rather unimpressive changes in policies is seen in the other studies and sources examining the practice of HRM in Britain which we referred to at the start of this section. In the brief account of them which follows, we begin with studies which have addressed the wider aspects of HRM like strategy, culture change and employee involvement and commitment, and then move on to ones which have focused on more specific areas such as training and reward policies.

Brewster and Smith (1990) found very little evidence that the concerns of personnel managers in Britain were becoming strategic at the end of the 1980s. Most organizations in their study, which covered all sectors of industry and commerce, had personnel directors and many of them were involved in developing corporate strategies. Yet about 40 per cent of organizations had no personnel or HR involvement at board or equivalent senior management level, and in the other three fifths of organizations with heads of personnel on their boards, only 62 per cent were involved in developing corporate strategies from the outset. There was clear evidence of some shifting of responsibility for various aspects of personnel management towards line managers. Only about four out of ten organizations had written HR strategies. In general, it was hard to discover whether the tendency for line managers to take over some personnel tasks, like training, were part of a trend for personnel to become more concentrated at top management level and hence more strategic and HRM-like, or whether it meant that personnel was being 'sidelined, with other senior managers determining the strategy and line managers taking over the personnel aspects of its implementation'. What was apparent was that there were no clear grounds for optimism from an HRM standpoint.

On the management of organizational culture, HRM style, Ogbonna (1992) reviewed existing UK studies along with his own data from retailing. He argued that the 'most important aspect of HRM appears to be...managing culture' because the achievement of HRM and new policy objectives demanded that employee attitudes and behaviour, and external perceptions of them, should be in tune with policy objectives and with each other. In his main case, a supermarket chain, managers were 'only able to generate behaviourial compliance from an indifferent workforce'. Checkout operators acted in friendly ways towards rude customers because they felt compelled to, but their 'values and assumptions remained intact' and were expressed in rude remarks about and away from them in store canteens. For Ogbonna 'strong cultures' could not be 'managed' or 'corrected' easily. Organizations *were* cultures: it was not sensible to think of them as *having* them (cf. Burrell and Morgan, 1979). Indeed managerialist attempts to impose 'culture' top down in organizations are sociologically, philosophically and politically naive.

224

All human artifacts - ideas, social institutions and three dimensional objects - are cultured, insofar as they form parts of whatever things belong to particular human collectivities and make them unique (Sorge and Warner, 1986; also Glover, 1992). To identify 'organizational cultures' only with governing ideas was to abuse and trivialize the whole notion of culture, partly by playing down historical and societal underpinnings and variety. For Anthony (1990) it was virtually always self-defeating because management attempts to develop and impose strong cultures on subordinates generally lacked the 'moral relationships and reciprocal obligations' of workplace subcultures or community cultures. The artificial and the unauthentic would always be in opposition to the natural and the authentic, and *vice-versa*, and managers who tried to use instruments of cultural control would almost always eventually isolate themselves from reality as well as from their subordinates.

Such evidence and argument is reinforced by the results of studies concerned with the possible growth of HRM style employee involvement and commitment. Kelly and Kelly (1991) reviewed 'seventeen case studies of share schemes, profit-sharing, quality circles and autonomous work groups which had reported relevant evidence on workers' attitudes. Workers had often welcomed the new techniques but because they had generally been imposed on them in the context of unequal power and status relations, managerial inconsistency and cynicism and lack of trust, and generally traditional 'them and us' attitudes to industrial relations had persisted. Marchington, Goodman, Wilkinson and Ackers (1992) examined evidence on attempts by managements to increase employee involvement, finding a very mixed picture associated with a great variety of reasons for management wanting to do so, but with little evidence of development of HRM style commitment on the part of employees. Similarly, Guest (1992b) found very little evidence of commitment in the British workforce either towards employees, or towards trade unions.

Still on the more general aspects of HRM, Blyton and Morris (1992) considered the role of workforce flexibility as a source of proactive organisational adaptation and thus competitive advantage. They emphasized how the pursuit of flexibility in practice almost always defined it 'in ways which match managerial objectives rather than ones which could represent possible areas of common ground with employees'. A 'high quality, flexible and committed workforce' could only be developed if 'a more equitable reciprocity' becomes the foundation of employment relationships. However 'state withdrawal from labour market regulations' weakened unions, and labour market conditions were being exploited by employers to impose numerical and financial flexibility in a 'hard' HRM approach, rather than functional flexibility in a 'softer' one.

More specific aspects of possible HRM style developments have been addressed in recent years by, among others, Poole and Mansfield, (1992); Keep, (1989); Smith, (1992); MORI, (1992) and Guest and Hoque, (1993). Poole and Mansfield found that attitudes consistent with HRM had been taken on board in the 1980s by British managers of most kinds, not only by those in personnel. Employee involvement in decision making and that of the financial kind were favoured as long as they were integrative. In 1990 compared with 1980, managers no longer felt as challenged from below by trade union power, and were more confident about their right and freedom to manage. Training and development were strongly supported in the late 1980s although in this instance no longitudinal data were available for a trend analysis. However Poole and Mansfield also argued that their evidence about somewhat more positive and proactive underlying attitudes towards 'human resources' amongst British managers was only that. Our reaction to their findings would interpret them as evidence of a combination of more broadly liberal and constructive attitudes to the employment relationship engendered by experience and improved management quality associated with competitive pressures and educational upgrading, and more confident attitudes engendered by labour market and political changes.

Keep (1989) argued that the commitment to training of a company was a central feature of any serious development of HRM in it. Training and development could generate loyalty, effort and commitment and serve as a crucial link between corporate and HR strategies, between managerial forecasting and career planning, for example. However, only 'a relatively limited group of larger companies .... competing in international markets' seemed to be aware of and to act on these points. Many companies preferred instead to operate in high volume standardized product markets using low skilled staff, or to shift productive capacity overseas, and so on, or to seek growth and profits by takeovers and divestments. Financial short termism, national and organizational, was also very relevant, as was the state's longstanding reluctance to develop a coherent national system of vocational education and training (cf. Sorge, 1979). Finally, employers' personnel policies were too informal. HRM demanded rigour, system and coherence of a kind which was traditionally missing in the relevant areas of management in Britain. Regarding the kind of systematic reward management which, through the use of performance related pay, might help to develop HRM style behaviour and commitment, Smith (1992) found that relevant developments generally had a piecemeal, *ad hoc* quality and that long term reward strategies designed to support training, development and performance were probably much less common than short term ones designed 'to drive down labour costs'. Also the very notion of HRM related reward management encapsulated a contradiction between individual rewards and team performance (Geary, 1992).

A large scale survey by Market Opinion and Research International (MORI, 1992) looked at the passing of personnel tasks to line managers. Personnel specialists seemed to be making great efforts to redefine their internal consultancy roles and to be doing far less to train, teach and otherwise help line managers to take over relevant functional personnel responsibilities. The results of the survey raise strong doubts about whether giving line managements HRM responsibilities is a wise thing to do, because line managers appeared to be so ill equipped to handle them.

Finally on the prevalence of HRM in Britain, Guest and Hoque (1993) used data from two large scale surveys to emphasise how very few British employers had changed the job titles of personnel to HR of relevant managers and staff. The use of HRM titles was more prevalent at head offices than at other establishments and the authors were careful to stress that personnel departments could, of course, have 'HRM' policies. However they were led to doubt, at least on the basis of their evidence, whether distinct and 'progressive' HRM policies and practices were in place in many organizations.

Recent discussions, recent disillusionment?

The evidence just described suggests that British managements preach HRM much more often and much more coherently than they practice it. Therefore, perhaps, it is not altogether surprising that recent British discussions of HRM have a critical and rather disillusioned quality. Sisson's (1990) 'definition' of HRM is very like ours at the start of this paper. We used the terms strategic, integrated, proactive and individualistic. He wrote of integration, domination by senior line management, individualism, and commitment and initiative. Guest (1987, 1990, 1991) produced a more policy goal centred definition, focusing on high commitment, high quality, flexibility and strategic integration. Guest had, in effect, offered a predictive 'theory' of HRM which has a normative, comprehensive and circular quality, making it difficult to falsify/test (cf. Boxall, 1992). Noon (1992) argued that the status of Guest's theory should be downgraded to that of a 'map' of ideas, a practical, diagnostic tool descriptive of a general style of management. Guest's desire to distinguish HRM from personnel management (cf. Armstrong, 1987) is excusable insofar as significant differences either exist or appear to exist, although the notion of personnel management's tasks being integrated with each other and with corporate strategy is several decades old, as indeed is the term human resource management (Storey, 1989, p. 4-5; see also Locke, 1996, on the history and on the strengths and weaknesses of American human relations management compared with German and Japanese philosophies; Armstrong, 1996, on the ideological character of much Anglo-American management thinking which depicts people as 'the' key resource; and Dingley, 1996, on some of the most important moral paradoxes which are interwoven with Anglo-Saxon management thought and practice).

The beginnings of much recent criticism of the HRM notion are at least partly apparent in Legge's (1989) distinction between its 'soft' and 'hard' elements or versions. The former has a more pluralist, developmental, humanistic emphasis (Fombrun, Tichy and Devanna, 1984). The latter is generally unitarist, managerialist, strategy-orientated and far more concerned with maximising the economic utilisation of human resources in the short run (cf. Hendry and Pettigrew, 1990). The most fundamental contradiction in all HRM thinking grows out of the fact that HRM, compared with personnel management, is demand rather than supply led, and ultimately concerned with efficiency above all else, so that there always seems to be an inherent conflict between short term financial criteria and the pursuit of long term employee development. This notion is fallacious in most respects, like the idea in manufacturing that there is an inevitable trade off between the cost of making things and the quality of work and of products.

Blyton and Turnbull (1992b) argued that HRM lacks both empirical support and that it has major conceptual weaknesses (as we have seen) but that it nevertheless threatens to be 'raised to the status of a new *lingua franca* among those teaching and researching in the areas of personnel management, industrial relations and organizational behaviour'. For Blyton and Turnbull, HRM was 'At best .... a series of practices which rose to prominence in management circles in the later 1980s'. In the early 1980s managements had been overly confrontational and inadequate in terms of obtaining the flexible cooperation of labour needed in the face of growing foreign competition. The political and economic conditions of the second half of the 1980s had provided a fundamental redefinition of the vocabulary of labour control and management, and the new rhetoric of HRM fitted a period of weak unions, strong foreign competition, and state encouragement of 'enterprise' and managerial power. Blyton and Turnbull went on to argue that HRM has been a blind alley in several key respects, one which attracted attention from central issues of industrial relations, albeit one which may usefully be retained as a descriptor of a set of management practices (with its own typical strengths and weaknesses) rather than as 'a more general theory of management'. HRM was *one* way in which managements might control labour. The old, 'core issues' of labour management, of 'power, control, conflict .... dependence, and so on', were as important as ever, and much more so than HRM.

Complementing these points, Keenoy and Anthony (1992) saw empirical testing of HRM as irrelevant, because rhetoric was its most important feature. HRM consisted of an attempt to redefine the meaning of work and of the employment relationship. It was a moral crusade which reflected and constituted an element of the enterprise culture. It was a mechanism for manufacturing meaning in the process of culture management. A philosophy of winning the heart and soul of the nation had informed its attempt to reconstruct employment relations. Its messages were far more important than the specific devices employed to transmit them, and its cultural impact far more important than the empirical reputation of its claims. There was no need to agonize about the conceptual clarity of HRM: to do so was irrelevant because it was just the latest of a long line of management metanarratives designed to legitimise management decisions and practice. Rhetoric was at the heart of HRM; because it is about the management of beliefs, comparison with management practice was not necessary for assessing its importance or effect. HRM was an ideology and it did not therefore collapse as a result of logical contradiction.

Since the subject matter was cultural construction, an effective critique needed to be cultural also. HRM sought to justify the prosaic aspects of the manipulation and control of labour and to deflect human responsibility to the hidden hand of the market so as to justify the means for achieving its ends of exploitation and domination. It should be subjected to moral scrutiny. Such scrutiny should address the moral ends of the product, images or narrative being 'sold'; the degree

228

of moral commitment deemed necessary to achieve these ends; the morality of the methods employed; and the moral consciences of its teachers.

The context reconsidered

We are inclined to agree with Keenoy and Anthony for three main reasons. First, the evidence discussed by us earlier shows how HRM rhetoric and reality are two very different things, thus lending effective support to a central part of their case. Second, the fact that HRM is logically contradictory and that many of its proponents continually ignore this is also, we consider, self-evident. Third, we agree with both them and Blyton and Turnbull that HRM as advocated in the UK in the last decade can be linked even more firmly than most management fads to a particular set of historical circumstances.

In an article with Reed, Anthony (Reed and Anthony, 1992) goes on to consider the morality of management education in Britain in recent years. Reed and Anthony 'define' management education very broadly, implicitly but effectively including almost anything taught to those who eventually manage others, and contrasting a 'technical competencies-based' and 'the creative professions/ethical' approaches to it. They discuss the very culturally, economically and socially fragmented character of British management and the related possibility for a 'fundamental re-evaluation of management education and its links with the professionalization of managerial work and its associated occupational structures'. They criticise the very instrumental character of business and management education for producing 'a barbarian elite' (see also Anthony, 1986). They go on to advocate a 'reformed management education' which generates self-awareness and responsibility in a context of concern for the real world, 'without the distracting and specious assistance of codes, competencies, catch phrases and mission statements'. Unreflective pragmatism and hucksterism, inherited from the unhappy and fragmented history of British educational-managerial relations 'since the ... industrial revolution', were producing managers and management without the sort of political and ethical foundation needed for coping with the growing complexity of their tasks and the need to secure the moral consent and involvement of subordinates. These arguments point some of the way towards a much more positive interpretation of HRM than that of the Keenoy and Anthony paper. First, however, a number of other, broader, aspects of the context of HRM need to be explored.

A weakness of the Reed and Anthony thesis is that they take the master occupational status category of manager for granted, albeit far from uncritically. They also accept and employ the modernist notions of a dramatic British industrial revolution and of organisational culture as consisting only of such things as values, ideas, beliefs, attitudes and patterns of behaviour. They do not appear to see that the very idea of management involves reification and implies estrangement, that is, it is a fundamentally alienating notion. They appear unaware that it is possible for resources to be managed successfully by very broadly educated, economically, socially and politically competent and responsible technical and other specialists who regard the notion of the generalist 'manager' with a certain amount of disdain. This is because such specialists think of someone who feels that he or she can manage 'oil, dishwashers, oranges and lemons, or mortgages' with "no intrinsic attachment to what happens to be his 'throughput' as 'a jack of all trades, delving in all kinds of things here and there, without serious dedication to a well defined lifetime activity" (Sorge, 1978). By accepting 'the manager' as the central character of contemporary economic life Reed and Anthony are indulging in a small amount of reification of their own. Further, they accept without serious demur the relevance of the mid-1980s debate about deficiencies in British 'management education' associated with the Management Charter Initiative, which relied on the perception that Britain experienced a deficit in such education, although in at least two of the countries with which relevant invidious comparisons were made, it tends to be conspicuous by its near-absence (cf. Glover and Kelly, 1993).

Reed and Anthony's apparent belief in the (historically somewhat anti industrial) notion of a British industrial revolution (cf. Fores, 1981) and in a rather trivial if widespread view of organizational culture are unimportant except insofar as they are evidence of their unnecessarily restricting the parameters of their arguments. What they should ideally have done is to follow their own precepts about critical understanding of the real world by stepping outside the boundaries of Anglo-Saxon management thought. By doing so they could have had pinned down contemporary notions of HRM much more comprehensively and firmly than either they or others have done so far.

The antecedents of HRM in Britain are more complicated than those of most of the other management level specialisms. This is only due in part to the fact that both the logic and the actual existence of HRM can be disputed very easily, as we have seen. The parent of HRM in the British context, is personnel management. The tasks and the roles of personnel management must initially form a very large part of virtually whatever we define HRM as, unless we take Keenoy and Anthony's criticisms to their logical conclusion and think of HRM as only having meaning as rhetoric and culture management. If HRM does eventually replace the term personnel management the latter is what much, probably most, of it will consist of. To understand the origins of HRM it is necessary to understand those of personnel management.

A cynical characterisation, perhaps even a caricature, of the history of British personnel management up to the mid-1970s, might have tried, as one of us once did at the time, to locate it in the evolving divisions of labour in British management. Thus, it was suggested, the history of British management in the first three quarters of the twentieth century, could with at least some truth be described:

in terms of engineers once having been dominant, but who because of an inability to make competitive products or to control costs, were partly replaced by accountants, who could control costs but who were technically ignorant and 'screwed up people'. and who were in their turn partly replaced by personnel specialists, 'failed academic do-gooders', who were expected to repair the human damage produced by the accountants, but who were both financially and technically ignorant, and not especially knowledgeable about people either (Paterson et al., 1988; Glover, 1976; see also Ackroyd and Lawrenson, 1996, in this book).

A more dispassionate account, one with less reliance on stereotypes, would cover the early twentieth century welfare emphasis of personnel work, the growth of a range of specific tasks like collective bargaining, recruitment and training along with 'industrial' social science, and the optimism and ambitions of the 1960s and 1970s. It would note how personnel management was quite significantly a repository of hope between the post-Robbins (1963) expansion of higher education (from a very low base) and the harsher years around 1980. For a time, it was quite widely felt, personnel techniques might offer relatively painless cures and help in constructing some kind of new and benign negotiated order in such problem areas as industrial relations and training. Second, it might offer constructive and to some degree 'caring' employment to some of the new graduates who were seeking appropriate employment in growing numbers following university and polytechnic expansion. However such aspirations were unlikely to do much to improve British economic performance: instead they were more typical of a then characteristic reluctance to attack problems at their source. British products and services were not marketable enough because of slow supply and poor quality. Effete if well meaning idealism and personal aspirations were partly irrelevant to this, and part of the problem themselves in some respects as well.

Unwillingness to get to the heart of things has been linked to two sets of master assumptions about work and employment, Business Management and *Technik* (Glover, 1992a). These are similar to Lane's (1989) negative and positive forms of capitalism and Albert's (1993) neo-American and Rhine models (the latter includes Japan as well as Western and North Western and continental Europe). The former is linked to the main English speaking developed countries and is 'associated with possessive individualism, with short term financial and/or trading priorities, antiproductivism, and rationally guided search behaviour', whereas the latter is 'associated with more collectivist forms of political economy, relatively long term economic priorities, respect for engineering and manufacturing, and arational problem solving, or, in other words, unpredictable ingenuity'. The former favours *laissez-faire* political economy and, in management, generalism and mobility, and the "technocratic *Technik* one emphasises specialism and stability in management [and in employment generally] and a relatively strong and consistent role for the state in most matters, including that of managing the 'human resource' at the national level" (Glover, 1992a, p. 2-3).

Many writers, some discussed above, have described how personnel specialists on both sides of the Atlantic have been seen as having failed to develop their specialism and to advance their interests since the 1960s so as to ensure improved utilisation of employees and their own place in the sun. HRM was therefore pushed as a way of succeeding where personnel failed, by using many personnel techniques but by also having a *strategic* approach to employing and developing people. Growing criticism of occupation based departmentalism in British and North American management and widespread advocacy of more flexibly integrated patterns of management helped to make the highly specialized personnel professional rather unfashionable in 1980s Britain. While HRM's vision of highly trained, highly committed and cost effective workforces is neither new nor specific to HRM or the personnel function, its explicit stress on competitive advantage and the pursuit of 1980s style 'excellence', using foreign and domestic examples of the latter, certainly was, at least as far as the personnel function was concerned.

HRM is predominantly a US notion and creation which was developed by employers as a way of heading off employee attempts to organise collectively, and in a context of low and declining levels of unionisation. American management thought grew up for reasons which make it very distinctively American, in a context in which its authors explicitly distanced themselves from what they saw as a corrupt Old World of Europe. They wanted to make America different from sinful Europe by using rational principles of natural law to 'overcome the particulars of history and become universal' (Noble, 1985). The American Dream of salvation through individual economic success and the American Way of management gave immigrants from diverse ethnic backgrounds a unifying ideology and helped to legitimise the process of developing a new nation, fending off the British, French and Spanish and dispossessing the Indians while occupying territory. US business education explicitly rejected 'rule of thumb': the theory and practice of management had to be systematic, nomothetic and generalisable. Both ends and means and causes and effects, had to be publicly visible and understood, not secretive and private in the bad old European ways. 'Relevant' knowledge was valued over all other types, and it was applied by 'expert power' in uniform ways in a wide variety of contexts. US textbook definitions of management have sought to teach future business managers to apply rules and formalizations across a wide range of situations in standardized ways. Similarly careers have been built around the idea of interfunctional and interorganizational mobility: and unlike ethnics, it has been thought, 'Americans' can manage anything (Fores, Glover and Lawrence, 1992).

Yet, different as the USA became, it was and still is, a country which was founded mainly by Englishmen, one whose language is English and whose legal and educational systems have several defining English characteristics. The powerful desire of Americans to be different can be understood as a development of English individualism and similarly American materialism can be interpreted as a development of English commercialism (Glover, 1985). In both nations too, there is a strong Arcadian rural ideal, and a strong belief that the less attractive jobs in factories should be managed at arms' length and performed by lesser breeds, such as immigrants or inhabitants of less fashionable regions or poor

232

foreign countries. Both countries have also institutionalized short termism in management, as expressed for example through banking practices, financial decision making on the part of corporations, the marketing concept which tends to favour what can be sold over what ought to be made to be sold, and the notion of HRM, which looks for organization level solutions to problems which are societal, to do with patterns of socialization in the family and elsewhere and with national systems of education and training.

A useful way of thinking about relevant national philosophies of education and training which helps to highlight the extent to which HRM style thinking is short termist was produced about fifteen years ago by Sorge (1979). He distinguished between 'state-school' and 'individualistic' philosophies, associating the former with France and Germany and the latter with Britain, and a kind of half-way house philosophy, the 'association' one, mainly with certain aspects of British and German practice. He explained how decisions by politicians and other members of governing elites about economic priorities, education, training, occupation formation, career and organisational structures, ways of classifying and using and developing knowledge and skills and soon, had extremely powerful effects on management and economic performance decades and centuries after they had been made, often long after the original reasons for them had been forgotten.

Thus, and following Sorge's line of thought, neglect of vocational education and training and state reluctance to impose comprehensive remedies for it have resulted in a wide range of *ad hoc* private, public and semi-public partial solutions being applied in the Business Management countries. Education for business and management have been bolted on to more specialized forms of education in ways which have often served to demean the latter (Armstrong, 1996). Fashion and opportunism have been powerful influences in this situation. In the late 1970s in Britain there was concern for a time about the lack of technical competence in British manufacturing management, but in the difficult political and economic context of the early 1980s concern shifted from British management's deficiencies to the world economy and to rather confused worrying about the impact of micro electronics on work and employment. The growth of large scale youth unemployment and otherwise valuable expansion of business and management education also diverted attention from the rather dull (in British eyes, anyway) but important issue of national educational and other neglect of engineering and manufacturing. Largely American led fearful fascination with Japanese management and rather vaguely defined 'management education' became major foci of contemporary Establishment attention in the mid to late 1980s, and resulted in the Management Charter Initiative in the late 1980s. This was explicitly uncritical of existing social and educational arrangements and very reliant on exhortation for action. Interest in HRM in 1980s' Britain grew up largely against such a background, one of concern, exhortation and so on. It was Anglo-Saxon managerialist insofar as it indicated top down manipulation of organizational behaviour, and it was short termist because it addressed organizational rather than societal issues for a society which has been so conspicuously lacking in serious

233

interest in the variety and complexity of manufacturing and of most other groupings of difficult specialist skills. Also its association with the obsessive, elitist and partly reactionary notion of excellence and with the conjuring up of managerial(ist) 'competencies' was not especially helpful.

The *Technik* set of assumptions, described earlier, are associated with very different habits and institutions. These assumptions include the notion of the human being as *homo faber*, as maker and doer, rather than Business Management's more restricted *homo sapiens*, the thinker or planner. It is connected with situations in which top job holders tend to be true technocrats, that is broadly educated technical or commercial and financial specialists whose experiences, but not all of their mental outlooks, tend to be specific to particular sectors of employment. These can be contrasted with two ideal-typical kinds of senior job holder in the Business Management countries, custodians and professionals. Custodians are typically academically educated people with liberal arts or natural or social science degrees, whose education has been academically more specialized than that received by technocrats but who have been presented as generalist philosopher-kings, or 'amateurs' of a kind, expected to have 'trained minds' for use in any sector of employment. The erstwhile 'second eleven' of professionals, who have supported and then increasingly supplemented them, has consisted of such people as engineers, accountants and marketing, natural and social scientific and personnel specialists whose collective upward social mobility projects have borrowed status from the various sciences which they have studied and in many cases helped to construct. The special prestige of science in the English speaking countries, in which science unlike engineering has been regarded as fit for a gentleman, was for a long time significantly useful to them in this way.

The notion of *Technik* subjects means, when interpreted most liberally, not only engineering and other making and doing ones such as those of business and commerce ones but also the arts of the state. The word has direct counterparts in all the main European languages except English. It is part of a threefold system of subject classification which is significantly more logical than the arts and natural (part and applied) and social science English language one. *Technik* subjects tend to be taught in specialist universities and other vocational institutions like Berlin Technical University of the *Ecole des Ponts et Chaussés* in Paris. Their outputs are valued in terms of utility: one asks does it work and what does it cost? *Wissenschaft* subjects, on the other hand, are valued in terms of truth. The word *Wissenschaft* means science, broadly interpreted to include all subjects concerned with truth and analysis, such as physics, sociology, and the *study* of literature (but creative writing is part of *Kunst*, below). Those subjects are taught in the traditional universities. *Kunst* means the fine and performing arts, such as painting, drama, and composing and performing music. These are judged by aesthetic and philosophical criteria: relevant questions regarding outputs include 'Is it beautiful?' and 'does it have universal relevance?'. These subjects are taught in special conservatoires, which are rather like British art colleges.

This is clearer than the English language classification of subjects into sciences and arts ones, in which the arts tend to be decorative and those which are more 'useful' are often hard to distinguish from each other and from so called applied science and without which the social sciences sit rather unhappily. It is not often associated with endless confused debates about the roles of natural and social scientific knowledge in industry, business and government. Such knowledge is simply thought of as a public good which anyone can use as they see fit. The prime source of creative activity is known to be unpredictable ingenuity. Whiggish ideas of an 'industrial' or 'modern' condition, specially dependent on rational forms of action, are well recognized for the propaganda that they are.

The *Technik* culture is not one in which Anglo-Saxon, or Anglo-American, HRM is particularly relevant (Sisson, 1989). This is not to deny that the idea of integrating 'people' and other aspects of management from the highest level downwards has some sort of universal validity and relevance for employers. However the strength of the *Technik* culture or approach is that the production and development of suitably educated, trained and divided labour is taken care of by governments before people become employees to a significantly greater extent than is the case with the Business Management approach. If larger Japanese organizations are to be thought of as examples of the *Technik* approach, they still broadly fit the pattern in spite of the fact that they have more responsibility for 'HR' management and development compared with continental European counterparts. In other words, they still differ from Business Management style organizations by routinely paying much more attention, over longer periods, to 'HR' development, and by focusing this much more directly on productive or other operations, i.e., they are not arm's length and they are not short termist.

Thus the main criticism of Business Management style HRM is that it is a (short term) ameliorative notion which cannot, by its nature, cure or even properly address the problems which confront it. In a context of skill shortages and confused and often misplaced aspirations, and of governmental confusion about actions needed, and as the consideration of the *Technik* has shown, it is both part of and a distraction from these more basic problems. It hands a set of tasks to employees which should have mainly been performed by parents and educators. It is a product of a grouping of free societies which sometimes seem willing to try any palliative or partial solution rather than attack the roots of their difficulties. For the Americans, in the land which invented it, HRM is a vision of the American Dream of success by hard work and self-improvement, facilitated by enlightened leadership (Guest, 1990). Foreign competition is the newest 'frontier', and widely cited HRM case studies are used as myths and legends to obscure the less pleasant aspects like 'downsizing' of companies and the assault of American businesses on their country's trade union movement. For Guest, HRM's British progress was relatively limited partly because British managers did not 'share the American Dream', although Thatcherite politics had included HRM related antiunion legislation and HRM-like individualistic forms of employee involvement (p. 393).

235

In both cases will and reactivity appear to have been substituted for thoughtful action.

Discussion and conclusion

Can HRM have, and/or does it deserve, a viable future? Virtually all extended definitions and discussions of it include consideration of all or most of old style personnel management, and more ambitious points about the strategic centrality of organization development and human resource issues. Thus HRM is clearly concerned with all or most aspects of managing the employment of people at both individual and organizational levels. Both of these practices are clearly underdeveloped, as indeed are theorizing about and the practical understanding of them. Both are influenced, in the nature of things, by historic and other disjunctions between technical and social divisions of labour, by all those situations in which the wrong kinds of people, with the wrong education and training are doing the wrong jobs in the wrong ways for the wrong reasons (Glover and Kelly, 1987). Both ought to be useful for helping to engender the reduction of such divisions, although a reading of most personnel and/or HRM textbooks of the period since 1945 would not be the most productive effort amongst those available for someone wanting to understand them. Personnel/HRM textbooks have been usefully prescriptive in a purely technical sense but they have not always articulated well with real world problems. Explaining how to interview is not the same as explaining how to choose creatively between job applicants in different settings before and after the interview stage.

HRM is arguably a better title than personnel management. Each is suspiciously long-winded and tautological. Personnel management might usefully be called Employment instead. That is what it means in practice, and would possess the same accuracy, brevity and confident ring as Accounts, Finance, Production, Sales or Marketing. HRM department could usefully be retitled the Work department: that would be really confident! However and in the imperfect world in which we are stuck with long-winded functional and occupational titles, HRM compared with personnel does often have some pleasing connotations of developing people as well as of using them. However we would emphasize the following points, with the aim of encouraging HRM to become more credible in practical and moral terms.

First, it must always be fully cognisant of societal factors. To expect employers to resolve all of the country's educational and skill deficiencies and moral and political issues is as naive as expecting the police to do the same with crime. Societal competence, in this regard, demands historical and comparative awareness, as we have suggested above. It means following Clint Eastwood, that famous critic of personnel managers, by knowing and living within one's limitations.

Second, a great deal of evidence suggests that the 'soft' approach to HRM is generally more productive than the ostensibly more hard nosed alternatives. Almost all that psychology tells us about learning, leadership and management styles, stress, motivation, and human growth and development, tells us that people perform better, for longer, when they are neither oppressed nor bullied on the one hand nor ignored and neglected on the other, but encouraged to learn and to work hard, treated as individuals, and generally developed through a judicious and individually relevant mixture of incentives and danger signals. We have been shown the folly of the 'pay em high, ride em hard', school of management in all sorts of accounts of German and Japanese versus UK and US management. All except the very simplest tasks involve learning, and harsh authoritarian management inhibits it. Also, to separate economic, moral and social phenomena from each other is to start dismantling the foundations of economic and social life. To develop people and to help them channel their energies and passions is a basic precondition of civilized living (Dingley, 1996). And to use an old but genuine example, we can see that in their day, one when their country's performances of most kinds were widely respected and admired, and by contemporary standards, Nelson and Wellington had conspicuously 'soft' approaches to 'HRM'. Administrative and managerial as well as naval and military competence was basic to their successes, just as administrative incompetence and callously selfish disregard for his followers' welfare led to the appalling disaster of Napoleon's excursion into Russia, in which, incidentally, far more French soldiers died from cold, starvation and disease before the infamous retreat from Moscow than died from the same things and the activities of the Cossacks during it. Thus UK people can use evidence from successful events in their own history as well as from other countries and from social science to justify decent treatment of employees on practical and moral grounds.

Third, HRM should be what the best personnel practice has tried to be, namely developmental above almost everything else. It should foster equal opportunities in the most positive ways that it can, in the pursuit of competence at all levels of employment and from all kinds of employee. The present British context, for example, is an extremely ageist one in which between 1972 and 1992 the proportion of males aged from 55 to 64 in full time employment fell from 88 to 33 per cent (Hallier, Glover and Lyon, 1993). Competent use of available energies and talents would demand that HRM address such facts, partly by working for the treatment of all employees as individuals and not as members of status or other social categories. In doing so it should address employment, development, promotion and termination issues, not only those connected with recruitment.

Fourth, education for HRM ought to move beyond outlining and discussing hypothetical examples of the use of practical techniques and covering social science theories and data, to systematic and direct concern with occupation- and sector-specific issues. Relevant courses should continually mix HRM thinking and techniques up with pertinent ideas and evidence from all of the social sciences, and with all relevant facts about specific people and situations (Glover and Kelly, 1986). Degrees for HRM specialists should use organization - and sector-specific examples routinely in this way. More specialized courses would generally consist of little else, while drawing heavily on rigorous academic theories and research.

The future development of education and training for HRM would largely consist of building up bodies of knowledge, and skills, for use in particular occupations and sectors. General HRM textbooks of the present type would be relegated, for example, to the early stages of degree and professional courses. Books and papers used for most HRM teaching would address such topics as human resource development in aeronautical engineering, appraising the performance of actuaries, converting professional footballers to team managers, management development for NHS consultants, and so on.

Finally, the problem with HRM at present is the amoral baggage associated with it through the abuse of terms like flexibility and commitment and the invention and use of such arguably evil euphemisms downsizing (rightsizing). When HRM is used as a political weapon in that kind of way it is a sign of lack of awareness by managers of the often harsh, even cruel, reality of many of their decisions. It is a political weapon used defensively as well as offensively, for rationalizing bad effects of decisions, for cooling out their own *angst* and the pain of others who are being exploited.

Keenoy and Anthony and Reed are very right to have drawn attention, in a number of publications over the last decade, to the morality of managerial behaviour in HRM (and other) contexts, and to suggest why people who are moral beings at rest and play become amoral ones at work, and how HRM as rhetoric helps them to block out ethical standards, social considerations, and so on, in ways which are sometimes disturbing (for some of the relevant background to this, see Dingley, 1996).

In part, this process also accounts for the ways in which personnel practitioners have begun to use the rhetoric of HRM in the last five years. Of course, personnel managers have long believed in their function's contributions to organizational performance as well as to employee well being. However, because of its language, HRM is perceived as the latest and perhaps best opportunity for the function to increase its status. Ironically, personnel managers have opted to tip the balance of their aims in favour of business goals at a time when the ethical issues facing the management of work are particularly acute due to rises in unemployment and job insecurity, and the demise of traditional career patterns from restructuring, flexibility initiatives and temporary working.

To some extent the acceptance of HRM rhetoric by personnel practitioners reflects their long established habit of adapting their roles to prevailing circumstances. In another sense the adoption of HRM language, if not much of its substance, can be construed mainly as a defensive tactic aimed at asserting their expertise in the strategic management of work as many of their routine functions become increasingly passed to line managers. As part of claiming a degree of ownership over strategic HR issues, the IPD launched a consultation document aimed at developing an agreed view among their membership of their new role(s) and in promoting personnel's business contribution among senior management (IPD, 1993). The substance of the document reveals the way the 'taken for granted' nature of HRM rhetoric enables personnel practitioners to overlook its problems and limitations. Thus, a definition of HRM is apparently unnecessary, the link between managing HR and competitiveness is believed to be widely understood, and the existence of empowerment, team working and flexibility is unproblematical. Although the document is designed to launch a debate among IPD members about the future direction of personnel work, it is clear that personnel practitioners regard the current climate as an opportunity to promote and legitimate their strategic business role. Confronting uncertainties, doubts and problems identified by academic writers and research has little to do, as far as they are concerned, with asserting and establishing influence in organizations.

While the acceptance of HRM's business values is a significant change in the aims of personnel specialists, it is difficult to be optimistic about the spread of HRM in companies or the raising of standards in the management of work and employment (Sisson, 1994). Although elements of HRM ideas will increasingly be adopted in work organizations, its real significance in the UK has been in the way in which personnel managers have begun to learn a business focused language to describe and legitimise their activities. Two outcomes may be expected to follow this.

One is that the prevalence of HRM rhetoric will tend to devalue the achievement of more modest but important goals. Already, many employers tend to express disappointment with anything less than strong organizational commitment on the part of employees. Because of the excessive unitarist aspirations of much HRM ideology, culture change and employee involvement initiatives are often expected to produce higher organizational commitment and performance rapidly if they are to be judged successful. The mere attainment of improved employee relations and communications are insufficient achievements in themselves.

Second, the promotion of HRM concepts will inevitably raise expectations regarding how the contributions of personnel specialists are judged. Keenoy and Anthony may be partly right to conclude that the rhetoric of HRM makes its practical outcomes irrelevant, but the same cannot be said of its potential effect on personnel management. Here both the problem and opportunity for the function lies in its justification and promotion mainly in business terms at a time when employers are directly evaluating the contribution of all roles and departments. Seen from this perspective the impact of HRM lies not with the extent of its presence or achievements in UK organizations. Of far greater significance has been the way in which aspects of the language of normative HRM models have been perceived by the personnel function as a source of increased business credibility. Within this aim lie the seeds either of success in achieving greater organizational status or failure from a gradual marginalization of personnel roles by line management. Either way, the personnel function's efforts to exhibit some features of general business management raise the very real possibility of greater informality and lower standards in personnel management. Therefore, and paradoxically, while the academic study of HRM is likely to grow, the future of the personnel function and the standards applied to the ways in which employees are managed are far less certain.

To sum up, HRM can have a viable future if it develops what it contributes by making it more specific in its details and more practical, and therefore more genuinely wide ranging in its application. Rhetoric, the selfish kind of ambition and politicking can only ever be short term substitutes for expertise and achievement.

References

Albert, M. (1993), *Capitalism versus Capitalism*, Whurr, London.

Anthony, P. (1977), *The Ideology of Work*, Tavistock, London.

Anthony, P. (1986), *The Foundation of Management*, Tavistock, London.

Anthony, P. (1990) "The Paradox of the Management of Culture or 'He who Leads is Lost'", *Personnel Review*, 19, 4: pp. 3-8.

Armstrong, M. (1987), *A Handbook of Personnel Management Practice*, Kogan Page, London.

Armstrong, P. J. (1996), 'The Expunction of Process Expertise from British Management Education and Teaching Syllabi: An Historical Analysis', Chapter 12 in this book.

Blyton, P. and Morris, J. (1992), 'HRM and the Limits of Flexibility', in Blyton, P. and Turnbull, P. (eds), *Reassessing Human Resource Management*, Sage, London, pp. 116-130.

Blyton, P. and Turnbull, P. (1992a), 'HRM: Debates, Dilemmas and Contradictions', in Blyton, P. and Turnbull, P. (eds), *Reassessing Human Resource Management*, Sage, London, pp. 1-15.

Blyton, P. and Turnbull, P. (1992b), 'Afterword', in Blyton, P. and Turnbull, P. (eds), *Reassessing Human Resource Management*, Sage, London, pp. 256-260.

Boxall, P. F. (1992), 'Strategic Human Resource Management: Beginnings of a New Theoretical Sophistication?', *Human Resource Management Journal*, Vol. 2, 3, pp. 60-79.

Boyatzis, R. E.(1982), *The Competent Manager: a model for effective performance*, Wiley, New Jersey.

Brewster, C. and Smith, C. (1990), 'Corporate Strategy: A No Go Area for Personnel', *Personnel Management*, July, pp. 36-40.

Burrell, G. and Morgan, G. (1979), *Sociological Paradigms and Organisational Analysis*, Heinemann, London.

Child, J. (1984), *Organization: A Guide to Problems and Practice*, Harper and Row, London.

Dingley, J. (1996), 'Durkheim, Professionals and Moral Integration', Chapter 7 in this book.

Fombrun, C., Tichy, N. M. and Devanna, M. A. (1984), *Strategic Human Resource Management*, John Wiley, Chichester.

Fores, M. (1981), 'The Myth of a British Industrial Revolution', *History*, June, pp. 181-198.

Fores, M., Glover, I. and Lawrence, P. (1992), 'Management Thought, the American Identity and the Future of European Labour Processes in 1992', Tenth Annual International Labour Process Conference, University of Aston, Birmingham.

Fowler, A. (1987), 'When Chief Executives Discover HRM', *Personnel Management*, January, p. 3.

Geary, J. F. (1992), 'Pay, control and commitment: linking appraisal and reward', *Human Resource Management Journal*, 2 (4), pp. 36-54.

Glover, I. A. (1976), 'Barely Managing with Academic Qualifications', *The Guardian*, 4 February, p. 15.

Glover, I. A. (1985), 'How the West was Lost? decline of Engineering and Manufacturing in Britain and the United States', *Higher Education Review*, 17, (3), pp. 3-34.

Glover, I. A. (1992a), "'But westward look, the land is bright'"? Reflections on what is to be learnt from British management education and practice', *Journal of Strategic Change*, 1, 6, Nov-Dec 1992, pp. 319-332.

Glover, I. A. (1992b), "'Technik', uncertainty and the ethical significance of human resource management", Proceedings of the Conference on Business Ethics, Sheffield Business School, Sheffield.

Glover, I. A. and Kelly, M. (1987), *Engineers in Britain: A Sociological Study of the Engineering Dimension*, Allen and Unwin, London.

Glover, I. A. and Kelly, M. (1993), 'Engineering Better Management', in Payne, G. and Cross, M. (eds), *Sociology in Action*, Macmillan, Basingstoke.

Guest, D. E. (1987), 'Human resource management and industrial relations', *Journal of Management Studies*, 24, (5), pp. 503-521.

Guest, D. E. (1989), 'Personnel and HRM: Can you Tell the Difference?', *Personnel Management*, January, pp. 48-51.

Guest, D. E. (1990), 'Human resource management and the American dream', *Journal of Management Studies*, 27, (4), pp. 377-397.

Guest, D. E. (1991), 'Personnel management: the end of orthodoxy?', *British Journal of Industrial Relations*, 29, (2), pp. 149-176.

Guest, D. E. (1992a) 'Human Resource Management in the United Kingdom', in Towers, B. (ed.), *The Handbook of Human Resource Management*, Blackwell, Oxford, pp. 3-26.

Guest, D. E. (1992b), 'Employee Commitment and Control', in Hartley, J. F. and Stephenson, G. M. (eds), *Employment Relations*, Blackwell, Oxford, pp. 111-135.

Guest, D. E. and Hoque, K. (1993), 'The Mystery of the Missing Human Resource Manager', *Personnel Management*, June, pp. 40-41.

Hallier, J. P., Glover, I. A. and Lyon, H. P. (1993), 'The Ageism Taboo in Human Resource Management Research', Eleventh Annual International Labour Process Conference, Blackpool.

Hendry, C. and Pettigrew, A. (1990) 'Human Resource Management: An Agenda for the 1990s', *International Journal of Human Resource Management*, Vol. 1, pp. 21-43.

Institute of Personnel and Development (IPD) (1993), *Managing People: The New Frontiers*, Consultative Document, Wimbledon, IPD.

Keenoy, T. (1990), 'HRM: a case of the wolf in sheep's clothing?', *Personnel Review*, 19, (2), pp. 3-9.

Keenoy, T. and Anthony, P. (1992), 'HRM: Metaphor, Meaning and Morality', in Blyton, P. and Turnbull, P. (eds), *Reassessing Human Resource Management*, Sage, London, pp. 233-255.

Keep, E. (1989) 'Corporate Training Strategies: The Vital Component?', in Storey, J. (ed.), *New Perspectives on Human Resource Management*, Routledge, London, pp. 109-125.

Kelly, J. and Kelly, C. (1991) "'Them and Us': Social Psychology and 'The New Industrial Relations'", *British Journal of Industrial Relations*, 29, 1, pp. 25-48.

Kelly, M. and Glover, I. A. (1987), "'Sociology for 'Technik'", *Higher Education Review*, 19, (3), pp. 24-36.

Lane, C. (1989), Management and Labour in Europe in *The Industrial Enterprise in Germany, Britain and France*, Edward Elgar, Aldershot.

Marchington, M., Goodman, J., Wilkinson, A. and Ackers, P. (1992), *New Developments in Employee Involvement*, Employment Department Research Services, No. 2, HMSO, London.

MORI (1992), *The Developing Role of Human Resource Management*, MORI, London.

Noble, D. W. (1985), *the End of American History*, University of Minnesota Press, Minneapolis.

Noon, M. (1992), 'HRM: A Map, Model or Theory?', in Blyton, P. and Turnbull, P. (eds), *Reassessing Human Resource Management*, Sage, London, pp. 16-32.

Ogbonna, E. (1992), 'Organization Culture and Human Resource Management: Dilemmas and Contradictions', in Blyton, P. and Turnbull, P. (eds), *Reassessing Human Resource Management*, Sage, London, pp. 74-96.

Paterson, B. E. (1996), 'Politics and Professionalism: Pursuing Managerialism in Personnel', in Glover, I. and Hughes, M. (eds), *Professions at Bay: Control and Encouragement of Ingenuity in British Management*, forthcoming, Avebury, Aldershot.

Paterson, B., Martin, G. and Glover, I. A. (1988), 'Who Incorporates Whom? Managerialism versus Professionalism amongst a Sample of Personnel Specialists in Scotland', presented at the Sixth Labour Process Conference, University of Aston, Birmingham.

Poole, M. and Mansfield, R. (1992), 'Managers' Attitudes to Human Resource Management: Rhetoric and Reality', in Blyton, P. and Turnbull, P. (eds), *Reassessing Human Resource Management*, Sage, London, pp. 200-214.

Reed, M. and Anthony, P. (1992), 'Professionalizing Management and Managing Professionalization: British Management in the 1980s', *Journal of Management Studies*, 29, 5, pp. 591-614.

Ritzer, G. and Harrison, M. (1970), 'A Mythical Occupational Image', *Human Mosaic*, Vol. 4, 2, pp. 69-78.

Sisson, K. (1989a), 'Personnel management in perspective', in Sisson, K. (ed.), *Personnel Management in Britain*, Blackwell, Oxford, pp. 3-21.

Sisson, K. (1989b), 'Personnel Management in Transition?', in Sisson, K. (ed.), *Personnel Management in Britain*, Oxford, Blackwell, pp. 22-52.

Sisson, K. (1990), 'Introducing the Human Resource Management Journal', *Human Resource Management Journal*, Vol. 1, (1), pp. 1-11.

Sisson, K. (1994), 'Personnel Management: Paradigms, Practice and Prospects', in Sisson, K. (ed.), *Personnel Management*, 2nd edition, Blackwell, Oxford, pp. 3-52.

Sisson, K., Edwards, P. and Hyman, R. (1992), 'Foreword' in Storey, J. *Developments in the Management of Human Resources*, Blackwell, Oxford.

Smith, I. (1992), 'Reward Management and HRM', in Blyton, P. and Turnbull, P. (eds), *Reassessing Human Resource Management*, Sage, London, pp. 169-184.

Sorge, A. (1978), 'The Management Tradition: A Continental View', in Fores, M. and Glover, I. A. (eds), *Manufacturing and Management*, HMSO, London, pp. 87-104.

Sorge, A. (1979), 'Engineers in Management: A Study of the British, German and French Traditions', *Journal of General Management*, 5, Summer, pp. 45-57.

Sorge, A. and Warner, M. (1986), *Comparative Factory Management*, Gower, Aldershot.

Storey, J. (1995), 'Human resource management: still marching on, or marching out?', in Storey, J. (ed.), *Human Resource Management: A Critical Text*, Routledge, London, pp. 3-32.

Storey, J. (1992), *Developments in the Management of Human Resources*, Blackwell, Oxford.

Timperley, S. and Sisson, K. (1989), 'From Manpower Planning to Human Resource Planning?', in Sisson, K. (ed.), *Personnel Management in Britain*, Blackwell, Oxford.

Torrington, D. (1989), 'Human Resource Management and the Personnel Function', in Storey, J. (ed.), *New Perspectives on Human Resource Management*, Routledge, London, pp. 56-66.

Torrington, D. and Hall, L. (1987), *Personnel Management*, A New Approach, Prentice Hall, London.

Watson, T. J. (1977), *The Personnel Managers: A Study in the Sociology of Work and Employment*, Routledge and Kegan Paul, London.

11 Traditional and emergent professions in the construction industry: competition and control over the building process

Mike Bresnen

Introduction

In the last decade, the architectural profession has come under increasing public scrutiny and, at times, attack. Well publicized critical observations made about modernist styles of architecture have been accompanied by increasing debate concerning the role of architects in responding to their clients' needs and the function of architecture in contributing towards the built environment. The obvious visibility of architects' contributions to the physical environment has always meant that the merits of competing styles of architecture have been hotly contested - both within the profession and also with the public at large. The difference nowadays is in the growing pressure for greater public accountability, associated with increasing dissatisfaction with the traditional client-architect relationship.

Important as they are, these developments are only a part of the problem as far as the architectural profession is concerned. For the best part of two decades, there have been equally significant changes occurring on what could be called the 'supply side' of the industry. Traditionally, architects have usually played a dominant role in the organization and management of construction projects, acting as main agents for their clients and having their rights and responsibilities formally set out in legal terms and conditions of contract. Yet there have been substantial modifications and departures from this basic model over the last two decades. In particular, new forms of contractual arrangement and the development of new management structures have substantially changed the locus of control and influence exercized by the various parties over the construction process. Architects now face competition from contractors and surveyors to undertake the leading role of project manager and have lost their former pre-eminent position as 'leader' of the construction project team.

It is with such changes to the structure of the project management team and their implications for the various actors involved that this chapter is concerned. It will explore recent changes in the pattern of roles and relationships amongst the participants in the project management process and attempt to relate these changes to changing economic conditions in the 1980s, processes of deregulation and organizational restructuring, the emergence of competition amongst the various professional groups and the key role played by building contractors' strategic manoeuvring.

As will be seen, the construction industry has historically been characterized by a complex division of labour between designers, builders and other participants which has led to a fragmented pattern of control over the construction process (e.g. Higgin and Jessop, 1965). Such a situation, it will be argued, has always provided the impetus behind attempts by each of the main parties concerned to extend their control over the total design/construction process - or at least to reduce their dependence on other parties to the contract (e.g. Ball, 1988; Bresnen, 1990). As such, the overall management and control of the design/construct process has long been the 'contested terrain' over which the various professional and other groups have sought to establish their hegemony (cf. Edwards, 1979; Johnson, 1972; Esland and Salaman, 1980). Consequently, changes in contractual and organizational arrangements can be interpreted as strategies adopted by the various groups to protect and/or extend their domains and jurisdictions (cf. Larson, 1977; Abbott, 1988). In particular, it will be argued that the emergence of project management has, in the context of heightened economic pressures and greater competition in the past decade, led to a significant realignment in the balance of power between the various groups involved in the construction process. Furthermore, that the main 'loser' in this process has been the traditionally dominant architectural profession.

To develop the argument, the paper will draw on secondary material and recently-collected primary data in order to chart recent developments in the industry and the associated discourse surrounding debates about the organizational forms deemed appropriate for the management of construction projects. In doing so, attention will be drawn to the manner in which the various professional bodies, the state and academics have contributed towards the debate by helping to define the nature of the problem, constructing the terms of reference for debate and acting as sources of legitimation for new and emergent organizational and contractual practices (cf. Zucker, 1977, 1983; Scott, 1987; DiMaggio and Powell, 1983).

The professions in the construction industry

The basic structure of the modern construction industry is the result of a long process of development that can be traced as far back as medieval times, when the industry was organized into a system of independent guilds, each representing one of the main specialist trades (bricklaying, carpentry, etc.). The period between the

246

seventeenth and early nineteenth centuries saw the establishment and consolidation of the major contemporary roles - of architect, engineer, quantity surveyor and main contractor (Higgin and Jessop, 1965). Architects initially came to the fore with the reconstruction that followed the great fire of London (Bowley, 1966). With the establishment of independent architects, design activity was effectively separated out from the construction process; and architects replaced 'master craftsmen' as coordinators of the building process with responsibility for the employment of specialist trades labour (Higgin and Jessop, 1965). Full professional status for architects came with the establishment, in 1834, of the Institute of British Architects - later to become the present day Royal Institute of British Architects (RIBA).

RIBA has traditionally acted as a classic professional institution (cf. Johnson, 1972), controlling entry to the profession through qualifications and training and providing codes of work practice and ethics (Stone, 1983). Until comparatively recently, terms and conditions for the provision of architectural services were rigidly specified by RIBA and chartered architects were not allowed to work in limited liability companies (Bowley, 1966, p. 342). Although RIBA membership is not mandatory, all practising architects nowadays have to be registered with the Architects' Registration Council (ARCUK), which was set up by Parliamentary legislation in 1931. Currently, there are nearly 32,000 registered architects, of which 21,000 are members of RIBA (Warne, 1993).

As the complexity of modern building work has increased, so too has the degree of specialization within the design process. Structural engineers have been employed within design teams since the nineteenth century, with responsibility for structural design aspects (Bowley, 1966, pp. 13-16). They have their own professional body - the Institute of Structural Engineers.[1] With the increasing sophistication of modern buildings in the twentieth century, specialist mechanical and electrical services engineers have also played an increasingly important role in design teams. They too have their own professional bodies, although their membership encompasses a much wider range of industries than construction. On some projects, such as the construction of petrochemical plants and other projects requiring complex engineering services, engineers might be called on to act as project managers instead of architects (NEDO, 1976). However, such projects are comparatively rare and the more usual situation is that architects perform this role, with engineers in the various disciplines contributing their services to the design process as part of an architect-led team (NEDO, 1976).

The role of quantity surveyor developed too at an early stage of industrialization: its origins can be found in the development of specialist 'measurers' who could negotiate on behalf of craftsmen with architects over payment for work done. As architects increasingly employed their own measurers in response and as the method of measuring work in advance from drawings developed, quantity surveying emerged as a distinct discipline (Higgin and Jessop, 1965). By the nineteenth century, quantity surveyors were already an important adjunct to the client's 'team'. Full professional status, however, came much later: it was only in 1868 that the Institute of Surveyors was founded - later to become the Royal Institute of Chartered Surveyors (RICS) in 1881.

The RICS set itself much the same task as RIBA, in terms of control over entry to the profession, specifying codes of professional practice and imposing limitations on members regarding employment in limited liability companies (Ball, 1988). However, its constituent membership has always been less precisely related to the organization of the construction industry. Firstly, membership has traditionally extended to the whole range of surveying functions relating to land development, including land and building surveying, and has not solely been restricted to quantity surveyors. Secondly, contractors' own quantity surveyors had, until recently, been effectively excluded from membership of RICS and many had joined a separate Institute of Quantity Surveyors (IQS) which was first established in 1938. In 1983, this historical split within the profession was ended with the merger of the two institutions.

Construction industry professionals are employed in a variety of ways by their clients. However, contracting-out professional services to consultants or using in-house design expertise have always been the two main alternative ways of organizing and managing projects. Clients in the industry range from smaller businesses who may be undertaking comparatively few projects and/or projects of insufficient scale to warrant investment in directly employed design staff; to major corporations and public authorities whose volume of work is sufficient to justify the direct employment of design staff. Public authorities, in particular, have traditionally operated a system in which their extensive housing and other construction programmes have been designed and managed by an architect-led multidisciplinary team of professional staff employed directly by the authority (NEDO, 1976).

For any particular organization, the tendency to employ direct or contract-out is likely to be based on a calculation that includes the relative costs of each option in relation to the volume of work and the more intangible costs and benefits associated with controlling the design process and making sure that client requirements are met (cf. Ouchi, 1980; Butler and Carney, 1983). There has long been a recognition within the industry that the use of external consultants to perform the work on the client's behalf has implications beyond the strictly financial ones, since it involves a loss of direct control over the design process. Not surprisingly, research has also shown how important existing knowledge of 'tried and tested' consultants is to the client (e.g. Bresnen, 1990). Indeed, such a concern with managing external relationships with consultants mirrors the problems identified in managing 'buyer-supplier' relations in other industries (e.g. Imrie and Morris, 1992). The general point here is that contracting out specialist design services has both positive and negative effects from the client's point of view. Potential problems of losing control over such activity are often responded to, as elsewhere, by the establishment of quasi-permanent interorganizational links between client and consultant. This is particularly pronounced in the private sector, where the use of consultants is both more common and not subject to the same public scrutiny as is the case with public sector work.

The effects of economic restructuring and deregulation in the 1980s

The 1980s saw substantial changes in the positions and comparative fortunes of the construction professions as a result of changed economic conditions. Over the decade there has been a substantial net reduction in the volume of new construction work, due to depressed economic conditions in the early 1980s and from the late 1980s onwards - culminating in publicly-expressed recent concerns about the lack of infrastructure investment and the depressed state of the housing market. For example, it has been estimated that the value of new architectural commissions (at 1985 prices) in the private sector fell from a peak of just under £15 million in 1989 to around £6 million in 1993.[2]

As a result, the number of professionals employed in the industry has fallen significantly, in line with the reduction in levels of employment within the industry as a whole. It has been estimated that, by July 1993, only about 63 per cent of registered architects were employed and that, between 1985 and 1993, there was a 15 per cent reduction in the numbers employed in architectural practices.[3] While the number of principal architects has remained fairly stable, there has been a substantial drop in the number of salaried architects and, especially, architectural assistants/technicians.[4] According to the Association of Consultant Architects, about 18,000 (45 per cent) architects and technicians were made redundant between 1990 and 1992.[5] A similar fall has occurred in the number of quantity surveyors employed, corresponding to an almost 50 per cent reduction in workload since 1988.[6] Employment of professionals in the public sector has also fallen, due to pressure to contain public expenditure. For example, new public sector commissions fell from around £2 million in 1989 to about £1.5 million in 1993.[7] On the other hand, although direct employment of architects by public authorities fell substantially during the 1980s, there has been little further reduction in staffing levels since 1990 (Matheou, 1992).

During the mid-1980s, there was also a substantial restructuring of employment within the industry associated with the decline in importance of public sector work and the growth of private sector speculative investment (Ball, 1988). As well as the direct effects of cuts in building programmes upon employment levels, public sector clients have also been forced to assess the feasibility of continuing to support the overheads associated with directly employing large, permanent design teams. As a result, many have increasingly looked to the market as a mechanism for procuring design services. Although the ratio of public to private sector work has increased in recent years due to the decline in private sector investment, the trend towards contracting-out professional services has continued. The net effect has been a steady erosion of the traditional institutional strongholds (namely, local authorities) of the design professionals in general, and of architects in particular.

For example, the Society of Chief Architects of Local Authorities (SCALA) has recently estimated that internal restructuring has led to a fall in the proportion of architect-led property and related departments in local authorities from 51 per cent in 1990 to 47 per cent in 1992 (Matheou, 1992).

In the private sector too, the much smaller number of inhouse professional design teams employed by larger client companies have become increasingly rare, as firms have responded to economic pressures in the 1980s by cutting their managerial overheads (e.g. Dopson and Stewart, 1990). Research conducted by the author at the height of the mid-1980s boom gives a flavour of the extent of contracting-out, as well as differences between private and public sectors (Bresnen and Haslam, 1991). Of 138 £1 million plus projects investigated, consultants were used for all professional services in 77 cases (56 per cent). In a further 16 cases (12 per cent), only an architect, surveyor or building services engineer was employed in-house. In only 20 of the cases (15 per cent) were all professional services supplied in-house - mainly on public sector housing contracts; although, even in the public sector, there were a significant number of projects where consultants were employed and the occasional case where an in-house architect was used primarily as project manager rather than designer.

Added to these shifts in employment have been major changes to the competitive structure for the provision of professional services. Since 1981, restrictions on architects holding directorships in construction firms and working for limited liability companies have effectively been removed and, in 1982, RIBA's mandatory fee scales were abolished, allowing architects to compete with one another on fees. Quantity surveyors have followed suit, with price competition being introduced in 1983 and restrictions on employment by limited liability companies being lifted in 1986. More recently, the process of deregulation seemed set to be taken a stage further, with the publication of a government report recommending the abolition of ARCUK as the architects' registration body and the abandonment of the title of 'chartered' architect (Warne, 1993). Although these recommendations have not been adopted, it is interesting to note the continuing pressure on the building professions - particularly architects - to open up to greater competition.

The background to these proposed changes forms the basis of this chapter and developments within the industry that are influencing changes to the roles of the main participants will be explored further below. In the meantime, it is interesting to note the reaction of the profession to these changes. In his recent inaugural speech as new RIBA president, Frank Duffy spoke of architects being 'under siege' and stressed the need for the profession to maintain its distinctive knowledge base and professional integrity and to redefine the role performed by the architect to preserve the profession's distinct contribution to the building process.[8] As will be seen, there is good reason for such a defensive reaction, albeit rather less cause for optimism that architects can retain their traditional professional status and role.

The traditional method of contracting

The emergence of the professional roles of architect, engineer and surveyor proceeded apace with the development of the contracting system which, by the nineteenth century, was firmly established as the common method of commissioning and organizing construction work. In the early nineteenth century, government regulations were introduced that specified that building operations should come under the control of a single 'contractor'. As a result, direct employment of specialist trades labour by the architect gave way to the emergence of the role of 'main contractor' - a general builder responsible for the entire construction process (Higgin and Jessop, 1965). This basic model is the precursor to today's system of contracting, in which a main contractor undertakes the building operations on behalf of the client, under the supervision and according to the specification of the client's architect (NEDO, 1978). The main contractor will undertake some of the work directly, although it has increasingly been the case that much of it is subcontracted (NEDO, 1988, p. 73).

In this standard arrangement, the contract is between the client and the main contractor. It includes design drawings and specifications prepared by the architect and other members of the design team, as well as a bill of quantities - prepared by the quantity surveyor - that measures and itemizes the work required and which forms the basis for the main contractor's estimate of contract price (e.g. Harris and McCaffer, 1989). The role and powers of the architect are set out in standard terms and conditions that also constitute part of the main contract (Turner, 1984). Such terms and conditions are set out and modified from time to time by the Joint Contracts Tribunal (JCT) - an industry body that was established in 1937 to provide a basis for regulating the relationship between clients, professionals and builders (Ball, 1988).

This 'traditional' (or 'JCT') model of construction contracting has a number of important features. Firstly, it reflects the independent but, at the same time, ambiguous role of the architect with respect to both client and contractor. On the one hand, the architect is there to protect their client's interests and to ensure that the work is carried out as specified; on the other hand, the architect has considerable discretion and can authorize additional work and decide whether contractors' claims for work done are 'reasonable'. According to Ball (1988, pp. 57-60), the maintenance of this independent position as mediator of the client-contractor relationship represents a 'remarkable political coup' by the architectural profession and one that has enabled it to stay beyond the direct influence of capitalist construction firms. However, it has also created a basic ambiguity in the architect's relationships with the main parties to the contract: it has long been observed that the architect's role as project manager *vis-a-vis* the main contractor does not correspond to the contractual relationship between the two (Chartered Institute of Building (CIOB), 1988).

Secondly, the architect has traditionally performed a dual role of both principal designer ('design team leader') and project manager. This has meant a heavy reliance being placed by clients upon their designers to manage the construction process and, again, considerable discretion being allowed architects in introducing design variations in the light of actual conditions on site. The main problem here is that the architect is expected to be both a specialist and a generalist at the same time. The architectural design of the building, though a key element, is only one aspect of the finished building and one element of the design process. Others include its structural components (the adequacy of foundations, strength of materials used, etc.); and - of particular importance to prospective users - the provision of services such as heating, lighting and ventilation. As noted above, each of these main areas is the separate province of a specialist engineering designer.

One implication of this is the increasing difficulty faced by architects in being able to understand fully, let alone control, key elements of the building process (Stone, 1983, p. 194). This is particularly so with the less cognate disciplines of building services design. Indeed, since the design for services is often dependent upon a complex process of interaction between building services designer(s) and the specialist subcontractors concerned (often nominated by the client), the process can become somewhat 'detached' from the overall design process. This has been commented upon by many observers of the industry, and research by the author has shown how it can be manifested in an almost distinct 'subculture' within the project management team (Bresnen, 1990). Another, related implication is that there is a latent conflict of interest between the architect's role as specialist designer and their role as generalist responsible for all aspects of the design of the building. Such a situation is a recipe for conflict within the design team and finds its expression in commonly reported difficulties of integrating aesthetic, structural and services elements (Bresnen, 1990).

Thirdly, the method of contracting based upon drawings, specifications and a bill of quantities has served to create a temporal disjuncture between design and construction processes, with the latter only proceeding when the former is well advanced. This has introduced a division which many regard as being at odds with the inherent uncertainty of the construction process and the close practical interdependence between design and construction (Higgin and Jessop, 1965; Crichton, 1966). Indeed, many commentators have suggested that the division of labour between designers and builders that has produced this divide has always led to inefficiencies in the industry and inhibited the introduction of new construction techniques (Bowley, 1966, p. 179). The basic problem is that architects' plans may be drawn up with only limited consideration given to the practical aspects of constructing the building on site. Again, the problem is heightened with the more complex designs associated with modern buildings. For example, building services often depend on detailed designs prepared by specialist subcontractors who may not be appointed until the main contract is let.

A final feature which receives somewhat less attention, but which deserves mention since it is implicit in many analyses of interprofessional and interorganizational relations in the industry, is the tendency that the established functional/professional division of labour has created towards distinct forms and cultures of organization (Bresnen, 1990). Many analyses have identified, not surprisingly, quite distinct structures, styles of management and modes of operation - especially between professional practices and construction firms (e.g. Morris, 1973). Added to these differences are the divergent orientations of different members of the professional team alluded to above. It is hardly surprising that such differences become important explanatory factors in investigations of common 'communication problems' experienced within the industry (Higgin and Jessop, 1965; Melchers, 1977).

In the 1960s and 1970s, the performance of the construction industry received considerable public attention, culminating in a series of governmental and other, independent reports which examined, amongst other things, the efficacy of traditional contractual and tendering arrangements (Emmerson, 1962; Banwell, 1964; Phelps-Brown, 1968; NEDO, 1970). Perceived widespread delays and cost over-runs were attributed, in part, to the inadequacies of the traditional method, with its confused system of responsibilities and its separation of design and construction processes. Commonly reported problems included: the lack of any builder's input into the design process; the difficulties caused by introducing and reaching agreement on design changes and additional work once the contract was signed; and the problems of coordination that occurred when there was any 'overlap' of the design process into the construction stage (Higgin and Jessop, 1965). Many commentators pointed to the lack of cooperation within the industry caused by the highly specialized division of labour and 'entrenched' institutional interests (e.g. Crichton, 1966, pp. 43-5).

Theoretical support for the proponents of change was provided by researchers at the Tavistock Institute and elsewhere (Higgin and Jessop, 1965; Crichton, 1966; Morris, 1973). Employing sociotechnical systems theory, researchers directed their attention towards problems at the 'design-construct interface'. A contradiction was observed between the 'technical system' requirements for a flexible and informal arrangement to allow for the coordination of complex, uncertain and interdependent design and construction processes; and the existing rigid institutional framework that was based upon a clear separation of design and construction activities. Crichton (1966), for instance, noted the 'sequential finality' that was implicit in the existing institutional framework and contrasted it with the need for a system that allowed for greater reciprocal interdependence between design and construction processes. Morris (1973) described the state of affairs as producing an 'hierarchic', as opposed to 'transformational', orientation to the project. Put more simply, it became received wisdom that a traditional contractual system did not allow for the increasing complexities and uncertainties associated with contemporary large scale, complex construction projects. Alternatives to the traditional arrangement had, in the meantime, already been developing, as contractors responded to increasing client preferences for a system that improved project coordination and created a simplified structure of contractual and managerial roles and relationships. These alternatives, to which the discussion now turns, are design-build and management/fee contracting.

Alternative forms of contracting

The basic idea behind design-build contracting is that the main contractor is employed by the client with full responsibility for both design and construction (NEDO, 1974; CIOB, 1988). This may be achieved by the contractor either employing their own in-house designers or hiring outside consultants. A variant of this 'package deal' approach is the system of develop and build, whereby the contractor prepares detailed designs on the basis of an outline design and performance specification provided by the client (NEDO, 1976). In both cases, it is argued by proponents that the method allocates clearer responsibility for total project performance, improves coordination between design and construction teams, allows 'fast-tracking' of projects by overlapping design and construction stages and increases the contractor's input into the design process.[9] Critics, on the other hand, argue that it can subordinate aesthetic design criteria to the objectives of time and cost and, as a result, can produce architecturally dull buildings and client dissatisfaction with the finished product (NEDO, 1976).

Management contracting, in contrast to design and build, retains the organizational separation of designers and builders, and instead involves a reconfiguration of relationships in such a way that the contractor becomes, in effect, part of the client's team. Management contractors subcontract all of the actual work on site and specialize in the management of the project, receiving a fee for their services (Carter, 1972). The principal benefits claimed for this system are similar to those claimed for design and construct. The main difference is that responsibility for the coordination of design and construction is made the province of a specialist managing contractor employed independently of those with prime responsibility for carrying out the work (CIOB, 1988). Again, there are critics of the method, whose main concerns centre around the extra cost involved and the possible greater ambiguity in relationships and responsibilities caused by putting the main contractor on an equal footing with members of the client's design team (NEDO, 1976).

Both forms of contractual arrangement have been used with greater frequency over the last twenty years. Evidence from the Wood Report on public sector clients highlighted how, at that time, traditional arrangements still continued to dominate public sector building programmes (NEDO, 1975). The report explicitly advocated that clients extend their choice to these alternative forms of 'delivery system' and make more use of associated alternative tendering arrangements, such as selective tendering and negotiated contracts. In the private sector, evidence at the time suggested that clients were beginning to exercise greater choice - particularly in the use of design-build contracts - and were reporting some greater satisfaction as a result (NEDO, 1974).

254

More recent research evidence suggests that, although these methods have gained some ground, there are still a substantial majority of clients that opt for the traditional method. For example, in the research referred to earlier, it was found that 68 per cent of the 138 projects investigated relied on a traditional JCT form of contract; 19 per cent involved a design-build contract or one of its variants; and only 13 per cent were let under a management form of contract (Bresnen and Haslam, 1991, p. 332). The main sources of explanation for variation in the use of different contract forms were in the tendency for alternative methods to be employed on larger-scale, more complex projects; and in the prevalence of the JCT method on public sector housing contracts. However, the research also pointed to a certain amount of 'institutional inertia', in the sense that most of the clients adopted an alternative method only in the case of unusually large, complex or untypical projects. Such findings help confirm many observations of the circumstances under which the various forms are expected to be adopted (Nahapiet and Nahapiet, 1985). However, they also suggest that, despite the increasing significance of alternatives to the JCT form of contract, their use is by no means as extensive as earlier proponents would perhaps have liked due, in part, to a tendency for clients to stick with their 'normal practice' (Bresnen and Haslam, 1991, p. 333). Other research, conducted more recently by RICS in 1989, confirms the continued extensive use of the JCT method.[10]

Nevertheless, the use of these alternatives has without doubt increased in recent years - particularly on larger scale, complex projects and particularly in the private sector. The crucial point about both these methods is that they seek to address the problem of coordination between complex and interdependent design and construction processes that the traditional method has failed to resolve. Design-build contracting does this by establishing a single point of responsibility for the whole design-construct process and internalizing the process of coordination within the contractor's administrative apparatus (Bresnen, 1990). As such, an interorganizational system of relationships based upon market exchange and a regulatory legal framework is partially substituted by an hierarchical, organizational system of control (Ouchi, 1980; Eccles, 1981). This is at its most evident where contractors directly employ their own design staff. Where contractors hire in consultants, a market mechanism is retained but the contractual position of the designer is changed to one of accountability to the main contractor, rather than to the client.

The management contracting system, in contrast, retains the market mechanism as well as the traditional architectural role, but attempts to specify more clearly the responsibility for project coordination as the main role of the management contractor. However, as research evidence suggests, the existing ambiguity surrounding the architect's role may at times be compounded by confused expectations surrounding the nature of the relationship between contractor and architect on a management contract (Bresnen, 1991). Moreover, in its greater reliance upon the use of nominated subcontractors, which have always created an ambiguity in the respective rights and responsibilities of the designer and main contractor (NEDO, 1976, pp. 16-17), such ambiguities may be increased. In this sense, the management contracting system solves only part of the perceived problem.

More pertinent to this discussion, however, are the consequences that follow for the participants in terms of their comparative roles, status, influence and effective control over the construction process. Both design-build and management contracting involve a change in the balance of influence within the project team away from the architect (and other members of the design team) and towards the main contractor. In design-build contracting, the architect is largely subordinated to the contractor - either being subject to direct hierarchical control, or being contracted-in to provide services. In management contracting, architects formally retain their independence. However, the specialization of the contractor in management effectively heightens their status and influence at the expense of the architect. In management contracting, the architect is expected to work with, rather than through, the main contractor - an orientation that is contrary to traditional expectations of the nature of the relationship and one that many architects still find difficult to cope with (NEDO, 1976). Research by the author, for instance, discovered how such conflicting expectations can have a dramatic impact upon the dynamics of relationships within the project team and upon project performance, particularly in the early stages of a contract (Bresnen, 1991).

Both design-build and management contracting are based on the presumption that an integrated project management approach is needed to deal with the complex problems of coordinating and controlling project work. Indeed, they both represent a separating out of the project management function from the specialist activities of design and (where work is all, or nearly all, subcontracted) construction as well. However, they also involve a partial transfer of this function away from the architect and towards the builder. The reason for this is not too difficult to see. In the traditional arrangement, it is not the existence of project complexity and uncertainty *per se* that causes problems for each of the parties; it is the fact that such complexity and uncertainty is influenced (some would say caused!) by the actions and decisions of other parties to the contract. From the contractor's point of view, their performance and commercial success is largely dependent upon the actions of an influential third party over whom they have no formal control - namely, the architect. From the architect's point of view, being able to realize their conceptual design is wholly dependent upon getting the contractor to undertake the work as specified.

On any particular project, of course, a range of factors are going to affect the nature and extent of any problems and conflicts that may occur as a result: most notably, the participants' precise aims and objectives on the project, the balance of commercial power between the main parties, the existence of any longer standing commercial relationship and the degree of personal cooperation between their representatives (Bresnen, 1990). However, in broad terms, it is not too difficult to see how the need to exert greater control over what might be described as 'critical functions' (cf. Crozier, 1964) has motivated contractors to develop

256

strategies aimed at extending their control further over the total design and construction process.

Of course, such strategies have to appeal to clients too, if they are to be adopted and become widespread. Without doubt, contractors which offer these types of contract have consciously and vigorously marketed their services and convinced some clients of their benefits. Indeed, it is hard not to see some element of conscious marketing in many of the industry reports which ostensibly simply describe the various forms available (e.g. CIOB, 1988). Conversely, it is not too difficult to see, in the criticisms noted earlier, an architect's response to the claimed benefits. However, their continued use also must lend testimony to the fact that clients find the ability to shorten lead times and more clearly locate accountability for actions and decisions of some benefit and worth the extra costs - at least for particular types of project. Consider, for example, the following accounts from two property service managers working for, respectively, a supermarket chain and a bank trust fund:

> Here at (the company) we use the design and build approach and we find that very satisfactory. In our earlier days, when we were using a JCT and appointed consultants to supervise the contract, we found that very unsatisfactory ... (Question: what sort of problems did you have?) ... Keeping a budget under control, projects going ahead with inadequate design, lots of variations - pretty well the full works. And now we use a project manager and design and build and I can't recall when we've had a project finish late or finish over budget. (The professionals) still like the old traditional methods of approach where the architect tends to run the project ... You come along and say, well, as a client, I like a design and build method of approach because I've really got then one backside to kick in the event that things go wrong. So, one of the principal advantages from my point of view, as a client on design and build, is that I've got one person to chase. And, by and large, that works fairly well.

Moreover, it is quite apparent too that clients are as much, and often more, concerned to produce a building on time and cost as they are to create an aesthetic masterpiece. The following comments are from another supermarket property manager and a property developer:

> The architect may decide that he is building a superstore which will be unrivalled in design to any other. Now, to be honest, we don't want that. We want something which is aesthetically correct - that may be an open term, but we want something which has an impact, but that doesn't cost us two million pounds on the aesthetics.
> It's always a hard job keeping the architect within the bounds of buildability and cost limits. And, invariably, most architects tend to guild the lily after they've won the job ... It is typical of an architect that he designs the thing in such a way that it's beautiful and very flashy, very smart, but it doesn't actually

fit within the cost parameters. And only by standing on his toes do you make it work.

In other words, a quite natural coincidence of client objectives and contractor's marketing strategy is more than likely to make an alternative approach a compelling one in some instances, with priority being given to commercial considerations at the possible expense of aesthetic criteria.

The development of alternative methods of contracting with their implications for control of the construction process has not gone unnoticed by the industry's professions and 'counter-strategies' have been developed to try to wrest back control from contractors. The first of these was a system of project management, initially developed at the Building Research Establishment in the late 1970s/early 1980s, called the Alternative Method of Management (AMM). Under this system, a main contractor was no longer employed and architects once again reverted back to the task of managing directly the work undertaken by specialist trades subcontractors. The system was based upon a recognition of the pervasiveness of subcontracting in practice (Leopold, 1982; Leopold and Leonard, 1983; Langford, 1985) and a desire to create a more direct link between designers and builders than could be achieved through a main contractor 'middle man'. It was used on a number of projects and by some local authorities in the early 1980s, but it effectively died out as a replacement for methods involving a main contractor. According to Ball (1988, pp. 208-9), the reason for this lies in its failure to address the inherent conflict in the relationship between architect and builder and their distinct orientations to the construction process. In other words, AMM did not remove the 'design-construct divide', it simply located it a little closer to the point of production.

A second development, that can be interpreted as a defensive counter-strategy, has been the growth of 'integrated practices' that combine within one organization all the professional disciplines relevant to the project management process (NEDO, 1976, p. 24). Many large design practices now offer the whole range of professional services, which enables them to provide a 'package deal' to clients who might be tempted by the alternative of going to a contractor instead of employing a number of separate professional consultants. As such, the problem of co-ordinating the design process is also internalized - this time within the design team organization; and the client is saved the potential problem of being drawn directly into wrangling between their professional representatives - a benefit that is made explicit in the following account by an industrial company client:

> From experience in the past, there had been confusion between the various professional representatives and it was decided at a very early stage that the architect appointed would be the professional supremo and it would be up to him to employ any other professions thought necessary, such as a structural engineer, mechanical and electrical engineer. The main idea was that there should be one person to whom the client could talk and get everything resolved.

258

There are limits to this option however. Firstly, it requires a sufficiently large practice with a sufficiently large workload to make the option economically feasible. Secondly, it contrasts with many clients' desires to retain their own independent consultant who can represent their interests. Thirdly, it does not address the crucial problem of the design-construct divide. Indeed, in allowing a more 'united front' to be presented on behalf of the designers, it may actually enhance the possibility of conflict to the extent that it evens up the power balance with the main contractor (Bresnen, 1990). Given what was noted above about clients' commercial priorities, it could actually be more in their interests to allow the contractor to exert some influence over their designers than to be constantly embroiled in head-to-head exchanges between the two of them.

A third strategy that has emerged in recent years has been a bid for the coveted title of project manager and an attempt to enter the competitive race with builders and surveyors to control the 'contested terrain' (cf. Edwards, 1979) at the heart of the building process through an emphasis on integrated project management. It is to a discussion of the emergence of project management as a distinct philosophy of organizing that the discussion now turns.

Project management and the construction process

As a working definition of project management in relation to the construction industry, the following is fairly typical:

> The overall planning, control and coordination of a project from inception to completion aimed at meeting a client's requirements and ensuring completion on time, within cost and to required quality standards (CIOB, 1988, p. 12).

Project management as a process is somewhat easier to define than it is to identify in practice, since the phrase is used extensively and at all levels of the industry (some site agents, for instance, are called project managers). Moreover, the common practice of clients appointing an individual employee to oversee the project from start to finish (e.g. an estates manager), ensures that project management in practice ranges from a 'loose' arrangement - where such an individual liaises with the design team and contractor about user needs; to a project management system proper - where either a consultant or internal project manager is employed.

Contractually, project management can take one of two generic forms: the 'executive' model - where the project manager has full responsibility for the project and contracts-in design and construction services; and the 'non-executive' model - where the project manager is employed separately to coordinate the design team and builders. Project managers employed separately under contract are a comparative rarity in the UK - except on very large scale, complex projects (CIOB, 1988). However, more limited forms - involving either a consultant hired to design and manage the project or an internal member of staff who is accountable for overall project performance - are increasingly common and do have important implications.

Project management as such is not new - many architects would argue that they have traditionally done this in their capacity as consultant to the client. What is new is its conceptualization as a specialized function distinct from the 'design team leader' role traditionally performed by the architect. It has developed as such in the context of increasing concern over time and cost performance and the growing opinion that the architect's traditional dual role was not suited to the task of both designing and managing complex contemporary construction projects. The question is inevitably raised of who should perform this function. According to a report prepared by the Chartered Institute of Building:

> A Project Manager must have an appreciative knowledge of all disciplines participating in the project and must demonstrate expertise and leadership. Experience of the industry is essential. The discipline from which the Project Manager comes is not significant since all disciplines can produce good Project Managers. A basic training in the industry with an understanding of financial and legal background is important but personal qualities are of considerable importance in producing a Project Manager of the right calibre and with the ability to lead the building team (CIOB, 1988, p. 12).

With a job description like that, it is hardly surprising to find that the role has been 'up for grabs'. There is a clear recognition that none of the main professional groups has a particular distinctive competence in the performance of the role, and more than a hint that architects are by no means the automatic choice.

In some quarters questions have been raised of whether architects actually possess the appropriate skills and capabilities needed to perform this type of role. For example, it is well established that, although architects spend a considerable amount of time engaged in management activity, they receive little in the way of management training and development.[11] A predisposition within the profession towards design and away from the practicalities of project management has always meant some degree of ambivalence towards their management role. Clients too have their strong views:

> I am not over keen on the architectural profession. I think quite often they're not strong enough to deal with the contractors and the contractors run rings around them to a major extent. And it's very difficult once a job gets behind to gear a contractor up to finish on time. If he can find any cause to claim an extension of time, he will do so and I've found few architects who are strong enough to resist that. Of course that means that the client is out of pocket. But we're learning - I think all project managers are learning - and we're now so arranging things that we do have much tighter control (Property Developer).

As a client, I have a concern that architects tend to come up with theoretical solutions - that the important aspect of their job is the finished product, whereas my concern is that I want to get the practical aspects of the job out of the way and I want someone that's going to have a total awareness of all the problems, from the services side, from the structural side - and co-ordinate them for me. If we need design advice, fine ... But I prefer it that way round to having an architect who is totally wrapped up in aesthetics and finishes, that tells the client he's got nothing to worry about because it's all under control - and yet doesn't understand what's happening further down the line (Property Services Manager, clearing bank).

Furthermore, it could be added that the continuing assumption that managing projects is precisely what architects have done and are continuing to do leaves them somewhat blind to the strategic moves of other interested parties. The recent establishment of a code of practice for project management by the CIOB, for instance, not only defines it as a distinct discipline, but also incorporates RICS conditions of engagement - making some within the architectural profession point out how they have been 'outflanked' by builders and surveyors.[12]

Although project management as a specialized contractual role is rare, project management in the more general sense of an orientation to the organization and management of projects is increasingly common. Coupled with the variety of forms of contract, there are a substantial number of possible organizational configurations which variously affect each party's role and responsibilities. As described earlier, contractors play a much greater part in the project management process in the case of design-build and management contracting. In addition, consultant quantity surveyors (QSs) are much more likely to act as the client's main consultant than formerly. As was once remarked by David Crawford, editor of *Chartered Surveyors Journal*, not without a hint of glee:

(Clients) are becoming more cost and budget conscious, and correspondingly anxious to ensure the best return on the construction element in their investment. They are, therefore, responsive to the presence of a cost-oriented profession which strikes them as having a management based approach and which has added to its traditional armoury of bills of quantities production and valuation such new skills as cost planning, project management and contract administration ... So, the present-day architect, whose 19th century predecessors voted to exclude quantity surveying activity from the ranks of their profession, can find himself reporting to a QS as the client's representative. This involves, of course, the discipline of designing within cost limits - something which is not necessarily to the taste of architects (*Financial Times*, 26 August 1981, p. 12).

These factors - a focus on cost and an orientation that matches the needs of the client - find expression in the following more recent accounts which demonstrate

261

the common interest that gives the profession a strong actual or potential foothold:

> The relationships between the main contractors, architects, QSs should always be considered very carefully in any project. It is the QS that has the controlling influence on cost and must relate more closely to the client than any other part of the design team if the costs are to be contained (Architectural Project Manager, hotel chain).

> (The QS) was my professional representative on this. I would lean on him very much to give his advice concerning all aspects of the contract. He was the only member of the team who was on my side, so I considered him to be very, very important (Managing Director, private hospital).

These views appear to be supported by other findings. For example, a survey conducted by Wilson, Large and Partners in 1990 found that 36 per cent of clients adjudged architectural project managers to be 'excellent' or 'good', 38 per cent found them 'acceptable' and 28 per cent rated them as 'poor'. However, 47 per cent of clients rated QSs as 'excellent' or 'good', 43 per cent rated them as 'acceptable' and only ten per cent rated them as 'poor'.[13]

The tendency for quantity surveyors to lead the team is particularly pronounced on design-build contracts.[14] However, the emphasis on nominated subcontracting on management contracts also lends itself to the heightened importance of a role which is specifically concerned with contract administration. Moreover, to the extent that many projects nowadays are, in effect, management-only since most of the work is subcontracted (NEDO, 1988, p. 73), then the pivotal role of quantity surveyors is enhanced. Indeed, it has been noted how quantity surveyors' status has grown substantially within the building team as their role as adviser to, and manager for, the client has steadily increased (Nahapiet and Nahapiet, 1985, p. 223; Faulkener and Day, 1986; NEDO, 1988, p. 71). Reports from within the profession also indicate how wholeheartedly quantity surveyors have embraced project management and how they see themselves becoming the 'natural choice' of clients to act as project manager, whatever the type of contractual system employed.[15]

It should also be noted that the focus on financial aspects dovetails much more closely too with the interests of the contractor, in so far as the two are 'talking the same language'. Contractor's own quantity surveyors and those employed by the client have necessarily always worked closely together - in producing evaluations for payment, for instance. Indeed, many would regard them as having their own distinct professional subculture - and one that bridges the contractual divide. Certainly, they share common techniques, a common language and a common frame of reference - if not common goals. This commonality has been remarked on to the author on numerous occasions by both contractors and surveyors, and been explicitly contrasted with the lack of common perspective each party shares with the architect, whose central concern is more with aesthetic aspects and whose language is that of the 'artist' or 'academic'. Although these are broad characterizations of the major participants, there is an important point here: namely, that contractors have potentially less of a problem with a project manager with whom they can 'communicate' and, as such, may implicitly prefer quantity surveyors to architects as project managers. Where clients, surveyors and contractors are all 'talking the same language', the possibility emerges of a tripartite system of influence in which the project's commercial considerations come to the fore and the architect is effectively marginalized. Early case study research by the author identified a number of circumstances in which such an outcome actually happened - irrespective of the formal powers vested in the participants by virtue of their contractual position (Bresnen, 1990, 1991).

A final trend worthy of note concerns the increasing tendency for clients to take a more proactive role themselves in the project management process. As noted earlier, client representatives have traditionally performed more of a liaison role between prospective users of the facility and the design team. However, there is increasing evidence of the tendency for clients to establish more sophisticated management structures in which project management plays a crucial part - particularly where alternative contractual arrangements are used. For example, in the research reported earlier (Bresnen and Haslam, 1991), 42 per cent of the projects had a designated individual assigned to the project by the client and, in a further 20 per cent of the projects, the client's chief executive played a direct role in conjunction with a consultant. The rationale for this is explained in the following account given by a project manager of a multinational company using a management contractor to build a new block of offices:

We maintained control here. We made our own decisions and we didn't allow the consultant team to occupy the role of supervising officer, where they could make design decisions without reference to the client and spend money without reference to the client ... They were expecting the normal role - the architect, for instance, expected to lead the project. I'd go so far as to say he'd actually called up the previous QS who had been involved in the previous project without our knowledge, without our consent, and we actually had to disengage that situation and say we are not using that QS ... He was expecting to lead the whole thing. So we had to change that and inform him quite firmly that we were leading - we took all the decisions ... We felt that we had to continue to run it, to lead the team, so that we could continue to balance the decisions to make sure we did maintain our budget. After all, if we had any of the other consultants actually leading it, with the best will in the world, they had a bias in either direction.

In other words, competition from other parties to perform the key role of project manager is added to by increasing constraints on the discretion exercized by the traditional architectural project manager due to heightened concern over project budgets and deadlines and a desire for greater accountability for project performance.

Concluding discussion

The above analysis has attempted to demonstrate how developments within the construction industry over the last decade have combined to influence dramatically the relative fortunes of the main parties traditionally involved in the building process. General economic conditions, together with specific government policies on public expenditure and the regulation of competition between providers of professional services, have had both direct and indirect effects upon the comparative position, status and influence of architects, surveyors and contractors. Direct consequences have included cuts and job losses in professional service establishments, especially in the public sector; and continuing deregulation leading to increased competition within the professions. Indirect effects have occurred through the influence of government policy on general economic conditions that have affected clients' orientations towards project objectives, project team organization and the decisions they make about methods of procuring projects.

In this context, the position of architects in particular has come under increasing threat. In line with changing client orientations and expectations, contractors have managed to develop strategies that lessen their former dependence upon the architectural profession and which, as a result, further weaken the firm grip that architects have traditionally had upon the project management process. As a further reflection of the emphasis on commercial objectives, quantity surveyors have emerged from the shadows and have begun to compete effectively with architects for the role of project manager. Long-standing problems within the industry of co-ordinating and controlling complex and uncertain design and construction processes have always supplied the impetus for such strategies: contractors, in particular, have always had the incentive to try to extend their control over the total process in order to reduce their dependence upon the designer. However, the ability of the two groups now to compete directly with architects is the result of a greater alignment of their aims with the expressed needs and expectations of clients, coupled with their ability to demonstrate these intentions to clients through their actions 'on the ground'.

Architects have historically been protected from such intrusions into their domain by their powerful position under the traditional system of contracting. However, the development of alternatives to that system, coupled with increasing client involvement in the project management process, has led to an undermining of their former power base. These trends have been legitimized by a well-established pattern of discourse within the industry that has served to privilege the more commercial and pragmatic aims of improved project coordination and control at the expense of the traditional powers and autonomy granted to the architect and other design professionals.

264

Ironically, the architect's former power and influence has always derived rather more from their generalist role as project manager - enshrined in law under general terms and conditions of contract - than from their role as specialist designer. The problem facing architects in this new scenario is the absence of any particular distinctive competence and specialized knowledge base that clearly enables the profession to claim the territory of project management. Many too would argue that architects have been unwilling to stake a firm claim and instead have relied too heavily upon their traditional approach to managing projects. In contrast, contractors and quantity surveyors have been willing and able to manoeuvre themselves into that role. Although the architect's role as project manager is still of great importance on many projects, they have lost the monopoly that they once had and some might regard them as now having a much more tenuous hold on the project management process and, in the extreme, a much more marginalized position within the client's team.

The trends identified above appear to be continuing. A study by consultants W.S. Atkins in conjunction with a consortium of European consultants recommended significant changes to the traditional UK model of consultancy in the context of the move towards a single European market (Matheou, 1993). The main recommendations of the study included: the need for the professions to 'adapt' their services to the range of different procurement procedures increasingly favoured by clients; the increased use of standardized, 'off-the-shelf' design specifications; greater stress being placed upon project management functions, as opposed to specialist design activity; the subordination of aesthetic design criteria to building services needs; the need for joint education and training of architects and engineers - especially in management skills; the need to develop appropriate arrangements for operating with contractors as clients or partners; and the need to consider organizational changes, such as more multidisciplinary practices, joint ventures and mergers (Matheou, 1993).

In the light of such developments, opinion from some quarters of the profession favours a more conscious attempt by architects to develop their project management capabilities in order to compete more effectively with other groups for the generalist role and to counter attempts at professional 'deskilling'. However, the evidence of the last ten years suggests that the profession has been slow to respond and that the more likely outcome is the continuing erosion of the architect's former status and influence as other groups intrude further into their 'territory'. There is therefore the distinct possibility that the redefinition of the architectural profession called for by the new RIBA president (see earlier) becomes a further gradual retreat into the narrower confines of architecture as pure design discipline.

Notes

1. Civil engineers, of course, predominate in all road and other infrastructure projects and have their own professional body.
2. *Architects' Journal*, 16 June 1993, p. 27.
3. *Architects' Journal*, July 1993, p. 7.
4. *Architects' Journal*, 16 June 1993, p. 27.
5. *Architects' Journal*, 3 Feb 1993, p. 8.
6. *Chartered Quantity Surveyor*, June 1992, p. 7.
7. *Architects' Journal*, 16 June 1993, p. 27.
8. *Architects' Journal*, July 1993, p. 7.
9. See, for instance, 'The rise and rise of design and build', *Contracts Journal*, March 1989.
10. *Chartered Quantity Surveyor*, Jan 1991, pp. 9-11. See also Nahapiet and Nahapiet, 1985.
11. *Architects' Journal*, 18 Nov 1992, p. 4.
12. *Architects' Journal*, 11 Nov 1992, p. 5.
13. *Chartered Quantity Surveyor*, Dec 1990, pp. 10-11.
14. *Contracts Journal*, July 1987. See also Bresnen and Haslam, 1991.
15. RICS, 1991. See also *Chartered Quantity Surveyor*, Dec/Jan 1992, pp. 17-26.

References

Abbott, A. (1988), *The System of Professions*, University of Chicago Press, Chicago.

Ball, M. (1988), *Rebuilding Construction: Economic Change in the British Construction Industry*, Routledge, London.

Banwell, H. (1964), *The Placing and Management of Contracts for Building and Civil Engineering Work*, HMSO, London.

Bowley, M. (1966), *The British Building Industry*, CUP, Cambridge.

Bresnen, M. J. (1990), *Organizing Construction*, Routledge, London.

Bresnen, M. J. (1991), 'Construction Contracting in Theory and Practice: A Case Study', *Construction Management and Economics*, Vol. 9, pp. 247-63.

Bresnen, M. J. and Haslam, C. O. (1991), 'Construction Industry Clients: A Survey of their Attributes and Project Management Practices', *Construction Management and Economics*, Vol. 9, pp. 327-42.

Butler, R. and Carney, M. G. (1983), 'Managing Markets: Implications for the Make-Buy Decision', *Journal of Management Studies*, Vol. 20, no. 2, pp. 213-31.

Carter, J. (1972), 'Management contracting', *Architects' Journal*, 13 Feb.

Chartered Institute of Building (CIOB) (1988), *Project Management in Building*, 3rd ed., Chartered Institute of Building, Ascot.

Crichton, C. (1966), *Interdependence and Uncertainty: A Study of the Building Industry*, Tavistock, London.

Crozier, M. (1964), *The Bureaucratic Phenomenon*, Tavistock, London.

DiMaggio, P. J. and Powell, W. W. (1983), 'The Iron Cage Revisited: Institutional Isomorphism and Collective Rationality in Organizational Fields', *American Sociological Review*, Vol. 48, pp. 147-60.

Dopson, S. and Stewart, R. (1990), 'What is Happening to Middle Management?', *British Journal of Management*, Vol. 1, no. 1, pp. 3-16.

Eccles, R. G. (1981), 'The Quasi-Firm in the Construction Industry', *Journal of Economic Behaviour and Organization*, Vol. 2, pp. 335-57.

Edwards, R. (1979), *Contested Terrain: The Transformation of the Workplace in the Twentieth Century*, Heinemann, London.

Emmerson, H. (1962), *A Survey of Problems before the Construction Industries*, HMSO, London.

Esland, G. and Salaman, G. (1980), *The Politics of Work and Occupations*, Open University Press, Milton Keynes.

Faulkener, A. C. and Day, A. K. (1986), 'Images of Status and Performance in Building Teams', *Construction Management and Economics*, Vol. 4, pp. 247-60.

Harris, F. and McCaffer, R. (1989), *Modern Construction Management*, BSP Professional Books, Oxford.

Higgin, J. and Jessop, N. (1965), *Communications in the Building Industry*, Tavistock, London.

Imrie, R. and Morris, J. (1992), 'A Review of Recent Changes in Buyer-Supplier Relations', *OMEGA International Journal of Management Science*, Vol. 20, No. 5/6, pp. 641-52.

Johnson, T. J. (1972), *Professions and Power*, Macmillan, London.

Langford, D. (1985), 'Labour-only subcontracting', *CIOB Technical Information Service*, occasional paper No. 57.

Larson, M. S. (1977), *The Rise of Professionalism: A Sociological Analysis*, University of California Press, California.

Leopold, E. (1982), 'Where have all the workers gone?', *Building*, 22 Oct, pp. 29-30.

Leopold, E. and Leonard, S. (1983), 'Reorganized labour', *Building*, 8 July.

Matheou, D. (1992), 'Council architects struggle under dual onslaught', *Architects' Journal*, Vol. 196, No. 23, p. 17.

Matheou, D. (1993), 'The real importance of the Architects' Council of Europe', *Architects' Journal*, Vol. 197, No. 22, p. 23.

Melchers, R. E. (1977), 'The Influence of Organization on Project Implementation', *ASCE Journal of the Construction Division*, Vol. 103, No. 4, pp. 611-25.

Morris, P. W. G. (1973), 'An Organizational Analysis of Project Management in the Building Industry', *Building International*, Vol. 6, pp. 595-615.

Nahapiet, H. and Nahapiet, J. (1985), 'A Comparison of Contractual Arrangements', *Construction Management and Economics*, Vol. 3, pp. 218-31.

NEDO (1970), *Large Industrial Sites*, HMSO, London.

NEDO (1974), *Before you Build: What a Client needs to know about the Construction Industry*, HMSO, London.

NEDO (1975), *The Public Client and the Construction Industries*, HMSO, London.

NEDO (1976), *The Professions in Construction*, HMSO, London.

NEDO (1978), *How Flexible is Construction?*, HMSO, London.

NEDO (1988), *Faster Building for Commerce*, HMSO, London.

Ouchi, W.G. (1980), 'Markets, Bureaucracies and Clans', *Administrative Science Quarterly*, Vol. 25, pp. 129-41.

Phelps-Brown, E. H. (1968), *Report of the Committee of Inquiry into Certain Matters Concerning Labour in Building and Civil Engineering*, HMSO, London.

Royal Institute of Chartered Surveyors (RICS) (1991), *Quantity Surveying 2000: The Future Role of the Chartered Quantity Surveyor*, Royal Institute of Chartered Surveyors, London.

Scott, W. R. (1987), 'The Adolescence of Institutional Theory', *Administrative Science Quarterly*, Vol. 32, pp. 493-511.

Stone, P. A. (1983), *Building Economy*, 3rd ed., Pergammon Press, Oxford.

Turner, D. F. (1984), *Standard Contracts for Building*, George Goodwin, Harlow.

Warne, E. J. D. (1993), *Review of the Architects (Registration) Acts 1931-1969*, HMSO, London.

Zucker, L. G. (1977), 'The Role of Institutionalization in Cultural Persistence', *American Sociological Review*, Vol. 42, pp. 726-43.

Zucker, L. G. (1983), 'Organizations as Institutions' in Bacharach, S.B. (ed.), *Research in the Sociology of Organizations: Volume 2*, JAI Press, Greenwich, CT.

12 The expunction of process expertise from British management teaching syllabi: an historical analysis

Peter Armstrong

Introduction: the content of management education as an issue

A recent canvas of employers by Her Majesty's Inspectorate has revealed that there is continuing disquiet over the content of the British MBA. As has happened in the past, the public response of the management education lobby has been to dismiss this disquiet as symptomatic of a backwoods disbelief in management education *per se*. The tacit assumption behind this manoeuvre is that the only sensible attitudes towards presently existing management education are either for it or against it, as if the nature of management and the education appropriate to it were settled matters. From at least the time of the Franks Report,[1] it has been assumed that strategic planning, financial control and behavioural science comprise the core disciplines of management. The fact that the education of managers in some of our most successful industrial competitors is very different is either ignored or regarded as a symptom-free cultural variation. There is a similar blindness to the historical specificity of the current content of British management education.

The object of the historical study presented here is to demonstrate that the British idea of what constitutes management, and of the education appropriate for it, has changed over time. In part, these changes can be seen as a response to changes in corporate structure and the consequent expansion of the scope of managerial activity. In part, however, the changes also appear to have been driven by the dynamics of the British 'management movement' itself, and in particular, by its determination to emancipate itself from its historical entanglement with engineering. To the extent that the latter has been the case, there is no reason to suppose that the current end result is particularly well adapted to the 'needs' of British industry. A sympathetic re-examination of the comments of industrialists

269

suggests that what they object to is precisely a conception of management, and of management education, which is detached, as a matter of principle, from expertise in the productive process. It is suggested that the burden on proof still lies upon those who argue (or assume) that British industrial performance will be improved by a further expansion of management education on the current pattern.

Current disquiets and historical contexts

'Management', in Anglo-Saxon thought, is a status as well as a function.[2] The claim that certain activities are managerial is simultaneously a claim that they are, or should be, superordinate to others. In this sense, management is prior to, and sets the context for the non-managerial.[3] In terms of the individual career, ambition must prioritize the managerial and avoid too intimate an association with the non-managerial. These correlates of the definition of management make it extremely important. It plays a considerable part in defining patterns of effort, of career movement and decision-making within business organizations.

Management education is implicated in this process, since it expresses and perpetuates the current conception of what is and what is not management. Wherever it is hard currency, for example, managerial education defines what the ambitious non-manager must acquire in order to become a manager.

Within the mainstream of management education thinking, such issues have become invisible within a broad consensus on the desirable content of management education. At least from the time of the Franks Report (1963), this has been regarded as more or less settled. Franks himself, for example, felt it unnecessary to argue the case for his 'framework knowledge' of applied economics, sociology and psychology or the 'skills and techniques' of operations research, linear programming, strategic planning, decision theory and computer techniques (ibid. pp. 8). Similarly, the Handy Report (1987, p. 16) stated that the subjects to be taught in the Diploma stage of the MBA should be the 'standard business topics of economics, accounting, finance, marketing, production and corporate strategy.' The confident assumptions behind these statements, however, have been persistently queried by spokespersons from industry. It is instructive to examine the responses which have been forthcoming from the management education establishment.

Typical, is the complaint of the manufacturing director of Lucas that a diet of the standard business topics is producing 'a whole generation of MBA students who will not go near a manufacturing strategy . . . they want to be in at the gin-and-tonic end with the financial strategy'(Parnaby, 1985). One response has employed the rhetoric of crisis. According to the Handy Report, for example, 'We cannot afford the luxury of a lengthy debate. Action is needed now' (Handy et al., 1987, p. v). Another tactic has been to stigmatize the reasoned misgivings of industrialists as symptomatic of a backwoods disbelief in management education *per se*. When a recent canvass of employer opinion by Her Majesty's Inspectorate revealed widespread dissatisfaction with the MBA, Andrew Lock, the Dean of

Management at Manchester Polytechnic countered thus: 'Views of this sort have been expressed by employers since business education was first introduced in the UK. There is a strong element of the old Guinness slogan, 'I've never tried it because I don't like it' (*The Higher* 5th June 1992).

These are the tactics of evasion. Whilst it is quite true that there are diehard intellectual Luddites amongst British employers, there is also a more nuanced body of opinion which regards the present *content* of management education as inappropriate to the work which many managers actually do.[4]

These misgivings on the part of employers provide a point of entry into the issue of the content of current teaching programmes, and the conception of management embodied in them. More, they raise the intriguing question of the origins of a pattern of provision which is regarded with suspicion by many employers. If the needs (or wishes) of industry have not been the driving force, what has? The question is the more interesting when set against early approaches to management education. From the first Institute of Industrial Administration syllabus of 1925 to the Urwick scheme of the 1940s, a knowledge of production technologies, work study, and other elements of the immediate management of processes was assumed to be a necessary part of the manager's toolkit. Whatever the other limitations of these early syllabi, their students could not have been accused, as current MBA.s are accused, of lacking in immediately useful abilities. Nor would they have been vulnerable to the Finniston accusation (1980) of ignorance of the crucial 'engineering dimension' of management.

These reflections lead to the particular questions to which this chapter is addressed. How and why did the engineering content of these early management syllabi disappear? Why are production engineering and method study now regarded as technical specialisms subordinate to management, rather than as integral to management itself? In effect we are enquiring into the accomplishment of a long run shift in the meaning of 'management'.

These matters are approached through an examination of the thinking of certain individuals who have been prominent in the development of British management education, and of the syllabi which they have produced. In no sense is it intended as a comprehensive history of British management education, still less of British management thought.[5] Rather, the intention is to identify two broad streams of thought and to enquire into the reasons for the gradual triumph of the one over the other.

As with the American Scientific management movement, the earlier 'industrial engineering' or 'shop management' tradition regarded engineering expertise as integral to the practice of management. For later 'enterprise management' thinkers, however, the priority was that trained managers should take over the direction of business as a whole. From this latter point of view, the entanglement of management with engineering appeared as an irrelevance, or worse, a hindrance to the development of a body of knowledge appropriate to the direction of enterprise. In important respects, it will be argued, the present pattern of British management education, and the associated conception of what management *is*, are the offspring of the ascendancy of the enterprise management view over the industrial engineering tradition.[6]

E T Elbourne and the shop management tradition

During the interwar years, the 'British management movement' was a small scale affair (Child, 1969). Its main institutional expression, the Institute of Industrial Administration (IIA) was founded in 1920, entered a coma in 1923, and only achieved a membership of 1000 in 1943 (Institute of Industrial Administration, 1954). The management teaching syllabi designed and sponsored by the IIA were taught only at the Regent Street Polytechnic and a few technical colleges. Of the Universities, only the London School of Economics and the Manchester College of Science and Technology offered full time courses in management (Rose, 1970 p. 1). Nevertheless these early British forays into management education are important. Their form was expressive of the notions of management held by that one-time minority who believed that management could be taught. In many respects they laid down the terms in which later developments in management education would be debated.

E. T. Elbourne, the founder of the IIA, was a member of the Institution of Mechanical Engineers. Like the American industrial engineers, (Elbourne had visited the USA as long ago as 1900), he approached management through his experience of factory administration. Like them, he is recognized as a pioneer of cost and management accountancy (Parker, 1969 p. 151).

There were profound differences between the industrial engineers' concept of management and that which is conventional today. A reading of Taylor (1947) conveys an instant impression of the transformation which has taken place. Vividly illustrated by explicit closeups of the transformed labour process, Taylor's writing is unencumbered by obfuscatory jargon and human relations sentimentality alike. When allowance is made for his productivist ideology, Taylor was straightforwardly honest about his intentions. By today's standards Taylorism was a kind of managerial hard porn which flaunted the sliderules and stopwatches of its engineering origins.

The direct influence of Taylorism on managerial practice in post-World War One Britain was minimal.[7] During Taylor's one visit to this country, he was invited to address the Institution of Mechanical Engineers on his innovations in machine tool technology but not on management (Urwick and Brech, 1963 pp. 132-3). Littler (1982 p. 95) suggests that the British distaste for Taylorism stemmed from the objections of Quaker employers to the debasement of the worker, a less high minded rejection of Taylor's high wage strategy and a lack of demand for standardized mass-products in British markets. Probably it was also important that British employers, unlike those in the USA, had traditionally been able to rely upon 'technically intelligent, highly skilled, widely experienced relatively cheap manpower rather than automatic or standardized machine processes' (Society for the Promotion of Engineering Education, 1931 p. 940).

The pioneers of British management education, however, were not typical of British employers as a whole. They were far more interested in the promise of a systematic theory of management. In consequence, Elbourne's first draft syllabus for the IIA reflected the influence of the Taylorite tradition of industrial engineering (Figure 12.1).

Design, Factory Planning, Estimating, Production control, Employment administration, Materials purchasing, Transport, Production statistics and costing.

Figure 12.1   Topics included in Elbourne's first draft syllabus for the IIA

Source: *IIA, p. 35*

The engineering emphasis was reproduced in the sample questions attached to this syllabus, which included such topics as tolerances and fitting. In fact the essential continuity of engineering and management was a thread which ran through most of Elbourne's work. In the widely published *Factory Administration and Accounts* (1914, p. 31) he had this to say: The works accountant ought not to be trained wholly as a clerk but ought really to be an engineer who has fitted himself for works accounting duties. The later text *Fundamentals of Industrial Administration* (1934) exhibited the same industrial engineering bias as Elbourne's first draft syllabus, although the early chapters were taken up with a somewhat unfocused portrait of capitalist industrial society, perhaps as a concession to the enterprise management view of management education, which will be discussed presently. There, too, Elbourne voiced his disapproval of managers who lacked technical knowledge:

A strong case can be made out for the recruiting of general managers from men with technological training and experience; but in actual fact it is the non-technical or so-called commercial man who is usually appointed (Elbourne, 1934, p. 562).

Apart from the current of shop management thinking within the IIA, as exemplified by Elbourne, there were other pressures to retain the engineering element in the teaching syllabi. In the small world of 1920s and 1930s British management education, the engineering institutions' courses in industrial administration were a major proportion of the whole national effort. Because this would confer recognition on the IIA, Elbourne was keen that the Institutions should adopt the IIA syllabus. Both the Mechanical and Electrical Engineering Institutions did so in 1933, but only after the syllabus had been adapted to their requirements

(Rose, 1970, p. 70).

This ability of the engineering institutions to influence British management syllabi persisted well into the postwar era. They were, for example, represented on the Urwick Committee which designed the first postwar national system of management education and on the United Kingdom Advisory Council on Education for Management which was created in 1960 to oversee the teaching of the Diploma in Management Studies in technical colleges. Their influence only appears to have ended with the advent of the MBA in the mid 1960s.

The limits of the shop management perspective

An important feature of Taylorism, frequently obscured by Taylor's extravagant claims of its universality, was that it fell a long way short of what would nowadays count as a comprehensive approach to management. This is Taylor, in an uncharacteristically ruminant mood:

> We, however, who are primarily interested in the shop, are apt to forget that success, instead of hinging upon shop management, depends in many cases mainly upon other elements, namely, the location of the company, its financial strength and ability, the efficiency of its business and sales departments, its engineering ability, the superiority of its plant and equipment, or the protection offered either by patents, combination or other partial monopoly (Taylor, 1947, p. 19).

Despite his confidence that administrative problems must yield to the onslaught of engineering rationality, Taylor gave no hint that these 'other elements', however crucial to business success, might also be amenable to rational management action. Today, of course, they are precisely the concerns of strategic management.

It could be that Taylor felt most at home on ground with which he had become familiar in his progression from workman to chargehand, and thence to factory manager. Taylor's biography, however, was as typical of early American industrial engineering as his view of management. It is significant that the first systematic theory of management was put together by men (Taylor modestly implicated '100 men or more' (Urwick, 1953a, p. 377) whose experience and conceptions of management stopped far short of business policy. The implication is that the source of this early myopia of the scientific management movement is to be found, not in the particularities of individual biography, but in the business context in which these theories evolved.

An indication that this was also the case in Great Britain is to be found in the somewhat later work of Sheldon, a British management thinker who wrote on the basis of his experience in the Cadbury family's factories:

The function of finance is outside the province of management. The control of finance is a matter for ownership. It is a function of capital, not of management. The latter is concerned only with the uses of capital (Sheldon, 1924, p. 52).

To the modern reader, confronted with the massive literature on financial management, it is apparent that Sheldon inhabited a different world. So did Taylor: Bethlehem Steel, where his work began, was owned by a group of locally-based businessmen whilst Midvale was owned by a group of financiers more interested in establishing monopolies and trusts than in the internal management of their factory (Rose, 1975). In neither case was Taylor in a position to influence company policy. Management thinkers like Taylor and Sheldon had little to say on the subject of business policy because, in their experience, these matters were not the province of salaried management but that of ownership and entrepreneurship. In that respect the shop management tradition was a product of the era of entrepreneurial capitalism (Chandler and Daems, 1974).

Bowie, Urwick and the enterprise management perspective

Bowie: Managerialism and the management teaching syllabus

(Elbourne's) draft syllabus' commented T G Rose, the official historian of the IIA, 'illustrates how engineering works management still dominated Elbourne's mind . . . The unsuitable nature of this syllabus was at once apparent to the Senior Industrialists who comprised the advisory council who had not been concerned with such matters for years ... (IIA, 1954 p. 33).

Whilst these are the comments of 1950s management thinking on that of the 1920s, they nevertheless indicate a tension within the management education movement which existed at least from the 1930s onwards.

First Year   **Background subjects**
1   The History and Evolution of Modern Industry
2   The Principles of Political Science and Sociology
3   Economics
4   Industrial Psychology
5   The Principles of Industrial Organization and Management

Second Year   **Tool subjects**
1   General Accounting
2   Cost Accounting
3   Business Statistics
4   Industrial Finance
5   Factory and Commercial Law
6   English Précis, Reports, and Correspondence.

Third Year   **Operative subjects**
1   Industrial Fatigue and Efficiency
2   Industrial Relations
3   Works Organization and Management
4   Office Organization and Management
5   Marketing
6   Transportation.

Figure 12.2   **Bowie's 'ideal' three year undergraduate course in industrial administration 1930**

Source: *Bowie, 1930, pp. 145-152*

In 1932, James Alexander Bowie, the first head of the Department of Industrial Administration at Manchester University Faculty of Technology, joined the IIA and was coopted onto the Council. There was a visionary quality in Bowie which was absent in Elbourne. To Bowie, the professionalization of management contained the potential to transform capitalist society. Writing in the depths of the 1930s slump, a decade before Burnham's better known *Managerial Revolution* (1941), he envisaged the withering away of class conflict in a new era of managerial efficiency which would be equally responsive to the claims of capital and labour. Obstructing the advent of this version of non-sectional managerialism (cf. Nichols, 1969) was the disruptive self-interest of ownership. Interestingly, Bowie's *Education for Business Management* contains a torrid excoriation of the attendant evil of nepotic incompetence (1930, p. 131 ff.).

276

Divisions of responsibility	Fundamentals Stage	Intermediate Stage	Final Stage
Basic	Industrial History. Elementary Economics. Management Theory.	Personnel Policy and Welfare	The Management Function. Industrial Relationships. Social Factors in Industry
Production	Production: General Principles	Production Planning and Material Control Production Measurement and Incentives	Specification, Tendering, including Material Control
Distribution	Distribution: General Principles	Sales Organization and Service	Sales Policy and Publicity
Development	Development: General Principles	Product Development and Quality Control	Market Research and Business Forecasting
Accounts and Finance	Management Graphics. Cost Accounts: General Principles	Financial Accounts, Industrial Accounts and Costing, including Management Graphics	Budgetary and Higher Control
Legal and Secretarial	Industrial Law. Office Organization	Office Organization and Methods	Business Organization and Finance

Figure 12.3   Institute of Industrial Administration syllabus of 1932

Source: *IIA, 1954*

These views were not an extraneous 'politics' tacked onto Bowie's ideas on management education. The two were of a piece. His 'broad' conception of management education made sense of his belief that management should take over most of the functions presently performed by owners and entrepreneurs. Moreover, the important social role which Bowie envisaged for managers, as arbiters between conflicting interests, prioritized the 'human aspects' of management far more than Elbourne's shop-management perspective. Partly for that reason, and partly because of the subsidiary place occupied by shop management in Bowie's thinking, he also differed from Elbourne in believing that engineering was *not* the best background for management. In Bowie's view, technical training led to a neglect of the vital 'human aspect'.[8] For all of these reasons, Bowie's idea of the 'ideal' three year undergraduate course in management (Figure 12.2) differed considerably from Elbourne's draft.

Despite the inclusion of topics on works and office organization in the third year, Bowie's graduates, would have been simply incapable of practising Scientific Management as the industrial engineers had understood it. On the other hand, the second-year 'Tool Subjects', in particular, are clearly directed towards the management of the enterprise rather than the production shop.

The actual teaching syllabi produced by the IIA during the 1920s and 1930s, reflected the variety of influences to which they were subject. In essence they were a compromise between the enterprise direction perspective, the shop management tradition and the need to attend to the requirements of the engineering institutions. A typical result is shown in Figure 12.3.[9]

Fayol: management as an abstract universal

Bowie's efforts notwithstanding, probably the major inspiration behind the enterprise management perspective in British management education from the 1930s onwards was Henri Fayol.

Though Fayol's career was roughly contemporary with Taylor's and though he too was an engineer by training, the context in which his theories were formed was an early instance of managerial capitalism. Fayol's experience as the director of a group of French mines led him to reflect, not on how he might redesign products and processes, but on how best to formulate and implement the overall policy of an enterprise. Quite unlike Taylor's, Fayol's prescriptions had nothing to say about changing production methods. Instead these were assumed in a set of prescriptions for a rational goal setting process acting through a unified structure of command. Fayol and his followers could (and did) claim that their methods of systematic planning and rational administration were applicable to all processes, and indeed to all organizations in which there was a division of labour.

Despite the supposed obsolescence of Fayol's 'principles of management',[10] the intellectual manoeuvre which underlay them endures in British and American management thought. The generality of Fayol's prescriptions depended on a process of abstraction in which management was defined so as to exclude much of the actual work of real life managers.

All industrial organizations - asserted Fayol - contain technical, commercial, financial, security, accounting and managerial activities. These activities are not performed by separate departments or individuals, but are combined, in various proportions, in the tasks which make up the total organization. In other words, real life managerial jobs contain both managerial and non-managerial elements. Managerial elements (i.e. those involving forecasting, organization, command, coordination and control) form a greater proportion of the whole tasks in the more senior positions. Nevertheless even quite junior positions may contain some managerial elements (Fayol, 1949, pp. 3, 9, and Chapter 5). Having defined management by this process of abstraction from real life tasks, Fayol then proceeded to discuss the managerial elements without reference to the particular activities in which they were enmeshed.

This latter-day version of the Platonic doctrine of forms is reproduced in the vast majority of management writing since Fayol's day. The resulting discussion of management *in vacuo* both depends on, and fosters, the belief that management is always and everywhere the same in essence. Though now a commonplace, such a view was probably novel in Fayol's time.[11] In England at least, an earlier generation of capitalists, when they thought about management at all, believed it to be mainly a matter of acquaintance with the process to be managed, or even with the particular factory. Management, in the sense of a common body of knowledge and code of behaviour remained industry-specific (Pollard, 1965, p. 158). The same was true, in a different sense, of Taylorism. Though Taylor certainly enunciated principles of scientific management, they were principles of *method*. In their application, they always depended on process-specific knowledge.

Despite the wide circulation of Fayol's work in his native France, his influence on English-speaking management education was not a direct one. It depended upon the labours of his great popularizer, Lyndall Urwick.

Urwick: teaching, professionalism and the abstract science of management[12]

Like Bowie, Urwick foresaw the coming domination of professionalized management. Urwick, however, saw it strictly within the framework of the market economy. Where Bowie envisaged the supersession of capitalist priorities, Urwick anticipated their articulation through modern strategic management.

> (A century of seller's markets and the development of new methods of production have) produced the world as it is today, a world in which on the whole business men have taken to thinking of production first and of distribution afterwards. They have come to regard the main function of distribution as selling what production happens to make. In this connection they have enormously developed the first three functions of the original market, transporting, selling and advertising.
>
> In doing so, they have to a large degree lost sight of the main function of those earlier markets - the informational function. The main job of distribution is not to get rid of what production makes, it is to tell production what it ought to make . ..

If this analysis is correct, if the long seller's market coupled with the development of machine production have resulted in the growth of an incorrect point of view so that business always thinks about production first and distribution second, the first and most essential thing is to break that habit . .. The first thing to be done is, therefore, the creation in every business of a new and separate main division of responsibility and duties which may be called the 'marketing division' . . .

This marketing division should not be placed 'over' production and sales. It should be a parallel department with its own clearly defined duties and functions of a planning and coordinating type, such as has been indicated. In the event of a failure in adjustment, the Managing Director should continue to exercise his function of control as at present (Urwick, 1933, pp. 85-93).

This passage is interesting in several respects. Not only does it explicitly attack the myopia of the shop management tradition, it also offers to account for the development of this 'incorrect point of view' in historical and technical terms. What was modern about Urwick's own approach in the Great Britain of the 1930s is that it was a conception of management addressed to the top level of control in capitalist enterprises. In that sense it was a product of the coming era of British managerial capitalism.

In Urwick's opinion, the materials for a body of knowledge appropriate to this expanded conception of management already existed in the work of Taylor and Fayol. He saw the two as complementary. Their obvious differences were, he believed, explicable in terms of their different starting points. Whereas Fayol had analysed the management process from the top down, Taylor had started from the bottom up - but both represented the same spirit of careful enquiry. The two approaches were bound, he believed, to meet in the middle.

In the main, Urwick's detailed writings on management were decidedly unoriginal. The unkind view of *Elements of Industrial Administration* (1947) would be that it consisted of little more than an elaboration of Fayol. On the other hand, his thinking at the strategic level on the prospects for the teaching of management and its professionalization made a number of important connections. Firstly his writings linked the idea of an expanded conception of management with the abstraction and generality of Fayol's administrative science. Secondly, the same abstract and general body of knowledge was seen as the basis both for the professionalization of management (Urwick, 1953b, p. 112) and for management education applicable to all types and levels of management (Urwick, 1964, pp. 7-8).

'A valid distinction cannot be drawn between the study of management for one purpose rather than another... ' wrote Urwick in the report which designed Britain's first national system of management education (Ministry of Education, 1947, p. 7). Though Urwick's formal administrative theory is no longer considered current knowledge, it nevertheless formed the first convincing foundation for claims that management could be a profession of universal application, for management education divorced from its context of application and for the rationale of the peripatetic management consultant (such as the partners of Urwick Orr and company).

Though Urwick was not formally involved in the IIA syllabi, until that of 1945, he probably exerted considerable influence on earlier versions. In 1926, he became the first Honorary secretary of the Management Research Group (of which Bowie was also a member). In 1928 he established the International Management Group based in Geneva and, shortly after this folded in 1933, he founded the consultancy firm of Urwick Orr and Partners. By the time of the Second World War, he was an eminent international management consultant with an intimate knowledge of American management practice and education. It was therefore natural that he should play a prominent role in the formation of British policy on management education in the immediate postwar years. Between 1942 and 1944 he served on the committee which establish the Administrative Staff College at Henley. When, in 1947, the British Institute of Management was founded on the recommendation of the Baillieu Committee, Urwick became its first chairman. When Atlee's Labour government despatched about sixty 'Productivity Teams' across the Atlantic under the Marshall Aid plan to report on the secrets of American industrial productivity, Urwick was a natural choice to lead the team which reported on American management education. Most important for the story of management education, he chaired the Ministry of Education Committee which designed Britain's first national system of management education (Ministry of Education 1947). Besides articulating Urwick's (or Fayol's) ideas on management, the report of this committee also drew extensively on Urwick's interpretation of developments in America. This latter, it will be argued, was coloured by his Fayolite preconceptions about the nature of management itself.

In 1947, however, the actual syllabi produced by the Urwick Committee (Figures 12.4 and 12.5) also reflected the continued influence of the engineering institutions. During the 1940s, it was the view of the government that a national syllabus for management education - or at least the intermediate stage of it - ought to cover the

Intermediate syllabus
Note: This was, in fact the first stage of study. The Committee decided that the term 'elementary' was inappropriate for a course in management and substituted the term 'intermediate'
Part A - Introductory Subjects
1. The evolution of the modern industrial organization
2. The nature of management
Part B - 'Background' Subjects
1. The economic aspects of industry and commerce
2. The legal aspects of industry and commerce
3. The psychological aspects of industry and commerce
Part C - 'Tool' Subjects
1. Financial accounting and cost accounting
2. Statistical method
3. Work measurement and incentives
4. Office organization and methods

1947 'Intermediate' stage syllabus for National Scheme of Management Studies (Urwick Scheme)

A2 The Nature of Management   (Extracts)
Development. Production. Materials and methods. Research. Designing for production. Organization of design department and flow of work.. Inspection.
Production Organization and interrelationship of the sections concerned with planning, estimating, rate-fixing, tool design and manufacture, manufacturing, progress, wages, costing, works engineering, labour bureau, welfare and canteens, routes of essential documents through the organization and of work through the shops.
C3 Work measurement and Incentives   (Extracts)
Motion Study ... Operation process chart, use in recording steps of the work. Flow process chart analysis, how and when used as a measuring tool. Improvements in factory layout and organization. Steps in motion analysis. Questioning technique. Developing the new method ...

Extracts from suggested examination syllabus for intermediate scheme

Figure 12.4   1947 'Intermediate' stage syllabus for National Scheme of Management Studies (Urwick Scheme)

Source: *Ministry of Education, 1947*

requirements of a wide range of 'managerial professions', which at that date were thought to include engineering. For this reason, Urwick's committee included representatives of the engineering institutions, and this leverage seems to have enabled them to influence the advanced as well as the intermediate stage. As a

Final stage in general management
1.   Factory Management
2.   Distribution
3.   Development and Design
4.   Purchasing, Storekeeping and Transportation
5.   Personnel management
6.   Higher Business Control
7.   Management - Principles
8.   Management - Practice

Final stage in specialized field of management
1-6.   Syllabus prescribed by the appropriate Management Professional Institution.
7.   Management - Principles
8.   Management - Practice

1947 'Final' stage syllabus for National Scheme of Management Studies (Urwick Scheme)

1.   Factory management
Functional responsibilities of departments within the factory.
a) Pre-production: Preparation of work to be done; approval and modification of design for manufacture; specifications, drawings and material schedules; determination of processes and machine operations; jig and tool design; rate-fixing; motion and time study; engineering estimation.

2.   Development and design
Purpose: to provide an appreciation of the principles governing efficient and progressive development and design of the product.
Research: Its relation to development and design; types of research - fundamental, applied and development.
Organization and personnel subjects.
Raw materials, processes, labour and markets ...

Extracts from suggested examination syllabus for final stage

Figure 12.5   1947 'Final' stage syllabus for National Scheme of Management Studies (Urwick Scheme)

Source: *Ministry of Education, 1947*

result, although the main outlines of Urwick's teaching syllabi are formal and abstract, the fine print of the examination syllabi still calls for some concrete grasp of the management of production processes. Urwick's own view of this continued entanglement of management and engineering will be considered in the next section of the chapter.

The emancipation of management from engineering

As a self-proclaimed inheritor of the scientific management tradition, Urwick could do no less than acknowledge 'Management's debt to the Engineer' (1953a). On the other hand he felt that management had now 'grown up (and) has its own organizations' (ibid. p. 379). For this reason he strongly disapproved of the continuation of the entanglement with engineering which management had inherited from Taylor:

> After, and even before, Taylor's death, a great many people adopted the profession of which he was the first exponent as advisers or counsellors to business undertakings that wished to improve their methods of management. Initially, the majority of these professional men described themselves as industrial engineers. Since most of then were engineers by training, they were usually employed in the manufacturing function of business and, most frequently, in the metallurgical industries. This was reasonable enough in the early stages. But as the concept of management has expanded, such counsellors have dealt with all kinds of business problems for which an engineering training is not necessarily the most appropriate discipline and for which, in certain cases, some other and different discipline may be mandatory. To continue to describe as industrial engineers firms engaged primarily in introducing psychological concepts into the selection and handling of personnel or statistical refinements into the handling of markets, is an obvious misnomer. The more modern and exact title of management consultant is tending to replace industrial engineer in these fields (Urwick, 1963, p. 1-5).

Urwick believed that the interpenetration of management and engineering was an historical accident which had occurred because engineers had been the only large group of salaried staff on hand at the time when there appeared new possibilities for logical thinking as applied to management problems (ibid. see also Urwick, 1953b, p. 15). However, the expansion of the technical content of engineering curriculae had created problems for the adequate treatment of management within them. The best solution for all concerned was a parting of the ways:

> The solution of this difficulty depends primarily on a sharper definition by engineers of the boundaries of their function as engineers and hence to a clear distinction between those functions in business for which full engineering training is desirable if not essential, and those functions which depend primarily

upon some other discipline although making use of engineering skills for the maintenance of equipment and so on ... There has from time to time been a recognisable tendency in some quarters to claim that industrial engineering is synonymous with management. It is not. Management owes an immense debt to engineering, but engineering as practised by the industrial engineer is only a part of the over-all work of managing. Engineering as a 'discipline' is concerned with physical forces and physical underlying sciences. Any title which includes the term engineering is strictly limited to dealing with things, because engineering knowledge does not include people (Urwick, 1963, pp. 1-6).

Like Bowie (see p. 10), Urwick reached this position by *defining* engineering in terms which excluded 'the human element'. Such a definition is by no means self-evident and it would probably be rejected by most practising engineers. Arguably it says as much about the ambitions of management educationalists as about the essential nature of engineering.[13] On the basis of such thinking, it was Urwick's view that the 1920s advent of management training conceptually divorced from engineering had effectively emancipated management from its origins. Though the syllabus of the Institute of Industrial Administration to which he refers in the following quotation was adopted by the Engineering Institutions as an educational requirement for certain routes to Associate Membership, to Urwick this signalled that management had been recognized as an independent body of knowledge rather than an aspect of engineering practice:

1927 was marked by another significant event, the starting of the lecture courses and examinations for the Diploma of the Institute of Industrial Administration professing that management was no longer the prerogative of the technically trained engineer however high his personal calibre, and testifying to the existence of a separate profession with its own principles, its own field of study, its own standards, capable of application throughout the length and breadth of industry.

To say that the story of education for management was now complete would be the antithesis of the truth. The story of the movement within the engineering profession was complete - not because the desired end was attained, but because the technical bias had ceased to be overwhelming. The struggle now beginning was that of education and training for management without restriction, the struggle for the recognition of the need for professional training and standards for management *per se*, and for the establishment of approved qualifications which would ensure for British industry a high standard of executive competence in all those to whom was entrusted responsibility for its governance (Urwick and Brech, 1959, p. 129).

It is clear from this quotation that, in Urwick's mind, the emancipation of management from engineering was *connected* with the identification of management (*per se*) with the governance of industry. The engineering design of work processes would no longer count as management in Urwick's sense. Instead it would henceforth become ghettoized within engineering curriculae and practice, notably those of work study and production engineering.

From the Urwick scheme to the diploma in management studies

The Urwick scheme was hardly a success. Though 100 technical colleges offered the Certificate course and 62 the Diploma, the number of awards over the fifteen years of the scheme's existence was only 810 and 640 respectively. Criticism centred upon the quality of the teaching, of the student intake, of the length of time it took to achieve diploma status (five years' part time study) and the dropout rate (Rose, 1970, p. 4). Moreover some employers appear to have been outraged by the temerity of those of their employees who pressed claims for promotion solely on the basis of possession of the Diploma (*The Manager*, May 1960, p. 335). Probably the main problem in the eyes of British advocates of management education, was that the diploma was offered in relatively low-status educational institutions.

In 1960 the Urwick scheme was replaced by the Diploma in Management Studies (DMS). This was adapted from the British Institute of Management's Associateship examination and initially administered jointly by the Institute and by the United Kingdom Advisory Council on Education for Management. Although, like the Urwick scheme, the diploma was to be taught in technical colleges, the Department of Education and Science's Circular 1/60 made it clear that the status of the award was to be maintained by requiring entrants to be of postgraduate standard.

This line proved impossible to hold. By the mid 1960s, in the author's personal experience, DMS courses were being taught to 18 year olds whose A-level results were too poor for admission on to degree courses. As a result, the DMS 'quickly fell into disrepute' (Whitley et al., 1981, p. 37). In a blistering report, J. W. Platt, the first chairman of the Advisory Council which had been appointed to oversee the Diploma, criticized the standards and methods of teaching, the quality of the student intake, the fragmentation of the course content and the diffusion of aim inherent in any national scheme of management study (Platt, 1968). He recommended that the DMS be discontinued forthwith in favour of MBA degrees on the American pattern.

The DMS, of course, survived this filicidal onslaught. As late as 1984/5, the annual output of Diploma-holders, at 1177, was still roughly equal to that from MBA courses (Council for National Academic Awards, 1984/5 Annual Report).

To advocates of University level management education, the DMS may appear to have been an evolutionary dead end. Its syllabus nevertheless represented a stage in the disengagement of British management education from industrial engineering. Figure 12.6 shows the model syllabus as it stood in 1968. Amongst many other differences from the Urwick scheme, it can be seen that the production engineering and work study elements of the Urwick syllabus have disappeared. A likely proximate reason was the appearance, in the intervening years, of institutions which claimed to represent management in general, and a consequent reduction in the weight attached to engineering opinion in official circles. In 1947 Urwick had to negotiate his syllabus with the engineering institutions. In 1960 the new national syllabus was the product of an agreement between the Department of Education and Science and the British Institute of Management - which of course, did not exist before 1947 (Department of Education and Science, 1968 p. 1).

Introductory Stage 1
... should be designed to give a general understanding of business, its environment, its problems and purpose and the human aspects involved and an introduction to two of its main tools, statistical analysis and accounting. For this the course should normally cover general economics, industrial sociology and psychology, elements of statistical methods and accounting (including an introduction to the quantitative aspects of decisions) all taught from the point of view of their relevance to business structure and problems and analytically rather than merely descriptively. A preliminary study of the main functional areas of management e.g. production, marketing, personnel, also has an appropriate place at this stage ...

Main body of course Stage 2
... the main functional areas of management should be studied, not from a specialist viewpoint, but to show their relevance to the process as a whole. The basic decision-making tools such as statistical method, costing methods and operational research techniques should be brought as far as is practical and relevant, into all parts of the course and linked with the human aspects, problems of leadership and decision implementing. Management principles and practice should be included as a study of organizational questions and methods that have been used to deal with them, not as a settled body of accepted rules. The study of industrial relations and financial control should also be taken in the broader business context.

Figure 12.6   Extracts from outline syllabus for Diploma in Management Studies 1968

Source: *DES memorandum on the DMS* (HMSO, 1968)

However, another reason for the absence of engineering elements in the D.M.S. syllabus may have been a hostility to the connection of management with engineering on the part of the scheme's administrators. Like Bowie and Urwick before him, J. W. Platt, chairman of the Advisory Council on Management

Education during the early 1960s, was no believer in engineering as a background for management:

> ...The undergraduate has to assess evidence and to think. But this does not fit him to be a businessman. I think the strongest case is that of the technologist and engineer, who is quite unfitted for a business career after graduating. If he is a really good technologist, he is likely to be kept in that job for too many years, and when he ultimately wants to get out it is too late; he has not the feeling for business problems (Robbins Report, Evidence Part 2, Vol. D, p. 1390).

The next major development in British management education, the MBA was self-consciously modelled on the American pattern. It was an import, however, which bore the thumbprints of the importers. In order to see this, it is necessary to sketch out the development of management education in America.

American models

American influence on the of the British management education movement had existed at least from the time of Elbourne's visit to the United States in 1900. Between the wars, prominent industrialists such as Herbert Austin (Church, 1979, p. 70) and Oliver Lucas (Nockolds, 1976, p. 183) also made the trip and returned as proselytes of the new methods - then industrial engineering and management accountancy.

We have already seen that the design of the 1947 Ministry of Education Committee was influenced by Urwick's knowledge of the American scene. The report contained an appendix on American management education to which it frequently referred in justification of its recommendations.

A generation later, the American MBA was the inspiration behind the establishment of its British counterpart. Following a visit to America by Keith Joseph and the graduation from Harvard Business School of John Bolton,[14] the two formed a 'management group' which met at the House of Commons. Together with J. W. Platt (whose disillusion with the DMS has already been noted), they established the Foundation for Management Education (FME). The objects were to press the case for university-level management education and to raise funds from industry for the purpose. By 1963, things were moving. It is impossible to improve upon the fine writing of Nind's account:

> (It was) during those twelve months that all the relevant sections of the British 'establishment' finally, unequivocally and irrevocably accepted management as a major thrust for education within the universities. A few ugly sisters would continue to lurk, even in some prominent corners; but the entrepreneurial spirit of Cinderella had prevailed.....the lone voices of the 1940s and 1950s had been

joined by others with increasing harmony; and a groundswell of sound began to be heard throughout the country (Nind, 1985, p. 19, 20).

Evidently these were exciting times. Dinners were held at the Savoy in order to promote management education. At one of these, the gathering hit upon the idea of asking Lord Franks to prepare a report. Franks succeeded both in 'surpass(ing) the council's best expectations' (Nind, 1985, p. 22) and in keeping his report commendably brief. This he achieved by the simple expedient of assuming his major conclusion - that university-level business schools should be established forthwith - and discussing only the details of how and where this might be done (Franks, 1963). For Franks, as for Urwick, the American experience was decisive. His clinching argument in favour of university-level business education was that the Americans did it that way (ibid. p. 5).

In the most important respect, the report served its purpose. In response to an appeal of 1964, industry stumped up to the tune of £5 million and the first British business schools were established at London and Manchester.

Sadly, even before a second appeal in 1969 netted enough to set up additional schools at Aston, Warwick and Bradford, disillusion had begun to set in. 'Industry' began complaining that the schools were too academic, out of touch with industry and were producing graduates who were arrogant and unemployable (Nind, 1985, pp. 40, 51). As was pointed out in the introduction, these plaints were the forerunners of a considerable literature of accusation and rebuttal, in the course of which the management education movement appeared to develop a sense of itself as apostolic elite with a mission to convert the atheistic mass of British industry. The cultural expression of this self-image was a discourse of go-getting dynamism in which attempts to debate the possible forms of management education were persistently trumped by appeals to the American example.[15] The prosperity of (some of) the United States and its massive programme of postgraduate management education were felt to provide all the argument necessary.

An interesting feature of the drive to import American style business education into the United Kingdom was that it ignored the fact that there have been *two* patterns of management education in the United States: a business school tradition, and an industrial engineering tradition which developed during the 1920s in the engineering schools. Though Urwick himself was well aware of this duality, most British advocacy of the American model has concentrated exclusively on the business school tradition.

Two traditions of American management education

Daniel (1971, pp. 66-7) was the first to point out that the Franks advocacy of postgraduate business education was based on a highly selective reading of the American experience. American undergraduate business degrees outnumber postgraduate qualifications by almost fifty-to-one. Furthermore there is a large volume of more rudimentary management instruction incorporated into engineering degrees (Rose, 1970, p. 129). It is far from clear why it should have been the graduate business schools rather than the larger volume of lower level work which have accounted for the productivity of American industry. During the immediate postwar years, in fact, there are grounds for believing that it was the engineering schools rather than the business schools which lay behind the American advantage. According to Locke (1984, p. 90-1) American productive superiority during the first half of the twentieth century had more to do with operational than strategic management. Furthermore the generation of American chief executives which accomplished the productivity miracle of World War Two, had backgrounds in manufacturing rather than sales or finance (Fligstein, 1978, Table 2), which suggests that they were largely products of the engineering, rather than the business schools.

Management education in American engineering schools

The interest of the American engineering schools in management, on a modest scale until the 1920s, expanded rapidly thereafter under the influence of Taylorism (Society for the Promotion of Engineering Education, 1931: Bulletin No. 11, pp. 549, 822). By 1930, 17 institutions were offering complete curriculae in engineering administration, commercial engineering and industrial engineering. Typically the 'management content' of such courses amounted to between 1/3 and 1/5 of the total teaching time, as compared to something under 1/10 in a normal technical degree of the day (Pierson et al., 1959, pp. 509, 513). Just as Taylorism itself approached management from a production engineering/shop management perspective, so the industrial engineering syllabi reflected a continuity between engineering and management (and a comparative neglect of the enterprise strategy aspects of management). The topics covered in the 1940s course at New York College of Engineering were:

Year 1 Technical
Year 2 Technical plus economics.
Year 3 Industrial administration, business history, organizational finance, factory planning.
Year 4 Time and motion, cost control, machine design, industrial psychology, social studies, engineering law.
(Source: Anglo-American Council on Productivity, 1951, p. 53).

By the time of the Anglo-American Productivity Teams, management education in the engineering schools was massively overshadowed by the output of the business schools: in 1949/50 these latter granted 76,530 degrees as compared to 3,650 from industrial engineering courses (Anglo-American Productivity Council, 1951, p. 47). Whilst this is some justification for Urwick's concentration on the business school model, it is still likely that the American record of productivity during World War Two owed as much to the industrial engineering tradition.

Beginning with the Wharton School at the University of Pennsylvania in 1881, most of the American business schools were founded on the initiative of university economics departments or of professional accounting bodies. For example, the New York University School of Commerce, Accounts and Finance was founded by the New York State Society of Certified Public Accountants, in order to prepare students for their professional examinations (Pierson et al., 1959, pp. 36-41).

In some cases, the schools' early syllabi seem to have been aimed more at the preparation of gilded youth for the management of investment portfolios or careers in the commercial professions than for corporate management as such. In 1916, the subjects represented in the Columbia School of Business (then an undergraduate institution), were accounting, banking, business organization, finance, insurance, business law and transport. At that stage, the neglect of production management within the School itself could be compensated by offering electives within the University's Department of Industrial Engineering. Later, this became less relevant. When, in 1949, the school changed to an all-graduate intake, emphasis shifted from functional specialization to the 'more vague but more exciting functions of the management of the business enterprise' (Van Metre, 1954, pp. 40-62).

Developments at Harvard followed a different route though the ultimate destination was the same. Designed from the outset as a preparation for corporate management, the first syllabi were aimed at specialized areas such as railways or banking. Quite soon, however, there was a trend, encouraged by the pattern of student enrolments on optional courses, away from functional and industrial specialization in favour of courses of the general administration type (Copeland, 1958, pp. 5, 18, 25, 42, 150, 159).

By the early 1920s, Harvard, like the other business schools, began to concentrate on 'certain broad functions of the business enterprise'. Teaching programmes solidified around six core subjects: business law, statistics, marketing, accounting, money and banking, and business and corporate finance. In the early 1920s, Harvard also pioneered the case study method of integrating these topics into the study of business decision-making (Pierson et al, 1959, p. 47-8).

The American business schools, then, unlike the engineering departments, approached management from a 'top down' perspective which concentrated upon enterprise-level decision making, particularly in its financial and marketing aspects.

There is some evidence, albeit sketchy, that the two approaches found themselves in competition in the arena of American practice, as well as the subject of demarcation disputes within the academies. Spokesmen for the accounting profession complained of 'charlatans calling themselves industrial engineers' who were competing for lucrative consultancies (Carey, 1969, p. 147). As we have seen, Urwick himself, in his aspect as an American management consultant, argued against the territorial encroachment of industrial engineering upon management. Within the academies, business schools and industrial engineering departments found themselves competing for the same students (Pierson et al., 1959, p. 522), which competition was increasingly resolved by arranging that the management requirements of engineering courses be serviced from the business schools and *vice versa* (e.g. Van Metre, 1954, p. 54).

As a consequence of this division of labour within the American academies, but also as a result of the conception of management embedded in their own traditions, the American business schools, from the 1920s onwards were *never* been concerned to prioritize manufacturing management. During the 1940s, just under 3 per cent of the management courses at a sample of American universities were in production, compared to 48 per cent in accounting and finance (Ministry of Education, 1947, p. 30). In the 1950s, about 60 per cent of undergraduate business schools offered no production major at all (Pierson et al., 1959, p. 494).

As a consequence of this line of evolution, a British observer such as Urwick, already predisposed to regard management as an abstract and general expertise, could find a sympathetic approach in the American business schools. In his characterization of management (administration), the Harvard University Emeritus Professor of Administration might have been quoting Urwick verbatim:

> Administration is operative at many levels in an organization, from foreman to president to chairman of the board, and at each level essentially the same process takes place and the same type of abilities are required (Copeland, 1958, p. 148).

This congeniality may have contributed to Urwick's concentration on the business school rather than the industrial engineering tradition as a model for the United Kingdom's first national scheme of management education. The 1960s 'Savoy Group', appears to have had a more limited knowledge of the American scene: their promotion of the MBA seems to have been based on the assumption that the business school tradition *was* American management education.

As a consequence of these mental sets and blindnesses, the 'American Model' which was imported into the United Kingdom during the mid-1960s was actually based on a very partial picture of American management and management education. Developments in the industrial engineering tradition which were so enthusiastically taken up by the Japanese in the immediate postwar period through the agency of W. Edwards Deming, were ignored both in the UK and the USA. The consequences live on. A typical 1980s syllabus from a highly rated British business school is shown in Figure 12.7.

YEAR 1

Term 1 Accounting, Finance, Law, Economics, Psychology, Sociology, Organizational Behaviour, Quantitative Methods.
Terms 2 and 3 Problem solving in resource allocation, policy making, decision making. Plus 10,000 word dissertation based on work in placement.

YEAR 2

Group project work on problems faced by real companies. examples of topics: operations management, industrial relations, entrepreneurship, international business.
Plus options in the main functional areas in management, the most popular being those in marketing and business finance, reflecting the students' view that rapid advancement is possible through these areas.

Figure 12.7   Outline of MBA Syllabus at Manchester Business School 1981

Source: *Whitley et al., 1981, pp. 51-2*

Conclusion and postscript

With the MBA we arrive at a stable and well institutionalized educational expression of an idea of management which excludes the traditional concerns of industrial engineering. It is not merely that the advent of managerial capitalism has led to an extension of the remit of management to include what were once entrepreneurial functions. The conception of management has contracted as well, in that it no longer includes the work of designing the products and processes of subordinate labour. Where the industrial engineers saw an organic relationship between the organization and supervision of labour on the one hand and the design of labour processes on the other, modern management thought draws a conceptual boundary between the two. Whereas the 'human' aspects of organization and supervision are counted as part of management, the intellectual labour of design is not. The following is from an American management text which is widely used in the UK and has now run through many editions:

> Failure to distinguish executive functions from nonmanagerial technical skills is another source of confusion . . . the manager . . . may or may not possess such technical skills. In his managerial capacity he certainly is not utilising such operating expertness (*sic*) (Koontz and O'Donnell, 1968, p. 55).

293

Similarly, from a popular management accounting text:

> From the viewpoint of systems development, the most important distinction
> between task control and management control is that many task control systems
> are *scientific*, whereas management control can never be reduced to a science.
> By definition, management control involves the behaviour of managers, and
> these behaviours cannot be expressed by equations. Serious errors are made
> when principles developed by management scientists for task control situations
> are applied to management control situations. In management control,
> managers interact with other managers; in task control, either human beings are
> not involved at all (as is the case with some automated production processes),
> or the interaction is between a managers and a nonmanager (Anthony, Dearden
> and Govindarajan, 1992, p. 16).

And from the most famous management guru of them all:

> Every manager does things which are not managing. He may spend most of his
> time on them. A sales manager makes a statistical analysis or placates an
> important customer. A foreman repairs a tool or fills in a production report.
> A manufacturing manager designs a new plant layout or tests new materials. A
> company president works through the details of a bank loan or negotiates a big
> contract - or spends dreary hours presiding at a dinner in honor of long service
> employees. All these things belong to a particular function. All are necessary
> and have to be done well. But they are apart from that work which every
> manager does whatever his function or activity, whatever his rank and position,
> work which is common to all managers and is peculiar to them (Drucker, 1955,
> p. 343).

An important corollary of this detachment of management from the design of
process is that it flattens out differences *within* management. Thus:

> the goal of managers as managers is fundamentally the same in business and
> non business enterprises. It is also the same at every level (Koontz and
> O'Donnell, 1968, p. 7).

and:

> ....managers perform the same function regardless of their place in the
> organizational structure or the type of enterprise in which they are engaged ...
> getting things done with or through people. The implications of this principle
> are several. In the first place it means that anything significant that is said
> about the functions of one manager applies to all managers... In the second
> place, the principle implies that management knowledge and experience are
> transferable from department to department and from enterprise to enterprise

294

(Koontz and O'Donnell, 1968, p. 54).

and:

> The management control system is basically similar throughout the organization; such similarity is essential so that the revenues and expenses of the organization can be aggregated into the summaries that managers need. By contrast, each types (*sic*) of task requires a different task control system. A production control system is quite different from a programme trading system. In management control, the focus is on organizational units; in task control, the focus is on specific tasks performed by these organizational units (Anthony, Dearden and Govindarajan, 1992, p. 20).

Thus the universalization of management follows from its abstraction. This feature of the conception of management built into most contemporary courses points towards the social sources of its stability. Firstly, management courses which promise open career prospects and transferability are attractive to students (recall the replacement of Harvard Business School's early course in Railroad Management by one in Management). Secondly, management schools can, with clear consciences, offer essentially the same syllabus to all industries and to all promotional levels. This application of the principle of variety reduction was spectacularly illustrated by Urwick himself in the 1940s, when he offered identical courses to foremen and top executives. Thirdly, the associated, but misleading, truism that management is essentially about the control of people, has made it possible for persons who are essentially behavioural scientists to assume the status of experts on management. Looking beyond the field of education, the universalized, abstract conception of management offers the perfect rationale for the peripatetic management consultant and the job hopping senior executive. This gridlock of vested interest operates to stabilize and maintain the contemporary definition of management, and the educational provision through which it is expressed.

None of these vested interests, it will be noted, depends immediately upon the actual performance of British industry. Nor is the belief that 'management' is detachable from the content of what is managed widespread in German and Japanese capitalism. In these respects, the questions being asked about presently-existing management education still await an answer.[16]

Notes

1. It was the Franks Report of 1963 which recommended the establishment of American style business schools at London and Manchester.
2. For the tendency of Anglo-Saxon managers to define themselves in terms of a general status rather than a particular function, see Mant (1978). For a good account of the peculiarities of the Anglo-Saxon conception of management, see Lawrence (1980).
3. Child et al. (1983) have discussed this tendency in terms of the professional authority of staff functions in British industry.
4. This should not be construed as an endorsement of the view that British management should be the ultimate judges of a programme of education aimed at its own improvement. This was implicit in the Griffiths and Murray (1985) proposal that business schools should be forced to subsist on fee income so as to make them more responsive to the needs of employers.
5. Brief overviews of the development of British management education are to be found in Wheatcroft (1970, Chapters 7 and 8) and Rose (1970). Major histories of management thought include Urwick and Brech (1963), Child (1969), George (1972), Wren (1972), and Pollard (1974, 1978) There is also a large number of relevant studies which sail under the flag of organizational behaviour (e.g. Pugh, Hickson and Hinings, 1971 and Rose, 1975), or concentrate on the ideological aspects of managerial thought (e.g. Bendix, 1956).
6. There are other, equally valid ways in which different approaches to management education might be categorized. In Vout's interesting study (1987), 'industrial engineering management' and 'executive training' paradigms are contrasted. The latter differed somewhat from the 'enterprise direction' approach discussed in the present paper, in that there was more emphasis on the skills and personal qualities deemed necessary for the direction of enterprise than on formal knowledge, as such. The most prominent exemplar of the 'executive training' approach was the Administrative Staffs College at Henley, and it is an ethos prominent in much in-company provision (Ascher, 1983), not to mention the 'outward bound' school of management development. For clarity this strand of thinking is not considered here, although it is an important part of the whole picture.
7. Notable exceptions included the Renold company in Manchester and Hopkinson's in Huddersfield.
8. Though Bowie, to his expressed regret, never held a position as a practising manager, this unflattering view of the engineer was based on a considerable acquaintance with engineers in their student phase. It must have taken some conviction to maintain such views in a technical institution.
9. The drift in the content of management teaching since these early IIA syllabi has also been examined by Anthony (1986), but his conclusions differ from those argued here. In Anthony's view, the dissociation between management

and expertise in the productive process has forced British managers to interpose layers of supervision between themselves and the workforce. The result has been a loss of 'leadership' of the productive process. Anthony's solution, however, is not a restoration of the lost expertise but a reliance on behavioural science. To the observation that contemporary management courses are stuffed with material on leadership, motivation, and the like, his response is that this is rendered useless by its banality. Whilst the banality is indisputable, the relevance of behavioural science to a problem caused by a deficit of expertise in the processes being managed is not obvious.

10. This observation may be premature. There are departments in Britain's newer Universities in which the undead Fayol speaks to a current generation through the medium of such textbooks as Hicks and Gullett (1976).

11. Interestingly, Fayol's position on this point was not entirely consistent. Despite his belief that the proportion of 'managerial' work at senior levels might approach 100 per cent, Fayol - a mining engineer who had been in charge of mines - also took it for granted that managers would be competent in the processes which they were to manage. Even in the managing director, he wrote (1949, pp. 72-3), 'lack of competence is inadmissible in the specialized activity characteristic of the business, technical in industry, commercial in commerce....'. This proviso tended to be forgotten in the writings of Urwick.

12. Urwick's reworking of Taylor and Fayol was also discussed by Armstrong (1991), in which an attempt was made to relate Urwick's demarcation of management from non-management to the Marxist distinction between productive and unproductive labour.

13. The definition of a professional engineer adopted by the Conference of Engineering Societies of Western Europe and the USA reads, in part:...His work is predominantly intellectual and varied and not of a routine mental and physical character. It requires the exercise of original thought and judgement 'and the ability to supervise the technical and administrative work of others' (quoted in Gerstl and Hutton, 1966, p. 4-5, italics added).

14. Both men were consequential in the development of British engineering as well as management. Sir Keith Joseph played a leading role in the decision not to create a statutory Engineering Authority charged with duty of promoting the 'engineering dimension' within British management, as had been recommended by the Finniston Report (1980). John Bolton, who later became the managing director of Solartron Electronics, played a more positive role. The advanced instrumentation and soft porn calendars produced by that company served British engineering well during early 1960s.

15. See Franks (1963, p. 5), for an example of the tendency to take for granted the desirability of the American business school model.

16. Mangham and Silver (1986) found no correlation whatsoever between company expenditure on management education and economic performance. This did not prevent them from joining the call for an urgent expansion of the former.

References

Anglo-American Council on Productivity (1951), *Education for Management*, Anglo-American Council on Productivity, London.

Anthony, P. D. (1986), *The Foundations of Management*, Tavistock, London.

Anthony, R. N., Dearden, J. and Govindarajan, V. (1992), *Management Control Systems*, 7th Edition, Irwin, Homewood, Ill.

Armstrong, P. (1991), 'The Divorce of Productive and Unproductive Management', Chapter 11 in Knights, D. and Willmott, H. (eds), *White Collar Work: the Non-Manual Labour Process*, Macmillan, London, pp. 241-261.

Ascher, K. (1983), *Managerial Training in Large UK Business Organizations: a Survey*, Harbridge House, London.

Bendix, R. (1956), *Work and Authority in Industry: Ideologies of Management in the Course of Industrialization*, Harper Row, New York.

Bowie, J. A. (1930), *Education for Business Management*, Oxford University Press, London.

Burnham, J. (1941), *The Managerial Revolution*, Day, New York.

Carey, J. L. (1969), *The Rise of the Accounting Profession: From Technician to Professional*, American Institute of Certified Public Accountants, New York.

Chandler, A. D. and Daems, H. (1974), 'The Rise of Managerial Capitalism and its Impact on Investment Strategy in the Western World and Japan', pp. 1-34 in Daems, H. and Van der Wee, H. (eds), *The Rise of Managerial Capitalism* Leuven University Press, Louvain.

Child, J. (1969), *British Management Thought: a Critical Analysis*, Allen and Unwin, London.

Child, J., Fores, M., Glover, I. and Lawrence, P. (1983), 'A Price to Pay? Professionalism and Work Organization in Britain and West Germany', *Sociology*, Vol. 17, 1, pp. 63-78.

Church, R. (1979), *Herbert Austin: The British Motor Car Industry to 1941*, Europa, London.

Copeland, M. T. (1958), *And Mark an Era: The Story of Harvard Business School*, Little & Brown, Boston.

Council for National Academic Awards (1984/5), *Annual Report*, Council for National Academic Awards, London.

Daniel, W.W. (1971) *Business Education at 18+: a survey of the HND in Business Studies*, PEP Broadsheet No. 524, London.

Department of Education and Science (1968), *A Memorandum on the Diploma in Management Studies*, Department of Education and Science, London.

Drucker, P. L. (1955), *The Practice of Management*, Heinemann, London.

Elbourne, E. T. (1914), *Factory Administration and Accounts*, (Page references to 1918 ed.), The Library Press Ltd. London.

Elbourne, E. T. (1934), *Fundamentals of Industrial Administration*, McDonald and Evans, London.

Fayol, H. (1949), *General and Industrial Management*, Pitman, London.

Finniston, Sir H. M. (Chairman), (1980), *Engineering our Future*, Cmnd 7794, HMSO London.

Fligstein, N. (1978), 'The Intraorganizational Power-Struggle: Rise of Finance Personnel to Top Leadership in Large Corporations, 1919-1979', *American Sociological Review*, Vol 52, pp. 44-58.

Franks (Lord) (1963), *British Business Schools*, British Institute of Management, London.

George, C. S. Jr (1972), *The History of Mangement Thought*, Prentice-Hall, New Jersey.

Gerstl, J. E. and Hutton, S. P. (1966), *Engineers: the Anatomy of a Profession.* Tavistock, London.

Griffiths, B. and Murray, H. (1985), *Whose Business? an analysis of the failure of British Business Schools and a radical proposal for their privatisation*, Institute of Economic Affairs, London.

Handy, C., Gow, I., Gordon, C., and Randlesome, C. (1987), *The Making of Managers: A Report on Management Education, Training and Development in the USA, West Germany, France, Japan and the UK*, National Economic Development Office, London.

Hicks, H. G. and Gullett, C. R. (1976), *Organisations: Theory and Behaviour*, McGraw-Hill, London.

Institute of Industrial Administration (1954), *A History of the Institute of Industrial Administration 1919-1951*, Institute of Industrial Administration, London.

Koontz, H. and O'Donnell, C. (1968), *Principles of Management: an Analysis of Managerial Functions*, 4th edition, McGraw-Hill, New York.

Lawrence, P. (1980), *Managers and Management in West Germany*, Croom Helm, London.

Littler, C. (1982), *The Development of the Labour Process in Capitalist Societies.* Heinemann, London.

Locke, R. R. (1984), *The End of the Practical Man: Entrepreneurship and Education in Germany, France and Great Britain 1880-1940*, JAI Press, London.

Mangham, I. L. and Silver, M. S. (1986), *Management Training: Context and Practice, School of Management*, University of Bath, Bath.

Mant, A. (1978), 'Authority and Task in the Manufacturing Operations of Multinationals', Paper 5 in Fores, M. and Glover, I. (eds), *Manufacturing and Management*, HMSO, London.

299

Ministry of Education (1947), *Education For Management Subjects in Technical and Commercial Colleges: Report of a Special Committee appointed by the Ministry of Education*, HMSO, London.

Nichols, W. A. T. (1969) *,Ownership, Control and Ideology*, Allen and Unwin, London.

Nind, P. F. (1985), *A Firm Foundation: the Story of the Foundation for Management Education*, Foundation for Management Education, Oxford.

Nockolds, H. (1976), *Lucas: The First Hundred Years*, David and Charles, London.

Parker, R. H. (1969), *Management Accounting: an Historical Perspective*, Macmillan, London.

Parnaby, J. Quoted in *The Engineer*, 5 Dec. 1985, p. 43-5.

Pierson, F. C. (and authors of individual chapters) (1959), *The Education of American Businessmen*, McGraw-Hill, New York.

Platt, J. W. (1968), *Education for Management: a Review of the Diploma in Management Studies*, Foundation for Management Education, London.

Pollard, H. (1974), *Developments in Management Thought*, Heinemann, London.

Pollard, H. (1978), *Further Developments in Management Thought*, Heinemann, London.

Pollard, S. (1965), *The Genesis of Modern Management*, Edward Arnold, London.

Pugh, D. S., Hichson, D. J. and Hinings, C. R. (1971), *Writers on Organisations*. 2nd edition, Penguin, London.

Robins (Lord, Chairman), *Report of the Committee on Higher Education*, HMSO, London.

Rose, H. (1970), *Management Education in the 1970s*, National Economic Development Office, London.

Rose, M. (1975), *Industrial Behaviour: Theoretical Developments since Taylor*, Allen Lane, London.

Sheldon, O. (1924), *The Philosophy of Management*, (1965 reprint) Pitman, London.

Society for the Promotion of Engineering Education (1931), *Report of the Investigation of Engineering Education 1923-1929*, Society for the Promotion of Engineering Education, Pittsburgh, Penn.

Taylor, F. W. (1947), *Scientific Management*, Harper Bros, New York.

Urwick, L. F. (1933), *Management of Tomorrow*, Nisbet, London.

Urwick, (1947), *Elements of Industrial Administration*, Pitman, London.

Urwick, L. F. (1953a), *Management Education in American Business*, American Management Association, New York.

Urwick, L. F. (1953b), 'Management's Debt to the Engineer', *Mechanical Engineering*, May. pp. 374-386.

Urwick, L. F. (1963), 'Development of Industrial Engineering', Chapter 1 in Maynard, H. B. (ed.), (1963), *Industrial Engineering Handbook*, 2nd edition, McGraw-Hill, New York.

Urwick, L. F. (1964), *Is Management a Profession?* Urwick Orr and Partners, London.

Urwick, L. F. (1965), *Elements of Industrial Administration*, 2nd edition, Pitman, London.

Urwick, L. F. and Brech, E. F. L. (1959), (page references to 1963 reprint) *The Making of Scientific Management, Vol. 1. Thirteen Pioneers*, Pitman, London.

Van Metre, T. W. (1954), *A History of the Graduate School of Business*, Columbia University, Columbia University Press, New York.

Vout, M. (1986), *The Schooling of Management in Britain: a Parallelogram of Forces 1920-50*, Unpublished Ms. Department of Economics and Public Administration, Nottingham Polytechnic, Nottingham.

Wheatcroft, M. (1970), *The Revolution in British Management Education*, Pitman, London.

Whitley, R., Thomas, A. and Marceau, J. (1981), *Masters of Business? Business Schools and Business Graduates in Britain and France*, Tavistock, London.

Wren, D. A. (1972), *The Evolution of Management Thought*, Ronald, New York.

Acknowledgements

This chapter is based on research carried out during 1986 and 1987, whilst the author was a visiting Fellow at the Industrial Research Unit at the University of Warwick. The author is grateful for the helpful criticism and advice freely given by members of the Unit.

Part IV

DISCUSSION

13 Towards a professional-managerial class?

Ian Glover and Michael Hughes

Introduction

In those societies in which the professional way of organizing senior occupations and management status, education, training and development are explicitly prevalent, a professional-managerial class comprises virtually all professional and managerial level jobs, and is more or less synonymous with expert and managerial labour. In Chapter One we depicted a professional-managerial class as lying between a managerial stratum (those who run things, whatever their backgrounds) of the kind consisting mainly of a mixture of liberal arts and pure science graduates and professional specialists, and a broadly educated and very highly qualified technocratic one. In the UK a professional-managerial class currently means a very heterogeneous mixture of professionally and managerially and otherwise qualified and experienced people. It contains many professionals who have taken management courses or who have undergone management training in one way or another. Most of all those involved have had some sort of managerial experience, and those non-specialist managers who work alongside, below and above professionals have usually had significant experiences of the main specialist roles and tasks of professionals without, of course, actually having performed them.

Also in Chapter One, we were concerned primarily as to whether it made sense to think of contemporary UK management as being in the pursuer mode, engaged in a 'catching up' exercise in terms of developing its expertise and knowledge compared with its counterparts in competitor societies. In the conclusion to Chapter One, we hinted that this was the case, although the process was gradual and fitful rather than fast and confident.

We will now consider those two issues, with more emphasis on the former, drawing on the previous chapters in this book. Our arguments are organized quite

305

simply, first by looking at each chapter, weighing up the extent to which it lends support to the idea that a professional-managerial class, in a pursuer mode and perhaps one containing a nascent technocracy, currently exists or is forming in the UK.

Towards a professional-managerial class?

In Chapter One we noted the growth, and the growing breadth, of higher vocational qualifications in the UK, and the increasingly vocational emphasis of the whole system of higher education. We noted how management controls, and sometimes general managers themselves, had been imposed on professionals during the 1980s and 1990s. This had been partly associated with the deregulation of professional and other markets. It had mixed effects on professionals, generally favouring their senior members and those with something to sell, and weakening the power, influence, incomes and status of those with relatively unattractive services to offer and of junior professionals in the public sector. There was also evidence of professionals asserting and reasserting themselves against management controls which, they feel, stifle their creativity and initiative. While many management fads had a shallow and short term quality, some such as quality of services and customer care were useful insofar as they helped to force professionals to raise the standards of their service provision over and above their efforts to improve the technical quality of their 'practices'. In general, there was a growing overlap of knowledge, understanding and in some cases skills, between the professional and other expert specialist occupations and functions within UK management. Lay, expert and practitioner understanding of what management level work consisted of and demanded had an increasingly accurate and holistic quality.

However, many Business-Management style weaknesses persisted. The USA, and Japan as often as not seen through US eyes, were still taken as sources of inspiration without much consideration being given to alternatives. Managerial over-control of professional creativity and innovation (what a wag once called Management by Paranoid Overkill) was too often in evidence. So too was financial short termism. Contemporary management fads like business process re-engineering, total quality management (TQM) and HRM seemed like no more than parts of what properly educated, trained and deployed managements should have been doing routinely.

Peter Lawrence, in Chapter Two, in his characterization of UK management, argued that UK managers were aware of themselves and their society being in a state of often painful transition, and of their consequent flexibility and sense of irony and humour. Lawrence also offers evidence, however, of a very persistent belief in the manager as a mobile generalist, and of a certain fear of conflict. This would suggest that uncertainty and insecurity are, at best, significant correlates of the long march from amateurism through professionalism and managerialism in the vague direction of some sort of rather footloose technocracy.

The wide-ranging argument and the many pieces of evidence discussed in Robert Locke's chapter are not really relevant in an immediate 'for' or 'against' debate about the growth of a professional-managerial class. Instead Locke offers a large number of background facts, ideas and arguments about important influences on recent and current trends, such as the post-1945 transfer of US ideas to the UK and elsewhere, and the reasons why the UK was more receptive than West Germany or Japan.

Similarly, Chapters Four, Five and Six, by Paul Jeffcutt, Michael Fores and Williams et al. respectively, belong to the book's Context section, and are most relevant as sources of background ideas, rather than of direct and readily focused evidence. Thus Paul Jeffcutt considers mainly Anglo-Saxon thinking about management, explains some of its growing unity and breadth of concern, while also exploring some of its important internal contradictions and flaws, but is not directly concerned with the social and material composition and evolution of UK management. Fores' offers evidence of the fundamentally one-sided and scientistic character of much Business Management related thinking, and of the dangers of self-aggrandizement in rationalist professionalism and managerialism. His arguments imply that these dangers are still real and likely to be so for a long time to come. Williams et al. provide a fascinating and powerful corrective to the pretensions of management everywhere, and point to the limitations of managerialism. However while all the arguments in the Context section of the book do have strong background relevance to the questions posed in this chapter, that is more or less all that they have for them.

More directly relevant pointers and facts are to be found in the Evidence section of the book. Thus the value of professional ideals and practices against the encroachments of apparently all-conquering commercialized managerialism is emphasized by James Dingley in Chapter Seven. His chapter constitutes, in itself, evidence of an increasing awareness of a need to temper management control and managerial assertiveness with actions to protect and develop high level skills and those who have them. His arguments are likely to convince most people about the value to society of responsible professional and craft or equivalent organization and skill. At the same time his chapter implies a great deal about the limitations of aggressively self-interested managerialism. It articulates how top down controlling behaviour, the heavy-handed exercise of the 'managerial' side of the professional-managerial equation, is likely to stifle the skill and commitment that enlightened management should foster and sustain. There is also much in Dingley's arguments that could be used in support of the creation of an enlightened technocracy.

Ackroyd and Lawrenson, in the eighth chapter, present a discussion which is largely historical, so that it appears to tell us little directly about the current composition, aspirations and abilities of UK managers. In fact it offers important evidence and insights into and explanations of the ways in which management and organization have developed in the UK throughout the twentieth century. The final point made by Ackroyd and Lawrenson is about the systemic, programmed inability of most UK managers to understand their own inadequacies, and the real possibility that attempts by managers and professionals to improve matters may generate conflict rather than constructive action. This makes a salutary point to set against some of the optimism that we ourselves expressed in Chapter One about a professional-managerial class with increasingly overlapping qualifications and increasingly shared aspirations and understanding.

The discussion of the experiences of NHS consultants and academic librarians in Chapter Nine, by Kirkpatrick, Whipp and Davies, is the most strongly and directly relevant for understanding how a professional-managerial class, with some proto-technocratic tendencies, may be forming. Its distinction between the executive and market phases of New Public Management (NPM) has relevance far beyond the management and organization of public sector employing units. It tells us about the evolving motives and values behind the various managerialist criticisms of professions and the widespread perceptions about how resources should be managed. The chapter is also very useful for its ideas about how professionals can (and do) reform and re-assert themselves, or lose out, or become incorporated, and so on, when attempts are made to control or subjugate them. In general this chapter says a lot about contemporary tensions between managerialism and professionalism, and how, in different circumstances and sectors, one 'side' could win decisively over the other and thus inhibit and retard the development of a professional-managerial class.

The notion of HRM is strongly anti-segmentalist in the terms used by Kanter (1984), being concerned with integrating the efforts of all those involved in managing work and employment. Glover and Hallier's discussion of HRM, in Chapter Ten, deals with several aspects of professionalism and managerialism as evinced and experienced by personnel, HR and other kinds of professional and manager. A sensible and useful coming together of professionalism and managerialism is seen in much of the practice as well as in the prescriptive notion of HRM. It is however also depicted as being, in part, evidence of the ongoing weaknesses of Business Management practice and thinking.

There is strong evidence of the development of parts of a professional-managerial class in one sector, construction, in the penultimate chapter by Bresnen. Here what is perhaps the most complacent and sometimes arrogant of its professional occupations is seen getting something of a comeuppance from the beneficiaries of its long-standing managerial and other weaknesses, the hitherto less powerful and prestigious construction professional occupations, such as surveyors, and from building contractors. Yet in a more pessimistic vein, Bresnen also offers evidence of continuing weaknesses in the management of 'his' sector, although partly, of course, in the process of explaining how certain remedies are being applied.

The relevance of Chapter Twelve, by Peter Armstrong, is very clear. He explains how the twentieth century development of UK management education away from and at the expense of engineering has so far had a positive and a negative effect on efforts to develop an enlightened technocracy through a professional-managerial class. Management education has, as Armstrong helps to show, gained significantly in both breadth and depth since losing those aspects which its origins in engineering once provided. However, continuing neglect of or antipathy towards engineering does not augur particularly well for a full-blown enlightened technocratic future. Some people might rejoice at this. We would not. We would suggest by quoting James Dingley that 'if so they only display their own limitations' (Chapter 7, p. 166).

Discussion

A number of related and varied themes and points emerge from the chapters and from thinking about their implications.

The first concerns the nature of the influence of the USA on the UK and *vice versa*. The unthinking way in which the UK has and continues to follow, US management practices goes much deeper than one might expect on the basis of their common language and historical experiences. For all the many real and superficial differences between the USA and the UK, the USA remains, in several key respects, an offspring of the UK (Glover, 1985). Apart from the shared language, the USA was founded by the English, and its educational and legal systems continue to display important marks of Englishness or Britishness or of reactions against them. So too do the USA's religious and political institutions, the individualism of its people, their tendency to believe in a rural ideal, the existence of the professional way of growing and organizing senior occupations, and the 'arts and sciences' way of classifying subjects for study and of thinking about the use of knowledge for practical ends. We would suggest that although most people in the UK rarely think of these things consciously, they are much more confident than they would be otherwise when they relate to the USA because of them. The 'special relationship' is not so special: it is a result of a partly shared history and of mutual interest, ancestry, exploitation and development. The USA is *not* a new and superior society, existing entirely apart from its European origins. Instead it is a middle-aged child of Europe, and especially, of the UK, neither superior nor inferior, but very different in some respects and almost identical in others. In retrospect, more (indeed often *some*) awareness within the UK of differences and similarities would have helped policy makers in business, education and government to make better decisions, to follow the USA less blindly and in different ways or not at all.

Our second point concerns 'the limits of management' arguments Williams et al. which is reinforced most by Lawrence, Locke, Jeffcutt, Dingley and Ackroyd and Lawrenson. The performance of any management team depends on such things as 'the characteristics of job holders (skills, attitudes, educational background and so on); resources available to them (finance, equipment, information); (the) management and organization of work, and the environments of employing units (markets, attitudes of governments, legal systems and so on)' (Glover and Kelly, 1987, p. 118). The abilities and the motivation of those who are managed form a very large part of the resources available to, and the environment of, management.

In this book we have focused almost entirely on managers and professionals, not on those whom they employ. Improvements to the standard of the former imply improvements to that of the latter. However there is plenty of evidence in the UK to indicate that improvements to the education and training of the approximately two-thirds of each cohort of school leavers which does not attend university continue to lag seriously behind that given to those who do. Education and training in the UK need to reach parts of the body, politic and economic, that have not yet been reached, or which have not been reached since the old, long era of apprenticeship combined with self-improvement of a generation and more ago.

A third point concerns purpose and morality. Improvements to the quality of a society's management ought to be accompanied by some notion as to the sort of society, economy and polity that its people wish to develop. There appears to be little currently in the UK in the way of consensus about the country's future role in the world and about how to articulate and perform it. We would have thought that the UK should at least be able to draw on its global experience and resources, however attenuated, to help the European Union (EU) link with other parts of the world, and that its special historic experience and partly detached geographical location would help the UK to act as a constructive and imaginative sort of devil's advocate within the EU itself. The UK does some of this already, and to do it all, and more consistently than hitherto, would be a definite step towards developing a new and positive future for itself.

Fourth, in order to think clearly about the UK's place in the world, it is necessary to continue to explore the meaning and direction of the world's economic and political development. Useful questions in this context would have included ones about societal convergence and divergence; about the extent of the globalization of human life; about the decline, the continued persistence, or of a country's history as a powerful influence on its management and work organization; and about the effects of the growth of regional economic trading blocs and sociopolitical groupings like the EU and its counterparts elsewhere.

Our last three points are much more specific to the concerns of the book. Thus, fifth, we feel that the development of management-level education beyond its current relatively pragmatic content, and through first and masters degree and at the doctoral level, should be to develop both the links between its specific components, and to broaden its scope to encompass all kinds of economic, historical, political and social experience. At the same time it should be deepened by drawing on the expertise and tacit knowledge of practitioners and articulating their experiences and understanding in the broadest philosophical terms. This would constitute a greening and maturing of higher vocational education.

Sixth, we think that as standards of education rise, managements should become less vulnerable to the sellers of management consultancy, fads and panaceas. We do envisage a future for management consultancies as such, in a situation in which divisions of labour and needs for specialist help continue to proliferate. However we expect those who try to sell the business and management counterparts of quack medical remedies to suffer in the face of increasing experience, sophistication and

310

scepticism on the part of potential buyers.

Seventh and finally, we expect professional-managerial relations to be a topic of keen interest and research for many decades to come, even if the webs of management-level and professional education, training, development, employment and work organization become ever more seamless. The process will almost certainly be a long and untidy one, with matters continually being recomplicated by the ongoing divisions of expert labour, by a process of economic, social and technical aspiration expanding the proportion of labour which makes itself expert, and probably by growth of increasingly varied forms of employment for the so-called 'third agers', people over fifty years old.

Conclusions

The *Technik* and Business Management approaches to management are not mutually incompatible: indeed they are the Yin and Yang of it in some respects and in their less extreme versions. Nor are they exclusive. The successes of various kinds of mainly nation-specific familial capitalism across the world demonstrate that. A more fruitful way of thinking about the *Technik*-Business Management relationship might be to see one as likely to succeed the other, in part, in the history of a nation. There is some historical evidence for this having happened. Both the UK and Japan became major financial centres after they industrialized and some elements of the opposite process can be seen in the economic history of the USA in the first half of the twentieth century.

The economic, educational and social priorities of UK governments since the 1960s and 1970s have generally tended to favour the Business Management approach although it is doubtful whether this would have been the case to so great an extent if more manufacturing and cognate sectors had been more successful. Elements of negativity have often pervaded the ways in which developments have occurred. Making money and useful work have often been contrasted unreasonably. So have making money and state provision of education, health and welfare.

More positive thinking would emphasize two things. The first would be to (continue to) 'green' business, management and professional courses, to use them as vehicles for producing citizens as well as highly knowledgeable and skilled individuals. Well known and documented deficiencies in professional and other courses, such as the neglect of the practical in architectural and of concern for the long run in accountancy ones and the limited commercial career ambitions of engineering ones, should not merely be addressed: they should be eradicated. All vocational courses should equip their recipients with an ability to manage their own practice and to make strong, broad and far-seeing contributions to management in their relevant sectors of employment. The proliferation of specialized vocational masters degrees should be encouraged within reason. So should the careful growth of vocational doctorates like the Doctor in Engineering, in Education, in Business

Administration and in Management, with the last designed for very experienced senior managers and professionals to articulate their tacit knowledge and the wider relevance of their experience. Such doctorates should be at least as difficult to obtain as the traditional kind, and more concerned with general educational and civilising benefits, *as well as* contributing to the development of academic discipline-based knowledge 'for its own sake'.

Second, there is still a strong need to recruit more able, flexible individuals with broad capabilities and outlooks into engineering. The UK's manufacturing and related sectors probably do not need very large numbers of highly qualified engineers, but they do need them to be outstandingly able. Moreover, science and engineering teaching should be made more imaginative and open-ended in their approach, so that many of those who might otherwise take arts subjects are attracted to engineering and scientific ones. Finally on this point, so-called 'management' subjects like accounting, economics, finance, HRM and marketing should be better integrated into engineering courses, so that they do not exacerbate the damaging, erroneous and already widespread perception that engineering is a natural handmaiden of management.

The evidence available in this book and that available elsewhere (see for example the chapters in Glover and Hughes (1996, forthcoming), and Leopold, Glover and Hughes (1996) just about favours the idea that the UK and those who manage its organizations are in the pursuer mode, striving to catch up with competitor countries, albeit with the *caveats* that this striving is not always successful even when they are, and that the latter are not standing still. The evidence certainly supports the idea that a professional-managerial class is forming and that it has at least some genuinely technocratic elements and qualities. More generally, we and some of the writers in this book have implicitly tried to respect, and at times referred to explicitly, the links that can and should exist between good professional practices, good management and good citizenship. These links are also discussed in Leopold, Glover and Hughes (1996, Chapter 13) and especially in Glover and Hughes (1996 forthcoming).

Finally, we would like to offer a small acid test to readers, for them to see how far they have understood what is, in our eyes at least, one of the main messages of the book. At the start of Armstrong's chapter he refers to a perception amongst advocates of management education of the 1960s, 1970s and 1980s, that any criticism of its content could only come from 'backwoodsmen'. One or two of the early reactions to his chapter seemed to show muted signs of wilful incomprehension and a distinct lack of interest. Who, these days, we would like to know, are the real backwoodsmen?

References

Glover, I. and Hughes, M. (1996), *Professions at Bay: Control and Encouragement of Ingenuity in UK Management*, forthcoming, Avebury, Aldershot.

Kanter, R. M. (1984), *The Change Masters*, Allen and Unwin, London.

Leopold, J., Glover, I. and Hughes, M., (1996), *Beyond Reason? The National Health Service and the limits of management*, Avebury, Aldershot.

Index

314

human conduct 115, 116, 121
Human Relations 13, 52, 63, 64, 84,
   165, 219, 227, 272
human resource management 22, 23, 48,
   80, 201, 215, 217, 222, 227, 240-243
human science 14, 89, 90, 93, 94, 99,
   100, 103
humour 12, 41, 46-48, 306

ideology of work 80, 240
Idols of the Market 109, 117-119, 122
industrial psychologists 220
industrial relations 9, 23, 88, 165,
   168, 184, 192, 212, 218, 221, 222,
   223, 225, 228, 231, 241, 242, 276,
   287, 292
industrial society 18, 92, 94, 104,
   157, 164, 167, 273
industrial unions 67
industrialization 13, 18, 65-68, 191,
   193, 247, 298
informal system 42
information technology 23, 78, 79,
   215
Institute of Industrial Administration
   299
interactive informality 40-42

Israel 11, 37, 39, 40, 42, 44, 48
Italy 44
ITT 46

Japanese collective consciousness 65
Japanese Employment System 68, 71,
   77, 80, 88
Japanese engineers 13, 66, 67
Jarratt Report 23
JIT 77, 78

job content analysis 188, 189
joint consultation 57, 59, 70
Joint Contracts Tribunal (JCT) 251
Just-in-Time 77

knowledge manipulation 111
knowledgewrights 109, 114
Krondratieff 172

Labour management relations 63, 64,
   67, 69, 76, 77, 81, 85
Labour process 31, 137, 145, 173,
   191, 192, 241, 242, 272, 298, 299
labour relations 13, 63, 64, 67-72, 82
Labour unions in Japan 67
labour utilization 130, 175
late capitalism 172
Law for the Protection of Labour 56,
   57
layers 39, 63, 297
leadership 33, 40, 44, 45, 59, 64,
   65, 73, 74, 79, 81, 84, 235, 236,
   236, 260, 287, 297, 299
lean production 16, 127, 132, 137,
   145, 148, 149, 151
legalism 68, 69
Lewchuk 177, 178, 183, 184, 192
line managers 204, 205, 210, 217,
   222-224, 226, 238

M-form organization 138
Mabbott 157, 169
manageability 14, 89, 98-100, 103
Management Charter Initiative 9,
   230, 233
management control 16, 20, 31, 55,
   72, 128, 138, 146, 191, 209, 294,
   295, 298, 307
management discourse 130, 148
management education 8, 10, 24,
   28-31, 54, 72, 220, 229, 230, 233,
   240, 241, 269-275, 277-281, 286,
   287, 288-290, 292, 295, 296, 298-
   301, 308, 312
management practices 127, 137, 151,
   199, 228, 266, 309
manager mobility 39
managerial capitalism 29, 52, 76, 78,
   278, 280, 293, 298

317

privatization 198
process expertise 240, 269
process of modernization 90, 95-97
product development 55, 78, 79, 277
production engineering 29, 271, 286, 287, 290
production engineers 187-189
productivity measurement 77, 128, 137, 148
Professional management 29, 55, 62
professional organization 97, 157, 158, 203
professional-managerial class 1, 3, 4, 23, 31, 305-308, 312
professionalism 3, 6, 16, 24, 25, 32, 39, 40, 45, 125, 187, 191, 201, 212, 214, 220, 242, 267, 279, 298, 306-308
professionals 3, 4, 5, 7-11, 15, 16, 21-23, 25, 26, 94, 101, 110, 155, 159, 160, 195, 197, 199, 201-203, 205, 206, 208-215, 234, 240, 248, 249, 251, 257, 264, 305, 306, 308, 310, 312
project management 27, 246, 252, 256, 258-267
proletarianization 209, 214
provincial 6, 7, 10, 115
public sector 5, 7, 9, 21, 22, 26, 31, 195-201, 204, 206, 208, 210-214, 221, 249, 250, 254, 255, 264, 306, 308
pursuer mode 1, 3, 4, 305, 306, 312

Quality control circle 73
quality improvement 199, 203
Quasi-markets 22, 23, 199, 202

rational-technical organization 95
rationality 14, 15, 32, 45, 91, 92, 98, 110, 112, 115, 117, 119, 122, 125, 155, 189, 267, 274
rationalization 10, 81, 92, 97, 98, 101, 116, 123, 183-185, 223
Reichstag 56-58, 69

Renault 132, 145, 151
reward management 226, 243
risk-taker 15
River Rouge 173
Rouge factory 145
Royal College of Surgeons 159
Royal Institute of Chartered Surveyors 268

scientific management 14, 51, 53, 82, 91, 92, 104, 106, 271, 274, 278, 279, 284, 300, 301
scientists 15, 16, 38, 66, 80, 109, 113, 117, 119-122, 124, 125, 156, 214, 294, 295
sectionalization 176, 178-180
self-interest 18, 19, 122, 157, 158, 161-164, 167, 276
self-regulation 18, 32, 160, 196, 197, 202, 203, 210
Sheldon 274, 275, 300
Shop floor 20, 50-52, 81, 84, 85, 178, 182
shop management 271-275, 278, 280, 290
Singer 117-121, 125, 184
Singer Motor Company 184
social responsibility 39
social solidarity 162-167
sociotechnical systems 253
solicitor 159
SOPS xiv, 43, 45
Specialism 38, 39, 47, 231, 232
specialist trades 26, 246, 247, 251, 258
Spencer 18, 90, 96, 157, 158, 162, 164, 166
Standard Motor Company 184
state welfare policy 196, 198
static build 20, 175, 176
stockholders 54, 55, 58, 61-63, 71, 72, 75, 76

319

strategic management 24, 30, 51,
185, 187, 189, 190, 220, 238, 274,
279, 290
strategic planning 28, 75, 269, 270
suicide 31, 163, 164, 168
Supervisory Board 58, 61-63, 83
Surveyors 6, 7, 25-27, 245, 247-250,
259, 261-265, 268, 308
Sweden 11, 39-42, 44, 48, 88
Swedish managers 41

Taylorism 51, 73, 77, 80, 82, 91-94,
97, 99, 173, 185, 272, 274, 279, 290
Technik 5, 8, 9, 11-13, 19, 32, 43, 44,
50, 82, 150, 231, 234, 235, 241,
242, 311
technocrats 7, 8, 21, 234
technology 8, 20, 23, 66, 67, 73,
78-81, 112, 116, 125, 150, 177,
183, 192, 208, 209, 215, 272, 276
Third Reich 55
Toynbee 102, 107
Toyota 74, 78, 85, 133-143, 145, 149
Transactional informality 42
transformation 86, 94, 100, 104, 121,
267, 272
Triumph 52, 182, 184, 271

Urwick 29, 271, 272, 274, 275,
279-292, 295-297, 300, 301
US business education 232
USA 4, 5, 8, 9, 11, 12, 16, 20, 21,
24, 28-30, 37-40, 42-44, 46, 131,
150, 172, 174, 179, 185, 188, 218,
219, 232, 272, 292, 297, 299, 306,
309, 311
utilitarianism 17, 18, 156, 157, 162,
164-166

value for money 22, 202, 203, 208
vertical disintegration 136, 140
vertically integrated hierarchies 22,
198, 199
vocational qualifications 306

Vorstand 43, 61, 83
VW 141

wage gradient 140, 142, 147
Wagner Act 52
Weber 15, 16, 33, 97-99, 115,
116, 122, 123, 125, 172, 193
Weimar Republic 58, 59
Western Europe 12, 49, 53, 67,
87, 88, 90, 297
Wharton School 291
Womack 127, 128, 137, 152
Wood Report 254
work intensification 92, 207, 208
works councils 58-61, 67, 81, 84
world class 81, 128, 149
World War II 54, 59, 180, 183, 185

Zaibatsu 72
Ziman 120, 121, 123, 126